Youth and Sociology

Prentice-Hall, Inc., Englewood Cliffs, New Jersey

Youth and Sociology

Edited by

Peter K. Manning
Michigan State University

Marcello Truzzi
New College

ISBN: P 0–13–982504–5
C 0–13–982512–6

Library of Congress Catalog Card No.: 71–172943

Printed in the United States of America
10 9 8 7 6 5 4 3 2 1

PRENTICE-HALL INTERNATIONAL, INC., London
PRENTICE-HALL OF AUSTRALIA, PTY. LTD., Sydney
PRENTICE-HALL OF CANADA, LTD., Toronto
PRENTICE-HALL OF INDIA PRIVATE LIMITED, New Delhi
PRENTICE-HALL OF JAPAN, INC., Tokyo

Contents

Preface

We want to thank the people who made this book first a possibility and later a reality. Al Lesure, friend and editor, created the conditions facilitating the book's appearance. Marlene Wilson, Nanette Davis, Janet Berryman, and Eleanor Hopping did the necessary typing, cutting, copying, and research with skill and a sense of humor.

Peter K. Manning, *East Lansing, Michigan*
Marcello Truzzi, *Sarasota, Florida*

Preliminary Note to the Instructor

As we will emphasize in the introductory essay, this book is intended to be an addition or supplement to an introductory sociology course, not a complete sociology of youth. Developing a sociology of youth is a more complex theoretical exercise, involving elaboration of a comprehensive perspective for explaining and illustrating the varieties of youthful experience. We hope with this book to provide materials to assist the presentation of some of the diverse theoretical approaches, concepts, and methods to the student first meeting sociology. The organization of the book parallels that of most introductory sociology textbooks so that it can easily be keyed to such texts.

Attempting to present a reasonably balanced, representative sample of sociological work, we have followed our own vision of the field to some degree. In the selections illustrating sociological analyses, the experiences of the middle-class urban white college student are predominant. Although some of the selections consider female roles (Riesman); blue collar or working class youth (Liebow, Hannerz, Psathas, Barker and Adams, among others in this volume); and political protest from the right and the major recent non-black protest movements (for example, Women's Liberation), these areas of social life are clearly under-represented. We have not, however, intentionally slighted these segments of American society. Selections were chosen as the most useful representatives of particular concepts, theories, or methods. The decisions resulted from our desire to provide material of pedagogical value. Finally, practical considerations such as size, depth, and balance create difficult editorial decisions inherent in any reader.

Some methods and theoretical approaches, such as the functionalist and symbolic interactionist perspectives, are more heavily represented among the readings than are representatives of the conflict, Marxian, or systems theory perspectives. The essay, the social survey, and the observational study are more common than are selections illustrating the use of unobtrusive measures (unknown to the people observed, or not involving face-to-face encounters between researcher and citizen), systematic behavioral observation (the "natural experiment"), or personal documents.

It seems to us that these emphases are approximately those shared by most sociologists. However, the purpose of this note is to make as clear as possible the focuses of this book. Instructors may find such clarification useful in deleting and/or supplementing the readings.

Introductory Essay: Youth and Sociology

This book is a collection of lively and relevant supplementary essays for introductory courses in sociology. It attempts to demonstrate the variety and scope of sociology by concentrating on the substantive area of youth. The book is not a comprehensive statement on youth; we do not seek to develop a sociology *of* youth, or even a youthful sociology. Instead we use the rich context of youth as a source of sociological examples and principles, of illustrative methods, theories, and concepts. Youth is merely one among many possible vehicles for illustrating the sociological enterprise. By studying youth, we can isolate concepts, principles, and data that reflect the larger aim of sociology: to understand society in a careful, disciplined, and systematic way. By pairing youth and sociology, then, we can draw on the behavior of youth to produce insight into social life in general. We could have used the aged, the middle-aged, or another social category for illustrations. Youth, however, is a timely topic, a rich source of sociological studies using a variety of methods, and a subject of personal interest to students and professors alike.

Let us define what we mean by the terms *youth* and *sociology.* In accord with a major contemporary sociological tradition, philosopher Ernst Cassirer defined man as a symbol-using animal. Man's most important symbol is clearly his language, for through language he defines his reality. Language includes categories, which sort reality into manageable parts. The use of language categories is a means of determining expectations and giving meaning to behavior. Once expectations and meanings are provided, mere behavior becomes conduct, directed toward a real or imagined audience. Things act; people conduct themselves. Taken together, language categories form "terminological screens" that select portions of reality which become salient to us, distract us from other portions, and make us indifferent to large parts of the world around us (Burke 1968). Movies such as *Rashomon, Belle De Jour,* and *Hiroshima Mon Amour* depict the importance of people's perspectives on their behavior and interpretation of given events. A perspective is a way of seeing things, but as Kenneth Burke has pointed out, the symbol —in this case language—is by definition selective, arbitrary, concealing, disguising, and dissembling as well as broad and inclusive, conventionalized, revealing, guising, and assembling. A way of seeing is also a way of not seeing (Burke 1965).[1]

Youth is a language category, applied to one segment of society by another segment with identifiable results, including the creation of social roles, attributes, and meanings for those to whom it is applied. Understanding youth in the context of American society involves an understanding of themes treated in this collection by Roszak, Friedenberg, and Eisenstadt. American society is technologically sophisticated, rapidly changing, and pluralistic. Technology runs almost unrestrained in American society, as the Keniston essay so dramatically shows. The wonder of the recent heart transplants is not that they have been successful, but that there is so little concern about the moral, social, and political implications of permitting physicians to decide not only about life and death, but also about the technological reconstruction and even creation of life. (We desire almost desperately to control life and to negate the power of death. Technology, like the shield of the crusaders, is our means.) Ours is a young society, both in fact (more than half the population is under 25, and the group from 15 through 25 is the fastest growing age category), and in spirit (Americans idolize their youth and youthfulness).

Stratification, or social ranking, in America is increasingly based on expertise rather than on age, race, sex, or family. In addition, new life styles and modes of expressive behavior (use of symbols to claim a social position) are cutting society into new social worlds. Our leisure styles as well as our participation patterns provide new clues to the emerging social order. Education, as Moller, Lofland, Flacks, and others in this book show, is one of the major forces for change. About 50 percent of the youths between 18 and 21 are enrolled in an institution of higher education. Only 26 percent attended comparable institutions in 1946. About six million students are now in college. Eventually, it is expected, all young people will go to college; indeed,

[1]For a general treatment of language, see Manning, in Douglas, 1971.

some consider college a right (Carnegie 1968, p. 4). Education, like most of our other activities, takes place within bureaucracies. A bureaucracy (although who needs a definition by now?) is a formally organized, legitimate system of rules and objectives that guide decisions and the flow of authority (see Weber 1947). Our lives are irrevocably tied to mass bureaucracies. Finally, it has been argued that our media-oriented society has created a new, nonlinear orientation to the world (McLuhan 1965). A growing number of people are more likely to be, experience, feel, and see than to cogitate, read, and intellectualize. The media have such a great effect because they operate in a society which has largely rejected the "great myths" of religion, utopias, and absolutistic belief in the future, government, progress, and fathers (Feuer 1969).[2]

The category of youth in the context of American society is a social creation, not a mere product of biology (see the Eisenstadt essay). Since the adults in a society possess the power to create and apply labels, "youth" comes into being when it is defined by the older generation. At one time the natural stages of development in America were infant, child, young adult, and adult. Then psychologist Stanley Hall created the term *adolescent.* He intended to underscore what he felt were the central attributes of this age group: dependence, prepubescence, sexual learning, and prelegal preparation for responsible social roles. In the last few years, the category of youth has been extended downward to include eight- to ten-year-old "teeny-boppers," and upward to include 30-year-old students. Some people feel that this social extension process has led to the creation of a youth or even of a counterculture with a special set of roles, beliefs, standards of behavior and feeling, and visions of the future. Roszak is one of the major advocates of this position (see also the papers of Berger, Friedenberg, and Lifton). Most importantly, as Erikson notes, "Youth . . . has been elaborated [as a category] as a set of differences from some standard human being, the norm, of course, being usually the normal adult male. The group is then judged on the basis of what it is *not* and will *never* be, or not quite yet, or is not anymore" (Erikson, in Erikson, ed. 1965, p. viii).

The category of youth is thus problematic and not a standard item in the cultural repertoire of all societies. We might speculate on the conditions under which the category of youth will be successfully applied to a social group, that is, under which a group of people will accept the labels conferred on them (see Lemert 1951; Becker 1963; Manning, forthcoming). These conditions probably include a sufficient mass or number, common experiences and interaction or contact, a concentration in special places (such as colleges and universities), and an increasingly uniform response of society to an otherwise differentiated social aggregate.[3] As many people have noted, youth mirrors many of the values, aspirations, and interests of the broader society. Whatever power youth has results from the latent support given

[2]For the effect of media on politics, see McLuhan 1965 and McGinnis 1970.

[3]These conditions are roughly similar to those described by Marx as the basis for class-consciousness.

youth by the values, attitudes, and behavior of adults. Although the central values of youth may appear to be inversions of adult values, they are in fact extreme exaggerations of the values held by the middle classes. Youth and parents agree in their ambivalence and disdain for work; their search for "kicks," or hedonistic pleasure; and their support of self-righteous violence. Matza and Sykes (1961) developed the thesis that youth is marginal, which was later elaborated in Matza's classic *Delinquency and Drift* (1966). Matza demonstrated that delinquent gangs, supposedly the extreme case of a youthful subculture, are actually perched precariously between the conventional and the nonconventional. Situational factors become highly significant predictors of resultant behavior. That is, finding the keys left in an automobile may be interpreted as an accident and ignored, or seen as an opportunity to "put one over" on an ignorant owner who is obviously asking to be ripped off. Whether a group of juveniles ignores a car or steals it may depend more on the way the situation is defined at that moment than upon frustration, lack of opportunity for middle-class employment, or their attitudes toward automobile theft as an abstract category unrelated to personal experiences.

Age is reflected in youth; the categories "youth" and "aged" are meaningful only as contrast conceptions, or counter-roles. The concord between youth and their parents emanates from their central agreement on the value of youth itself: we worship youth and youthfulness almost as much as money (Williams 1964). They agree about the worrisome effects of rapid change, the erosion of old moralities and absolutist conceptions of right and wrong; they share a love for the "drugged escape"; it could be said that youths act, while adults react. Because this equation is so dynamic, it is seldom possible to capture it fully and to the satisfaction of the parties involved.

Some of the major problems sociologists face in trying to "capture" youth arise from sociologists' own continuing commitment to the timely essay, the quick observation, the witty remark. The essayist continues to occupy high status in the profession. The problem of "capturing" the youth scene also arises from changes in contemporary social events and from the observers' changing relationship to that scene. In the early 1960s, the era of civil rights activity, of southern sit-ins and legal tests, and of southern summers, the image of the young was favorable; they were considered idealistic. Richard Flacks describes and contrasts that earlier situation with the tone of the times in the early seventies.

> The first waves of student protest met with quite general approval, since they signified the end of a decade of political stagnation and outright fear. Listen, for example, to the Governor of California, speaking in 1961, expressing quite directly the mood of those years: "I say, Thank God for the spectacle of students picketing—even when they are picketing me at Sacramento and I think they are wrong, for students protesting and Freedom Riding, . . . going out to the fields with our migratory workers, and marching off to jail with our segregated Negroes. At least we're getting somewhere. The colleges have become bootcamps for citizenship and citizen-leaders are marching out of them. For a while it will be hard on us as administrators. Some students are going to be wrong and some people will want to deny them the right to make mistakes. . . . But let us stand up and be proud of our students."

> Four and a half years later to the day, the same Governor Pat Brown was sending state police to the campus of the University of California to drag 800 students off to jail because they had taken control of the Administration Building in an effort to secure their right to organize on the campus the very kinds of activity the Governor had formerly celebrated. Since Berkeley, of course, public attitudes toward student protest have greatly hardened, including the attitudes of liberal educators and administrators. (Flacks 1968, pp. 1–2)

The generation of the 1950s, on the other hand, was called the silent or apathetic generation, faulted for its conservatism, its careerist future plans, and its stodgy and stable view of the world. Prior to that generation, youths were the "wild ones" freed by the war (see Aries 1968 for a general discussion of the image of youth).

Yet sociologists have failed miserably to predict or even to anticipate the major social upheavals of the past 20 years. They were surprised by the civil rights movement, by the various permutations and combinations of the still changing black movements that followed, by the student movements and the various tortured courses they have taken, and by the violence and ugliness characterizing the present campus scene. Professors have looked in wonder at the changes in the hippie, radical, and anarchist youth movements. Any attempt to characterize comprehensively such a rapidly changing social phenomenon is highly likely to be time-bound and short on predictive value. We have not yet developed a perspective on our times as an interconnected, holistic phenomenon divorced from our own intense personal involvement in the events we are describing. So this collection should not be viewed as an encyclopedic and exhaustive survey. We will only scratch the surface.

Let us now examine the second term, *sociology*. We do not assume that the students who read this book are familiar with the content of sociology. Sociology may be a new field to most who read the book; its concepts may be new, its style difficult, its theories obtuse. Several principles guided us in writing this introductory section: sociology is in the process of becoming a science; it is rapidly developing a paradigm; it has a body of theory, concepts, and methods. We shall discuss the content of the book in relation to those principles. In so doing, we hope to help readers understand (1) the rationale for including each selection, and (2) the main themes of the papers.

Science is, very simply, a way of looking at objects in the world. A scientific way of looking at objects involves at least four components: paradigm, theory, concepts, and method. Once we have these tools we can look meaningfully at any number of sociological studies.

A paradigm is a model, a near-ideal basis for conceiving of and pursuing problems. Thomas Kuhn wrote a dramatic and illuminating monograph entitled "The Structure of Scientific Revolutions" (1962), which created a minor revolution. The existence of paradigms was the central idea of his book. Kuhn's thesis was that scientific revolutions occur when there are shifts in the paradigms, the underlying assumptions about the way science is done. The implicit assumptions of a science—natural, physical, or social—are the fundamental bases for the growth and development of that science. Usually one major piece of scientific work sets the paradigm, but accumulated research, debate, and agitation are required to bring a new paradigm into being. In the case of sociology, it is clear that methods, theories, and even the "facts" are in dispute.

> I assume no one would question the statement, "There is a body of thought which can be referred to as 'sociology', and there are people whose interest it is to 'do sociology'." However, I might encounter objections if I presumed to define what "doing sociology" *really is.* That philosophers have long ago abandoned the quest for what *is* would not constitute a reasonable objection, since sociology has become a 'science', and long ago sorted its own problems from those of the philosophers. I do not think it necessary, however, to cease the work of laying out sociological perspectives because it is not in any philosophical sense possible to say what sociology *really is.* I am inclined, as will become clear below, to accept Wittgensteinian notions that what *is* is not as important as language used in discussing what people experience socially. (Manning 1967, p. 1)

Faced with this situation, most sociologists feel that students learn more quickly about an aspect of society if they have examples of "doing sociology" which illustrate what society is like. Uncovering society involves invoking the principle Peter Berger (1963) suggests: ". . . the first wisdom of sociology is . . . things are not what they seem." To perform the operation of revealing social life, sociologists rely on concepts—basic units of thought and tools for inquiry (Gould and Kolb, eds., pp. 120–21). The major concepts in sociology include those headings (including formal and informal education) found in the table of contents of this book: social organization, culture, socialization, stratification, deviance and collective behavior, ecology and population, religion, power (politics), and social change.[4]

These central concepts provide sociologists with guidance and focus. To establish the continuing utility of their concepts and theories, sociologists are committed to subject their ideas to an empirical test. Research is a critical part of sociology. Methods, or systematic means of obtaining information, are necessary to substantiate theories and concepts. The selections that follow show that a range of methods has been employed to gather and analyze sociological information. We have tried to represent in the selections sociological concepts first and methodological approaches second. Thus we have certainly slighted some methods (see the preliminary note to the instructor) and have provided in-depth treatment of others.

The commitment to fact and observable evidence is supplanted by the use of abstract concepts such as values, attitudes, and norms—inferences from behavior, used to explain behavioral regularities. The dictum of the late sociologist Howard P. Becker was to keep your eyes on the things that are out of sight. Without attention to abstractions, captured and systematized in theory, the social sciences would be reduced to reporting, editorializing, or mere tabulation of public opinion. For example, a belief common in the early

[4]For basic definitions and illustrations of these concepts, see the introductions to the sections or J. Gould and W. Kolb, eds., *International Dictionary of the Social Sciences* (New York: The Free Press, 1964).

fifties was that "separate but equal" schools, albeit segregated, had no damaging effects on black children. Sociologists, social psychologists, and other social scientists assembled evidence documenting the adverse effect that segregated schools were having on the learning potential of black youth. This evidence was gathered at the request of the Supreme Court of the United States and was one of the bases for the *Brown* v. *Board of Education* decision that made segregated schooling illegal. This evidence was gathered scientifically and did not rely on the unexamined beliefs of the layman. It led to one of the most important decisions in the history of the Supreme Court. Thus a commitment to science not only makes some aspects of society more clearly understood, but can also be the basis for sweeping changes in social policy.

One informal sort of method is the conceptual essay (Eisenstadt, Roszak, Friedenberg, Berger, Davis, Parsons, Riesman, Goode, Brown, Lofland, and Flacks). Within an established scholarly form—the essay—the authors attempt to develop a critical stance toward an intellectual problem. The evidence marshaled by essayists is generally individualistic; indeed, why else read an essay? The passions, idiosyncracies, and sensitivities of the writers give spirit and life to such works. However, at least one purpose of the scientific essay is to create what Blumer calls "sensitizing concepts" (1969, pp. 140–52). Sensitizing concepts provide the source of new schemes, hypotheses, and research. Many important early sociologists and social scientists were "mere essayists," for example, Simmel, Ross, Comte, and Sumner. Contemporary sociological essayists, however, are of two broad types. They have either done extensive research, which has previously been carefully reported for the professional audience, and now they are turning to a new writing style to communicate to the public at large; or they are planning such research and have begun to think out loud in the form of an essay. Their usual aim is to redirect the concepts into the scientific research process for critical empirical weighing and assessment.

Somewhat related to the essay is another form represented in the selections, the participant observer's report of his activities in the everyday, anyday world. Like the essay, participant observation demands much of the self of the writer (assuming that the writer is also the researcher). The self of the observer is intimately and continuously involved in gathering and analyzing data. The selections from Liebow, Hannerz, Keiser, and Becker demonstrate the centrality of the self-as-instrument. Some people argue that participant observation can be done only by "certain kinds of people." If this were true, of course, observation would be a very limited aspect of scientific work. It is perhaps more accurate to say that successful participant observation requires a sensitivity to the social world and an ability to interpret and organize observations that may initially have been gathered in a relatively unsystematic fashion. When the observer plunges into the social world to observe it close at hand, to develop concepts reflecting the actor's view (the perspective of the observed), and to generate new concepts, he moves in areas where there are few clear markers of success or failure and a paucity of accumulated standards for judging validity and reliability of the data (see Lofland 1971). By plunging into the social world he is actively breaking down the tendency of the sciences to dehumanize and objectify the people studied. The sciences tend to make people objects, not subjects with will and reason. Occasionally the "objects" strike back. The following poem was returned as an answer to sociologists surveying religious attitudes at a midwestern university. Many people feel that participant observation requires an image of man not found explicitly elsewhere in sociology: of man creative and adaptive, not simply responding to this world, but creating it, shaping it, and molding it according to the meanings he attributes to it (Bruyn 1966; Lofland 1971).

A Note from the Underground

By Respondent No. 5542

The little men in untold legions
Descend upon the private regions.
Behold, my child, the questionnaire,
And be as honest as you dare.

"As briefly as possible, kindly state
Age and income, height and weight.
Sex (M or F); sex of spouse
(or spouses—list).

Do you own your house?
How much of your income goes for rent?
Give racial background, by percent.
Have you had, or are you now having
Orgasm? Or thereunto a craving?
Will Christ return? If so, when?
(kindly fill this out in pen)
Do you masturbate? In what style?
(fill and return the enclosed vial)
Do you eat, or have you eaten
Feces? Whose?

And were you beaten?
Was your mother? Sister? Dog?
(attach descriptive catalogue)
Have you mystic inspiration?
Our thanks for your co-operation."

Distended now with new-got lore,
Our plump and pleasant men-of-war
Torture whimsey into fact,

And then, to sanctify the act,
Cast in gleaming, ponderous rows,
Ingots of insipid prose,
A classic paper! Soon to be
Rammed down the throats of such as we.[5]

Two case studies are among the selections. They resemble the case study, the essay, and the participant observational style of sociological work. Sociological case studies may examine organizations, movements, groups, or the like; however, they usually involve generalizations or comparisons directed to the social entity as the unit of analysis (see Appendix I in Lipset et al., *Union Democracy,* 1962). However, social–psychological or psychological case studies typically focus on the life history or development of persons.

The case study by Lifton (based on interviews with Japanese, Chinese, and American youth) aims to explicate the relationships between individuals and their social context. The psychohistorical method employed by Lifton seeks to enlarge the study of social history to include psychological dynamics. The psychological dimension is either based on extended interviews or inferred from diaries, journals, documents, and the written observations of others. The individual is seen in the context of the major social forces surrounding him. Erikson's work on great men such as Gandhi and Luther illustrates this method well (Erikson 1958, 1969). It continues the Freudian interest in great men (for example, Da Vinci and Moses) and history but expands it to include modern sociological concepts and insights. This method is the new social history of our times, a new mode of reinterpreting the events of the past from within the contemporary frame of reference.

Historical sociology is the attempt to apply sociological concepts and methods to past events (see Lipset and Hofstadter, eds. 1968). This is an admittedly difficult exercise, but Kanter's article on communes illustrates the value of such investigations. Using her survey of 21 communes, or utopian communities, of the past (see Kanter 1968) and the correlates of success (defined in terms of survival), she predicts possible sources of strength or weakness in modern communes. She uses the lessons of the past to suggest the future of an emerging social form, the commune.

Moller's demographic analysis is an example of a more formal method. Demographers use the regularities in statistical findings about a social group, area, or region to characterize the social dynamics of that unit. The social processes that produce such order are the ultimate concern of the demographer, not the actual regularity itself.[6] Thus Moller first presents figures on the demography of youth in the modern world and then infers the social consequences of such changes.

[5]Submitted anonymously in lieu of anonymous questionnaire in a study of student values and campus religion at the University of Wisconsin by N. J. Demerath III

[6]Jack Douglas (1967) traces this logic in historical terms in his seminal discussion of Durkheim's suicide. See also Douglas 1971.
and Kenneth G. Lutterman.

The standard sociological digging tool is the survey interview and its intimate companion, the survey questionnaire (Riesman and Benney in Riesman 1965). The strategy of administering a survey is to select a theoretical problem, to choose a population from which to gather data relevant to the theory, and then to sample a group of potential interviewees. Once the data are in, with assumed homogeneity of meanings, comparability of responses, and uniform administration of the instrument, statistical analysis is typically applied. This approach rivals the conceptual essay as a leading sociological style. The great flexibility of the survey method is attested to by the wide range of statistical techniques used to analyze survey data in the various selections: factor analysis and analysis of variance (Psathas), correlation (Coleman), tests of means (Braungart), tests of association (Orum and Orum), and percentage comparisons (Coleman and Campbell). In quotations found in the selections, interview material is also used to illustrate the argument.

The range of methods and techniques in this book is fairly representative of the approaches sociologists have used. From these selections you should be able to determine both the weaknesses and the strengths of contemporary sociology.

List of References Cited

(This list does not include selections in the book.)

Aries, Phillip. *Centuries of Childhood.* Translated by R. Baldick. New York: Vintage, 1968.

Becker, Howard S. *Outsiders.* New York: The Free Press, 1963.

Berger, Peter. *Invitation to Sociology: A Humanistic Perspective*, New York: Doubleday Anchor Books, 1963.

Blumer, Herbert. *Symbolic Interactionism.* Englewood Cliffs, N.J.: Prentice-Hall, 1969.

Bruyn, Severyn. *The Human Perspective in Sociology: The Methodology of Participant Observation.* Englewood Cliffs, N.J.: Prentice-Hall, 1966.

Burke, Kenneth. *Permanence and Change.* 2d rev. ed. Indianapolis, Ind.: Bobbs-Merrill, 1965.

———. "A Definition of Man." In *Language as Symbolic Action.* Berkeley, Calif.: University of California Press, 1968.

Carnegie Commission. *Quality and Equality: New Levels of Federal Responsibility for Higher Education.* New York: McGraw-Hill, 1968.

Douglas, Jack. *The Social Meanings of Suicide.* Princeton, N.J.: Princeton University Press, 1967.

———. *American Social Order.* New York: The Free Press, 1971.

Erikson, Erik. *The Young Man Luther.* New York: W. W. Norton, 1958.

———. *Gandhi's Truth.* New York: W. W. Norton, 1969.

———, ed. *The Challenge of Youth.* New York: Doubleday Anchor Books, 1965.

Feuer, Lewis. *The Conflict of Generations.* New York: Basic Books, 1969.

Flacks, Richard. "Student Power and the New Left: The Role of the SDS." Paper presented to the American Psychological Association, 1968.

Gould, Julius, and Kolb, W. L., eds. *International Dictionary of the Social Sciences.* New York: The Free Press, 1964.

Kanter, Rosabeth M. "Commitment and Organization: A Study of Commitment Mechanisms in Utopian Communities." *American Sociological Review* 33 (August 1968):499–517.

Kuhn, Thomas. *The Structure of Scientific Revolutions.* Chicago: University of Chicago Press, 1962.

Lemert, Edwin. *Social Pathology.* New York: McGraw-Hill, 1951.

Lipset, S. M., Trow, M., and Coleman, J. *Union Democracy.* New York: Doubleday Anchor Books, 1962.

Lipset, S. M., and Hofstadter, R., eds. *Sociology and History: Methods.* New York: Basic Books, 1968.

Lofland, John. *Analyzing Social Settings.* Belmont, Calif.: Wadsworth, 1971.

Manning, Peter K. "Sociology as a Game of Games." Unpublished paper. East Lansing, Mich.: Michigan State University, 1967.

———. "Language, Meaning and Action." In Jack Douglas, ed., *Introduction to Sociology: Situation and Structures.* New York: The Free Press, 1971.

———. *Explaining Deviance.* New York: Random House, forthcoming.

Matza, David. *Delinquency and Drift.* New York: John Wiley, 1966.

Matza, David, and Sykes, G. "Delinquency and Subterranean Values." *American Sociological Review* 26 (October 1961):712–19.

McGinnis, Joseph. *The Selling of the President 1968.* New York: Bantam Books, 1970.

McLuhan, Marshall. *Understanding Media.* New York: McGraw-Hill, 1965.

Riesman, D., and Benney, M. "The Sociology of the Interview." In David Riesman, ed., *Abundance for What?* New York: Doubleday Anchor Books, 1965.

Weber, Max. *Theory of Economic and Social Organization.* Translated by T. Parsons and A. M. Henderson. London and New York: Oxford University Press, 1947.

Williams, Robin. *American Society.* New York: Alfred A. Knopf, 1964.

1 Youth and Social Organization

A society's organization, its division of labor, its significant values, its norms and symbols, all profoundly influence how youth is defined and depicted. The nature of youth, the period of transition to adulthood, is not uniformly defined in all societies. When and how the period occurs, and what psycho-social attributes are said to attach to youth, are closely associated with the link between the family and family roles and the requirements made of adults and adult roles.

S. N. Eisenstadt is author of one of the most comprehensive comparative treatments of youth as a period of transition, *From Generation to Generation* (1956).[1] In the article included in this section, he summarizes much of the evidence related to one of the central problems of sociology: how societies insure their own continuity. He focuses on the character of youth's movement from socially defined *non-responsible* roles into socially defined *adult* roles. Using evidence from preliterate, industrial, and modernizing societies, Eisenstadt shows that definitions of youth are not simply biological or

[1]All references are listed in the bibliography at the end of the book.

chronological but are also social and cultural; they are intimately related to the division of labor (the complex process by which people are assigned social roles), the process of identity formation, and the attribution of "primordial" qualities such as strength, vigor, powers, and so forth. *Archetype* means in this context a fundamental or essential aspect of youth passage. The archetypal pattern to which Eisenstadt refers is the passage of members of the category of "youth" into adult roles. The pattern can be studied in any society. The most dramatic cases of initiation are the *rites de passage* conducted by primitive groups, but their dramatic imagery should not obscure the universality of the process itself.

Because the family provides the basic socializing unit in all societies (although the definition of "family" may differ), the fit between familial roles and social roles is critical. In societies where kinship provides neither the sole criterion for assigning full social status nor the basis for organizing major social functions, other bases have been developed. Where differentiated political, economic, and religious structures exist, kinship no longer holds sway. Youth cultures tend to develop in that type of complex, non-kinship–based society. The tendency toward the development of a transitional stage to ease the induction process is more likely, according to Eisenstadt, where rapid modernization, urbanization, migration, and mobility are present. Eisenstadt also discusses the conditions under which one or another concrete form of youth group will emerge. His analysis supports the argument that social arrangements in the United States are ripe for supporting a full-scale youth movement, but that the specific content and future of such a movement require further investigation.

One of Eisenstadt's concerns is the image attributed to youth by their elders. Friedenberg also takes up this issue, arguing that the primordial qualities we attribute to youth—sexuality, spontaneity, creativity, and expressive capacity—make people both fearful of and attracted to the young. The stereotype of American youth includes a "hot-blooded" sensuality, spontaneity, and potential freedom from the fetters of "civilized" existence. Friedenberg's interpretation of adult repression of youth, especially in the schools, is based on the assumption that adults fear the sexuality of youth. Friedenberg's position follows the Freudian view that men are constrained, fettered, and repressed by society. The Freudian view, implicit in Friedenberg, has the following tenets: (1) the price of civilized life is repression of the basic sexual drives; (2) society is essentially repressive and dehumanizing, although it may strive to ameliorate these tendencies; (3) youth represents the relatively free and unsocialized version of man; and (4) the aging process involves a progressive deterioration of youthful lust and excitement for life.

According to Friedenberg, by means of law, educational institutions, and perhaps increasingly by police force, Americans attempt to desexualize, objectify, and repress youth. People fear most that youths may not become the desexualized, committed functionaries that post-industrial society demands. Although schools may attempt to educate and free the individual, they are most concerned with rule-following, with order, with discipline.

Friedenberg applies the specific stresses suggested by Eisenstadt to the American experience. Is it essentially American to repress and desexualize youth, or is that a feature of all industrial societies?

Roszak's selection, taken from his popular book *The Making of a Counter Culture* (1969), is an insightful description of the conditions under which the youth culture has reached its present prominence in the United States. Roszak sees several important trends in recent American sociopolitical organization as critical to the rise of youth culture, its politics, and what he calls the "adolescentization of dissent." These trends are (1) the growing numbers of young people from 15 to 29, and a correlated self-awareness of their numbers; (2) the expansion of higher education; (3) the growth of the non-student population; (4) change from a production-oriented society to one emphasizing consumption and "permissiveness" in child rearing; and (5) the extension of adolescence, both downward to the "teeny-bopper" age group and upward to students of 30 and over.

Most of these trends have been obvious since the end of World War II, but sociologists had not anticipated the dramatic rise of the youth movement in the late sixties. The same facts had been used to explain the apathy of the youth of the fifties. It is interesting to note further that Friedenberg advocates, implicitly at least, the very thing Roszak considers problematic and difficult—the "adolescentization" of many social activities. In other words, the demand for immediate solutions, for instant utopias, for confrontational tactics, and the glamorization of the moment have typically been considered adolescent traits in our society, but they are more common now in all forms of dissent. The rhetoric of youth has been adopted by a number of groups, with no small stimulus from advertisers who have seized the colorful vocabulary of the young as a medium for stimulating consumption. The media thus glorify the "political–sexual" image of youth suggested by Friedenberg and Roszak.

The dramatization of assorted images of youth has been an apparent public trend during the past few years. The images themselves, as well as the attributes assigned to members of the category of youth, have changed rapidly and dramatically. These years, then, are an abundant source of evidence for the view that what is taken to be youth and youthful is *cultural.* Our selections may provide a framework for assessing the conditions under which this labeling process occurs.

Archetypal Patterns of Youth

S. N. Eisenstadt

Youth constitutes a universal phenomenon. It is first of all a biological phenomenon, but one always defined in cultural terms. In this sense it constitutes a part of a wider cultural phenomenon, the varying definitions of age and of the differences between one age and another.[1] Age and age differences are among the basic aspects of life and the determinants of human destiny. Every human passes through various ages, and at each one he attains and uses different biological and intellectual capacities. At each stage he performs different tasks and roles in relation to the other members of his society: from a child, he becomes a father; from a pupil, a teacher; from a vigorous youth, a mature adult, and then an aging and "old" man.

This gradual unfolding of power and capacity is not merely a universal, biologically conditioned, and inescapable fact. Although the basic biological processes of maturation (within the limits set by such factors as relative longevity) are probably more or less similar in all human societies, their cultural definition varies from society to society, at least in details. In all societies, age serves as a basis for defining the cultural and social characteristic of human beings, for the formation of some of their mutual relations and common activities, and for the differential allocation of social roles.

The cultural definitions of age and age differences contain several different yet complementary elements. First, these definitions often refer to the social division of labor in a society, to the criteria according to which people occupy various social positions and roles within any society. For instance, in many societies certain roles—especially those of married men, full citizens, independent earners—are barred to young people, while others—as

[1] A general sociological analysis of the place of age in social structure has been attempted in S. N. Eisenstadt, *From Generation to Generation* (Chicago: The Free Press of Glencoe, Illinois, 1956).

certain military roles—are specifically allocated to them. Second, the cultural definition of age is one important constituent of a person's self-identity, his self-perception in terms of his own psychological needs and aspirations, his place in society, and the ultimate meaning of his life.

Within any such definition, the qualities of each age are evaluated according to their relation to some basic, primordial qualities, such as vigor, physical and sexual prowess, the ability to cope with material, social, and supernatural environment, wisdom, experience, or divine inspiration. Different ages are seen in different societies as the embodiments of such qualities. These various qualities seem to unfold from one age to another, each age emphasizing some out of the whole panorama of such possible qualities. The cultural definition of an age span is always a broad definition of human potentialities, limitations, and obligations at a given stage of life. In terms of these definitions, people map out the broad contours of life, their own expectations and possibilities, and place themselves and their fellow men in social and cultural positions, ascribing to each a given place within these contours.

The various qualities attributed to different ages do not constitute an unconnected series. They are usually interconnected in many ways. The subtle dialectics between the unfolding of some qualities and the waning of others in a person is not a mere registration of his psychological or biological traits; rather, it constitutes the broad framework of his potentialities and their limits throughout his life span. The characteristics of any one "age," therefore, cannot be fully understood except in relation to those of other ages. Whether seen as a gradually unfolding continuum or as a series of sharp contrasts and opposed characteristics, they are fully explicable and understandable only in terms of one another. The boy bears within himself the seeds of the adult man; else, he must as an adult acquire new patterns of behavior, sharply and intentionally opposed to those of his boyhood. The adult either develops naturally into an old man—or decays into one. Only when taken together do these different "ages" constitute the entire map of human possibilities and limitations; and, as every individual usually must pass through them all, their complementariness and continuity (even if defined in discontinuous and contrasting terms) become strongly emphasized and articulated.

The same holds true for the age definitions of the two sexes, although perhaps with a somewhat different meaning. Each age span is defined differently for either sex, and these definitions are usually related and complementary, as the "sexual image" and identity always constitute basic elements of man's image in every society. This close connection between different ages necessarily stresses the problem of transition from one point in a person's life to another as a basic constituent of any cultural definition of an "age." Hence, each definition of age must necessarily cope with the perception of time, and changes in time, of one's own progress in time, one's transition from one period of life to another.

This personal transition, or temporal progress, or change, may become closely linked with what may be called cosmic and societal time.[2] The attempt to find some meaning in personal temporal transition may often lead to identification with the rhythms of nature or history, with the cycles of the seasons, with the unfolding of some cosmic plan (whether cyclical, seasonal, or apocalyptic), or with the destiny and development of society. The nature of this linkage often constitutes the focus round which an individual's personal identity becomes defined in cultural terms and through which personal experience, with its anguish, may be given some meaning in terms of cultural symbols and values.

The whole problem of age definition and the linkage of personal time and transition with cosmic time become especially accentuated in that age span usually designated as youth. However great the differences among various societies, there is one focal point within the life span of an individual which in most known societies is to some extent emphasized: the period of youth, of transition from childhood to full adult status, or full membership in the society. In this period the individual is no longer a child (especially from the physical and sexual point of view) but is ready to undertake many attributes of an adult and to fulfill adult roles. But he is not yet fully acknowledged as an adult, a full member of the society. Rather, he is being "prepared," or is preparing himself for such adulthood.

This image of youth—the cultural definition of youth—contains all the crucial elements of any definition of age, usually in an especially articulated way. This is the stage at which the individual's personality acquires the basic psychological mechanism of self-regulation and self-control, when his self-identity becomes crystallized. It is also the stage at which the young are confronted with some models of the major roles they are supposed to emulate in adult life and with the major symbols and values of their culture and community. Moreover, in this phase the problem of the linkage of the personal temporal transition with cosmic or societal time becomes extremely acute. Any cultural definition of youth describes it as a transitory phase, couched in terms of transition toward something new, something basically different from the past. Hence the acuteness of the problem of linkage.

The very emphasis on the transitory nature of this stage and of its essentially preparatory character, however, may easily create a somewhat paradoxical situation. It may evolve an image of youth as the purest manifestation and repository of ultimate cultural and societal values. Such an image is rooted first in the fact that to some extent youth is always defined as a period of "role moratorium," that is, as a period in which one may play with various roles without definitely choosing any. It does not yet require

[2]The analysis of personal, cosmic, and societal time (or temporal progression) has constituted a fascinating but not easily dealt with focus of analysis. For some approaches to these problems, see *Man and Time* (papers from the Eranos Yearbooks, edited by Joseph Campbell; London: Routledge & Kegan Paul, 1958), especially the article by Gerardus van der Leeuw. See also Mircea Eliade, *The Myth of the Eternal Return.* Translated by W. R. Trask. New York: Pantheon Books, 1954 (Bollingen Series).

the various compromises inherent in daily participation in adult life. At the same time, however, since it is also the period when the maximum identification with the values of the society is stressed, under certain conditions it may be viewed as the repository of all the major human virtues and primordial qualities. It may then be regarded as the only age in which full identification with the ultimate values and symbols of the society is attained—facilitated by the flowering of physical vigor, a vigor which may easily become identified with a more general flowering of the cosmos or the society.

The fullest, the most articulate and definitive expression of these archetypal elements of youth is best exemplified in the ritual dramatization of the transition from adolescence to adulthood, such as the various *rites de passage* and ceremonies of initiation in primitive tribes and in ancient civilizations.[3] In these rites the pre-adult youth are transformed into full members of the tribe. This transformation is effected through:

1. a series of rites in which the adolescents are symbolically divested of the characteristics of youth and invested with those of adulthood, from a sexual and social point of view; this investment, which has deep emotional significance, may have various concrete manifestations: bodily mutilation, circumcision, the taking on of a new name or symbolic rebirth;
2. the complete symbolic separation of the male adolescents from the world of their youth, especially from their close attachment to their mothers; in other words, their complete "male" independence and image are fully articulated (the opposite usually holds true of girls' initiations) ;
3. the dramatization of the encounter between the several generations, a dramatization that may take the form of a fight or a competition, in which the basic complementariness of various age grades—whether of a continuous or discontinuous type—is stressed; quite often the discontinuity between adolescence and adulthood is symbolically expressed, as in the symbolic death of the adolescents as children and their rebirth as adults.
4. the transmission of the tribal lore with its instructions about proper behavior, both through formalized teaching and through various ritual activities; this transmission is combined with:
5. a relaxation of the concrete control of the adults over the erstwhile adolescents and its substitution by self-control and adult responsibility.

Most of these dramatic elements can also be found, although in somewhat more diluted forms, in various traditional folk festivals in peasant communities, especially those such as rural carnivals in which youth and marriage are emphasized. In an even more diluted form, these elements may

[3]For a fuller exposition of the sociological significance of initiation rites, see Mircea Eliade, *Birth and Rebirth* (New York: Harper & Brothers, 1958) and *From Generation to Generation.*

be found in various spontaneous initiation ceremonies of the fraternities and youth groups in modern societies.[4] Here, however, the full dramatic articulation of these elements is lacking, and their configuration and organization assume different forms.

The transition from childhood and adolescence to adulthood, the development of personal identity, psychological autonomy and self-regulation, the attempt to link personal temporal transition to general cultural images and to cosmic rhythms, and to link psychological maturity to the emulation of definite role models—these constitute the basic elements of any archetypal image of youth. However, the ways in which these various elements become crystallized in concrete configurations differ greatly from society to society and within sectors of the same society. The full dramatic articulation of these elements in the *rites de passage* of primitive societies constitutes only one—perhaps the most extreme and articulate but certainly not the only—configuration of these archetypal elements of youth.

In order to understand other types of such configurations, it is necessary to analyze some conditions that influence their development. Perhaps the best starting point is the nature of the social organization of the period of adolescence: the process of transition from childhood to adulthood, the social context in which the process of growing up is shaped and structured. There are two major criteria that shape the social organization of the period of youth. One is the extent to which age in general and youth in particular form a criterion for the allocation of roles in a society, whether in politics, in economic or cultural activity—aside from the family, of course, in which they always serve as such a criterion. The second is the extent to which any society develops specific age groups, specific corporate organizations, composed of members of the same "age," such as youth movements or old men's clubs. If roles are allocated in a society according to age, this greatly influences the extent to which age constitutes a component of a person's identity. In such cases, youth becomes a definite and meaningful phase of transition in an individual's progress through life, and his budding self-identity acquires content and a relation to role models and cultural values. No less important to the concrete development of identity is the extent to which it is influenced, either by the common participation of different generations in the same group as in the family, or conversely by the organization of members of the same age groups into specific, distinct groups.

The importance of age as a criterion for allocating roles in a society is closely related to several major aspects of social organization and cultural orientation. The first aspect is the relative complexity of the division of labor. In general, the simpler the organization of the society, the more influential age will be as a criterion for allocating roles. Therefore, in primitive or traditional societies (or in the more primitive and traditional sectors

[4]See Bruno Bettelheim, *Symbolic Wounds, Puberty Rites and the Envious Cirois* (Chicago: The Free Press of Glencoe, Illinois, 1954).

of developed societies) age and seniority constitute basic criteria for allocating social, economic, and political roles.

The second aspect consists of the major value orientations and symbols of a society, especially the extent to which they emphasize certain general orientations, qualities, or types of activity (such as physical vigor, the maintenance of cultural tradition, the achievement and maintenance of supernatural prowess) which can be defined in terms of broad human qualities and which become expressed and symbolized in specific ages.

The emphasis on any particular age as a criterion for the allocation of roles is largely related to the concrete application of the major value orientations in a society. For instance, we find that those primitive societies in which military values and orientations prevail emphasize young adulthood as the most important age, while those in which sedentary activities prevail emphasize older age. Similarly, within some traditional societies, a particular period such as old age may be emphasized if it is seen as the most appropriate one for expressing major cultural values and symbols—for instance, the upholding of a given cultural tradition.

The social and cultural conditions that determine the extent to which specific age groups and youth groups develop differ from the conditions that determine the extent to which age serves as a criterion for the allocation of roles. At the same time, the two kinds of conditions may be closely related, as we shall see. Age groups in general and youth groups in particular tend to arise in those societies in which the family or kinship unit cannot ensure (it may even impede) the attainment of full social status on the part of its members. These conditions appear especially (although not uniquely[5]) in societies in which family or kinship groups do not constitute the basic unit of the social division of labor. Several features characterize such societies. First, the membership in the total society (citizenship) is not defined in terms of belonging to any such family, kinship group, or estate, nor is it mediated by such a group.

Second, in these societies the major political, economic, social, and religious functions are performed not by family or kinship units but rather by various specialized groups (political parties, occupational associations, etc.), which individuals may join irrespective of their family, kinship, or caste. In these societies, therefore, the major roles that adults are expected to perform in the wider society differ in orientation from those of the family or kinship group. The children's identification and close interaction with family members of other ages does not assure the attainment of full self-identity and social maturity on the part of the children. In these cases, there arises a tendency for peer groups to form, especially youth groups; these can serve as a transitory phase between the world of childhood and the adult world.

This type of the social division of labor is found in varying degrees in different societies, primitive, historical, or modern. In several primitive tribes

[5]A special type of age groups may also develop in familistic societies. See *From Generation to Generation,* ch. 5.

such a division of labor has existed,[6] for example, in Africa, among the chiefless (segmentary) tribes of Nandi, Masai, or Kipsigis, in the village communities of Yako and Ibo, or in more centralized kingdoms of the Zulu and Swazi, and among some of the Indian tribes of the Plains, as well as among some South American and Indian tribes.

Such a division of labor likewise existed to some extent in several historical societies (especially in city states such as Athens or Rome), although most great historical civilizations were characterized mainly by a more hierarchical and ascriptive system of the division of labor, in which there were greater continuity and harmony between the family and kinship groups and the broader institutional contexts. The fullest development of this type of the social division of labor, however, is to be found in modern industrial societies. Their inclusive membership is usually based on the universal criterion of citizenship and is not conditioned by membership in any kinship group. In these societies the family does not constitute a basic unit of the division of labor, especially not in production and distribution, and even in the sphere of consumption its functions become more limited. Occupations are not transmitted through heredity. Similarly, the family or kinship group does not constitute a basic unit of political or ritual activities. Moreover, the general scope of the activities of the family has been continuously diminishing, while various specialized agencies tend to take over its functions in the fields of education and recreation.

To be sure, the extent to which the family is diminishing in modern societies is often exaggerated. In many social spheres (neighborhood, friendship, informal association, some class relations, community relations), family, kinship, and status are still very influential. But the scope of these relations is more limited in modern societies than in many others, even if the prevalent myth of the disappearance of the family has long since been exploded. The major social developments of the nineteenth century (the establishment of national states, the progress of the industrial revolution, the great waves of intercontinental migrations) have greatly contributed to this diminution of scope, and especially in the first phase of modernization there has been a growing discontinuity between the life of the children, whether in the family or the traditional school and in the social world with its new and enlarged perspectives.

Youth groups tend to develop in all societies in which such a division of labor exists. Youth's tendency to coalesce in such groups is rooted in the fact that participation in the family became insufficient for developing full identity or full social maturity, and that the roles learned in the family did not constitute an adequate basis for developing such identity and participation. In the youth groups the adolescent seeks some framework for the development and crystallization of his identity, for the attainment of personal autonomy, and for his effective transition into the adult world.

Various types of youth organizations always tend to appear with the

[6]For fuller details, see *From Generation to Generation,* especially chs. 3 and 4.

transition from traditional or feudal societies to modern societies, along with the intensified processes of change, especially in periods of rapid mobility, migration, urbanization, and industrialization. This is true of all European societies, and also of non-Western societies. The impact of Western civilization on primitive and historical-traditional peoples is usually connected with the disruption of family life, but beyond this it also involves a change in the mutual evaluation of the different generations. The younger generation usually begin to seek a new self-identification, and in one phase or another this search is expressed in ideological conflict with the older.

Most of the nationalistic movements in the Middle East, Asia, and Africa have consisted of young people, students, or officers who rebelled against their elders and the traditional familistic setting with its stress on the latters' authority. At the same time there usually has developed a specific youth consciousness and ideology that intensifies the nationalistic movement to "rejuvenate" the country.

The emergence of the peer group among immigrant children is a well-known phenomenon that usually appears in the second generation. It occurs mainly because of the relative breakdown of immigrant family life in the new country. The more highly industrialized and urbanized that country (or the sector absorbing the immigrants) is, the sharper the breakdown. Hence, the family of the immigrant or second-generation child has often been an inadequate guide to the new society. The immigrant child's attainment of full identity in the new land is usually related to how much he has been able to detach himself from his older, family setting. Some of these children, therefore, have developed a strong predisposition to join various peer groups. Such an affiliation has sometimes facilitated their transition to the absorbing society by stressing the values and patterns of behavior in that society—or, on the contrary, it may express their rebellion against this society, or against their older setting.

All these modern social developments and movements have given rise to a great variety of youth groups, peer groups, youth movements, and what has been called youth culture. The types and concrete forms of such groups vary widely: spontaneous youth groups, student movements, ideological and semipolitical movements, and youth rebellions connected with the Romantic movement in Europe, and, later, with the German youth movements. The various social and national trends of the nineteenth and twentieth centuries have also given impetus to such organizations. At the same time there have appeared many adult-sponsored youth organizations and other agencies springing out of the great extension of educational institutions. In addition to providing recreative facilities, these agencies have also aimed at character molding and the instilling of civic virtues, so as to deepen social consciousness and widen the social and cultural horizon. The chief examples are the YMCA, the Youth Brigades organized in England by William Smith, the Boy Scouts, the Jousters in France, and the many kinds of community organizations, hostels, summer camps, or vocational guidance centers.

Thus we see that there are many parallels between primitive and historical societies and modern societies with regard to the conditions under which the various constellations of youth groups, youth activities, and youth images have developed. But these parallels are only partial. Despite certain similarities, the specific configurations of the basic archetypal elements of the youth image in modern societies differ greatly from those of primitive and traditional societies. The most important differences are rooted in the fact that in the modern, the development of specific youth organizations is paradoxically connected with the weakening of the importance of age in general and youth in particular as definite criteria for the allocation of roles in society.

As we have already said, the extent to which major occupational, cultural, or political roles are allocated today according to the explicit criterion of age is very small. Most such roles are achieved according to wealth, acquired skills, specialization, and knowledge. Family background may be of great importance for the acquisition of these attributes, but very few positions are directly given people by virtue of their family standing. Yet this very weakening of the importance of age is always connected with intensive developments of youth groups and movements. This fact has several interesting repercussions on the organization and structure of such groups. In primitive and traditional societies, youth groups are usually part of a wider organization of age groups that covers a very long period of life, from childhood to late adulthood and even old age. To be sure, it is during youth that most of the dramatic elements of the transition from one age to another are manifest, but this stage constitutes only part of a longer series of continuous, well-defined stages.

From this point of view, primitive or traditional societies do not differ greatly from those in which the transition from youth to adulthood is not organized in specific age groups but is largely effected within the fold of the family and kinship groups. In both primitive and traditional societies we observe a close and comprehensive linkage between personal temporal transition and societal or cosmic time, a linkage most fully expressed in the *rites de passage*. Consequently, the transition from childhood to adulthood in all such societies is given full meaning in terms of ultimate cultural values and symbols borne or symbolized by various adult role models.

In modern societies the above picture greatly changes. The youth group, whatever its composition or organization, usually stands alone. It does not constitute a part of a fully institutionalized and organized series of age groups. It is true that in many of the more traditional sectors of modern societies the more primitive or traditional archetypes of youth still prevail. Moreover, in many modern societies elements of the primitive archetypes of youth still exist. But the full articulation of these elements is lacking, and the social organization and self-expression of youth are not given full legitimation or meaning in terms of cultural values and rituals.

The close linkage between the growth of personality, psychological maturation, and definite role models derived from the adult world has become greatly weakened. Hence the very coalescence of youth into special groups only tends to emphasize their problematic, uncertain standing from the point of view of cultural values and symbols. This has created a new constellation of the basic archetypal elements of youth. This new constellation can most clearly be seen in what has been called the emergence of the problems and stresses of adolescence in modern societies. While some of these stresses are necessarily common to adolescence in all societies, they become especially acute in modern societies.

Among these stresses the most important are the following: first, the bodily development of the adolescent constitutes a constant problem to him (or her). Since social maturity usually lags behind biological maturity, the bodily changes of puberty are not usually given a full cultural, normative meaning, and their evaluation is one of the adolescent's main concerns. The difficulty inherent in attaining legitimate sexual outlets and relations at this period of growth makes these problems even more acute. Second, the adolescent's orientation toward the main values of his society is also beset with difficulties. Owing to the long period of preparation and the relative segregation of the children's world from that of the adults, the main values of the society are necessarily presented to the child and adolescent in a highly selective way, with a strong idealistic emphasis. The relative unreality of these values as presented to the children—which at the same time are not given full ritual and symbolic expression—creates among the adolescents a great potential uncertainty and ambivalence toward the adult world.

This ambivalence is manifest, on the one hand, in a striving to communicate with the adult world and receive its recognition; on the other hand, it appears in certain dispositions to accentuate the differences between them and the adults and to oppose the various roles allocated to them by the adults. While they orient themselves to full participation in the adult world and its values, they usually attempt also to communicate with this world in a distinct, special way.

Parallel developments are to be found in the ideologies of modern youth groups. Most of these tend to create an ideology that emphasizes the discontinuity between youth and adulthood and the uniqueness of the youth period as the purest embodiment of ultimate social and cultural values. Although the explicitness of this ideology varies in extent from one sector of modern society to another, its basic elements are prevalent in almost all modern youth groups.

These processes have been necessarily accentuated in modern societies by the specific developments in cultural orientations in general and in the conception of time that has evolved in particular. The major social developments in modern societies have weakened the importance of broad cultural qualities as criteria for the allocation of roles. Similarly, important changes in the conception of time that is prevalent in modern societies have occurred. Primordial (cosmic-mythical, cyclical, or apocalyptical) conceptions of time have become greatly weakened, especially in their bearing on daily activities. The mechanical conception of time of modern technology has become much more prevalent. Of necessity this has greatly weakened the possibility of the direct ritual links between personal temporal changes and cosmic or societal progression. Therefore, the exploration of the actual meaning of major cultural values in their relation to the reality of the social world becomes one of the adolescent's main problems. This exploration may lead in many directions—cynicism, idealistic youth rebellion, deviant ideology and behavior, or a gradual development of a balanced identity.

Thus we see how all these developments in modern societies have created a new constellation of the basic archetypal elements of youth and the youth image. The two main characteristics of this constellation are the weakened possibility of directly linking the development of personality and the personal temporal transition with cosmic and societal time, on the one hand, and with the clear role models derived from the adult world, on the other.

In terms of personality development, this situation has created a great potential insecurity and the possible lack of a clear definition of personal identity. Yet it has also created the possibility of greater personal autonomy and flexibility in the choice of roles and the commitment to different values and symbols. In general, the individual, in his search for the meaning of his personal transition, has been thrown much more on his own powers.

These processes have provided the framework within which the various attempts to forge youth's identity and activities—both on the part of youth itself and on the part of various educational agencies—have developed. These attempts may take several directions. Youth's own activities and attempts at self-expression may first develop in the direction of considerable autonomy in the choice of roles and in commitment to various values. Conversely, they may develop in the direction of a more complete, fully organized and closed ideology connected with a small extent of personal autonomy. Second, these attempts may differ greatly in their emphasis on the direct linkage of cultural values to a specific social group and their view of these groups as the main bearers of such values.

In a parallel sense, attempts have been made on the part of various educational agencies to create new types of youth organizations within which youth can forge its identity and become linked to adult society. The purpose of such attempts has been two-fold: to provide youth with opportunities to develop a reasonably autonomous personality and a differentiated field of activity; and to encompass youth fully within well-organized groups set up by adult society and to provide them with full, unequivocal role models and symbols of identification. The interaction between these different tendencies of youth and the attempts of adult society to provide various frameworks for youth activities has given rise to the major types of youth organizations, movements, and ideologies manifested in modern societies.

These various trends and tendencies have created a situation in which, so far as we can ascertain, the number of casualties among youth has become very great—probably relatively much greater than in other types of societies. Youth's search for identity, for finding some place of its own in society, and its potential difficulties in coping with the attainment of such identity have given rise to the magnified extent of the casualties observed in the numerous youth delinquents of varying types. These failures, however, are not the only major youth developments in modern societies, although their relatively greater number is endemic in modern conditions. Much more extensive are the more positive attempts of youth to forge its own identity, to find some meaningful way of defining its place in the social and cultural context and of connecting social and political values with personal development in a coherent and signfiicant manner.

The best example in our times of the extreme upsurge of specific youth consciousness is seen in the various revolutionary youth movements. They range from the autonomous free German youth movements to the less spectacular youth movements in Central Europe and also to some extent to the specific youth culture of various more flexible youth groups. Here the attempt has been made to overcome the dislocation between personal transition and societal and cultural time. It is in these movements that the social dynamics of modern youth has found its fullest expression. It is in them that dreams of a new life, a new society, freedom and spontaneity, a new humanity and aspirations to social and cultural change have found utterance. It is in these youth movements that the forging of youth's new social identity has become closely connected with the development of new symbols of collective identity or new social-cultural symbols and meanings.

These movements have aimed at changing many aspects of the social and cultural life of their respective societies. They have depicted the present in a rather shabby form; they have dubbed it with adjectives of materialism, restriction, exploitation, lack of opportunity for self-fulfillment and creativity. At the same time they have held out hope for the future—seemingly, the not very far off future—when both self-fulfillment and collective fulfillment can be achieved and the materialistic civilization of the adult world can be shaken off. They have tried to appeal to youth to forge its own self-identity in terms of these new collective symbols, and this is why they have been so attractive to youth, for whom they have provided a set of symbols, hopes, and aims to which to direct its activities.

Within these movements the emphasis has been on a given social group or collectivity—nation, class, or the youth group itself—as the main, almost exclusive bearer of the "good" cultural value and symbols. Indeed, youth has at times been upheld as the sole and pure bearer of cultural values and social creativity. Through its association with these movements, youth has also been able to connect its aspiration for a different personal future, its anxiety to escape the present through plans and hopes for a different future within its cultural or social setting.

These various manifestations have played a crucial part in the emergence of social movements and parties in modern societies. Student groups have been the nuclei of the most important nationalistic and revolutionary movements in Central and Eastern Europe, in Italy, Germany, Hungary, and Russia. They have also played a significant role in Zionism and in the various waves of immigration to Israel. Their influence has become enormous in various fields, not only political and educational but cultural in general. In a way, education itself has tended to become a social movement. Many schools and universities, many teachers, have been among the most important bearers of collective values. The very spread of education is often seen as a means by which a new epoch might be ushered in.

The search for some connection between the personal situation of youth and social-cultural values has also stimulated the looser youth groups in modern societies, especially in the United States, and to some extent in Europe as well—though here the psychological meaning of the search is somewhat different. The looser youth groups have often shared some of the characteristics of the more defined youth movements, and they too have developed an emphasis on the attainment of social and cultural change. The yearning for a different personal future has likewise become connected with aspirations for changing the cultural setting, but not necessarily through a direct political or organized expression. They are principally important as a strong link with various collective, artistic, and literary aspirations aimed at changing social and cultural life. As such they are affiliated with various cultural values and symbols, not with any exclusive social groups. Thus they have necessarily developed a much greater freedom in choice of roles and commitment to values.

Specific social conditions surround the emergence of all these youth groups. In general, they are associated with a breakdown of traditional settings, the onset of modernization, urbanization, secularization, and industrialization. The less organized, more spontaneous types of youth organization and the more flexible kind of youth consciousness arise when the transition has been relatively smooth and gradual, especially in societies whose basic collective identity and political framework evince a large degree of continuity and a slow process of modernization. On the other hand, the more intensive types of youth movements tend to develop in those societies and periods in which the onset of modernization is connected with great upheavals and sharp cleavages in the social structure and the structure of authority and with the breakdown of symbols of collective identity.

In the latter situation the adult society has made many efforts to organize youth in what may be called totalistic organizations, in which clear role models and values might be set before youth and in which the extent of choice allowed youth is very limited and the manifestations of personal spontaneity and autonomy are restricted. Both types of conditions appeared in various European societies and in the United States in the nineteenth and early twentieth centuries, and in Asian and African societies in the second half of the twentieth century. The relative predominance of each of these conditions varies in different periods in these societies. However, with the progress of modernization and the growing absorption of broad masses within the framework of society, the whole basic setting of youth in modern society has changed—and it is this new framework that is predominant today and in which contemporary youth problems are shaped and played out.

The change this new framework represents is to some extent common both to the fully organized totalistic youth movements and to the looser youth groups. It is connected mainly with the institutionalizing of the aims and values toward the realization of which these movements were oriented, with the acceptance of such youth organizations as part of the structure of the general educational and cultural structure of their societies.

In Russia youth movements became fully institutionalized through the organization of the Komsomol. In many European countries the institutionalizing of youth groups, agencies, and ideologies came through association with political parties, or through acceptance as part of the educational system—an acceptance that sometimes entailed supervision by the official authorities. In the United States, many (such as the Boy Scouts) have become an accepted part of community life and to some extent a symbol of differential social status. In many Asian and African countries, organized youth movements have become part of the nationalistic movements and, independence won, have become part of the official educational organizations.

This institutionalizing of the values of youth movements in education and community life has been part of a wider process of institutionalizing various collective values. In some countries this has come about through revolution; in others, as a result of a long process of political and social evolution.

From the point of view of our analysis, these processes have had several important results. They have introduced a new element into the configuration of the basic archetypal elements of youth. The possibility of linking personal transition both to social groups and to cultural values—so strongly emphasized in the youth movements and noticeable to some extent even in the looser youth culture—has become greatly weakened. The social and sometimes even the cultural dimension of the future may thus become flattened and emptied. The various collective values become transformed. Instead of being remote goals resplendent with romantic dreams, they have become mundane objectives of the present, with its shabby details of daily politics and administration. More often than not they are intimately connected with the processes of bureaucratization.

All these mutations are associated with a notable decline in ideology and in preoccupation with ideology among many of the groups and strata in modern societies, with a general flattening of political-ideological motives and a growing apathy to them. This decline in turn is connected with what has been called the spiritual or cultural shallowness of the new social and economic benefits accruing from the welfare state—an emptiness illustrated by the fact that all these benefits are in the nature of things administered not by spiritual or social leaders but, as Stephen Toulmin has wittily pointed out, "the assistant postmaster." As a consequence, we observe the emptiness and meaninglessness of social relations, so often described by critics of the age of consumption and mass society.

In general, these developments have brought about the flattening of the image of the societal future and have deprived it of its allure. Between present and future there is no ideological discontinuity. The present has become the more important, if not the more meaningful, because the future has lost its characteristic as a dimension different from the present. Out of these conditions has grown what Riesman has called the cult of immediacy. Youth has been robbed, therefore, of the full experience of the dramatic transition from adolescence to adulthood and of the dramatization of the difference between present and future. Their own changing personal future has become dissociated from any changes in the shape of their societies or in cultural activities and values.

Paradoxically enough, these developments have often been connected with a strong adulation of youth—an adulation, however, which was in a way purely instrumental. The necessity of a continuous adjustment to new, changing conditions has emphasized the potential value of youth as the bearers of continuous innovation, of noncommitment to any specific conditions and values. But such an emphasis is often couched in terms of a purely instrumental adaptability, beyond which there is only the relative emptiness of the meaningless passage of time—of aging.[7]

Yet the impact on youth of what has been called postindustrial society need not result in such an emptiness and shallowness, although in recent literature these effects appear large indeed. It is as yet too early to make a full and adequate analysis of all these impacts. But it should be emphasized that the changes we have described, together with growing abundance and continuous technological change, have necessarily heightened the possibility of greater personal autonomy and cultural creativity and of the formation of the bases of such autonomy and of a flexible yet stable identity during the period of youth.

These new conditions have enhanced the possibility of flexibility in linking cultural values to social reality; they have enhanced the scope of personal and cultural creativity and the development of different personal culture. They have created the possibility of youth's developing what may be called a nonideological, direct identification with moral values, an awareness of the predicaments of moral choice that exist in any given situation, and individual responsibility for such choices—a responsibility that cannot be shed by relying on overarching ideological solutions oriented to the future.

These new social conditions exist in most industrial and postindustrial societies, sometimes together with the older conditions that gave rise to the more intensive types of youth movements. They constitute the framework within which the new configuration of the archetypal elements of youth and the new possibilities and problems facing youth in contemporary society develop. It is as yet too early to specify all these new possibilities and trends: here we have attempted to indicate some of their general contours.

[7]For an exposition of this view, see Paul Goodman, "Youth in Organized Society," *Commentary*, February 1960, pp. 95–107; and M. R. Stein, *The Eclipse of Community* (Princeton: Princeton University Press, 1960), especially pp. 215ff.; also, the review of this book by H. Rosenberg, "Community, Values, Comedy," *Commentary*, August 1960, pp. 150–157.

The Image of the Adolescent Minority

Edgar Z. Friedenberg

In our society there are two kinds of minority status. One of these I will call the "hot-blooded" minorities, whose archetypical image is that of the Negro or Latin. *In the United States, "Teen-agers" are treated as a "hot-blooded" minority.* Then, there are the "long-suffering minorities," whose archetype is the Jew, but which also, I should say, includes women. Try, for a second, to picture a Jewish "teen-ager," and you may sense a tendency for the image to grate. "Teen-agers" err on the hot side; they talk jive, drive hot-rods and become juvenile delinquents. Young Jews talk volubly, play the violin, and go to medical school, though never on Saturday.

The minority group is a special American institution, created by the interaction between a history and an ideology which are not to be duplicated elsewhere. Minority status has little to do with size or proportion. In a democracy, a dominant social group is called a majority and a part of its dominance consists in the power to arrange appropriate manifestations of public support; while a subordinate group is, by the logic of political morality, a minority. The minority stereotype, though affected by the actual characteristics of the minority group, develops to fit the purposes and expresses the anxieties of the dominant social group. It serves as a slimy coating over the sharp realities of cultural difference, protecting the social organism until the irritant can be absorbed.

Now, when one is dealing with a group that actually is genetically or culturally different from the dominant social group, this is perhaps to be expected. It is neither desirable nor inevitable, for xenophobia is neither desirable nor inevitable; but it is not surprising.

What is surprising is that the sons and daughters of the *dominant* adult group should be treated as a minority group merely because of their age. Their papers are in order and they speak the language adequately. In any society, to be sure, the young occupy a subordinate or probationary status while under tutelage for adult life. But a minority group is not merely subordinate; it is not under tutelage. It is in the process of being denatured; of becoming, under social stress, something more acceptable to

Reprinted by permission of *Dissent Magazine* 10 (Spring 1963): 149–58.

the dominant society, but essentially different from what its own growth and experience would lead to. Most beasts recognize their own kind. Primitive peoples may initiate their youth; we insist that ours be naturalized, though it is what is most natural about them that disturbs adults most.

The court of naturalization is the public school. A high school diploma is a certificate of legitimacy, not of competence. A youth needs one today in order to hold a job that will permit even minimal participation in the dominant society. Yet our laws governing school attendance do not deal with education. They are not *licensing* laws, requiring attendance until a certain defined minimum competence, presumed essential for adult life, has been demonstrated. They are not *contractual,* they offer no remedy for failure of the school to provide services of a minimum quality. A juvenile may not legally withdraw from school even if he can establish that it is substandard or that he is being ill-treated there. If he does, as many do, for just these reasons, he becomes *prima facie* an offender; for, in cold fact, the compulsory attendance law guarantees him nothing, not even the services of qualified teachers. It merely defines, in terms of age alone, a particular group as subject to legal restrictions not applicable to other persons.

Second-Class Citizen

Legally, the adolescent comes pretty close to having no basic rights at all. The state generally retains the final right even to strip him of his minority status. He has no right to *demand* the particular protection of *either* due process or the juvenile administrative procedure—the state decides. We have had several cases in the past few years of boys sixteen and under being sentenced to death by the full apparatus of formal criminal law, who would not have been permitted to claim its protection had they been accused of theft or disorderly conduct. Each of these executions has so far been forestalled by various legal procedures, but none in such a way as to establish the right of a juvenile to be tried as a juvenile; though he long ago lost his claim to be treated as an adult.

In the most formal sense, then, the adolescent is one of our second class citizens. But the informal aspects of minority status are also imputed to him. The "teen-ager," like the Latin or Negro, is seen as joyous, playful, lazy, and irresponsible, with brutality lurking just below the surface and ready to break out into violence.[1] All these groups are seen as childish and

[1]A very bad—indeed, vicious—but remarkably ambivalent reenactment of the entire fantasy on which the minority-status of the teen-ager is based can be seen in the movie *13 West St.* Here, the legal impotence of the "teen-ager" is taken absolutely for granted, and sadistic hostility of adults against him, though deplored, is condoned and accepted as natural. Occasional efforts are made to counterbalance the, in my judgment, pornographic picture of a brutal teen-age gang by presenting "good" teen-agers unjustly suspected, and decent police trying to resist sadistic pressure from the gang's victim, who drives one of its members to suicide. But despite this, the picture ends with a scene of the gang's victim—a virile-type rocket scientist—beating the leader of the gang with his cane

excitable, imprudent and improvident, sexually aggressive, and dangerous, but possessed of superb and sustained power to satisfy sexual demands. *West Side Story* is not much like *Romeo and Juliet;* but it is a great deal like *Porgy and Bess.*

The fantasy underlying this stereotype, then, is erotic; and its subject is male. The "hot-blooded" minorities are always represented by a masculine stereotype; nobody asks "Would you want your *son* to marry a Negro?" In each case, also, little counter-stereotypes, repulsively pallid in contrast to the alluring violence and conflict of the central scene, are held out enticingly by the dominant culture; the conscientious "teener" sold by Pat Boone to soothe adults while the kids themselves buy *Mad* and *Catcher;* the boy whose Italian immigrant mother sees to it that he wears a clean shirt to school every day on his way to the Governor's mansion; *Uncle Tom.* In the rectilinear planning of Jonesville these are set aside conspicuously as Public Squares, but at dusk they are little frequented.

One need hardly labor the point that what the dominant society seeks to control by imposing "hot-blooded" minority status is not the actual aggressiveness and sexuality of the Negro, the Latin, or the JD, but its own wish for what the British working classes used to call "a nice game of slap and tickle," on the unimpeachable assumption that a little of what you fancy does you good. This, the well-lighted Public Squares cannot afford; the community is proud of them, but they are such stuff as only the driest dreams are made of. These are not the dreams that are wanted. In my experience, it is just not possible to discuss adolescence with a group of American adults without being forced onto the topic of juvenile delinquency. Partly this is an expression of legitimate concern, but partly it is because only the JD has any emotional vividness for them.

I would ascribe the success of *West Side Story* to the functional equivalence in the minds of adults between adolescence, delinquency, and aggressive sexuality. Many who saw the show must have wondered, as I did, why there were no Negroes in it—one of the best things about Juvenile Delinquency is that, at least, it is integrated. Hollywood, doubtless, was as usual reluctant to show a member of an enfranchised minority group in an unfavorable light. But there was also a rather sound artistic reason. Putting a real Negro boy in *West Side Story* would have been like scoring the second movement of the *Pastorale* for an eagle rather than flute. The provocative, surly, sexy dancing kids who come to a bad end are not meant realistically. Efforts to use real street-adolescents in *West Side Story* had to be abandoned; they didn't know how to act. What was depicted here was neither Negro nor white nor really delinquent, but a comfortably vulgar middle-class dream of a "hot-blooded" minority. In dreams a single symbolic boy can represent them all; let the symbol turn real and the dreamer wakes up screaming.

---

and attempting to drown the boy in a swimming pool—which the police dismiss as excusable under the circumstances. A Honolulu paper, at least, described this scene of attempted murder as "an old-fashioned caning that had the audience cheering in its seats."

Adolescents are treated as a "hot-blooded" minority, then, because they seem so good at slap-and-tickle. But a number of interesting implications flow from this. Slap-and-tickle implies sexual vigor and attractiveness, warmth and aggression, salted with enough conventional perversity to lend spice to a long dull existence. Such perversity is a kind of exuberant overflow from the mainstream of sexuality, not a diversion of it. It is joyous excess and bounty; extravagant foreplay in the well-worn marriage-bed; the generosity of impulse that leads the champion lover of the high school to prance around the shower-room snapping a towel on the buttocks of his team-mates three hours before a hot date, just to remind them that life can be beautiful.

Experience Repressed

When a society sees impulsiveness and sexual exuberance as minority characteristics which unsuit the individual for membership until he is successfully naturalized, it is in pretty bad shape. Adolescents, loved, respected, taught to accept, enjoy, and discipline their feelings, grow up. "Teen-agers" don't; they pass. Then, in middle-age, they have the same trouble with their former self that many ethnics do. They hate and fear the kinds of spontaneity that remind them of what they have abandoned, and they hate themselves for having joined forces with and having come to resemble their oppressors.[2] This is the vicious spiral by which "hot-blooded" minority status maintains itself. I am convinced that it is also the source of the specific hostility—and sometimes sentimentality—that adolescents arouse in adults. The processes involved have been dealt with in detail by Daniel Boorstin, Leslie Fiedler, Paul Goodman, and especially Ernest Schachtel.[3] Their effect is to starve out, through silence and misrepresentation, the capacity to have genuine and strongly felt experience, and to replace it by the conventional symbols that serve as the common currency of daily life.

Experience repressed in adolescence does not, of course, result in amnesia, as does the repression of childhood experience; it leaves no temporal gaps in the memory. This makes it more dangerous, because the adult is then quite unaware that his memory is incomplete, that the most significant components of feeling have been lost or driven out. We at least know that we no longer know what we felt as children. But an adolescent boy who asks his father how he felt on the first night he spent in barracks or with a woman will be told what the father now thinks he felt because he ought to have; and this is very dangerous nonsense indeed.

[2]Cf. Abraham Kardiner and Lionel Ovesey's classic, *The Mark of Oppression* (New York: Norton, 1951), for a fascinating study of these dynamics among American Negroes.

[3]Daniel Boorstin, *The Image*. New York: Atheneum, 1962; Leslie Fiedler, "The Fear of the Impulsive Life." *WFMT Perspective,* October, 1961, pp. 4–9; Paul Goodman, *Growing Up Absurd*. New York: Random House, 1960, p. 38; Ernest Schachtel, "On Memory and Childhood Amnesia." Widely anthologized, cf. the author's *Metamorphosis*. New York: Basic Books, 1959, pp. 279–322.

Whether in childhood or in adolescence, the same quality of experience is starved out or repressed. It is still the spontaneous, vivid and immediate that is most feared, and feared the more because so much is desired. But there is a difference in focus and emphasis because in adolescence spontaneity can lead to much more serious consequences.

This, perhaps, is the crux of the matter; since it begins to explain why our kind of society should be so easily plunged into conflict by "hot-blooded" minorities in general and adolescent boys in particular. We are consequence-oriented and future-oriented. Among us, to prefer present delights is a sign of either low or high status, and both are feared. Schachtel makes it clear how we go about building this kind of character in the child —by making it difficult for him to notice his delights when he has them, and obliterating the language in which he might recall them joyfully later. This prepares the ground against the subsequent assault of adolescence. But it is a strong assault, and if adolescence wins, the future hangs in the balance.

The Adolescent Girl

In this assault, adolescent boys play a very different role from adolescent girls; and are dealt with unconsciously by totally different dynamics. Adolescent girls are not seen as members of a "hot-blooded" minority, and to this fact may be traced some interesting paradoxes in our perception of the total phenomenon of adolescence.

Many critics of the current literature on adolescence—Bruno Bettelheim[4] perhaps most cogently—have pointed out that most contemporary writing about adolescents ignores the adolescent girl almost completely. Bettelheim specifically mentions Goodman and myself; the best novels about adolescents of the past decade or so have been, I think there would be fair agreement, Salinger's *The Catcher in the Rye,* John Knowles' *A Separate Peace,* and Colin MacInnes' less well known but superb *Absolute Beginners.* All these have adolescent boys as heroes. Yet, as Bettelheim points out, the adolescent girl is as important as the adolescent boy, and her actual plight in society is just as severe; her opportunities are even more limited and her growth into a mature woman as effectively discouraged. Why has she not aroused more interest?

There are demonstrable reasons for the prominence of the adolescent boy in our culture. Conventionally, it is he who threatens the virtue of our daughters and the integrity of our automobiles. There are so many more ways to get hung up on a boy. "Teen-agers," too, may be all right; but would you want your daughter to marry one? When she doesn't know anything about him except how she feels—and what does that matter when they are both too young to know what they are doing; when he may never have the makings of an executive, or she of an executive's wife?

For this last consideration, paradoxically, also makes the *boy,* rather

[4]In "Adolescence and the Conflict of Generations," *Daedalus,* Winter, 1962, p. 68.

than the girl, the focus of anxiety. He alone bears the terrible burden of parental aspirations; it is his capacity for spontaneous commitment that endangers the opportunity of adults to live vicariously the life they never managed to live personally.

Holden, Finny, and the unnamed narrator of *Absolute Beginners,* are adolescent boys who do not pass; who retain their minority status, their spontaneous feelings, their power to act out and act up. They go prancing to their destinies. But what destiny can we imagine for them? We leave Holden in a mental hospital, being adjusted to reality; and Finny dead of the horror of learning that his best friend, Gene, had unconsciously contrived the accident that broke up his beautifully articulated body. The Absolute Beginner, a happier boy in a less tense society, fares better; he has had more real contact with other human beings, including a very satisfactory father, and by his time there is such a thing as a "teen-ager," little as it is, for him to be. On this basis the Beginner can identify himself; the marvelous book ends as he rushes out onto the tarmac at London Airport, bursting through the customs barrier, to stand at the foot of the gangway and greet a planeload of astonished immigrants by crying, "Here I am! Meet your first teen-ager."

Political Disinterest

There are still enough Finnys and Holdens running around free to give me much joy and some hope, and they are flexible enough to come to their own terms with reality. But the system is against them, and they know it well. Why, then, do they not try to change it? Why are none of these novels of adolescence political novels? Why have their heroes no political interests at all? In this respect, fiction is true to American life; American adolescents are notably free from political interests. I must maintain this despite the recent advances of SANE kids and Freedom Riders; for, though I love and honor them for their courage and devotion, the causes they fight for are not what I would call political. No controversy over basic policy is involved, because nobody advocates atomic disaster or racial persecution. The kids' opponents are merely in favor of the kind of American society that these evils flourish in, and the youngsters do not challenge the system itself, though they are appalled by its consequences.

Yet could they, as adolescents, be political? I don't think so; and I don't know that I would be pleased if they were. American politics is a cold-blooded business indeed. Personal clarity and commitment are not wanted in it and not furthered by it. I do not think this is necessarily true of all politics; but it becomes true when the basic economic and social assumptions are as irrational as ours.

Political effectiveness in our time requires just the kind of caginess, pseudo-realism, and stereotyping of thought and feeling; the same submergence of spontaneity to the exigencies of collective action that mark the ruin of adolescence. Adolescents are, inherently, anti-mass; they take things personally. Sexuality, itself, has this power to resolve relationships into the immediate and interpersonal. As a symbol the cocky adolescent boy stands, a little like Luther, an obstacle to compromise and accommodation. Such symbols stick in the mind, though the reality can usually be handled. With occasional spectacular failures we do manage to assimilate the "teen-age" minority; the kids learn not to get fresh; they get smart, they dry up. We are left then, like the Macbeths, with the memory of an earlier fidelity. But Lady Macbeth was less resourceful than ourselves; she knew next to nothing about industrial solvents. Where she had only perfume we have oil.

The Girl As Woman

This is how we use the boy, but what about the girl? I have already asserted that, since she is not perceived as a member of the "hot-blooded" minority she cannot take his place in the unconscious, which is apt to turn very nasty if it is fobbed off with the wrong sex. Is she then simply not much involved by our psychodynamics, or is she actively repressed? Is she omitted from our fantasies or excluded from them?

It may seem very strange that I should find her so inconspicuous. Her image gets so much publicity. Drum-majorettes and cheerleaders are ubiquitous; *Playboy* provides businessmen with a new *playmate* each month. Nymphets are a public institution.

Exactly, and they serve a useful public function. American males are certainly anxious to project a heterosexual public image, and even more anxious to believe in it themselves. None of us, surely, wishes to feel obligated to hang himself out of respect for the United States Senate; it is, as Yum-Yum remarked to Nanki-Poo, such a stuffy death. I am not questioning our sincerity; the essence of my point is that in what we call maturity we feel what we are supposed to feel, and nothing else. But I am questioning the depth and significance of our interest in the cover or pin-up girl. Her patrons are concerned to experience their own masculinity; they are not much interested in her: I reject the celebration of "babes" in song and story as evidence that we have adolescent girls much on our minds; if we did we wouldn't think of them as "babes." I think, indeed, that in contrast to the boy, of whom we are hyperaware, we repress our awareness of the girl. She is not just omitted, she is excluded.

The adolescent heroine in current fiction is not interpreted in the same way as the adolescent hero, even when the parallel is quite close. Her adolescence is treated as less crucial; she is off-handedly accepted as a woman already. This is true even when the author struggles against it. *Lolita,* for example, is every bit as much a tragic heroine of adolescence as Holden is a hero—she isn't as nice a girl as he is a boy, but they are both victims of the same kind of corruption in adult society and the same absense of any real opportunity to grow up to be themselves. Lolita's failure is the classic failure of identity in adolescence; and Humbert knows this and accepts responsibility for it; this is the crime he expiates. But this is not the way Lolita—the character, not the book—is generally received. Unlike Holden, she has no cult and is not vouchsafed any dignity. It is thought to be comical that, at fourteen, she is already a whore.

A parallel example is to be found in Rumer Godden's *The Greengage Summer*. Here the story is explicitly about Joss's growing up. The author's emphasis is on the way her angry betrayal of her lover marks the end of her childhood; her feelings are now too strong and confused, and too serious in their consequences, to be handled with childish irresponsibility; she can no longer claim the exemptions of childhood. But what the movie presented, it seemed to me, was almost entirely an account of her rise to sexual power; Joss had become a Babe at last.

One reason that we do not take adolescent growth seriously in girls is that we do not much care what happens to people unless it has economic consequences: what would Holden ever be, since he never even graduates from high school; who would hire him? He has a problem; Lolita could always be a waitress or something, what more could she expect? Since we define adulthood almost exclusively in economic terms, we obviously cannot concern ourselves as much about the growth of those members of society who are subject from birth to restricted economic opportunity. But so, of course, are the members of the "hot-blooded" minorities; though we find their hot-bloodedness so exciting that we remain aware of them anyway.

But girls, like Jews, are not supposed to fight back; we expect them, instead, to insinuate themselves coyly into the roles available. In our society, there are such lovely things for them to be. They can take care of other people and clean up after them. Women can become wives and mothers; Jews can become kindly old Rabbis and philosophers and even psychoanalysts and lovable comic essayists. They can become powers behind the power; a fine old law firm runs on the brains of its anonymous young Jews just as a husband's best asset is his loyal and unobtrusive wife. A Jewish girl can become a Jewish Mother, and this is a role which even Plato would have called essential.

Effects of Discrimination

Clearly, this kind of discrimination is quite different from that experienced by the "hot-blooded" minorities; and must be based on a very different image in the minds of those who practice it and must have a different impact upon them. Particularly, in the case of the adolescent, the effect on the adult of practicing these two kinds of discrimination will be different. The adolescent boy must be altered to fit middle-class adult roles, and when he has been he becomes a much less vital creature. But the girl is merely squandered, and this wastage will continue all her life. Since adolescence is, for boy and girl alike, the time of life in which the self must be established, the girl suffers as much from being wasted as the boy does from being cut down; there has recently been, for example, a number of tragic suicides reported among adolescent girls, though suicide generally is far less common among females. But from the point of view of the dominant society nothing special is done to the female in adolescence—the same squeeze continues throughout life, even though this is when it hurts most.

The guilts we retain for our treatments of "hot-blooded" and "long-suffering" minorities therefore affect us in contrasting ways. For the boy we suffer angry, paranoid remorse, as if he were Billy the Kid, or Budd. We had to do our duty, but how can we ever forget him? But we do not attack the girl; we only neglect her and leave her to wither gradually through an unfulfilled life; and the best defense against this sort of guilt is selective inattention. We just don't see her; instead, we see a caricature, not brutalized as in the case of the boy, to justify our own brutality; but sentimentalized, roseate, to reassure us that we have done her no harm, and that she is well contented. Look: she even has her own telephone, with what is left of the boy dangling from the other end of the line.

A Lonely Ride

This is the fantasy; the reality is very different, but it is bad enough to be a "Teen-ager." The adolescent is now the only totally disfranchised minority group in the country. In America, no minority has ever gotten any respect or consistently decent treatment until it began to acquire political power. The vote comes before anything else. This is obviously true of the Negro at the present time; his recent advances have all been made under—sometimes reluctant—Federal auspices because, nationally, Negroes vote, and Northern Negroes are able to cast a ballot on which their buffeted Southern rural fellows may be pulled to firmer political ground. This is what makes it impossible to stop Freedom Rides; just as the comparative militance of the Catholic Church in proceeding toward integration in Louisiana may have less to do with Louisiana than Nigeria, which is in grave danger of falling into the hands of Black Muslims. People generally sympathetic with adolescents sometimes say, "Well, it really isn't fair; if they're old enough to be drafted, they're old enough to vote," which is about as naive as it is possible to get.

Can the status of the "teen-ager" be improved? Only, presumably, through increased political effectiveness. Yet, it is precisely here that a crucial dilemma arises. For the aspirations of the adolescent minority are completely different from those of other minorities. All the others are struggling to obtain what the adolescent is struggling to avoid. They seek and welcome the conventional American middle-class status that has been partially or totally barred to them. But this is what the adolescent is left with if he gives in and goes along.

In the recent and very moving CORE film, *Freedom Ride,* one of the heroic group who suffered beatings and imprisonment for their efforts to end segregation says, as nearly as I can recall, "If the road to freedom leads through the jails of the South, then that's the road I'll take." It may be the road to freedom; but it is the road to suburbia too. You can't tell which the people are headed for until they are nearly there; but all our past ethnic groups have settled for suburbia, and the people who live there bear witness that freedom is somewhere else.

I am not sure there *is* a road to freedom in America. Not enough people want to go there; the last I can recall was H. D. Thoreau, and he went on foot, through the woods, alone. This still may be the only way to get there. For those with plenty of guts, compassion, and dedication to social justice, who nevertheless dislike walking alone through the woods, or feel it to be a Quixotic extravagance, a freedom ride is a noble enterprise. Compared to them, the individual boy or girl on a solitary journey must seem an anachronism. Such a youngster has very little place in our way of life. And of all the criticisms that might be directed against that way of life, this is the harshest.

The Making of a Counter Culture

Theodore Roszak

The fact is, it is the young who have in their own amateurish, even grotesque way, gotten dissent off the adult drawing board. They have torn it out of the books and journals an older generation of radicals authored, and they have fashioned it into a style of life. They have turned the hypotheses of disgruntled elders into experiments, though often without the willingness to admit that one may have to concede failure at the end of any true experiment.

When all is said and done, however, one cannot help being ambivalent toward this compensatory dynamism of the young. For it is, at last, symptomatic of a thoroughly diseased state of affairs. It is not ideal, it is probably not even good that the young should bear so great a responsibility for inventing or initiating for their society as a whole. It is too big a job for them to do successfully. It is indeed tragic that in a crisis that demands the tact and wisdom of maturity, everything that looks most hopeful in our culture should be building from scratch—as must be the case when the builders are absolute beginners.

Beyond the parental default, there are a number of social and psychic

Reprinted by permission of Doubleday Anchor Books from *The Making of the Counter Culture,* by Theodore Roszak, 1969, pp. 26–41.

facts of life that help explain the prominence of the dissenting young in our culture. In a number of ways, this new generation happens to be particularly well placed and primed for action.

Most obviously, the society is getting younger—to the extent that in America, as in a number of European countries, a bit more than 50 per cent of the population is under twenty-five years of age. Even if one grants that people in their mid-twenties have no business claiming, or letting themselves be claimed for the status of "youth," there still remains among the authentically young in the thirteen to nineteen bracket a small nation of twenty-five million people. (As we shall see below, however, there is good reason to group the mid-twenties with their adolescent juniors.)

But numbers alone do not account for the aggressive prominence of contemporary youth. More important, the young seem to *feel* the potential power of their numbers as never before. No doubt to a great extent this is because the market apparatus of our consumer society has devoted a deal of wit to cultivating the age-consciousness of old and young alike. Teen-agers alone control a stupendous amount of money and enjoy much leisure, so, inevitably, they have been turned into a self-conscious market. They have been pampered, exploited, idolized, and made almost nauseatingly much of. With the result that whatever the young have fashioned for themselves has rapidly been rendered grist for the commercial mill and cynically merchandised by assorted hucksters—*including* the new ethos of dissent, a fact that creates an agonizing disorientation for the dissenting young (and their critics) and to which we will return presently.

The force of the market has not been the only factor in intensifying age-consciousness, however. The expansion of higher education has done even more in this direction. In the United States we have a college population of nearly six million, an increase of more than double over 1950. And the expansion continues as college falls more and more into the standard educational pattern of the middle-class young.[1] Just as the dark satanic mills of early industrialism concentrated labor and helped create the class-consciousness of the proletariat, so the university campus, where up to

[1]The rapid growth of the college population is an international phenomenon, with Germany, Russia, France, Japan, and Czechoslovakia (among the developed countries) equaling or surpassing the increase of the United States. UNESCO statistics for the period 1950–64 are as follows:

	1950	*1964*	*Increase*
U.S.A.	2.3 million	5 million	2.2×
U.K.	133,000	211,000	1.6×
U.S.S.R.	2.2 million	3.6 million	3.0×
Italy	192,000	262,000	1.3×
France	140,000	455,000	3.3×
W. Germany	123,000	343,000	2.8×
W. Berlin	12,000	31,000	2.6×
Czechoslovakia	44,000	142,000	3.2×
Japan	391,000	917,000	2.3×
India	404,000	1.1 million	2.2×

thirty thousand students may be gathered, has served to crystallize the group identity of the young—with the important effect of mingling freshmen of seventeen and eighteen with graduate students well away in their twenties. On the major campuses, it is often enough the graduates who assume positions of leadership, contributing to student movements a degree of competence that the younger students could not muster. When one includes in this alliance that significant new entity, the non-student—the campus roustabout who may be in his late twenties—one sees why "youth" has become such a long-term career these days. The grads and the non-students easily come to identify their interests and allegiance with a distinctly younger age group. In previous generations, they would long since have left these youngsters behind. But now they and the freshmen just out of high school find themselves all together in one campus community.

The role of these campus elders is crucial, for they tend to be those who have the most vivid realization of the new economic role of the university. Being closer to the technocratic careers for which higher education is supposed to be grooming them in the Great Society, they have a delicate sensitivity to the social regimentation that imminently confronts them, and a stronger sense of the potential power with which the society's need for trained personnel endows them. In some cases their restiveness springs from a bread-and-butter awareness of the basic facts of educational life these days, for in England, Germany, and France the most troublesome students are those who have swelled the numbers in the humanities and social studies only to discover that what the society really wants out of its schools is technicians, not philosophers. In Britain, this strong trend away from the sciences over the past four years continues to provoke annoyed concern from public figures who are not the least bit embarrassed to reveal their good bourgeois philistinism by loudly observing that the country is not spending its money to produce poets and Egyptologists—and then demanding a sharp cut in university grants and stipends.[2]

Yet at the same time, these non-technicians know that the society cannot do without its universities, that it cannot shut them down or brutalize the students without limit. The universities produce the brains the technocracy needs; therefore, making trouble on the campus is making trouble in one of the economy's vital sectors. And once the graduate students—many of whom may be serving as low-level teaching assistants—have been infected with qualms and aggressive discontents, the junior faculty, with whom they overlap, may soon catch the fevers of dissent and find themselves drawn into the orbit of "youth."

The troubles at Berkeley in late 1966 illustrate the expansivenes of youthful protest. To begin with, a group of undergraduates stages a sit-in against naval recruiters at the Student Union. They are soon joined by a

[2]In his 1967 Reith Lectures, Dr. Edmund Leach seeks to account for the steady swing from the sciences. See his *Runaway World*, British Broadcasting Company, 1968. For reflections on the same phenomenon in Germany, see Max Beloff's article in *Encounter*, July 1968, pp. 28–33.

contingent of non-students, whom the administration then martyrs by selective arrest. A non-student of nearly thirty—Mario Savio, already married and a father—is quickly adopted as spokesman for the protest. Finally, the teaching assistants call a strike in support of the menaced demonstration. When at last the agitation comes to its ambiguous conclusion, a rally of thousands gathers outside Sproul Hall, the central administration building, to sing the Beatles' "Yellow Submarine"—which happens to be the current hit on all the local high-school campuses. If "youth" is not the word we are going to use to cover this obstreperous population, then we may have to coin another. But undeniably the social grouping exists with a self-conscious solidarity.

If we ask who is to blame for such troublesome children, there can be only one answer: it is the parents who have equipped them with an anemic superego. The current generation of students is the beneficiary of the particularly permissive child-rearing habits that have been a feature of our postwar society. Dr. Spock's endearing latitudinarianism (go easy on the toilet training, don't panic over masturbation, avoid the heavy discipline) is much more a reflection than a cause of the new (and wise) conception of proper parent-child relations that prevails in our middle class. A high-consumption, leisure-wealthy society simply doesn't need contingents of rigidly trained, "responsible" young workers. It cannot employ more than a fraction of untrained youngsters fresh out of high school. The middle class can therefore afford to prolong the ease and drift of childhood, and so it does. Since nobody expects a child to learn any marketable skills until he gets to college, high school becomes a country club for which the family pays one's dues. Thus the young are "spoiled," meaning they are influenced to believe that being human has something to do with pleasure and freedom. But unlike their parents, who are also avid for the plenty and leisure of the consumer society, the young have not had to sell themselves for their comforts or to accept them on a part-time basis. Economic security is something they can take for granted—and on it they build a new, uncompromised personality, flawed perhaps by irresponsible ease, but also touched with some outspoken spirit. Unlike their parents, who must kowtow to the organizations from which they win their bread, the youngsters can talk back at home with little fear of being thrown out in the cold. One of the pathetic, but, now we see, promising characteristics of postwar America has been the uppityness of adolescents and the concomitant reduction of the paterfamilias to the general ineffectuality of a Dagwood Bumstead. In every family comedy of the last twenty years, dad has been the buffoon.

The permissiveness of postwar child-rearing has probably seldom met A. S. Neill's standards—but it has been sufficient to arouse expectations. As babies, the middle-class young got picked up when they bawled. As children, they got their kindergarten finger paintings thumbtacked on the living room wall by mothers who knew better than to discourage incipient artistry. As adolescents, they perhaps even got a car of their own (or control of the family's), with all of the sexual privileges attending. They passed through school systems which, dismal as they all are in so many respects, have nevertheless prided themselves since World War II on the introduction of "progressive" classes having to do with "creativity" and "self-expression." These are also the years that saw the proliferation of all the mickey mouse courses which take the self-indulgence of adolescent "life problems" so seriously. Such scholastic pap mixes easily with the commercial world's effort to elaborate a total culture of adolescence based on nothing but fun and games. (What else could a culture of adolescence be based on?) The result has been to make of adolescence, not the beginning of adulthood, but a status in its own right: a limbo that is nothing so much as the prolongation of an already permissive infancy.

To be sure, such an infantization of the middle-class young has a corrupting effect. It ill prepares them for the real world and its unrelenting if ever more subtle disciplines. It allows them to nurse childish fantasies until too late in life; until there comes the inevitable crunch. For as life in the multiversity wears on for these pampered youngsters, the technocratic reality principle begins grimly to demand its concessions. The young get told they are now officially "grown up," but they have been left too long without any taste for the rigidities and hypocrisies that adulthood is supposed to be all about. General Motors all of a sudden wants barbered hair, punctuality, and an appropriate reverence for the conformities of the organizational hierarchy. Washington wants patriotic cannon fodder with no questions asked. Such prospects do not look like fun from the vantage point of between eighteen and twenty years of relatively carefree drifting.[3]

Some of the young (most of them, in fact) summon up the proper sense of responsibility to adjust to the prescribed patterns of adulthood; others, being incorrigibly childish, do not. They continue to assert pleasure and freedom as human rights and begin to ask aggressive questions of those forces that insist, amid obvious affluence, on the continued necessity of discipline, no matter how subliminal. This is why, for example, university administrators are forced to play such a false game with their students, insisting on the one hand that the students are "grown-up, responsible men and women," but on the other hand knowing full well that they dare not entrust such erratic children with any power over their own education. For what can one rely upon them to do that will suit the needs of technocratic regimentation?

The incorrigibles either turn political or drop out. Or perhaps they fluctuate between the two, restless, bewildered, hungry for better ideas about grown-upness than GM or IBM or LBJ seem able to offer. Since they are improvising their own ideal of adulthood—a task akin to lifting oneself by one's bootstraps—it is all too easy to go pathetically wrong. Some become ne'er-do-well dependents, bumming about the bohemias of America and

[3]Even the Young Americans for Freedom, who staunchly champion the disciplined virtues of the corporate structure, have become too restive to put up with the indignity of conscription. With full support from Ayn Rand, they have set the draft down as "selective slavery." How long will it be before a conservatism that perceptive recognizes that the ideal of free enterprise has nothing to do with technocratic capitalism?

Europe on money from home; others simply bolt. The FBI reports the arrest of over ninety thousand juvenile runaways in 1966; most of those who flee well-off middle-class homes get picked up by the thousands each current year in the big-city bohemias, fending off malnutrition and venereal disease. The immigration departments of Europe record a constant level over the past few years of something like ten thousand disheveled "flower children" (mostly American, British, German, and Scandinavian) migrating to the Near East and India—usually toward Katmandu (where drugs are cheap and legal) and a deal of hard knocks along the way. The influx has been sufficient to force Iran and Afghanistan to substantially boost the "cash in hand" requirements of prospective tourists. And the British consul-general in Istanbul officially requested Parliament in late 1967 to grant him increased accommodations for the "swarm" of penniless young Englishmen who have been cropping up at the consulate on their way east, seeking temporary lodgings or perhaps shelter from Turkish narcotics authorities.[4]

One can flippantly construe this exodus as the contemporary version of running off with the circus; but the more apt parallel might be with the quest of third-century Christians (a similarly scruffy, uncouth, and often half-mad lot) for escape from the corruptions of Hellenistic society: it is much more a flight *from* than *toward.* Certainly for a youngster of seventeen, clearing out of the comfortable bosom of the middle-class family to become a beggar is a formidable gesture of dissent. One makes light of it at the expense of ignoring a significant measure of our social health.

So, by way of a dialectic Marx could never have imagined, technocratic America produces a potentially revolutionary element among its own youth. The bourgeoisie, instead of discovering the class enemy in its factories, finds it across the breakfast table in the person of its own pampered children. To be sure, by themselves the young might drift into hopeless confusion and despair. But now we must add one final ingredient to this ebullient culture of youthful dissent, which gives it some chance of achieving form and direction. This is the adult radical who finds himself in a plight which much resembles that of the bourgeois intellectual in Marxist theory. In despair for the timidity and lethargy of his own class, Marx's middle-class revolutionary was supposed at last to turn renegade and defect to the proletariat. So in postwar America, the adult radical, confronted with a diminishing public among the "cheerful robots" of his own generation, naturally gravitates to the restless middle-class young. Where else is he to find an audience? The working class, which provided the traditional following for radical ideology, now neither leads nor follows, but sits tight and plays safe: the stoutest prop of the established order. If the adult radical is white, the ideal of Black Power progressively seals off his entrée to Negro organizations. As for the exploited masses of the Third World, they have as little use for white Western ideologues as our native blacks—and in any case they are far distant. Unless he follows the strenuous example of a Regis Debray, the white American rad-

[4]For the statistics mentioned, see *Time,* September 15, 1967, pp. 47–49; *The Observer* (London), September 24, 1967; and *The Guardian* (London), November 18, 1967.

ical can do little more than sympathize from afar with the revolutionary movements of Asia, Africa, and Latin America.

On the other hand, the disaffected middle-class young are at hand, suffering a strange new kind of "immiserization" that comes of being stranded between a permissive childhood and an obnoxiously conformist adulthood, experimenting desperately with new ways of growing up self-respectfully into a world they despise, calling for help. So the radical adults bid to become gurus to the alienated young or perhaps the young draft them into service.

Of course, the young do not win over all the liberal and radical adults in sight. From more than a few their readiness to experiment with a variety of dissenting life styles comes in for severe stricture—which is bound to be exasperating for the young. What are they to think? For generations, left-wing intellectuals have lambasted the bad habits of bourgeois society. "The bourgeoisie" they have insisted, "is obsessed by greed; its sex life is insipid and prudish; its family patterns are debased; its slavish conformities of dress and grooming are degrading; its mercenary routinization of existence is intolerable; its vision of life is drab and joyless; etc., etc." So the restive young, believing what they hear, begin to try this and that, and one by one they discard the vices of their parents, preferring the less structured ways of their own childhood and adolescence—only to discover many an old-line dissenter, embarrassed by the brazen sexuality and unwashed feet, the disheveled dress and playful ways, taking up the chorus, "No, that is not what I meant. That is not what I meant at all."

For example, a good liberal like Hans Toch invokes the Protestant work ethic to give the hippies a fatherly tongue-lashing for their "consuming but noncontributing" ways. They are being "parasitic," Professor Toch observes, for "the hippies, after all accept—even demand—social services, while rejecting the desirability of making a contribution to the economy."[5] But *of course* they do. Because we have an economy of cybernated abundance that does not need their labor, that is rapidly severing the tie between work and wages, that suffers from hard-core poverty due to maldistribution, not scarcity. From this point of view, why is the voluntary dropping-out of the hip young any more "parasitic" than the enforced dropping-out of impoverished ghetto dwellers? The economy can do abundantly without all this labor. How better, then, to spend our affluence than on those minimal goods and services that will support leisure for as many of us as possible? Or are these hippies reprehensible because they seem to enjoy their mendicant idleness, rather than feeling, as the poor apparently should, indignant and fighting mad to get a good respectable forty-hour-week job? There are criticisms to be made of the beat-hip bohemian fringe of our youth culture —but this is surely not one of them.

[5]Hans Toch, "The Last Word on the Hippies," *The Nation,* December 4, 1967. See also the jaundiced remarks of Eric Hoffer in the New York *Post Magazine,* September 23, 1967, pp. 32–33; Milton Mayer writing in *The Progressive,* October 1967; and Arnold Wesker's "Delusions of Floral Grandeur" in the English magazine *Envoy,* December 1967.

It would be a better general criticism to make of the young that they have done a miserably bad job of dealing with the distortive publicity with which the mass media have burdened their embryonic experiments. Too often they fall into the trap of reacting narcissistically or defensively to their own image in the fun-house mirror of the media. Whatever these things called "beatniks" and "hippies" originally were, or still are, may have nothing to do with what *Time, Esquire, Cheeta,* CBSNBCABC, Broadway comedy, and Hollywood have decided to make of them. Dissent, the press has clearly decided, is hot copy. But if anything, the media tend to isolate the weirdest aberrations *and* consequently to attract to the movement many extroverted poseurs. But what does bohemia do when it finds itself massively infiltrated by well-intentioned sociologists (and we now all of a sudden have specialized "sociologists of adolescence"), sensationalizing journalists, curious tourists, and weekend fellow travelers? What doors does one close on them? The problem is a new and tough one: a kind of cynical smothering of dissent by saturation coverage, and it begins to look like a far more formidable weapon in the hands of the establishment than outright suppression.

Again, in his excellent article on the Italian students quoted above, Nicola Chiaromonte tells us that dissenters

> must detach themselves, must become resolute "heretics." They must detach themselves quietly, without shouting or riots, indeed in silence and secrecy; not alone but in groups, in real "societies" that will create, as far as possible, a life that is independent and wise. . . . It would be . . . a nonrhetorical form of "total rejection."

But how is one to develop such strategies of dignified secrecy when the establishment has discovered exactly the weapon with which to defeat one's purposes: the omniscient mass media? The only way anybody or anything stays underground these days is by trying outlandishly hard—as when Ed Saunders and a group of New York poets titled a private publication *Fuck You* to make sure it stayed off the newsstands. But it can be quite as distortive to spend all one's time evading the electronic eyes and ears of the world as to let oneself be inaccurately reported by them.

Yet to grant the fact that the media distort is not the same as saying that the young have evolved no life style of their own, or that they are unserious about it. We would be surrendering to admass an absolutely destructive potential if we were to take the tack that whatever it touches is automatically debased or perhaps has no reality at all. In London today at some of the better shops one can buy a Chinese Army-style jacket, advertised as "Mao Thoughts in Burberry Country: elegant navy flannel, revolutionary with brass buttons and Mao collar." The cost: £28 . . . a mere $68. Do Mao and the cultural revolution suddenly become mere figments by virtue of such admass larks?

Commercial vulgarization is one of the endemic pests of twentieth-century Western life, like the flies that swarm to sweets in the summer. But the flies don't create the sweets (though they may make them less palatable); nor do they make the summer happen. It will be my contention that there is, despite the fraudulence and folly that collects around its edges, a significant new culture a-borning among our youth, and that this culture deserves careful understanding, if for no other reason than the sheer size of the population it potentially involves.

But there *are* other reasons, namely, the intrinsic value of what the young are making happen. If, however, we want to achieve that understanding, we must insist on passing over the exotic tidbits and sensational case histories the media offer us. Nor should we resort to the superficial snooping that comes of cruising bohemia for a few exciting days in search of local color and the inside dope, often with the intention of writing it all up for the slick magazines. Rather, we should look for major trends that seem to outlast the current fashion. We should try to find the most articulate public statements of belief and value the young have made or have given ear to; the thoughtful formulations, rather than the off-hand gossip. Above all, we must be willing, in a spirit of critical helpfulness, to sort out what seems valuable and promising in this dissenting culture, as if indeed it mattered to us whether the alienated young succeeded in their project.

Granted this requires a deal of patience. For what we are confronted with is a progressive "adolescentization" of dissenting thought and culture, if not on the part of its creators, then on the part of much of its audience. And we should make no mistake about how far back into the early years of adolescence these tastes now reach. Let me offer one illuminating example. In December of 1967, I watched a group of thirteen-year-olds from a London settlement house perform an improvised Christmas play as part of a therapeutic theater program. The kids had concocted a show in which Santa Claus had been imprisoned by the immigration authorities for entering the country without proper permission. The knock at official society was especially stinging, coming as it did instinctively from some very ordinary youngsters who had scarcely been exposed to any advanced intellectual influences. And whom did the thirteen-year-olds decide to introduce as Santa's liberators? An exotic species of being known to them as "the hippies," who shiva-danced to the jailhouse and magically released Father Christmas, accompanied by strobelights and jangling sitars.

However lacking older radicals may find the hippies in authenticity or revolutionary potential, they have clearly succeeded in embodying radical disaffiliation—what Herbert Marcuse has called the Great Refusal—in a form that captures the need of the young for unrestricted joy. The hippy, real or as imagined, now seems to stand as one of the few images toward which the very young can grow without having to give up the childish sense of enchantment and playfulness, perhaps because the hippy keeps one foot in his childhood. Hippies who may be pushing thirty wear buttons that read "Frodo Lives" and decorate their pads with maps of Middle Earth (which happens to be the name of one of London's current rock clubs). Is it any wonder that the best and brightest youngsters at Berkeley High School (just to choose the school that happens to be in my neighborhood) are already coming to class barefoot, with flowers in their hair, and ringing with cowbells?

Such developments make clear that the generational revolt is not likely to pass over in a few years' time. The ethos of dissaffiliation is still in the process of broadening down through the adolescent years, picking up numbers as time goes on. With the present situation we are perhaps at a stage comparable to the Chartist phase of trade unionism in Great Britain, when the ideals and spirit of a labor movement had been formulated but had not reached anything like class-wide dimensions. Similarly, it is still a small, if boisterous minority of the young who now define the generational conflict. But the conflict will not vanish when those who are now twenty reach thirty; it may only reach its peak when those who are now eleven and twelve reach their late twenties. (Say, about 1984.) We then may discover that what a mere handful of beatniks pioneered in Allen Ginsberg's youth will have become the life style of millions of college-age young. Is there any other ideal toward which the young can grow that looks half so appealing?

"Nothing," Goethe observed, "is more inadequate than a mature judgment when adopted by an immature mind." When radical intellectuals have to deal with a dissenting public that becomes this young, all kinds of problems accrue. The adolescentization of dissent poses dilemmas as perplexing as the proletarianization of dissent that bedeviled left-wing theorists when it was the working class they had to ally with in their effort to reclaim our culture for the good, the true, and the beautiful. Then it was the horny-handed virtues of the beer hall and the trade union that had to serve as the medium of radical thought. Now it is the youthful exuberance of the rock club, the love-in, the teach-in.

The young, miserably educated as they are, bring with them almost nothing but healthy instincts. The project of building a sophisticated framework of thought atop those instincts is rather like trying to graft an oak tree upon a wildflower. How to sustain the oak tree? More important, how to avoid crushing the wildflower? And yet such is the project that confronts those of us who are concerned with radical social change. For the young have become one of the very few social levers dissent has to work with. This is that "significant soil" in which the Great Refusal has begun to take root. If we reject it in frustration for the youthful follies that also sprout there, where then do we turn?

2 Youth Cultures

American society is pluralistic; that is, on the major issues and problems of the times, there is no consensus. A range of values and norms, arising from different experiences and behaviors, conflict and contrast on the American scene. After we have claimed for 50 to 60 years that the great Americanization process was proceeding apace to grind down, assimilate and absorb, co-opt and otherwise diminish distinctive styles of life, we now have a new appreciation of the persistent pluralism of our society. This pluralism is reflected in youth cultures. Any given type of youth culture, far from providing a single pathway from childhood to adulthood, has a variety of routes. From the violent and disaffected through the more passive and self-destructive, to the middle-class cultural and political dissenters, American society contains widely varied young people.

Bennett Berger describes youth cultures as characteristic patterns of norms, not necessarily correlated with age. This is an essential distinction: Berger does not obviate the explanations of other writers, but expands our vision of youth cultures to include what might better be called "youthful cultures." These are groups whose central themes are reflected in norms sanctioning "hedonism," "expression," and "irresponsibility," which provide the motif of youthfulness and are found in a variety of social strata, aggregates, age groups, and occupations. "Adolescent rebellion," or dramatic and visible attachment to youthful norms, occurs only where the broader society sanctions and supports it.

The teenager, or pre-college youth, is usually characterized by his tastes in music, dress, and automobiles. His tastes, especially in music, are exploited widely by commercial radio and record businesses. Robinson and Hirsch (1969), for example, show that even within the high school culture, race and region affect listening patterns. Instead of getting a single message from music, the different taste groups within a youth culture further refine and interpret the meanings of music.

American high schools seem to have developed their own subculture. Popular magazines portray it as a locus of sex, fun, and football (with the lurking shadow of political radicalism, disruption, and violence). The Coleman article is one of the important recent attempts to analyze the content of adolescent values and their impact on behavior. From a survey of 10 midwestern high schools, Coleman drew some important conclusions about the impact of student values on academic achievement.

When asked how they would like to be remembered after they left school, male students solidly chose star athlete over brilliant or most popular student. When Coleman examined the choices of boys who were considered the "leading crowd" in the schools, he found that they chose star athlete more often than the rest of the boys. One of the implications of these value statements is that behavior will be patterned to seek certain rewards. If a social system rewards athletics over other activities, a greater proportion of athletically talented people should be drawn into the arena. The same proposition should hold true for academics: is there an association between rewards for academic performance and actual behavior? When academic excellence was defined as the frequency with which students mentioned good grades as a means for getting into the leading crowd, and performance was defined in terms of the relative I.Q. superiority of A students over the remainder of their school, there was an association between rewards and performance by school. This finding applied to both boys and girls. (You might refer to this article when you read the Campbell and Coleman article included in this book, which shows the *negligible* effect of curriculum, staff, and financing on standardized intelligence test results.)

A striking contrast is provided by the study previously mentioned, showing the centrality of the star athlete image in virtually all schools. Coleman infers that the involvement of schools in interscholastic athletics stimulates community pride, reward, and sanction, and that there are no parallel rewards for intellectual accomplishment. He suggests developing interscholastic academic games and competition to bring rewards, values and behavior in line with the expressed purposes of education.

Other status groups that can form the basis for a youth culture are included in following selections. Liebow's study of a black group living near a corner carry-out store in Washington, D.C. indicates a set of shared relationships that is more nearly a network than a cultural group. There are shared friendships and values, but no overall belief system and friendship-interaction pattern which would indicate a strong, binding solidarity among Tally and his friends. The ties that are most characteristic of the middle-class young, generated by educational experience, shared affluence, and resources supplied by the nuclear family, are not found among the blacks in Liebow's study. Members of street networks are denied personal worth and self-esteem by the society within which they live. They lack economic stability to undergird their relationships, to give them predictability and continuity. To attain a modicum of success, Tally and his friends must persist in the face of almost insurmountable odds. The concrete and vicious nature of institutionalized racism can be seen in other chapters of *Tally's Corner:* stereotypes of the black man keep him from work, allow him to be exploited while at work, and redound to his dismay in interpersonal relationships with peers of the same and the opposite sex.

Most of the friendships Liebow identified were based on locality and kinship, fictive or real. The paucity of their personal and social resources and the instability of the men's ties to the larger society through work make personal or primary group ties central to them. Primary groups are a filter of the larger society in all strata and are the center of social life for most people. The failures of friendship networks built up by Tally and his friends are even more critical because they lack many of the other social ties shared by members of the middle class.

Roszak describes non-students as an important aspect of the youth movement; they are street people, like the people described by Liebow. What differentiates them from students or from other youth groups dramatically present now? Watts and Whittaker (1967), in an ingenious study, attempted to match a group of non-students living near the Berkeley campus of the University of California with the student group. By comparison, the non-students were alienated and estranged from society and family, a pattern seen in the Braungart and Flacks selections. They were not as oriented to a career or to the "work game," as were the students sampled, and they preferred the more creative fields. Although they participated in political actions, they doubted the efficacy of those actions in changing the social system. Are they dropouts because of prior socializing experiences, or did they become dropouts only after they saw that their attempts at political action were futile? Perhaps the most salient characteristic of this non-student group is their dissatisfaction with higher education. They are marginal: they are apparently alienated from education, yet they value it and the careers it permits. As opposed to the radical activist, who aggressively attempts to promote social change, and the cultural radical, who passively moves to create an alternative, the non-student hangs precipitously between action and inaction, between politics and culture. He is a product of a society which can support, and in fact encourages, a long period of education, adolescence, and social puberty.

The pluralism of American society, reflected in youthful cultures, will doubtless be with us as long as affluence and technology continue to facilitate alternative life styles. In the youthful cultures described by Berger, in the high schools described by Coleman, and in the streets, pluralism and value diversity are likely to persist and to underlie other potential conflicts based on age, sex, class, or race.

On the Youthfulness of Youth Cultures

Bennett M. Berger

For more than twenty years now, sociologists have increasingly concerned themselves with the study of "youth culture." Talcott Parsons' very influential article, published in 1942,[1] with its much quoted characterization of youth culture as "more or less specifically irresponsible" has become a point of departure for an enormous amount of research and discussion on youth. Parsons' characterization of youth culture, however, inadvertently suggests that whatever it is that constitutes the "youthfulness" of youth culture may have less to do with chronology than with culture. To characterize youth culture as "irresponsible" or to describe its "dominant note" as "having a good time" or to say that it has "a strong tendency to develop in directions which are on the borderline of parental approval or beyond the pale . . ." (note 1) clearly excludes those large numbers of adolescents who have had no important experience in anything remotely resembling such a milieu. Many, and probably most young persons, while they experience the classic problems of adolescent psychology described in the textbooks, seem to make their way through to full adult status without grave cultural damage, without getting into serious trouble, without a dominating hedonism, and without generalized attitudes of rebellion toward parents and the world.

These introductory remarks are not intended as a preface to a "defense" of adolescents against the bad press they have been getting in recent years. I intend, rather, to suggest that 1) "youth culture" should refer to the normative system of *youthful* persons, not necessarily of young ones; and 2) since whatever it is that is normatively distinctive about youth culture is

Reprinted by permission of *Social Research* 30 (Autumn 1963):319–42.

[1]"Age and Sex in the Social Structure of the United States," *American Sociological Review* (October 1942).

probably not characteristic of all or even most adolescents, it is not attributable solely or even primarily to chronological age; and hence 3) that the definitive characteristics of youth culture are relevant to groups other than the age-grade we call adolescence.

While Frederick Elkin and William A. Westley believe they have exploded "The Myth of Adolescent Culture"[2] with survey data showing that a sample of middle class adolescents comply with the norms of deferred gratification, get along well with their parents, without hostility or resentful feelings that "they don't understand us," what they have actually done is present evidence that certain adolescents do not share the norms of youth culture. By thus implicitly distinguishing the facts of chronological age from the phenomena of culture, they invite us to consider the hypothesis that what we are in the habit of calling "youth culture" is the creature of some young and some not so young persons. If hedonism or irresponsibility or rebelliousness are essential features of youth culture, then it may be unwise as well as unnecessary to restrict the consideration of youth culture to adolescent groups—since these qualities are dominant in several adult groups as well; and the fact that this is so is probably not fortuitous. I am suggesting, in short, that youthfulness, like fertility, is unequally distributed in society, and not satisfactorily explained by reference to chronological age. This essay is an attempt to explore theoretically some of the conceptual problems that an investigation of the structure and dynamics of youth culture will encounter.

Youth Cultures of the Young

TWO IMAGES OF THE YOUNG: "TEENAGERS" AND "AMERICAN YOUTH."[3] To begin, let us note a recurrent ambiguity in the images with which American adolescents are usually conceived. The "teenagers" are those who, in Dwight McDonald's apt ethnography,[4] spend an hour a day on the phone and two hours a day listening to disc jockeys; they are the most assiduous moviegoers in the nation, preferring especially films about monsters, rock and roll music, and teenagers like themselves. More than half of them "go steady" and practice the sexual or proto-sexual intimacies implied by that phrase. The boys are very car-conscious, and spend a good deal of their leisure reading about, talking about, and working on hot rods. They read *Mad,* and its imitators *Frenzy* and *Thimk;* they don't read the Bible, don't go to church regularly, are bored by politics, ignorant of the Bill of Rights, and so on.

If one shifts one's perspective for a moment, and begins to think of the adolescents who populate Boy Scouts, Youth for Christ, 4H clubs, Future Farmers of America, and other groups of this sort, McDonald's characteriza-

[2]*American Sociological Review* (December 1955).

[3]I am indebted to Barbara Williams for the terms of this distinction.

[4]See his two-part "profile" of Eugene Gilbert in *The New Yorker* (November 22 and 29, 1958).

tion (based in part upon the results of Remmers' work[5] and Eugene Gilbert's youth polls) has a rather jarring effect. These doers of good deeds and raisers of prize pigs and winners of essay contests on Americanism are clearly not the adolescents who have seemingly become a permanent "problem" on the American scene.

"Teenagers" and "American youth" are, of course, images, and as such, they may be little more than stereotypes; we may, and likely will, find rock and rollers belonging to the FFA. But it is also likely that these distinctive images express differences in social and demographic variables like class, region, ethnicity, and religion. In any case, the initial distinction between "teenagers" (the adolescents publicly worried about) and "American youth" (the adolescents publicly praised) does suggest the useful banality that some adolescents engage in ways of life essentially at odds with or indifferent to the official desires and expectations of "responsible" adults, whereas other adolescents comply with or actively pursue the aims and expectations set down for youth by adult authorities.

TRANSITIONAL STAGE AND SUBCULTURE. One way of extending this distinction between types of adolescents is to contrast two ideas that are frequently used in psychological and sociological discussions of youth. Most standard works on the social psychology of adolescence speak of it as a "transitional stage" between childhood and adulthood, a period of years ridden with conflicts and tensions stemming partly from an acceleration in the individual's physical and cultural growth but also from the age-grading norms of our society that withhold from adolescents most of the opportunities, rights, and responsibilities of adults. When sexual desires are more powerful than they will ever again be, sexual opportunities are fewest; obedience and submission are asked of adolescents at precisely the time when their strength, energy, and desire for autonomy are ascendant; responsible participation in the major institutions are denied them at the moment when their interest in the world has been poignantly awakened.[6] Such tensions, generated by our age-grading system and exacerbated by a decline in parental control and a world in a state of permanent crisis, are frequently cited as the major source of adolescent difficulty. Conceived as a "transitional stage," adolescence is a very difficult period; it is described—and caricatured—as a time of awkwardness and embarrassment and trouble and pain—something to be got out of as soon as possible by orienting oneself primarily toward eventual membership in the adult community.

For many years, apparently, this conception of adolescence as a difficult transitional stage was the dominant framework in which adolescent problems were discussed. As recently as 1944, Caroline Tryon could write, "we have a tendency to disregard or to minimize the educational significance of

[5]H. H. Remmers and D. H. Radler, *The American Teenager* (Indianapolis, Ind.: The Bobbs-Merrill Co., 1957).

[6]These are a few of the "discontinuities" made famous by Ruth Benedict in her celebrated article "Continuities and Discontinuities in Cultural Conditioning," *Psychiatry* (May 1938). See also Kingsley Davis' related discussions: "Adolescence and the Social Structure," *The Annals* (November 1944) and "The Sociology of Parent-Youth Conflict," *American Sociological Review* (August 1940).

the child's experience in his peer group."[7] Today, this statement strikes the eye as incredible; certainly it is no longer true. Very few contemporary discussions of youth fail to mention the significance of the involvement of young persons in their own age-graded peer groups. The emphasis in these discussions, however, is quite different from that contained in discussions of adolescence as a transitional stage; the stress is on the orientation of adolescents to their peers. From this perspective emerged the idea of an adolescent subculture[8] as a "way of life" relatively autonomous, and controlled internally by a system of norms and sanctions largely antithetical or indifferent to that offered by parents, teachers, and clergymen—the official representatives of the adult world.

By itself, the subcultural view of adolescence suggests nothing *inherently* transitional, except in the sense that all experience is transitional, representing, as it does, the passage from what one was to what one is about to become. But oddly enough, it is precisely this element that is missing from the conventional usage of the concept of "transitional stage." To suggest that adolescence is "a stage they go through"—something that adolescents "grow out of," is to violate much of what we know about the permanent effects of socialized experience. It is as if adolescence, frequently designated "the formative years," formed nothing, but was simply a rather uncomfortable period of biding one's time until the advent of one's twenty-first birthday or that one's graduation from school induces the adult world to extend a symbolic invitation to join it. But if the transitional view of adolescence minimizes the permanent influences of adolescent experience, the subcultural view exaggerates the degree to which adolescents create an insulated, autonomous milieu in which they may with impunity practice their anti-adult rites. No large scale study of high school youth, for example, has successfully demonstrated the existence of a really deviant system of norms which governs adolescent life.[9]

The point I wish to stress here, however, is that our understanding of the varieties of adolescent experience depends heavily upon whether adolescent group life is primarily conceived in the vocabulary of development psychology as a transitional stage, or in the sociological vocabulary of subcultures. Conceived as a transitional stage, adolescence is typically described in ways which make its termination devoutly to be wished.[10] When adolescence

[7]Caroline Tryon, "The Adolescent Peer Culture," *43rd Yearbook of the National Society for the Study of Education* (Chicago, Ill.: University of Chicago Press, 1944).

[8]This is not the place to go into the problems of applying the concept of "subculture," developed on ethnic models, to age groups. See, however, J. Milton Yinger, "Contraculture and Subculture," *American Sociological Review* (October 1960) and my own comments in "Adolescence and Beyond," *Social Problems* (Spring 1963).

[9]The most ambitious attempt to demonstrate this is James Coleman, *The Adolescent Society* (New York: The Free Press of Glencoe, 1961).

[10]The characterization of adolescence as "the awkward age" full of pimples and embarrassment has validity only for the very early teen years. It may merely be a survival from a period when adolescents were completely dependent and completely subordinate. Today, high school students, free and relatively affluent, frequently feel that they are currently living what they expect will be the best years of their lives.

is discussed in subcultural terms, no such implication is carried with it. The literature on youth culture most consistently describes it in terms of hedonistic, irresponsible, and "expressive" behavior. Although most adults may believe that this behavior and the norms that constrain it *ought* to be terminated at the threshold of adulthood, it is by no means self-evident that a group which can "get away with" a life of hedonism (read: fun, kicks), irresponsibility (read: freedom, license), and expressiveness (read: immediate gratification, ego enhancement) may be expected to terminate it easily in exchange for the mixed blessing of recognition as adults, and the sometimes baleful responsibilities that this entails. Objectively—and at the very least, adolescence is a portion of a life lived—*formative* attitudes and orientations, talents and commitments, capacities, *and incapacities* develop that affect adolescents' various modes of adaptation into adult worlds, which more or less facilitate or obstruct their eventual recruitment into a specific adult milieu. If the child is father of the man, an understanding of the varieties of experience adolescents undergo, the varieties of milieu they touch, should contribute to the understanding of the kind of adults they are likely to become—and *not* to become.

CHRONOLOGICAL AGE AND YOUTHFULNESS. Before attempting to describe the groups that might fit the categories of "teenagers" and "American youth," and the groups that might be usefully analyzed with the concepts of "transitional stage" and "subculture," I wish to make explicit one more distinction alluded to earlier, and conceptually parallel to the two sets of distinction I have already made. To say that youthfulness is far from perfectly correlated with chronological age is to imply that some adolescents are more youthful than others. Once the distinction is made, we can speak categorically of youthful young men, unyouthful young men, youthful old men and unyouthful old men. This fourfold classification suggests, perhaps over-sharply, that chronological age and the culture-personality variables associated with it may be analytically separated. To render the distinction fruitful, however, it is necessary to specify what is meant by youthfulness. Rather than approach this problem directly, it may be wiser to do it indirectly, by contrasting with it the relative lack of youthfulness in "American youth."

In this connection, let me draw attention to a book called *The Vanishing Adolescent* in which Edgar Friedenberg argues that adolescence as a stormy decade of identity-seeking and as a distinctive stage of human development is disappearing in the United States largely as a result of premature socialization primarily in the high schools.[11] Without digressing into a discussion of Friedenberg's thesis, we *can* say that we have all known adolescents of the kind about which he is concerned. They do well enough in school, are "well-adjusted," popular with their peers, have few great conflicts with their parents or other authorities, and in general have few if any serious quarrels with the value system into which they are being socialized or with the institutions representing these values. Grant this image some validity; then let us ask: in what sense are these young persons youthful?

[11](Boston, Mass.: The Beacon Press, 1959).

Certainly they are young and probably inexperienced in the affairs of the world. But adolescents who respond docilely to the expectations of school authorities, who accept as legitimate the limits imposed on them by their parents,[12] who engage in the activities that are deemed appropriate by adult authorities, are more aptly described as going through the final phase of their pre-adult socialization, as junior grown-ups, rather than as incarnations of youthfulness. For when, in common usage, we describe persons as "youthful," we mean not primarily that they are obviously young, and hence relatively naive and inexperienced; we mean that they tend to manifest certain qualities in their behavior, and that although these qualities do seem to be empirically *associated* with tender years, they are not *exclusively* age-graded. Regardless of chronological age, youthful persons tend to be impulsive, spontaneous, energetic, exploratory, venturesome, and vivacious; they tend to be candid, colorful, blunt in speech (having not acquired the skill and habit of dissimulation); they are often irreverent, frequently disrespectful; extreme, immoderate, they know no golden mean; they are "action seekers"[13] rather than seekers of stable routine. They joke a lot; the play motif dominates much of their activity—which they tend to transform into games, even in the most apparently unpropitious of circumstances. Lacking caution and judiciousness, they tend to throw themselves with full passion and sexually alert intensity into those activities that promise thrills and excitement, which they tend to pursue with little regard for consequences.

Notice that these are primarily the qualities of persons, not roles, and certainly not rationalized, bureaucratic roles—although they may become quasi-institutionalized as "deviant" roles. Notice too that they are all very active—one might say erotic. When abstracted from behavior and become conscious, qualities such as these assert themselves on *ideological* grounds. When, that is, they take on the character of moral imperatives, we can properly speak of a system of subcultural norms.[14] Such norms underlie the content of youth culture. Clearly, they are dangerous: from the perspective of the major institutions of social order, youthfulness is excess; it is implicit or incipient disorder; for society, it is a "problem" that requires handling, control, co-optation, or channeling in socially approved directions.

Society has at its disposal a great armory of means to control this implicit threat of disorder. I mean not the police and the courts or the more informal sanctions wielded by parents and other authorities; I mean the

[12]There actually are many adolescents who respond to questionnaires with the opinion that teenagers are not really old enough to smoke or drink or in general to know what is good for them.

[13]The term "action seeker" is taken from Herbert Gans' characterization of some working-class Bostonians. See his *The Urban Villagers* (New York: The Free Press of Glencoe, 1962).

[14]For modern formulations of this ideology, see Norman Brown, *Life Against Death* (New York: Random House, 1960); Herbert Marcuse, *Eros and Civilization* (Boston, Mass.: The Beacon Press, 1959) and Paul Goodman, *Growing Up Absurd* (New York: Random House, 1960).

community youth center, the chaperoned dance, organized sports, school-sponsored extracurricular clubs, and the junior auxiliaries of business, religious, fraternal and veterans' associations—for adults have learned that adolescents will frequently accept from their peers the same norms they may reject from adults. But the effectiveness of these organizational weapons in coping with youth varies with the location of particular youths in the social structure. Where, for example, adult leadership is poor and community facilities limited, as in urban slums and certain new suburbs; or where sudden discontinuities in style of life create inter-generation tensions and anxieties, and disqualify parents as models worthy of emulation and respect, as frequently occurs in immigrant or highly mobile families; or where failure or anticipated failure in academic competition leaves the failer with the perception of a bleak future and with no approved alternative sources of self-respect, as frequently occurs among ethnic and working class boys in schools dominated by middle class norms—where these and other early experiences of incipient social disaffection can mobilize ideological supports and some degree of structural insulation from the major institutions, there we are likely to find fertile ground in which the seeds of youthful excess and disorder can grow, and, eventually, bear the exotic flower called "youth culture."

VARIETIES OF YOUTH CULTURE. The flower has many blooms; the varieties of youth culture are as wide as the variety of cultural contexts and opportunity systems offered by a pluralistic society. At its broadest and most innocuous, the youth cultures of the young touch the fringes of what is called "teenage culture": popular songs, rock and roll, disc jockeys, juke boxes, portable phonographs, movie stars, dating, and romantic love; hot rods, motorcycles, drag racing, and sports cars, panty raids and water fights, drive-in hamburgers and clandestine drinking, football games, basketball games, dances and parties, and clubs and cliques, and lovers' lanes. At its delinquent extreme, youth culture is black leather jackets, gang rumbles and switch blades, malicious mischief, and joy riding in stolen cars. Politically, it is expressed in sit-ins, freedom rides, peace marches, and folk songs; it is Jazz at Newport, vacations at Fort Lauderdale—and their attendant riots. And it is also bohemians and beatniks and beards and hipsters, and coffee shop desperadoes plotting everything from literary magazines to assaults on the House Committee on Un-American Activities.[15]

I intend by this apparently formless catalogue of symbols to suggest how wide a variety of group styles and expressions the youth cultures of the young include. Intimations[16] of youth culture will be found more frequently among "teenagers" than among "American youth," more frequently among "conflict" and "retreatist" delinquent gangs than among the "ra-

[15]For a very similar formulation, see David Matza, "Subterranean Traditions of Youth," *The Annals* (November 1961) in which Matza argues that radicalism, bohemianism, and delinquency are the three basic forms which subterranean traditions (that is, subcultures) of youth take.

[16]I say "intimations" because "teenage culture" is what David Matza calls a "conventionalized version" of what I would call a genuine youth culture.

tional" criminal delinquents,[17] more among "bohemian" and "collegiate" undergraduates than among academically or vocationally oriented college students,[18] and more among politically militant and extreme student groups than among the student adherents of "moderate" sentiment within the two major political parties. The wide social spectrum represented by these groups should reassure the skeptical that I have no ideological axes to grind; few of those prone to moral judgments of youth could unambiguously approve or disapprove of *all* of these groups at the same time. But what delinquents and bohemians and campus radicals and even some high school hot rodders and college fraternity boys have in common is, I am suggesting, their youthfulness, that is, their tendency to behave in patterned ways normatively hedonistic, irresponsible, and expressive.

In spite of the wide variety of dissimilar forms in which it is expressed, it seems reasonable and useful—and also more objective—initially to designate this normative behavior as "youthful" (rather than, say, "deviant" or "delinquent" or "alienated"—although it may *become* these) because it is in large part the autonomous creature of sub-societies of the recalcitrant young. Although, as I have suggested above and will argue at some length below, it is also selected from, supported by, and modeled after a long cultural tradition, nourished by several contemporary subcultures of adults, and is hence in principle viable into adulthood and beyond. The youth cultures of the young are an adaptive response by *some* adolescents to problems presented to them by their parent society and culture (for example, contradictions or imbalances in norms, blockage of opportunity, inadequately defined roles, ambiguities of age-grading, the prospect of meaningless work), and the forms they take in specific groups reflect a choice from traditions available to them. To see the matter this way takes account of both the autonomous character of the subculture and its linkage to important traditions which antedate it. The significance of the adjective in the term "youth culture," however, rests not in the fact that many of its participants are young, but in the fact that their selective interaction with one another, under the difficult conditions generated by our age-grading norms and in contexts that limit the exercise of adult supervision and control, may sustain a set of more or less counter-norms which encourage and support, however ambivalently, a pattern of behavior at odds with the official norms of the culture in which it is located, but *adaptive* in the sense that it can provide —not just temporarily—a more or less viable way of life.

Adult Youth Cultures

THE PRESERVATION OF YOUTH CULTURE: ITS LINKS WITH THE ADULT WORLD. Earlier, I criticized the usage of the concept of "transitional stage" be-

[17]See Richard Cloward and Lloyd Ohlin, *Delinquency and Opportunity* (New York: The Free Press, 1960) for a discussion of these types of gangs.

[18]See the typology of college student orientations in Martin A. Trow and Burton Clark, "Determinants of College Student Subcultures," in *The Study of College Peer Groups,* T. M. Newcomb and E. K. Wilson, eds. (Forthcoming).

cause it did not sufficiently specify the differential impact of adolescent experience upon subsequent careers. We already know that adolescents eventually become adults; but we do not know much about the ways in which variations in adolescent experience affect subsequent adult adaptations. The concept of "transitional stage" is often employed largely as a palliative for society's functional problems of recruiting and integrating youth into adult worlds: if it's merely "a stage they're going through," then adults need not frankly confront the problems their behavior raises because, after all, "they'll grow out of it."

Most of them, it is true, do grow out of it, and the fact that they do is testimony not only to the power of adult agencies of socialization but to the vulnerability to co-optation of "teenage culture"—to its lack of resources to sustain it in crisis and insulate it from attack.[19] But some do not or cannot grow out of it. What becomes of those young persons whose "youthful rebelliousness" turns out to be not "a stage they're going through," but a series of subculturally rewarding experiences that subjectively validate their initial opposition to or irritation with the official demands of adults? And what becomes of those whose participation in political, delinquent, and bohemian forms of youth culture leaves permanent stigmata that render them permanently visible to a henceforth skeptical and suspicious world? Delinquency statistics, the "beatnik" craze, student militance and riots suggest that for substantial numbers (how many, no one knows) adolescence is not simply an awkward but benign transitional stage, and it is these facts to which we refer when we speak of youth and their growing up as a "social problem." To the extent that we can conceive of growing up as a *career* (and in this psychoanalytical age it is not difficult to do so), "*not* growing up" (that is, the preservation of the essential features of youth culture in later life) can also be considered as a career. Although there is a certain joylessness in the idea of "maturity" (identified, as it is, with sober responsibilities and solemn commitments), there are relatively few niches in the adult social structure where "youthfulness" does not receive severe negative sanctions, and those adolescents whose peer group experience has developed in them trained incapacities for growing up or perhaps even conscientious objections to it may be expected to gravitate toward them.

Those adolescents among whom youthful attributes are weakest—for example, those studied by Elkin and Westley, the prematurely socialized type described by Friedenberg, and the bulk of adolescents only superficially involved in teenage culture—will probably have the least difficulty in making the transition to the typical adult careers offered in a highly industrialized, bureaucratized society. On the other hand, those in whom youthful

[19]It is this lack which distinguishes "teenage culture" from more genuine subcultures such as ethnic communities, delinquent gangs in urban slums, and bohemias. Ethnic communities frequently have a full blown institutional structure to shield its members from the society's encroachment; delinquent gangs emphasize the inviolability of "turf" for good sociological reason; bohemias are usually ecological communities as well as subcultures, and even political radicals have, at the very least, a strong ideology to sustain them. Teenagers have very little.

attributes are strong will have the greatest difficulty in making those sacrifices of youthfulness that most executive and professional and other prestigious adult careers require.

What kinds of adult occupations and milieu are likely to reward or at least to tolerate youthfulness, and thus normatively support an attempt not to grow up or an inability to grow up? If it is true that some adolescents are more youthful than others, it is also true that some adults are more youthful than others, and it is likely that some of the important forces that sustain youthfulness in those who are no longer young may be found in the norms of the occupations they choose (or which choose them) and in the milieu that those norms help create.[20] What are some of these types of occupations?

YOUTHFUL CAREERS. I submit the following short list for illustrative purposes. My best hope is that it will be taken as suggestive of one way of theoretically linking the content of adolescent youth cultures with important subterranean or deviant traditions in the adult world, and hence of linking certain kinds of youthful experience in the adolescent milieu with the subsequent taking up of adult careers.

BOHEMIAN BUSINESS. By bohemian businessmen, I mean the proprietors or managers of small enterprises that cater to the needs, tastes, and desires of bohemians. These enterprises range all the way from those that are central to bohemian subcultures (*espresso* coffee houses, small art galleries, sandal and leather shops, pottery shops, jewelry shops, and so on) to other marginal businesses serving other markets as well ("art" theaters, paperback bookstores, small night clubs specializing in modern jazz, accessory and specialty shops for women, and so on). Wherever a "deviant" community exists (in this case a bohemian community), a business community is likely to exist to supply the wants that symbolize and define its deviance—in a sense analogous to that in which organized crime is symbiotically interrelated with government, law enforcement agencies, and parts of the legitimate business community. Bohemian business enterprise is one of the relatively few types of careers available to persons who, having had their basic orientations to the world shaped by experience in an adolescent subculture, have developed trained incapacities for pursuing more conventional kinds of business or professional or "bourgeois" careers—although the ironic and economically "reactionary" character of bohemian enterprise is that it gives its entrepreneurs the status of shopkeeper.

But their status as shopkeepers is less important and less revealing than the fact that they are likely to be bohemians. Bohemian businessmen, that is, are more like their customers than like other small businessmen. Even in their strictly economic capacities, bohemian businessmen are likely to reflect the habits of their customers. They may, for example, be expected

[20]Statuses other than occupational ones, of course, may also help sustain youthfulness: bachelor, divorcé(e), student, for example. Periodicals such as *Esquire* and *Playboy* are apparently directed at youthful adult audiences, and an analysis of their readers might provide evidence of youthful adult statuses.

to keep irregular hours, to open their shops late in the day, and remain open late in the evening. Located primarily in the "Latin quarter" of large cities or near university campuses, they frequently take long summer vacations or move their shops to summer resorts of the "art colony" type. They are not likely to keep rigorous books and their prices are frequently not standardized—sometimes because their wares are not. Often, they do not have a primarily commercial or instrumental orientation to what they sell, but rather an expressive one.[21] Dealing mainly in beauty—in esthetic objects or experience—they are not likely to think of themselves primarily as businessmen, but either as craftsmen or as esthetic functionaries performing services for the community of avant-garde good taste. However they think of themselves, bohemian businessmen (recruited largely from the student bohemian world of craftsmen, failed or insufficiently talented artists, and hangers-on and camp followers of the cultural avant-garde) live in a milieu that tolerates and rewards a youthful adaptation to the world. Bohemian business offers a moderately viable niche in the adult world for those unable or unwilling to grow out of youth culture.

Perhaps an *image* of a viable niche in the world would be a more accurate statement. For it is, of course, true that the actual opportunities for a successful career in bohemian business are probably not very good. Although it is a theoretically open milieu, the rate of business failure seems high, and the population of bohemia is probably not large enough to support the commercial enterprises of very many of those young persons who are more or less successfully resisting or evading middle-class socialization. Nevertheless, the image of an adult bohemian life is culturally fertile and ambiguously seductive to many. Bohemia is always newsworthy; its consistent coverage in the mass media, its consistent status as a "tourist attraction" means that it is of great interest to the vicarious lives of large numbers of people. For every core bohemian there are probably five fringe bohemians; for every fringe bohemian there are probably five "weekend bohemians"; and for every weekend bohemian there are probably scores of Walter Mittys each of whom might be secretly flattered to have one of his perhaps idiosyncratic habits labeled "bohemian" by a suspicious and surly neighbor. My point is simply that although full-time bohemianism as a career may not be viable very long for very many, its part-time or fantasy appeal is apparently much stronger than the actual opportunities it offers. But it is the existence of this appeal and the ambiguous possibilities represented by it that enable it to serve for the youthful as a *milieu of orientation* tolerant of their behavior and to which they may look for permanent sustenance.

SHOW BUSINESS. Many actors, singers, dancers, musicians, comedians, and other entertainers inhabit a world suffused by the myth of youth—a world in which grandmothers and grandfathers are noted for their sex ap-

[21]As an example a customer walks into an "art mart" to purchase a teapot that goes with a set of china that the customer knows the shop stocks. With some hauteur, the proprietress informs the customer that she does not sell the teapot (although she sells all the other pieces in the set) because it is "poorly designed."

peal. The professional milieu of jazz musicians interpenetrates with the hipster and bohemian varieties of youth culture, bonded by a common antipathy to "squares." Much like the jazz milieu, the world of the off-Broadway theater is heavily populated with aspiring actors and actresses, committed to their expressive art, who live on the fringe of bohemia. The celebrity world of Hollywood stars is, for public consumption at least, "La Dolce Vita," with its dominating motifs of sex, speed, alcohol, drugs, and perversion set in a context of luxury. Most of the "new" American comedians have come up from the dark basement clubs catering to bohemian-intellectual audiences into the bright glare of the legitimate stage and the TV studio to continue, somewhat diluted, their savage satires of the routine, the usual, the ordinary (that is, the "adult")—but now to the masochistic audience upon whose lives and opinions their material is based. Finally, teenage pop singers, despite their ritual affirmation of God, Home, and Mother, and their pious promises to "continue their education" (directed, one supposes, at the parents of their admirers), create a professional image compounded or thinly disguised erotica and forlorn adolescent alienation, and, with the help of publicity, transform their slum or otherwise poverty-stricken backgrounds into a romantic determination to "be somebody." ("I want to become a really good actor instead of just a teenage singer.")

That show business careers and similar occupations are in fact subject to much the same economic circumstances and bureaucratic controls as are other occupations, and that many show folk in fact live model middle-class lives are less important than the carefully nurtured Dionysian images of show business life, the persistent myth that careers are made "overnight," that its durable stars are ageless, and that "expressive" opportunities are offered by the public spotlight. Like other "creative" occupations, show business tends to be tolerant of irregular, spontaneous, unpredictable, exhibitionistic behavior—indeed, these are sometimes built into the very conditions of employment; more, show business expects this kind of behavior, and sometimes rewards it (in publicity, if nothing else—and publicity is seldom nothing else), at least among its stars. The hedonism and public irresponsibility of show business celebrities is disingenuously mythologized as "artistic temperament," suggesting that in those industries in which "creativity" is a basic commodity, perversities of other sorts must also be accepted: great beauty, great talent, great acclaim imply great vices. Thus Ava Gardner (a living Lady Brett) leaves a trail of discarded lovers across the bull rings of Spain; thus Maria Callas sails the Mediterranean in her Greek billionaire's yacht, telling the press at Riviera ports that they are "just friends"; thus Ingrid Bergman illegitimately conceives a child on a volcanic Aegean island to the merely temporary dismay of her fans; thus Lana Turner rears a daughter who becomes the killer of her mother's gangster-lover; thus Eddie leaves Debbie for Liz and Liz leaves Eddie for Richard to a breathless watching world of column readers. Billie Holliday, the greatest jazz singer of the era, wasted from years of addiction to heroin, dies under guard in a hospital; idols of teenage girls get picked up for homosexuality; Dean Martin nurtures a lucrative public image built on a reputation for alcoholism, and the Frank Sinatra clique spread across the night life of the country their money, their liquor, their arrogance, and their talent to delight the press.

With this newsreel, I intend neither a documentation of the lurid nor a righteous cry of decadence but only a vivid suggestion that, manufactured or not, the image of show business careers exists in a milieu in which Dionysian excess has a long tradition and an honored place—a cautious and implicit honor (given its dependence on the whims of public opinion), but a milieu in which one neither loses face nor gets fired for scandalous behavior, a milieu in which the only bad publicity is no publicity at all. The extremes to which the public behavior of show business celebrities is constrained are, like that of gang delinquents, justified by the "rep" it engenders; the Dionysian comings and goings of middle-aged Frank Sinatra and his middle-aged friends are apparently regarded by the public with the same chuckling benignity reserved for the pranks of teenagers. There is a normative kinship between the Dionysian motifs of the celebrity world of show biz and the hedonistic, expressive values of youth culture. A substantial part of the material content of youth culture is provided and sustained by the industries of mass entertainment and a large part of the entertainment business depends upon youth for its markets. Notice also that show business careers (and satellite show business careers such as disc jockeying and modeling) are virtually the *only* occupations or occupational images offered to adolescents in the pages of the "teenage magazines." Like bohemian business, show business offers the image of a career to talented young people with trained incapacities for business or the bureaucratized professions. People with "artistic talent" have, according to legend, no "business sense," and show business careers are often said to require the kind of single-minded dedication that is unable even to imagine another kind of future. Like bohemian business, show business tolerates or rewards a youthful orientation to the world and offers the inducement of "romantic" or "glamorous" careers to those unable or unwilling to "grow up."[22]

Like bohemian business too, show business has an important component of vicarious appeal; there is a sense in which show business is everyman's vicarious business; there are probably thousands of Americans who sit in front of their TV sets quietly confident that they can sing as well, dance as well, tell jokes as well, ride a horse and sling a gun as well as those merely lucky ones on the screen. Show business not only involves the audience in the imaginary worlds it creates, it involves them vicariously in show business itself. This may be one of the reasons for the proverbial interest of Americans in the private lives of celebrities, and why professional, in-group

[22]Moss Hart, who should know, writes, "I would hazard a guess . . . that the temperament, the tantrums, and the utter childishness of theater people in general, is neither accidental nor a necessary weapon of their profession. It has nothing to do with so-called 'artistic temperament.' The explanation, I think, is a far simpler one. For the most part they are impaled in childhood like a fly in amber." Moss Hart, *Act One* (New York: Random House, 1959).

banter and jokes about show business is virtually the only kind of esoteric humor of interest to out-groups. So that in addition to the promise of an actual career, show business, again like bohemia, offers an abundance of vicarious careers to the imperfectly socialized, and is thus, in an oddly perverse sense, functional to the extent that, by mollifying largely unfulfilled yearnings for a freer, more spontaneous, that is, more youthful life, it softens the tensions and frustrations engendered by socialization without internalization. Like the Horatio Alger myth, which told us that we too could succeed, the myths of the adult milieu which combine the exciting with the unsavory tell us that our lives need not be routine and colorless. The Alger myth succored an age of economic growth preoccupied with objective success; the youthfulness myth succors an age of psychology preoccupied with subjective "fulfillment."

WORKING-CLASS OCCUPATIONS. Many of the adolescents whom I have called "youthful"—the high school rebels, the flouters of adult authority, the claimers of autonomy for adolescents—are likely to be of working-class background, especially ethnics, culturally "deprived," without much talent, who drop out of high school or do poorly in it, and are probably headed not for the glamorous careers I have mentioned but for the lower reaches of the manual labor force. Nevertheless, there are good reasons for believing that many working-class occupations and the subcultural norms associated with some of them are more supportive of youthful orientations than most middle-class occupations.

Several otherwise disparate intellectual traditions converge in their characterizations of working-class life in terms akin to my conception of youthfulness. The Marxist tradition, for example, confers upon labor the innocent dignity of useful work, the tragedy of exploitation and alienation, and the heroic mission of carrying within it the seeds of a bright and revolutionary future. Having nothing to lose but their chains, the proletariat can take dramatic and passionate steps in its own interest. Sabotage, walkouts, general strikes, the Marxist myth of a militant working class—bold, defiant, resentful of its oppressors, impatient to bring down the system of authority which victimizes it—strikingly partakes of much the same spirit and imagery as rebellious adolescents *vis-à-vis* the world of adults. Both groups claim for themselves, in the strident tones characteristic of those without a parliamentary voice, autonomy, freedom from their illegitimate subordination to an authority they never chose, that consigns them to a future they do not want.

There is also a literary tradition more than 150 years old that bestows upon laborers—especially rural laborers—greater energy, vitality, and sexuality than the pale, thin, beardless, repressed pencil pushers who inhabit the offices of the world. In this literary tradition, workers are impulsive, strong, intuitive, passionate—capable of great anger and great tenderness; above all, they are, like adolescents, *personal,* largely alienated from and disgusted with the rationales and rationalizing of the impersonal bureaucratic world.

Paralleling these two romanticisms of working-class life is a third intellectual tradition that emphasizes the common values and long history of both the highest and the lowest classes of traditional Europe, which the despised, calculating minds of the *arriviste* middle class could never share: aristocrats and peasants share a tendency to violence, to alcoholic excesses, and to blood sports. This kinship between the highest and the lowest may be rather forced, but the peculiar combination of aristocratic and vulgar motifs, or élite and egalitarian themes which crystallize around a disdain for middle class life has persisted for nearly two hundred years.[23] The intellectual core of this tradition is the belief that the powers, privileges, and immunities of aristocratic life, and the passion, desperation, and anarchy of life in the depths are both preferable to the calculated moderation and mediocrity inherent in bourgeois definitions of maturity and responsibility. Each extreme is, in its different way, transcendent; the middle class is forever earthbound. Translating this tradition into my own terms, the lower classes and the upper classes are more youthful than the middle class.

Finally, recent empirical descriptions of working-class culture by sociologists lend considerable support to these romanticized versions of working-class life. These studies show a highly remarkable but generally unremarked upon similarity to standard descriptions of youth culture. Thus workers tend to be hedonistic, unable to plan ahead or defer gratification; they are highly expressive rather than instrumental in their basic orientations, given to violent and extreme views, irrational, anti-intellectual, "person-centered" (rather than "role-centered"), and generally neglectful of their civic responsibilities.[24] Certain working-class occupations, then, especially *lower* ones, are likely to require much less in the way of sacrifice of youthfulness than most other occupations, and it should come as no surprise that recalcitrant youth without academic ability or usable deviant talents should gravitate toward these jobs.

Conclusion

What I have offered here is in a sense a conceptual model for the analysis of adolescent behavior and the youthful adult milieu to which, under certain conditions, it may lead. There are youthful occupations and milieu

[23]Especially strongly in the bohemian literary tradition from, say, Diderot to Norman Mailer. One is reminded that "teddy boys" affect the garments of Edwardian gentlemen and the manners of hoodlums. Leslie Fiedler has argued at some length that "highbrow" and "lowbrow" culture have more in common than either has with "middlebrow" culture. See his, "Both Ends Against the Middle," reprinted in Rosenberg and White (eds.), *Mass Culture* (New York: The Free Press, 1957) .

[24]See, for example, William F. Whyte, *Street Corner Society* (Chicago, Ill.: University of Chicago Press, 1943); S. M. Miller and Frank Riessman, "The Working Class Subculture," *Social Problems* (Summer 1961); Richard Hoggart, *The Uses of Literacy* (London: Chatto and Windus, 1957); A. K. Cohen and H. M. Hodges, "Characteristics of the Lower-Blue-Collar Class," *Social Problems* (Spring 1963); Herbert J. Gans (Note 13), and Seymour Martin Lipset, "Working Class Authoritarianism," in *Social Controversy,* W. Petersen and D. Matza, eds. (Belmont, Calif.: Wadsworth Publishing Co., 1963).

other than those I have described. I have not, for example, mentioned free lance art or the military or professional sports, nor have I mentioned several niches in the academic and intellectual worlds that support youthful orientations. But I think that by now my major point should be clear: I have tried to suggest that the successful socialization of children into the dominant value system is always problematic especially in pluralistic societies, that recalcitrance can be spotted early, and that what I have called youth culture begins when adolescent rebellion against dominant adult norms takes on ideological supports from existing deviant traditions. For many adolescents, of course, this is only "a stage they go through," and most of them eventually internalize or at least comply with the norms constrained on them by the major agencies of socialization. At the same time, it is important to recognize that many adolescents do not, that the experience of many in adolescent subcultures shapes their futures by incapacitating them for bureaucratic roles. Most of these, it is true, wind up at the lower end of the occupational hierarchy, especially those who are unable to survive high school. But those who do survive and who are fortunate enough to discover the other face of their trained incapacities—in college or elsewhere—are uniquely enabled to take advantage of the few sheltered places a pluralistic society offers in its occupational structure which will permit them, as adults, to sustain that normative variation without which pluralism is emptied of its cultural meaning. This leaves a society highly differentiated on the level of social structure but homogeneous on the level of culture.

With this analysis, I am not offering only a more differentiated view of socialization—substituting a frame of reference emphasizing conformity to milieu rather than to general cultural norms. I mean also to emphasize that groups differ in the extent to which they tolerate or encourage normative dissension, and the extent to which this is true is directly relevant to the *roles* that inveterate dissenters can find in the social structure. In groups which require a high degree of uniformity, dissenters are constrained to yield or to withdraw from active participation; but in groups that place a high value on innovation—and many youthful groups are prominent among these—dissenters are much more likely to be able to retain the privileges of active association.[25]

This analysis also bears upon the problem of adaptation to failure, and casts a little light on the ingenious way in which society provides for the comfort of its failures while using its own failure to socialize some of its members as a way of easing the tensions engendered by its excessive success with others: those who are relegated to the bottom of the occupational heap, for example, are heir to a ready-made ideology, a myth that invidiously contrasts their own vigor, vitality, and authentic humanity with the repressions, the deskboundness, and the futile status-seeking of the successful. Society uses the luckier ones too—those who are able to find loftier, more glamorous, youthful adult niches. These feed the vicarious appetites

[25]For empirical data on this point, see Yrjo Littunen, "Deviance and Passivity in Radio Listener Groups," *Acta Sociologia* (Vol. 4).

of the nation, and are living testimony to the bored, the alienated from work, and the otherwise vaguely dissatisfied that exciting careers *do* exist. And the definition of these careers as newsworthy by the mass media peculiarly fits them for the strategic role they play in the vicarious lives of others.

The Adolescent Subculture and Academic Achievement[1]

James S. Coleman

Industrial society has spawned a peculiar phenomenon, most evident in America but emerging also in other Western societies: adolescent subcultures, with values and activities quite distinct from those of the adult society—subcultures whose members have most of their important associations within and few with adult society. Industrialization, and the rapidity of change itself, has taken out of the hands of the parent the task of training his child, made the parent's skills obsolescent, and put him out of touch with the times—unable to understand, much less inculcate, the standards of a social order which has changed since he was young.

By extending the period of training necessary for a child and by encompassing nearly the whole population, industrial society has made of high school a social system of adolescents. It includes, in the United States, almost all adolescents and more and more of the activities of the adolescent himself. A typical example is provided by an excerpt from a high-school newspaper in an upper-middle-class suburban school:

> SOPHOMORE DANCING FEATURES CHA CHA
>
> Sophomores, this is your chance to learn how to dance! The first day of sophomore dancing is Nov. 14 and it will begin at 8:30 A.M. in the Boys' Gym. . . .
>
> No one is required to take dancing but it is highly recommended for both boys and girls. . . .

Reprinted by permission of the publisher, the University of Chicago Press, from the *American Journal of Sociology* 65 (January 1960):337–47.

[1]The research discussed in this paper was carried out under a grant from the United States Office of Education; a full report is contained in "Social Climates and Social Structures in High Schools," a report to the Office of Education. The paper was presented at the Fourth World Congress of Sociology, Milan, Italy, September, 1959.

If you don't attend at this time except in case of absence from school, you may not attend at any other time. Absence excuses should be shown to Miss ——— or Mr. ———.

In effect, then, what our society has done is to set apart, in an institution of their own, adolescents for whom home is little more than a dormitory and whose world is made up of activities peculiar to their fellows. They have been given as well many of the instruments which can make them a functioning community: cars, freedom in dating, continual contact with the opposite sex, money, and entertainment, like popular music and movies, designed especially for them. The international spread of "rock-and-roll" and of so-called American patterns of adolescent behavior is a consequence, I would suggest, of these economic changes which have set adolescents off in a world of their own.

Yet the fact that such a subsystem has sprung up in society has not been systematically recognized in the organization of secondary education. The theory and practice of education remains focused on *individuals;* teachers exhort individuals to concentrate their energies in scholarly directions, while the community of adolescents diverts these energies into other channels. The premise of the present research is that, if educational goals are to be realized in modern society, a fundamentally different approach to secondary education is necessary. Adults are in control of the institutions they have established for secondary education; traditionally, these institutions have been used to mold children as individuals toward ends which adults dictate. The fundamental change which must occur is to shift the focus: to mold social communities as communities, so that the norms of the communities themselves reinforce educational goals rather than inhibit them, as is at present the case.

The research being reported is an attempt to examine the status systems of the adolescent communities in ten high schools and to see the effects to these status systems upon the individuals within them. The ten high schools are all in the Midwest. They include five schools in small towns (labeled *0–4* in the figures which follow), one in a working-class suburb (*6*), one in a well-to-do suburb (*9*), and three schools in cities of varying sizes (*5, 7,* and *8*). All but No. *5,* a Catholic boys' school, are coeducational, and all but it are public schools.

The intention was to study schools which had quite different status systems, but the similarities were far more striking than the differences. In a questionnaire all boys were asked: "How would you most like to be remembered in school: as an athletic star, a brilliant student, or most popular? The results of the responses for each school are shown in Figure 1,[2] where the left corner of the triangle represents 100 per cent saying "star athlete"; the top corner represents 100 per cent saying "brilliant student"; and the right corner represents 100 per cent saying "most popular." Each school is

[2]I am grateful to James A. Davis and Jacob Feldman, of the University of Chicago, for suggesting such graphs for presenting responses to trichotomous items in a population.

representedly a point whose location relative to the three corners shows the proportion giving each response.

The schools are remarkably grouped somewhat off-center, showing a greater tendency to say "star athlete" than either of the other choices. From each school's point is a broken arrow connecting the school as a whole with its members who were named by their fellows as being "members of the leading crowd." In almost every case, the leading crowd tends in the direction of the athlete—in all cases *away* from the ideal of the brilliant student. Again, for the leading crowds as well as for the students as a whole, the uniformity is remarkably great; not so great in the absolute positions of the leading crowds but in the direction they deviate from the student bodies.

This trend toward the ideal of the athletic star on the part of the leading crowds is due in part to the fact that the leading crowds include a great number of athletes. Boys were asked in a questionnaire to name the best athlete in their grade, the best student, and the boy most popular with girls. In every school, without exception, the boys named as best athletes were named more often—on the average over twice as often—as members of the leading crowd than were those named as best students. Similarly, the boy most popular with girls was named as belonging to the leading crowd more

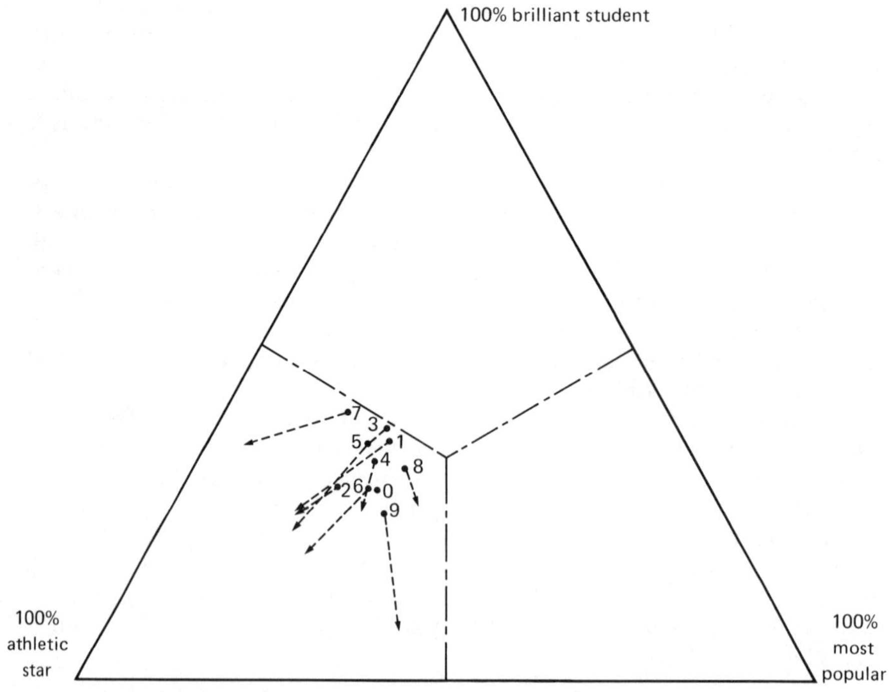

Fig. 1. Positions of schools and leading crowds in boys' relative choice of brilliant student, athletic star, and most popular

often than the best student, though in all schools but the well-to-do suburb and the smallest rural town (schools *9* and *0* on Fig. 1) less often than the best athlete.

These and other data indicate the importance of athletic achievement as an avenue for gaining status in the schools. Indeed, in the predominantly middle-class schools, it is by far the most effective achievement for gaining a working-class boy entrée into the leading crowd.

Similarly, each girl was asked how she would like to be remembered: as a brilliant student, a leader in extracurricular activities, or most popular. The various schools are located on Figure 2, together with arrows connecting them to their leading crowd. The girls tend slightly less, on the average, than the boys to want to be remembered as brilliant students. Although the alternatives are different, and thus cannot be directly compared, a great deal of other evidence indicates that the girls—although better students in every school—do not want to be considered "brilliant students." They have good reason not to, for the girl in each grade in each of the schools who was most often named as best student has fewer friends and is less often in the leading crowd than is the boy most often named as best student.

There is, however, diversity among the schools in the attractiveness of the images of "activities leader" and "popular girl" (Fig. 2). In five (*9, 0, 3,*

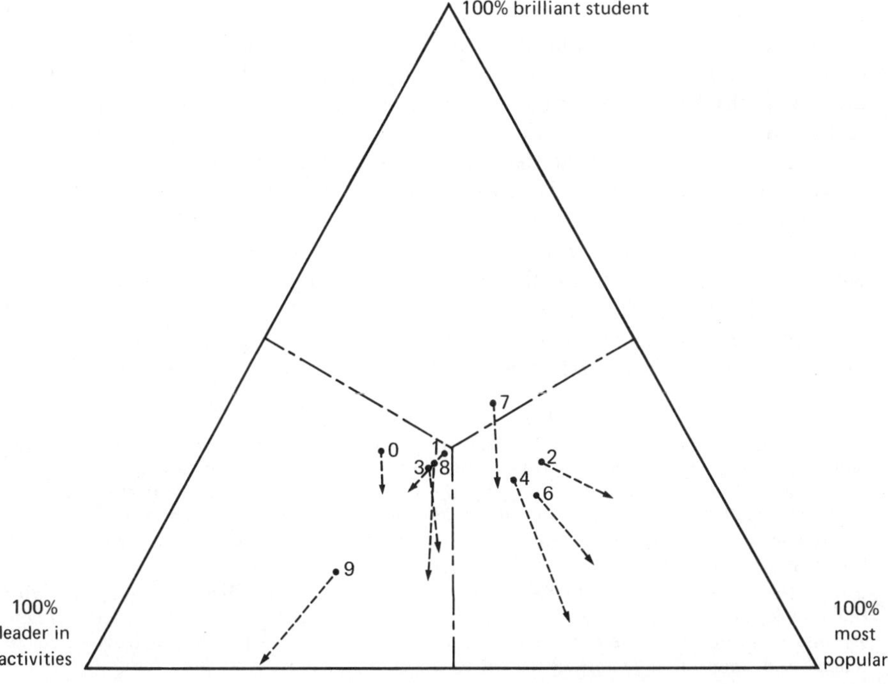

Fig. 2. Titles as in Fig. 6, but without last parentheses

8, and *1*), the leader in activities is more often chosen as an ideal than is the popular girl; in four (*7, 6, 2,* and *4*) the most popular girl is the more attractive of the two. These differences correspond somewhat to class background differences among the schools: *2, 4, 6,* and *7,* where the activities leader is least attractive, have highest proportion of students with working-class backgrounds. School *9* is by far the most upper-middle-class one and by far the most activities-oriented.

The differences among the schools correspond as well to differences among the leading crowds: in schools *2, 4,* and *6,* where the girls as a whole are most oriented to being popular, the leading crowds are even more so; in the school where the girls are most oriented to the ideal of the activities leader, No. *9,* the leading crowd goes even further in that direction.[3] In other words, it is as if a pull is exerted by the leading crowd, bringing the rest of the students toward one or the other of the polar extremes. In all cases, the leading crowd pulls away from the brilliant-student ideal.

Although these schools vary far less than one might wish when examining the effects of status systems, there are differences. All students were asked in a questionnaire: "What does it take to get into the leading crowd?" On the basis of the answers, the relative importance of various activities can be determined. Consider only a single activity, academic achievement. Its importance for status among the adolescents in each school can be measured simply by the proportion of responses which specify "good grades," or "brains" as adolescents often put it, as a means of entrée into the leading crowd. In all the schools, academic achievement was of less importance than other matters, such as being an athletic star among the boys, being a cheerleader or being good-looking among the girls, or other attributes. Other measures which were obtained of the importance of academic achievement in the adolescent status system correlate highly with this one.[4]

If, then, it is true that the status system of adolescents *does* affect educational goals, those schools which differ in the importance of academic achievement in the adolescent status system should differ in numerous other ways which are directly related to educational goals. Only one of those, which illustrates well the differing pressures upon students in the various schools, will be reported here.

In every social context certain activities are highly rewarded, while others are not. Those activities which are rewarded are the activities for

[3]This result could logically be a statistical artifact because the leaders were included among students as a whole and thus would boost the result in the direction they tend. However, it is not a statistical artifact, for the leading crowds are a small part of the total student body. When they are taken out for computing the position of the rest of the girls in each school, schools *2, 4, 6,* and *7* are still the most popularity-oriented, and school *9* the most activities-oriented.

[4]Parenthetically, it might be noted that the measures correlate on imperfectly with the proportion of boys or girls who want to be remembered as brilliant students. These responses depend on the relative attractiveness of other ideals, which varies from school to school, and upon other factors unrelated to the status system.

which there is strong competition—activities in which everyone with some ability will compete. In such activities the persons who achieve most should be those with most potential ability. In contrast, in unrewarded activities, those who have most ability may not be motivated to compete; consequently, the persons who achieve most will be persons of lesser ability. Thus in a high school where basketball is important, nearly every boy who might be a good basketball player will go out for the sport, and, as a result, basketball stars are likely to be the boys with the most ability. If in the same school volleyball does not bring the same status, few boys will go out for it, and those who end up as members of the team will not be the boys with most potential ability.

Similarly, with academic achievement: if a school where such achievement brings few social rewards, those who "go out" for scholarly achievement will be few. The high performers, those who receive good grades, will not be the boys whose ability is greatest but a more mediocre few. Thus the "intellectuals" of such a society, those defined by themselves and others as the best students, will not in fact be those with most intellectual ability. The latter, knowing where the social rewards lie, will be off cultivating other fields which bring social rewards.

To examine the effect of varying social pressures in the schools, academic achievement, as measured by grades in school, was related to I.Q. Since the I.Q. tests differ from school to school, and since each school had its own mean I.Q. and its own variation around it, the ability of high performers (boys who made *A* or *A*— average)[5] was measured by the number of standard deviations of their average I.Q.'s above the mean. In this way, it is possible to see where the high performers' ability lay, relative to the distribution of abilities in their school.[6]

The variations were great: in a small-town school, No. *1,* the boys who made an *A* or *A*— average had I.Q.'s 1.53 standard deviations above the school average; in another small-town school, No. *0,* their I.Q.'s were only about a third this distance above the mean, .59. Given this variation, the

[5]In each school but *3* and *8*, those making *A* and *A*— constituted from 6 to 8 per cent of the student body. In order to provide a correct test of the hypothesis, it is necessary to have the same fraction of the student body in each case (since I.Q.'s of this group are being measured in terms of number of standard deviations above the student body). To adjust these groups, enough *6*'s were added (each being assigned the average I.Q. of the total group of *6*'s) to bring the proportion up to 6 per cent (from 3 per cent in school *3*, from 4 per cent in school *8*).

[6]The I.Q. tests used in the different schools were: (*0*) California Mental Maturity (taken seventh, eighth, or ninth grade); (*1*) California Mental Maturity (taken eighth grade); (*2*) SRA Primary Mental Abilities (taken tenth grade); (*3*) California Mental Maturity (taken ninth grade; seniors took SRA PMA, which was tabulated as a percentile, and they have been omitted from analysis reported above); (*4*) Otis (ninth and tenth grades; taken eighth grade); Kuhlman Finch (eleventh and twelfth grades, taken eighth grade); (*5*) Otis (taken ninth grade); (*6*) California Mental Matúrity (taken eighth grade); (*7*) California Mental Maturity (taken eighth grade); (*8*) Otis (taken ninth or tenth grade); and (*9*) Otis (taken eighth grade).

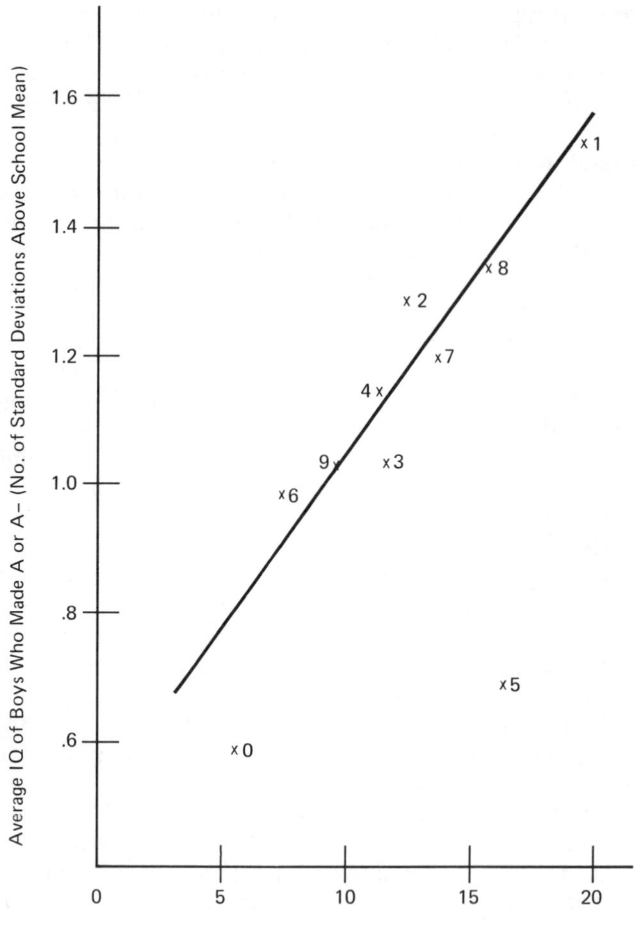

Fig. 3. I.Q.'s of high achieving boys by importance of good grades among other boys

question can be asked: Do these variations in ability of the high performers correspond to variations in the social rewards for, or constraints against, being a good student?

Figure 3 shows the relation for the boys between the social rewards for academic excellence (i.e., the frequency with which "good grades" was mentioned as a means for getting into the leading crowd) and the ability of the high performers, measured by the number of standard deviations their average I.Q.'s exceed that of the rest of the boys in the school. The relation is extremely strong. Only one school, a parochial boys' school in the city's slums, deviates. This is a school in which many boys had their most important associations outside the school rather than in it, so that its student body constituted far less of a social system, less able to dispense social rewards and punishments, than was true of the other schools.

Similarly, Figure 4 shows for the girls the I.Q.'s of the high performers.[7] Unfortunately, most of the schools are closely bunched in the de-

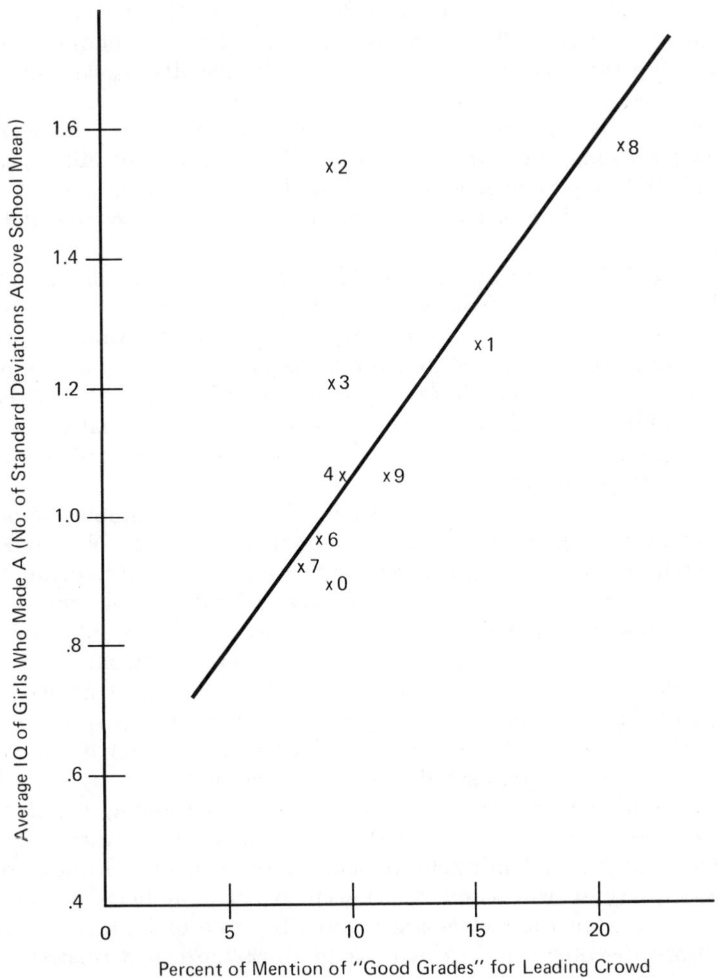

Fig. 4. I.Q.'s of high achieving girls by importance of good grades among other girls

[7]For the girls, only girls with a straight-*A* average were included. Since girls get better grades than boys, this device is necessary in order to make the sizes of the "high-performer" group roughly comparable for boys and for girls. Schools differed somewhat in the

gree to which good grades are important among the girls, so that there is too little variation among them to examine this effect as fully as would be desirable. School *2* is the one school whose girls deviate from the general relationship.

The effect of these values systems on the freedom for academic ability to express itself in high achievement is evident among the girls as it is among the boys. This is not merely due to the school facilities, social composition of the school, or other variables: the two schools highest in the importance of scholastic achievement for both boys and girls are *1* and *8*, the first a small-town school of 350 students and the second a city school of 2,000 students. In both there are fewer students with white-collar backgrounds than in schools *9* or *3*, which are somewhere in the middle as to value placed on academic achievement, but are more white-collar than in schools *7* or *4*, which are also somewhere in the middle. The highest expenditure per student was $695 per year in school *9*, and the lowest was little more than half that, in school *4*. These schools are close together on the graphs of Figures 3 and 4.

It should be mentioned in passing that an extensive unpublished study throughout Connecticut, using standard tests of achievement and ability, yielded consistent results. The study found no correlation between per pupil expenditure in a school and the achievement of its students relative to their ability. The effects shown in Figures 3 and 4 suggest why: that students with ability are led to achieve only when there are social rewards, primarily from their peers, for doing so—and these social rewards seem little correlated with per pupil expenditure.

So much for the effects as shown by the variation among schools. As mentioned earlier, the variation among schools was not nearly so striking in this research as the fact that, in all of them, academic achievement did not count for as much as other activities. In every school the boy named as best athlete and the boy named as most popular with girls was far more often mentioned as a member of the leading crowd, and as someone to "be like," than was the boy named as the best student. And the girl named as best dressed, and the one named as most popular with boys, was in every school far more often mentioned as being in the leading crowd and as someone "to be like," than was the girl named as the best student.

The relative unimportance of academic achievement, together with the effect shown earlier, suggests that these adolescent subcultures are generally deterrents to academic achievement. In other words, in these societies of adolescents those who come to be seen as the "intellectuals" and who come to think so of themselves are not really those of highest intelligence but are only the ones who are willing to work hard at a relatively unrewarded activity.

---

proportion of *A*'s, constituting about 6 per cent of the students in the small schools, only about 3 per cent in schools *6* and *7*, 1 per cent in *8*, and 2 per cent in *9*. In *8* and *9*, enough girls were added and assigned the average grade of the 7 (*A*−) group to bring the proportion to 3 per cent, comparable with the other large schools. The difference, however, between the large and small schools was left.

The implications for American society as a whole are clear. Because high schools allow the adolescent subcultures to divert energies into athletics, social activities, and the like, they recruit into adult intellectual activities people with a rather mediocre level of ability. In fact, the high school seems to do more than allow these subcultures to discourage academic achievement; it aids them in doing so. To indicate how it does and to indicate how it might do differently is another story, to be examined below.

Figures 1 and 2, which show the way boys and girls would like to be remembered in their high school, demonstrate a curious difference between the boys and the girls. Despite great variation in social background, in size of school (from 180 to 2,000), in size of town (from less than a thousand to over a million), and in style of life of their parents, the proportion of boys choosing each of the three images by which he wants to be remembered is very nearly the same in all schools. And in every school the leading crowd "pulls" in similar directions: at least partly toward the ideal of the star athlete. Yet the ideals of the girls in these schools are far more dispersed, and the leading crowds "pull" in varying directions, far less uniformly than among the boys. Why such a diversity in the same schools?

The question can best be answered by indirection. In two schools apart from those in the research, the questionnaire was administered primarily to answer a puzzling question: Why was academic achievement of so little importance among the adolescents in school *9*? Their parents were professionals and business executives, about 80 per cent were going to college (over twice as high a proportion as in any of the other schools), and yet academic excellence counted for little among them. In the two additional schools parental background was largely held constant, for they were private, coeducational day schools whose students had upper-middle-class backgrounds quite similar to those of school *9*. One (No. *10*) was in the city; the other (No. *11*), in a suburban setting almost identical to that of No. *9*. Although the two schools were added to the study to answer the question about school *9*, they will be used to help answer the puzzle set earlier: that of the clustering of schools for the boys and their greater spread for the girls. When we look at the responses of adolescents in these two schools to the question as to how they would like to be remembered, the picture becomes even more puzzling (Figs. 5 and 6). For the boys, they are extremely far from the cluster of the other schools; for girls, they are intermingled with the other schools. Thus, though it was for the boys that the other schools clustered so closely, these two deviate sharply from the cluster; and for the girls, where the schools already varied, these two are not distinguishable. Furthermore, the leading crowds of boys in these schools do not pull the ideal toward the star-athlete ideal as do those in almost all the other schools. To be sure, they pull away from the ideal of the brilliant student, but the pull is primarily toward a social image, the most popular. Among the girls, the leading crowds pull in different directions and are nearly indistinguishable from the other schools.

The answer to both puzzles, that is, first, the great cluster of the boys and now, in these two additional schools, the greater deviation, seems to lie in one fact: the boys' interscholastic athletics. The nine public schools are

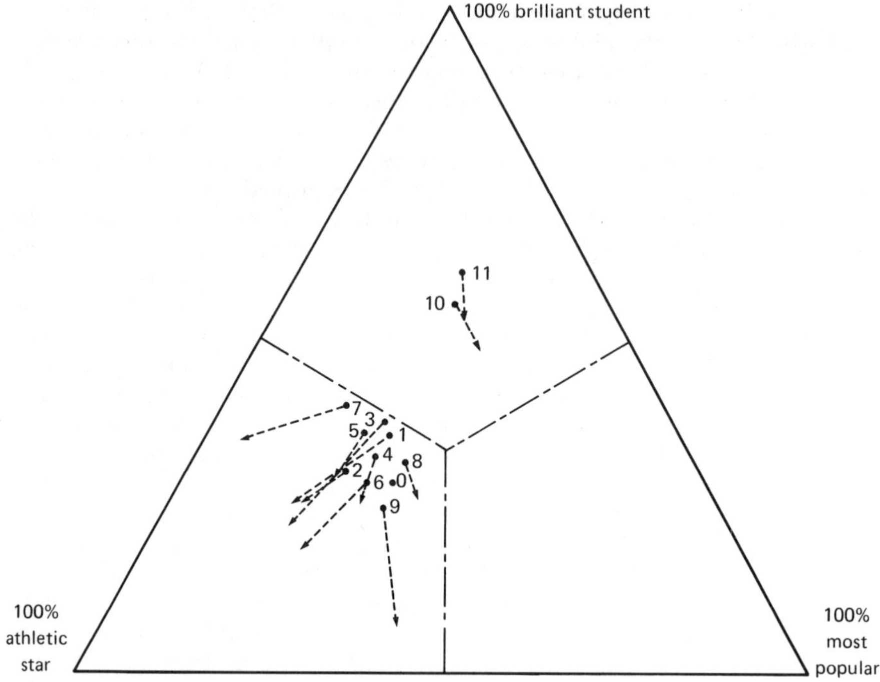

Fig. 5. Title as in Fig. 1, but with added: (two private schools [*10, 11*] included)

all engaged in interscholastic leagues which themselves are knit together in state tournaments. The other school of the first ten, the Catholic school, is in a parochial league, where games are just as hotly contested as in the public leagues and is also knit together with them in tournaments.

Schools *10* and *11* are athletically in a world apart from this. Although boys in both schools may go in for sports, and both schools have interscholastic games, the opponents are scattered private schools, constituting a league in name only. They take no part in state or city tournaments and have almost no publicity.

There is nothing for the girls comparable to the boys' interscholastic athletics. There are school activities of one sort or another, in which most girls take part, but no interscholastic games involving them. Their absence and the lack of leagues which knit all schools together in systematic competition means that the status system can "wander" freely, depending on local conditions in the school. In athletics, however, a school and the community surrounding it, cannot hold its head up if it continues to lose games. It *must* devote roughly the same attention to athletics as do the schools surrounding it, for athletic games are the only games in which it engages other schools and, by representation, other communities.

These games are almost the only means a school has of generating internal cohesion and identification, for they constitute the only activity in which the school participates as a school. (This is well indicated by the fact that a number of students in school *10,* the private school which engages in no interscholastic games, has been concerned by a "lack of school spirit.") It is as a consequence of this that the athlete gains so much status: he is doing something for the school and the community, not only for himself, in leading his team to victory, for it is a school victory.

The outstanding student, in contrast, has little or no way to bring glory to his school. His victories are always purely personal, often at the expense of his classmates, who are forced to work harder to keep up with him. It is no wonder that his accomplishments gain little reward and are often met by ridiculing remarks, such as "curve-raiser" or "grind," terms of disapprobation which have no analogues in athletics.

These results are particularly intriguing, for they suggest ways in which rather straightforward social theory could be used in organizing the activities of high schools in such a way that their adolescent subcultures would encourage, rather than discourage, the channeling of energies into directions of learning. One might speculate on the possible effects of city-wide or state-wide "scholastic fairs" composed of academic games and tourna-

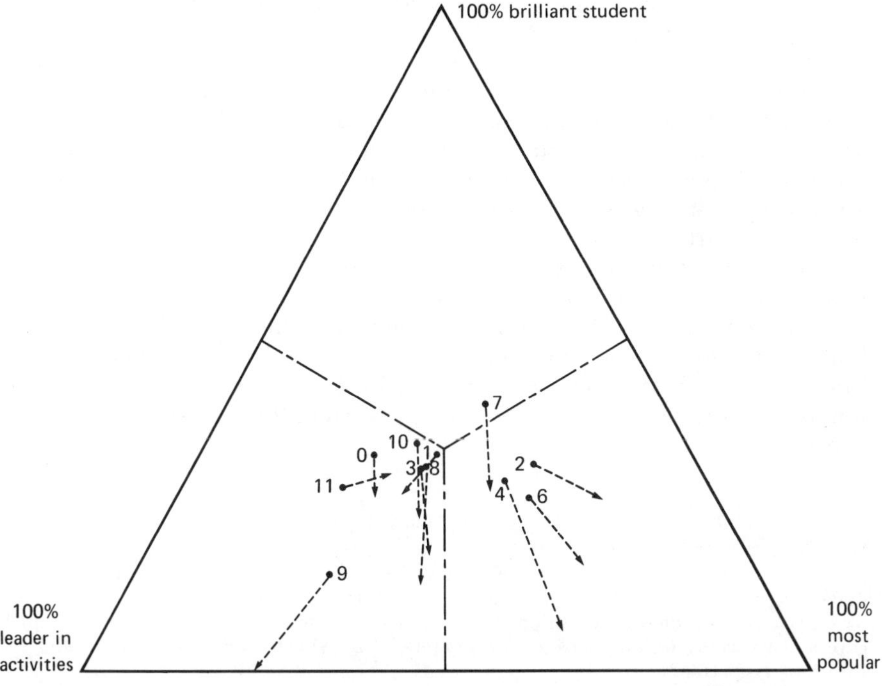

Fig. 6. Positions of schools and leading crowds in girls' relative choice of brilliant student, activities leader, and most popular (two private schools [*10, 11*] included)

ments between schools and school exhibits to be judged. It could be that the mere institution of such games would, just as do the state basketball tournaments in the midwestern United States, have a profound effect upon the educational climate in the participating schools. In fact, by an extension of this analysis, one would predict that an international fair of this sort, a "Scholastic Olympics," would generate interscholastic games and tournaments within the participating countries.

Friends and Networks

Elliot Liebow

More than most social worlds, perhaps, the streetcorner world takes its shape and color from the structure and character of the face-to-face relationships of the people who live in it. Unlike other areas in our society, where a large portion of the individual's energies, concerns and time are invested in self-improvement, career and job development, family and community activities, religious and cultural pursuits, or even in broad, impersonal social and political issues, these resources in the streetcorner world are almost entirely given over to the construction and maintenance of personal relationships.

On the streetcorner, each man has his own network of these personal relationships and each man's network defines for him the members of his personal community.[1] His personal community, then, is not a bounded area but rather a web-like arrangement of man–man and man–woman relationships in which he is selectively attached in a particular way to a definite number of discrete persons. In like fashion, each of these persons has his own personal network.[2]

[1]I have borrowed this term from Jules Henry and taken the liberty of defining it differently and limiting its scope (to exclude, for example, from a man's personal community, his employer, the policeman on the beat, or other agents of local, state and national governments whom he may look to for support). See "The Personal Community and Its Invariant Properties."

[2]"A network is a social configuration in which some, but not all, of the component external units maintain relationships with one another. The external units do not make up a larger social whole. They are not surrounded by a common boundary." Elizabeth Bott, *Family and Social Network,* pp. 216–17.

At the edges of this network are those persons with whom his relationship is affectively neutral, such as area residents whom he has "seen around" but does not know except to nod or say "hi" to as they pass on the street. These relationships are limited to simple recognition. Also at the edges are those men and women, including former friends and acquaintances, whom he dislikes or fears or who dislike or fear him. These relationships are frequently characterized by avoidance but the incumbents remain highly visible and relevant to one another.

In toward the center are those persons he knows and likes best, those with whom he is "up tight": his "walking buddies," "good" or "best" friends, girl friends, and sometimes real or putative kinsmen. These are the people with whom he is in more or less daily, face-to-face contact, and whom he turns to for emergency aid, comfort or support in time of need or crisis. He gives them and receives from them goods and services in the name of friendship, ostensibly keeping no reckoning. Routinely, he seeks them out and is sought out by them. They serve his need to be with others of his kind, and to be recognized as a discrete, distinctive personality, and he, in turn, serves them the same way. They are both his audience and his fellow actors.

It is with these men and women that he spends his waking, nonworking hours, drinking, dancing, engaging in sex, playing the fool or the wise man, passing the time at the Carry-out or on the street-corner, talking about nothing and everything, about epistemology or Cassius Clay, about the nature of numbers or how he would "have it made" if he could have a steady job that paid him $60 a week with no layoffs.

So important a part of daily life are these relationships that it seems like no life at all without them. Old Mr. Jenkins climbed out of his sickbed to take up a seat on the Coca-Cola case at the Carry-out for a couple of hours. "I can't stay home and play dead," he explained, "I got to get out and see my friends."

Friendship is sometimes anchored in kinship, sometimes in long-term associations which may reach back into childhood. Other close friendships are born locally, in the streetcorner world itself, rather than brought in by men from the outside. Such friendships are built on neighbor or co-worker relationships, or on a shared experience or other event or situation which brings two people together in a special way.

In general, close friendships tend to develop out of associations with those who are already in one's network of personal relationships: relatives, men and women who live in the area and spend much of their time on the street or in public places, and co-workers. The result is that the streetcorner man, perhaps more than others in our society, tends to use the same individuals over and over again: he may make a friend, neighbor and co-worker of his kinsman, or a friend, co-worker and kinsman of his neighbor. A look at some of the personal relationships can illustrate the many-stranded aspects of friendship and the bi-directional character of friendship on the one hand, and kinship, neighbor, co-worker and other relationships on the other.

When Tonk and Pearl got married and took an apartment near the Carry-out, Pearl's brother, Boley, moved in with them. Later, Pearl's nephew, J.R., came up from their hometown in North Carolina and he, too, moved in with them. J.R. joined Tonk and Boley on the streetcorner and when Earl told Tonk of some job openings where he worked, Tonk took J.R. with him. These three, then, were kinsmen, shared the same residence, hung out together on the streetcorner, and two of them—for a time at least—were co-workers.

Preston was Clarence's uncle. They lived within a block of each other and within two blocks of the Carry-out. Clarence worked on a construction job and later got Preston a job at the same place. Tally, Wee Tom and Budder also worked at the same construction site. The five men regularly walked back from the job to the streetcorner together, usually sharing a bottle along the way. On Friday afternoons, they continued drinking together for an hour or so after returning to the streetcorner. Tally referred to the other four men as his "drinking buddies."

Tally had met Wee Tom on the job. Through Tally, Wee Tom joined them on the walk home, began to hang around the Carry-out and finally moved into the neighborhood as well. Budder had been the last to join the group at the construction site. He had known Preston and Clarence all along, but not well. He first knew Tally as a neighbor. They came to be friends through Tally's visits to the girl who lived with Budder, his common-law wife, and his wife's children. When Tally took Budder onto the job with him, Budder became a co-worker and drinking buddy, too. Thus, in Tally's network, Wee Tom began as co-worker, moved up to drinking buddy, neighbor and finally close friend; Budder from neighbor and friend to co-worker. Importantly, and irrespective of the direction in which the relationships developed, the confluence of the co-worker and especially the neighbor relationship with friendship deepened the friend relationship.

One of the most striking aspects of these overlapping relationships is the use of kinship as a model for the friend relationship. Most of the men and women on the streetcorner are unrelated to one another and only a few have kinsmen in the immediate area. Nevertheless, kinship ties are frequently manufactured to explain, account for, or even to validate friend relationships. In this manner, one could move from friendship to kinship in either direction. One could start with kinship, say, as did Preston and Clarence or Boley and Tonk and build on this, or conversely, one could start with friendship and build a kin relationship.

The most common form of the pseudo-kin relationship between two men is known as "going for brothers." This means, simply, that two men agree to present themselves as brothers to the outside world and to deal with one another on the same basis. Going for brothers appears as a special case of friendship in which the usual claims, obligations, expectations, and loyalties of the friend relationship are publicly declared to be at their maximum.

Sea Cat and Arthur went for brothers. Sea Cat's room was Arthur's home so far as he had one anywhere. It was there that he kept his few clothes and other belongings, and it was on Sea Cat's dresser that he placed the pictures of his girl friends (sent "with love" or "love and kisses"). Sea Cat and Arthur wore one another's clothes and, whenever possible or practical, were in one another's company. Even when not together, each usually had a good idea of where the other was or had been or when he would return. Generally, they seemed to prefer going with women who were themselves friends; for a period of a month or so, they went out with two sisters.

Sea Cat worked regularly; Arthur only sporadically or for long periods not at all. His own credit of little value, Arthur sometimes tried to borrow money from the men on the corner, saying that the lender could look to his "brother" for payment. And when Sea Cat found a "good thing" in Gloria, who set him up with a car and his own apartment, Arthur shared in his friend's good fortune. On the streetcorner or in Sea Cat's room, they laughed and horsed around together, obviously enjoying one another's company. They cursed each other and called each other names in mock anger or battle, taking liberties that were reserved for and tolerated in close friends alone.[3]

A few of the men on the corner knew that Sea Cat and Arthur were, in fact, unrelated. A few knew they were not brothers but thought they were probably related in some way. Others took their claim to kinship at face value. Even those who knew they were merely going for brothers, however, accepted this as evidence of the special character of their friend relationship. In general, only those who are among the most important in one's personal network can distinguish between real and pseudo-kin relationships, partly because the question as to whether two men are really brothers or are simply going for brothers is not especially relevant. The important thing for people to know in their interaction with the two men is that they say they are brothers, not whether they are or not.

The social reality of the pseudo-kinship tie between those who are "going for brothers" is clearly evident in the case of Richard and Leroy. Richard and Leroy had been going for brothers for three months or so when Leroy got in a fight with a group of teenagers and young adults. Leroy suffered serious internal injuries and was hospitalized for more than a month. One week after the fight, Richard and one of the teenagers who had beaten up Leroy, and with whom both he and Leroy had been on friendly terms, got into a fight over a private matter having nothing to do with Leroy, and Richard killed the teenager. Richard was immediately arrested and the police, acting on information from the dead boy's friends, relatives, and others in the community, charged him with first degree murder for the premeditated revenge killing of one who had beaten up "his brother." But when it was established that Leroy and Richard were not related in any way, the charge was dropped to murder in the second degree. The dead boy's friends and relatives were outraged and bewildered. To them, and even to some of Richard and Leroy's friends, it was clearly a premeditated, deliber-

[3]Once, in his room, Sea Cat complained that a can of hair spray cost him more than $3.00, but that, with Arthur around, a can didn't even last a week. Arthur seemed not to have heard. Slowly, he got up from the bed, took a can of hair spray from the dresser, ostentatiously loosened his belt, pulled his pants away from his waist and with great deliberation sprayed his genitals, looking at Sea Cat with an air of blank innocence all the while. Sea Cat shook his head: "See what I mean?" he said, but he couldn't quite suppress his laughter.

ate killing. Hadn't Richard and Leroy been going for brothers? And hadn't Leroy been badly beaten by this same boy just eight days earlier?

Pseudo-kinship ties are also invoked in certain man–woman relationships. Stoopy first met Lucille in the kitchen of an officers' club in Virginia where they both worked. They became friends and later, when Lucille and her teenage son were looking for a place to live, Stoopy told her of a place in the Carry-out area and Lucille moved in. As neighbors as well as co-workers, Stoopy and Lucille's friendship deepened and they "went for cousins." Stoopy and Lucille saw a lot of one another. They frequently went back and forth to work together. They borrowed money from each other and freely visited each other in their homes. Lucille came to know Stoopy's wife through her Saturday morning visits with the children, and Stoopy's relationship with Lucille's son was conspicuously warm and avuncular.[4]

At no time in their relationship was there ever the slightest suggestion of any romantic or sexual connection between them. Indeed, this seems to be the primary purpose behind "going for cousins." It is a way of saying, "This woman [man] and I are good friends but we are not lovers." Given the taboo against cousin marriage,[5] going for cousins permits an unrelated man and woman to enter into a close-friend relationship without compromising their romantic or sexual status in any way. It is a public disclaimer of any romantic or sexual content in a cross-sex, close-friend relationship.

The social utility of going for cousins is evident when one compares Stoopy and Lucille with Tally and Velma. Tally and Velma were good friends, but unlike Stoopy and Lucille, they were not going for cousins.[6] On several occasions Tally and Velma attended parties as part of a foursome, each bringing his own partner. On such occasions, Tally often spoke of his friendship with Velma, noting that he had several times slept in her home but had "never laid a hand on her." Skeptical or even uninterested listeners were dragged before Velma who verified Tally's description of their relationship.

In contrast, Stoopy and Lucille were under no such pressure to validate the asexual nature of their relationship. The question never came up. They were going for cousins. That was enough.

[4]Later, after Lucille moved out, she sometimes visited Stoopy and others in the Carry-out area. During this period, she and Stoopy continued to go for cousins.

[5]The aura of incest associated with sex relationships between (first) cousins may explain the following episode. In this particular case, even a sexual relationship with one's cousin's spouse appears as an unthinkable proposition. Wee Tom and I had been in Nancy's place. Among the others there, were a man and woman neither of us knew. Later the same evening we met them again on a streetcorner. The man went into a drugstore. The woman tried to kiss me and I pushed her away. "What do you want with him? You already got your man," said Wee Tom, pointing to the man in the drugstore. "Him?" she said, indignantly. "He's married to my cousin. How could he be my man?"

[6]I do not know why Tally and Velma did not go for cousins. Perhaps they did not see enough of each other (Velma lived across the river in Virginia) to warrant taking this step. Perhaps they were not prepared to commit themselves to the obligations that such a formalization of their relationship would entail. Perhaps they did not want to preclude the possibility that their relationship might develop along romantic lines. Or finally, perhaps they were beginning the process of going for cousins.

Sometimes pseudo-kinship is invoked in more casual terms, apparently to sharpen and lend formal structure to a relationship which is generally vague. Occasionally, one hears that "he just call her his sister," or that "they just call it brother and sister," or even "they just go for brother and sister." Such was the case with Stanton. His young daughter was living with a married woman whom most people, including Stanton, referred to as his sister. But Stanton, "he just call her his sister." In caring for his child, the woman was, of course, doing what sisters sometimes do. The assignment of the label "sister" to one already performing a function which frequently appears in association with that label was an easy step to take. A vague relationship was rendered specific; it was simplified, and the need for explanations was reduced. This may also have served to discourage public suspicion about the nature of this relationship. In these respects, perhaps going for cousins would have served them equally well. And as in the case of going for brothers, whether Stanton and this woman were in fact brother and sister was less important than the fact that they "called" themselves so. The woman's husband, we must assume, knew they were not related. But since Stanton and the man's wife called themselves brother and sister, the husband's vested interests and public status were not jeopardized, not even by Stanton's visits to his home when he himself was not present.

Most friendships are thus born in propinquity, in relationships or situations in which individuals confront one another day by day and face to face. These friendships are nurtured and supported by an exchange of money, goods, services and emotional support. Small loans, ranging from a few pennies up to two or three dollars, are constantly being asked for and extended. Leroy watches Malvina's children while she goes out to have a few drinks with a friend. Tonk and Stanton help Budder move the old refrigerator he just bought into his apartment. Robert spends an evening giving Richard a home process. Preston lends Stoopy forty cents for bus fare to go to work. Pearl and Tonk throw a party, supplying all of the food and much of the liquor themselves. When Bernice leaves Stanton, Leroy consoles him telling him of how Charlene is always doing this too, but always coming back. Leroy borrows a bottle of milk for the baby from Richard and Shirley. Sara gives Earl three dollars to get his clothes out of the cleaners. Sea Cat and Stoopy find Sweets knocked unconscious on the sidewalk, carry him home and put him to bed. Tonk and Richard go down to the police station to put up five dollars toward Tally's collateral. Clarence returns from his father's funeral where Tally and Preston hung onto him throughout, restraining him physically where necessary and comforting him in his shock as best they could. Back at Nancy's place, Clarence nurses his grief in silence and nonparticipation. Tally urges him again and again to "Come on, Baby, show me you're a man," but Clarence shakes his head no. Tally keeps trying. Finally, taking the glass of whiskey offered him, Clarence sloughs off his mourner's status by dancing with Nancy. Tally laughs with pleasure at his own handiwork. "O.K. now?" he asks, and Clarence smiles back that yes, everything's O.K. now.

In ways such as these, each person plays an important part in helping and being helped by those in his personal network. Since much of the cooperation between friends centers around the basic prerequisites of daily living, friends are of special importance to one's sense of physical and emotional security. The more friends one has or believes himself to have, and the deeper he holds these friendships to be, the greater his self-esteem and the greater the esteem for himself he thinks he sees in the eyes of others.

The pursuit of security and self-esteem push him to romanticize his perception of his friends and friendships. He wants to see acquaintances as friends, and not only as friends but as friends with whom he is "up tight," "walking buddies," "best friends," or even brothers. He prefers to see the movement of money, goods, services and emotional support between friends as flowing freely out of loyalty and generosity and according to need rather than as a mutual exchange resting securely on a quid pro quo basis. He wants to believe that his friendships reach back into the distant past and have an unlimited future; that he knows and is known by his friends intimately, that they can trust one another implicitly, and that their loyalties to one another are almost unbounded. He wants to see himself as Pythias to other Damons.

"Wee Tom's my best friend," said Tally, two months after they first met. He put his hand on Wee Tom's shoulder. "Him and me are up tight. Nothing I have is too good for him." Wee Tom said the same went for him.

When Arthur was shot to death by the shopkeeper whom he was trying to hold up, Richard said that the shopkeeper had, in effect, killed himself as well as killed Arthur. Arthur was his—Richard's—friend and neither he nor Arthur's other friends would let their buddy's death go unavenged. When Shirley protested that the man killed Arthur in self-defense, that Arthur was in the wrong, and what about the consequences of revenge to Richard, herself and the children, Richard dismissed her with a shrug. "I can't break it down for you. You just don't understand [how it is between friends]."

Leroy said he and all the roomers in the house didn't pay Malvina any fixed amount of rent. Everybody just gave what they could when they could. They were all friends, you know, and it was oh, so informal: from each according to his ability, to each according to his need.

But Tally and Wee Tom did have things that were "too good" for each other, and their friendship was gradually eroded by arguments over money[7] and a variety of other things, including the relative priority of friendship claims against those of the husband–wife relationship.[8]

[7]Such as the time Tally hit the number for a quarter ($135.00) and not only refused to give Wee Tom $5 or $10 (which Wee Tom didn't really expect) but also refused to lend him more than $5.00.

[8]Wee Tom and I were in Tally's room, waiting for Tally to finish dressing. As Tally peeled off his undershirt, he began berating Wee Tom for leaving him and the others after they got paid. Wee Tom protested that "You can't always do what you want to do. Sometimes you do what you gotta do, and I had to get home. My old lady needed the money to pay the rent and we had a lot to talk about. That don't mean we're not friends. I just had to go home, that was all." Tally sneered at this. "A woman's got to come up to a man," he answered. "If a woman don't come up to me, fuck her. Throw her ass out." Wee Tom was annoyed and angry but he said nothing.

And Richard, who did not go to Arthur's funeral,[9] never again mentioned avenging his friend's death, even when the subject of Arthur came up.

As for Leroy's contention that Malvina and the others he was living with at the time were one big family, sharing one hearth, one pot, the fact is that each person or couple purchased their own food and kept it under lock and key in one of the four refrigerators in the kitchen in the basement. Everyone had the right to use the toilet on the second floor, the kitchen, and the handful of pots, pans and dishes lying dirty in the sink or on the drainboard, but nothing else was held in common. Moreover, careful mental accounts were kept, not only of rent, but of less formal exchanges as well, nor were the figures rounded off. Here is Leroy reconstructing on tape the events leading up to his last break with Malvina and others in the house.[10] Charlene had told Leroy that Malvina said she wanted the money he owed her for rent and other expenses:

> So when I got paid I went down there. I said, "Malvina, here is your twelve ninety-five . . ." I said, "Now, I want a dollar and a half from you for your haircut; I want two dollars for the money I gave you to buy the liquor and I want a dollar and seventy-five cents for the money you got the other day." Then I said, "Malvina, I want five dollars from you from where I got the groceries and I want the four dollars that you got then."
>
> [Caricaturing Malvina] "Well, I ain't got it right now."
>
> I said, "Then I'll wait until you get paid. When you all get paid I'm gonna come down here and I'm gonna have my list ready. When we get to five dollars, you subtract that money from what you all owe me and have my money ready."
>
> So when they got the money, they said, "We got to pay the rent."
>
> I said, "I don't know nothing about that. My rent's paid. All I wants is my money. If I don't get my money, you can take that on my rent. I ain't paying the rent for the next three weeks."
>
> So I didn't pay no rent for the next three weeks. We kept on arguing. Then last night, Malvina jumped up . . .

Friendship is at its romantic, flamboyant best when things are going well for the persons involved. But friendship does not often stand up well to the stress of crisis or conflict of interest, when demands tend to be heaviest and most insistent. Everyone knows this. Extravagant pledges of aid and comfort between friends are, at one level, made and received in good faith. But at another level, fully aware of his friends' limited resources and the demands of their self-interest, each person is ultimately prepared to look to himself alone.

The recognition that, at bottom, friendship is not a bigger-than-life relationship is sometimes expressed as a repudiation of all would-be friends

[9] He later gave as his reason the fact that he did not have the money to get his hair fixed.

[10] "It is only when the relationship breaks down that the underlying obligations are brought to light." William Foote Whyte, *Street Corner Society,* p. 257.

("I don't need you or any other mother-fucker") or as a cynical denial that friendship as a system of mutual aid and support exists at all. When Tally threatened to withdraw his friendship from Richard, Richard dismissed this as no real loss. "Richard's the only one who ever looked out for Richard," he said.

A similar attitude leads to the assessment of friendship as a "fair weather" phenomenon. John had just been fired from his job. Bernice, Betty and I were speculating about the reason for it. I told them what I had heard on the corner.

> "I know who told you that, but they all talk about John behind his back," said Bernice.
>
> I said that the person who told me what I had repeated to them considered himself John's friend.
>
> "He ain't no friend of John's. He never was," retorted Bernice. "I know who told you and I know he's not John's friend."
>
> Betty said, "None of them's John's friend. All those boys—Sea Cat, Richard, Tally, Leroy—they're the ones cost John his job. They're not his friends. You know, when a person's up, the whole world's up with him. But when a person's down, you're down alone."

Attitudes toward friends and friendships are thus always shifting, frequently ambivalent, and sometimes contradictory. One moment, friendship is an almost sacred covenant; the next, it is the locus of cynical exploitation: "Friends are [good only] for money."

These shifts and apparent contradictions arise directly out of the structure and character of the individual's network of personal relationships. They arise from the fact that, at any given moment, the different relationships that comprise the individual's network of personal relationships may be at widely different stages of development or degeneration. They arise, too, from the easy quickness with which a casual encounter can ripen into an intense man–man or man–woman relationship, and the equal ease with which these relationships break down under stress.

One gains a feeling for the fluidity and processual character of personal relations and their networks by looking at one such network over time.

. . .

The overall picture is one of a broad web of interlocking, overlapping networks in which the incumbents are constantly—however irregularly—shifting and changing positions relative to one another. This fluidity and change which characterizes personal relationships is reflected in neighbor and kin relationships, in family, household, indeed in the whole social structure of the streetcorner world which rests to so large an extent precisely on the primary, face-to-face relationships of the personal network.[11]

[11]"Were [William F.] Whyte to return today to the cornervilles of America, he would probably find much less evidence of what he called 'highly organized and integrated' patterns of slum life." Richard A. Cloward and Lloyd E. Ohlin, *Delinquency and*

In support of the economic, social and psychological forces arrayed against the stability of personal networks is the intrinsic weakness of friendship itself. Whether as cause, effect, or both, the fact is that friendships are not often rooted in long-term associations nor do the persons involved necessarily know anything of one another's personal history prior to their association.[12] The man would like to think—and sometimes says—that his friendship with so-and-so goes back several years or even into childhood—but this is not often the case in fact.[13] Their relationship rests almost entirely in present time. A man may have detailed knowledge of his friend's present circumstances and relationships but little else. He knows from the fact that his friend is on the street, and he knows, from looking into himself, the gross characteristic features of the friend's personal history. He knows his friend was raised principally by women and that he holds these women dearly, that he was brought up to love and fear God, that he's had little formal education, that he has few if any job skills and has worked in different towns and cities, that in one or more of these towns he fathered a child whom he has probably never seen, that he first came here because he has an uncle or aunt here, or because he met this girl, or because he heard about this job, or because he was wanted by the police or someone else wherever he used to live. But he does not know the particulars. He does not know whether it was his mother, grandmother or father's sister who raised him, how far he went in school, which towns and which cities he's lived and worked in, and what crucial experiences he had there, and so forth. Of course, much of this comes out as unsolicited, incidental information in the course of casual talk and hanging around, but much does not.[14]

Opportunity: A Theory of Delinquent Gangs, p. 210. On p. 172 of the same work, vertical and geographic mobility, housing and changing land use are identified as some of "the many forces making for instability in the social organization of some slum areas. . . . Forces of this kind keep a community off balance, for tentative efforts to develop social organization are quickly checked. *Transiency and instability become the overriding features of social life.*" (Emphasis added.) Whyte himself points out the importance of distinguishing between relatively stable slum communities (such as his own Street Corner Society) and unstable slum districts. He notes that Margaret Chandler, in "The Social Organization of Workers in a Rooming House Area," found that "an acquaintance of a week might be described as an old friend, so rapidly did the ties shift" "On Street Corner Society," p. 257).

[12]Oscar Lewis found that "in some villages, peasants can live out their lives without any deep knowledge or understanding of the people whom they 'know' in face to face relationships" ("Further Observations on the Folk-Urban Continuum and Urbanization with Special Reference to Mexico City," p. 12).

[13]When Leroy, for example, appeared as a character witness at Richard's murder trial, he testified that he had known Richard since they were kids. Leroy later protested that this was a minor exaggeration and shook his head in disbelief and wonderment when he was reminded that he did not meet Richard until the winter of 1961.

[14]Not even their last names. One evening Richard was sitting in his apartment lamenting his present circumstances. He was reminded that he had a lot of friends (he had been the janitor in his apartment house for five or six months). Richard snorted and said that if the police were to pick him up and allow him his one phone call, he wouldn't know what to do with it because he doesn't even know anyone's last name. This was not entirely true, but it clearly points up his own contemptuous assessment of the depths of

Especially lacking is an exchange of secret thoughts, of private hopes and fears.

Friendship thus appears as a relationship between two people who, in an important sense, stand unrevealed to one another. Lacking depth in both past and present, friendship is easily uprooted by the tug of economic or psychological self-interest or by external forces acting against it.

The recognition of this weakness, coupled with the importance of friendship as a source of security and self-esteem, is surely a principal source of the impulse to romanticize relationships, to upgrade them, to elevate what others see as a casual acquaintanceship to friendship, and friendship to close friendship. It is this, perhaps, that lies behind the attempt to ascribe a past to a relationship that never had one, and to borrow from the bony structure of kinship ("going for brothers") to lend structural support to a relationship sorely in need of it. It is as if friendship is an artifact of desire, a wish relationship, a private agreement between two people to act "as if," rather than a real relationship between persons.

---

the friendships he had formed in the Carry-out neighborhood. The quality of these friendships contrasted sharply with those he had formed in his hometown (1960 population: 1,100), where his family knew all the other Negro families and was known by them, and where his friends were young men and women he had known from infancy.

3 Youth, the Family, and Socialization

The nuclear family—that is, the family living isolated from kin, whose basic unit consists of mother, father, and children—underlies many of the problems characteristically associated with the socialization of youth in American society. The articles in this section begin with an analysis of parent-child conflict in any society (Kingsley Davis) and then spell out some of the implications of the Davis article.

Hannerz, who investigated a black community in Washington, D.C., contends that Liebow's description of family life among blacks is only partially true. Hannerz claims that Liebow, who found an unconnected, almost independent development of males, failed to recognize a variety of socializing influences. The family grows through contacts with the larger environment; Hannerz identifies the influence of women on the masculinity of young males and the import of the solidarity of male street groups. Remember that Hannerz is discussing interaction, while Liebow shows that idealized descriptions and expectations are fictive and that superficial interaction does not provide support and continuity. In short, the black male, particularly the one in the street, faces many of the stresses of adolescence within the larger society while also facing the street demands for independence, masculinity, and aggressiveness. This is the implicit message of "The Roots of Black Manhood." The ghetto is a mixture of two cultural streams, both of which present obstacles to socialization into adulthood.

Riesman's "Permissiveness and Sex Roles" outlines several of the positive and negative features of the American nuclear family constellation, with its tendency to foster independence at an early age. He sensitively anticipates the present youth culture and the women's liberation movement, showing how the drives for independence create great demands on women, both intellectually and emotionally. In effect, Riesman demonstrates how, when rapid change occurs—in this case, alternative opportunities for females—unaccompanied by new patterns of support from significant social groups, it exacerbates the process of socialization. He further advocates the value of the youth culture in supporting the adolescent through a transitional period where he can "play" with identities and roles.

That the commune is a growing American institution indicates both the failure of conventional post-industrial society to offer attractive and satisfying roles, and the strength of that society to support new forms of "occupation." In "Communes," Rosabeth Kanter compares the present communes with a group of historical communes and finds the present groups wanting. She judges that the failure of today's communes to create beliefs and practices that insure commitment to the group, and to socialize the young into these beliefs and practices, suggests a short existence for the communes.

A number of trends—including communes; the spread of what was once seen as a lower-class life style (for example, common-law marriage, cohabitation, and bearing and keeping illegitimate children); and the reported instability of the black family—indicate that the nuclear family is undergoing several subtle but possibly profound changes. Although the nuclear family remains at present the fundamental source of identities, one may ask what are the possible family forms of the future? (See Moore 1965.)

The Sociology of Parent-Youth Conflict

Kingsley Davis

It is in sociological terms that this paper attempts to frame and solve the sole question with which it deals, namely: Why does contemporary Western civilization manifest an extraordinary amount of parent–adolescent conflict?[1] In other cultures, the outstanding fact is generally not the rebelliousness of youth, but its docility. There is practically no custom, no matter how tedious or painful, to which youth in primitive tribes or archaic civilizations will not willingly submit.[2] What, then, are the peculiar features of our society which give us one of the extremest examples of endemic filial friction in human history?

Our answer to this question makes use of constants and variables, the constants being the universal factors in the parent-youth relation, the variables being the factors which differ from one society to another. Though one's attention, in explaining the parent–youth relations of a given milieu, is focused on the variables, one cannot comprehend the action of the variables without also understanding the constants, for the latter constitute the structural and functional basis of the family as a part of society.

THE RATE OF SOCIAL CHANGE. The first important variable is the rate of social change. Extremely rapid change in modern civilization, in contrast to

Reprinted by permission of the author and the publisher, The American Sociological Association, from *American Sociological Review* 5 (August 1940):523–35.

[1]In the absence of statistical evidence, exaggeration of the conflict is easily possible, and two able students have warned against it. E. B. Reuter, "The Sociology of Adolescence," and Jessie R. Runner, "Social Distance in Adolescent Relationships," both in *The American Journal of Sociology*, November 1937, 43:415–16, 437. Yet sufficient nonquantitative evidence lies at hand in the form of personal experience, the outpour of literature on adolescent problems, and the historical and anthropological accounts of contrasting societies to justify the conclusion that in comparison with other cultures ours exhibits an exceptional amount of such conflict. If this paper seems to stress conflict, it is simply because we are concerned with this problem rather than with parent–youth harmony.

[2]Cf. Nathan Miller, *The Child in Primitive Society* (New York: 1928); Miriam Van Waters, "The Adolescent Girl Among Primitive Peoples," *Journal of Religious Psychology*, 1913, 6:375–421 (1913) and 7:75–120 (1914); Margaret Mead, *Coming of Age in Samoa* and "Adolescence in Primitive and Modern Society," *The New Generation* (ed. by V. F. Calverton and S. Schmalhausen); A. M. Bacon, *Japanese Girls and Women*.

most societies, tends to increase parent–youth conflict, for within a fast-changing social order the time-interval between generations, ordinarily but a mere moment in the life of a social system, become historically significant, thereby creating a hiatus between one generation and the next. Inevitably, under such a condition, youth is reared in a milieu different from that of the parents; hence the parents became old-fashioned, youth rebellious, and clashes occur which, in the closely confined circle of the immediate family; generate sharp emotion.

That rapidity of change is a significant variable can be demonstrated by three lines of evidence: a comparison of stable and nonstable societies,[3] a consideration of immigrant families; and an analysis of revolutionary epochs. If, for example, the conflict is sharper in the immigrant household, this can be due to one thing only, that the immigrant family generally undergoes the most rapid social change of any type of family in a given society. Similarly, a revolution (an abrupt form of societal alteration), by concentrating great change in a short span, catapults the younger generation into power—a generation which has absorbed and pushed the new ideas, acquired the habit of force, and which, accordingly, dominates those hangovers from the old regime, its parents.[4]

THE BIRTH-CYCLE, DECELERATING SOCIALIZATION, AND PARENT–CHILD DIFFERENCES. Note, however, that rapid social change would have no "power to produce conflict were it not for two universal factors: first, the family's duration; and second, the decelerating rate of socialization in the development of personality. "A family" is not a static entity but a process in time, a process ordinarily so brief compared with historical time that it is unimportant, but which, when history is "full" (i.e., marked by rapid social change), strongly influences the mutual adjustment of the generations. This "span" is basically the birth-cycle—the length of time between the birth of one person and his procreation of another. It is biological and inescapable. It would, however, have no effect in producing parent–youth conflict, even with social change, if it were not for the additional fact, intimately related and equally universal, that the sequential development of personality involves a constantly decelerating rate of socialization. This deceleration is due both to organic factors (age—which ties it to the birth-cycle) and to social factors (the cumulative character of social experience). Its effect is to make the birth-cycle interval, which is the period of youth, the time of major socialization, subsequent periods of socialization being subsidiary. . . .

Given these constant features, rapid social change creates conflict because *to* the intrinsic (universal inescapable) differences between parents and children it adds an extrinsic (variable) difference derived from the acquisition at the same stage of life, of differential cultural content by each

[3]Partially done by Mead and Van Waters in the works cited above.

[4]Soviet Russia and Nazi Germany are examples. See Sigmund Neumann, "The Conflict of Generations in Contemporary Europe from Versailles to Munich," *Vital Speeches of the Day*, August 1, 1939. Parents in these countries are to be obeyed only so long as they profess the "correct" (i.e., youthful, revolutionary) ideas.

successive generation. Not only are parent and child, at any given moment, in different stages of development, but the content which the parent acquired at the stage where the child now is, was a different content from that which the child is now acquiring. Since the parent is supposed to socialize the child, he tends to apply the erstwhile but now inappropriate content (see Diagram). He makes this mistake, and cannot remedy it, because, due to the logic of personality growth, his basic orientation was formed by the experiences of his own childhood. He cannot "modernize" his point of view, because *he* is the product of those experiences. He can change in superficial ways, such as learning a new tune, but he cannot change (or *want* to change) the initial modes of thinking upon which his subsequent social experience has been built. To change the basic conceptions by which he has learned to judge the rightness and reality of all specific situations would be to render subsequent experience meaningless, to make an empty caricature of what had been his life.

Although, in the birth-cycle gap between parent and offspring, astronomical time constitutes the basic point of disparity, the actual sequences, and hence the actual differences significant for us, are physiological, psychosocial, and sociological—each with an acceleration of its own within, but to some degree independent of, sideral time, and each containning a divergence between parent and child which must be taken into account in explaining parent–youth conflict.

Physiological differences. Though the disparity in chronological age remains constant through life, the precise physiological differences between parent and offspring vary radically from one period to another. The organic contrasts between parent and *infant,* for example, are far different from those between parent and adolescent. Yet whatever the period, the organic differences produce contrasts (as between young and old) in those desires which, at least in part, are organically determined. Thus, at the time of adolescence the contrast is between an organism which is just reaching its

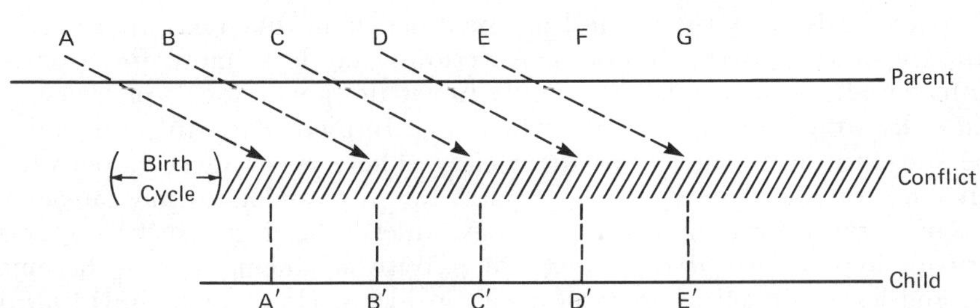

The birth-cycle, social change, and parent-child relations at different stages of life

full powers and one which is just losing them. The physiological need of the latter is for security and conservation, because as the superabundance of energy diminishes, the organism seems to hoard what remains.

Such differences, often alleged (under the heading of "disturbing physiological changes accompanying adolescence") as the primary cause of parent–adolescent strife, are undoubtedly a factor in such conflict, but, like other universal differences to be discussed, they form a constant factor present in every community, and therefore cannot in themselves explain the peculiar heightening of parent–youth conflict in our culture.

The fact is that most societies avoid the potential clash of old and young by using sociological position as a neutralizing agent. They assign definite and separate positions to persons of different ages, thereby eliminating competition between them for the same position and avoiding the competitive emotions of jealousy and envy. Also, since the expected behavior of old and young is thus made complementary rather than identical, the performance of cooperative functions is accomplished by different but mutually related activities suited to the disparate organic needs of each, with no coercion to behave in a manner unsuited to one's organic age. In our culture, where most positions are *theoretically* based on accomplishment rather than age, interage competition arises, superior organic propensities lead to a high evaluation of youth (the so-called "accent on youth"), a disproportionate lack of opportunity for youth manifests itself, and consequently, arrogance and frustration appear in the young, fear and envy, in the old.

Psychosocial differences: adult realism versus youthful idealism. The decelerating rate of socialization (an outgrowth both of the human being's organic development, from infant plasticity to senile rigidity, and of his cumulative cultural and social development), when taken with rapid social change and other conditions of our society, tends to produce certain differences of orientation between parent and youth. Though lack of space makes it impossible to discuss all of these ramifications, we shall attempt to delineate at least one sector of difference in terms of the conflict between adult realism (or pragmatism) and youthful idealism.

Though both youth and age claim to see the truth, the old are more conservatively realistic than the young, because on the one hand they take Utopian ideals less seriously and on the other hand they take what may be called operating ideals, if not more seriously, at least more for granted. Thus, middle-aged people notoriously forget the poetic ideals of a new social order which they cherished when young. In their place, they put simply the working ideals current in the society. There is, in short, a persistent tendency for the ideology of a person as he grows older to gravitate more and more toward the status quo ideology, unless other facts (such as a social crisis or hypnotic suggestion) intervene.[5] With advancing age, he becomes less and less bothered by inconsistencies in ideals. He tends to judge ideals according to whether they are widespread and hence effective in thinking about practical life, not according to whether they are logically consistent.

[5]See Footnote 11 for necessary qualifications.

Furthermore, he gradually ceases to bother about the *untruth* of his ideals, in the sense of their failure to correspond to reality. He assumes through long habit that, though they do not correspond perfectly, the discrepancy is not significant. The reality of an ideal is defined for him in terms of how many people accept it rather than how completely it is mirrored in actual behavior.[6] Thus, we call him, as he approaches middle age, a realist.

The young, however, are idealists, partly because they take working ideals literally and partly because they acquire ideals not fully operative in the social organization. Those in authority over children are obligated as a requirement of their status to inculcate ideals as a part of the official culture given the new generation.[7] The children are receptive because they have little social experience—experience being systematically kept from them (by such means as censorship, for example, a large part of which is to "protect" children). Consequently, young people possess little ballast for their acquired ideals, which therefore soar to the sky, whereas the middle-aged, by contrast, have plenty of ballast.

This relatively unchecked idealism in youth is eventually complicated by the fact that young people possess keen reasoning ability. The mind, simply as a logical machine, works as well at sixteen as at thirty-six.[8] Such logical capacity, combined with high ideals and an initial lack of experience, means that youth soon discovers with increasing age that the ideals it has been taught are true and consistent are not so in fact. Mental conflict thereupon ensues, for the young person has not learned that ideals may be useful without being true and consistent. As a solution, youth is likely to take action designed to remove inconsistencies or force actual conduct into line with ideals, such action assuming one of several typical adolescent forms—from religious withdrawal to the militant support of some Utopian scheme—but in any case consisting essentially in serious allegiance to one or more of the ideal moral systems present in the culture.[9]

A different, usually later reaction to disillusionment is the cynical or sophomoric attitude; for, if the ideals one has imbibed cannot be reconciled

[6]When discussing a youthful ideal, however, the older person is quick to take a dialectical advantage by pointing out not only that this ideal affronts the aspirations of the multitude but that it also fails to correspond to human behavior either now or (by the lessons of history) probably in the future.

[7]See amusing but accurate article, "Fathers Are Liars," *Scribner's,* March 1934.

[8]Evidence from mental growth data which point to a leveling off of the growth curve at about age 16. For charts and brief explanations, together with references, see F. K. Shuttelworth, The Adolescent Period, Monographs of the Society for Research in Child Development, III, Serial No. 16 (Washington, D. C., 1938), Figs. 16, 230, 232, 276, 285, 308.

Maturity of judgment is of course another matter. We are speaking only of logical capacity. Judgment is based on experience as well as capacity; hence, adolescents are apt to lack it.

[9]An illustration of youthful reformation was afforded by the Laval University students who decided to "do something about" prostitution in the city of Quebec. They broke into eight houses in succession one night, "whacked naked inmates upon the buttocks, upset beds and otherwise proved their collegiate virtue. . . ." They ended by "shoving the few remaining girls out of doors into the cold autumn night." *Time,* October 19, 1936.

and do not fit reality, then why not dismiss them as worthless? Cynicism has the advantage of giving justification for behavior that young organisms crave anyway. It might be mistaken for genuine realism if it were not for two things. The first is the emotional strain behind the "don't care" attitude. The cynic, in his judgment that the world is bad because of inconsistency and untruth of ideals, clearly implies that he still values the ideals. The true realist sees the inconsistency and untruth, but without emotion; he uses either ideals or reality whenever it suits his purpose. The second is the early disappearance of the cynical attitude. Increased experience usually teaches the adolescent that overt cynicism is unpopular and unworkable, that to deny and deride all beliefs which fail to cohere or to correspond to facts, and to act in opposition to them, is to alienate oneself from any group.[10] because these beliefs, however unreal, are precisely what makes group unity possible. Soon, therefore, the youthful cynic finds himself bound up with some group having a system of working ideals, and becomes merely another conformist, cynical only about the beliefs of other groups.[11]

While the germ of this contrast between youthful idealism and adult realism may spring from the universal logic of personality development, it receives in our culture a peculiar exaggeration. Social change, complexity, and specialization (by compartmentalizing different aspects of life) segregate ideals from fact and throw together incompatible ideologies, while at the same time providing the intellectual tools for discerning logical inconsistencies and empirical errors. Our highly elaborated burden of culture, correlated with a variegated system of achieved vertical mobility, necessitates long years of formal education which separate youth from adulthood, theory from practice, school from life. Insofar, then, as youth's reformist zeal or cynical negativism produces conflict with parents, the peculiar conditions of our culture are responsible.

SOCIOLOGICAL DIFFERENCES: PARENTAL AUTHORITY. Since social status

[10]This holds only for expressed cynicism, but so close is the relation of thought to action that the possibility of an entirely convert cynic seems remote.

[11]This tentative analysis holds only insofar as the logic of personality development in a complex culture is the sole factor. Because of other forces, concrete situations may be quite different. When, for example, a person is specifically trained in certain rigid, other worldly, or impractical ideals, he may grow increasingly fanatical with the years rather than realistic, while his offspring, because of association with less fanatical persons, may be more pragmatic than he. The variation in group norms within a society produces persons who, whatever their orientation inside the group, remain more idealistic than the average outsider, while their children may, with outside contacts, become more pragmatic. Even within a group, however, a person's situation may be such as to drive him beyond the everyday realities of that group, while his children remain undisturbed. Such situations largely explain the personal crises that may alter one's orientation. The analysis, overly brief and mainly illustrative, therefore represents a certain degree of abstraction. The reader should realize, moreover, that the terms "realistic" and "idealistic" are chosen merely for convenience in trying to convey the idea, not for any evaluative judgments which they may happen to connote. The terms are not used in any technical epistemological sense, but simply in the way made plain by the context. Above all, it is not implied that ideals "unreal" to observer and actor are complex indeed. See Talcott Parsons, *The Structure of Social Action,* 396, and V. Pareto, *The Mind and Society,* III: 1300–1304.

and office are everywhere partly distributed on the basis of age, personality development is intimately linked with the network of social positions successively occupied during life. Western society, in spite of an unusual amount of interage competition, maintains differences of social position between parent and child, the developmental gap between them being too clear-cut, the symbiotic needs too fundamental, to escape being made a basis of social organization. Hence, parent and child, in a variety of ways, find themselves enmeshed in different social contexts and possessed of different outlooks. The much publicized critical attitude of youth toward established ways, for example, is partly a matter of being on the outside looking in. The "established ways" under criticism are usually institutions (such as property, marriage, profession) which the adolescent has not yet entered. He looks at them from the point of view of the outsider (especially since they affect him in a restrictive manner), either failing to imagine himself finding satisfaction in such patterns or else feeling resentful that the old have in them a vested interest from which he is excluded.

Not only is there differential position, but also *mutually* differential position, status being in many ways specific for and reciprocal between parent and child. Some of these differences, relating to the birth-cycle and constituting part of the family structure are universal. This is particularly true of the super- and subordination summed up in the term *parental authority*.

Since sociological differences between parent and child are inherent in family organization, they constitute a universal factor potentially capable of producing conflict. Like the biological differences, however, they do not in themselves produce such conflict. In fact, they may help to avoid it. To understand how our society brings to expression the potentiality for conflict, indeed to deal realistically with the relation between the generations, we must do so not in generalized terms but in terms of the specific "power situation." Therefore, the remainder of our discussion will center upon the nature of parental authority and its vicissitudes in our society.

Because of his strategic position with reference to the new-born child (at least in the familial type of reproductive institution), the parent is given considerable authority. Charged by his social group with the responsibility of controlling and training the child in conformity with the mores and thereby insuring the maintenance of the cultural structure, the parent, to fulfill his duties, must have the privileges as well as the obligations of authority, and the surrounding community ordinarily guarantees both.

The first thing to note about parental authority, in addition to its function in socialization, is that it is a case of authority within a primary group. Simmel has pointed out that authority is bearable for the subordinate because it touches only one aspect of life. Impersonal and objective, it permits all other aspects to be free from its particularistic dominance. This escape, however, is lacking in parental authority, for since the family includes most aspects of life, its authority is not limited, specific, or impersonal. What, then, can make this authority bearable? Three factors associated with the familial primary group help to give the answer: (1) the child is socialized within the family, and therefore knowing nothing else and being utterly dependent, the authority of the parent is internalized, accepted; (2) the family, like other primary groups, implies identification, in such sense that one person understands and responds emphatically to the sentiments of the other, so that the harshness of authority is ameliorated;[12] (3) in the intimate interaction of the primary group control can never be purely one-sided; there are too many ways in which the subordinated can exert the pressure of his will. When, therefore, the family system is a going concern, parental authority, however inclusive, is not felt as despotic.

A second thing to note about parental authority is that while its duration is variable (lasting in some societies a few years and in others a lifetime), it inevitably involves a change, a progressive readjustment, in the respective positions of parent and child—in some cases an almost complete reversal of roles, in others at least a cumulative allowance for the fact of maturity in the subordinated offspring. Age is a unique basis for social stratification. Unlike birth, sex, wealth, or occupation, it implies that the stratification is temporary, that the person, if he lives a full life, will eventually traverse all of the strata having it as a basis. Therefore, there is a peculiar ambivalence attached to this kind of differentiation, as well as a constant directional movement. On the one hand, the young person, in the stage of maximum socialization, is, so to speak, *moving into* the social organization. His social personality is expanding, i.e., acquiring an increased amount of the cultural heritage, filling more powerful and numerous positions. His future is before him, in what the older person is leaving behind. The latter, on the other hand, has a future before him only in the sense that the offspring represents it. Therefore, there is a disparity of interest, the young person placing his thoughts upon a future which, once the first stages of dependence are passed, does not include the parent, the old person placing his hopes vicariously upon the young. This situation, representing a *tendency* in every society, is avoided in many places by a system of respect for the aged and an imaginary projection of life beyond the grave. In the absence of such a religio-ancestral system, the role of the aged is a tragic one.[13]

Let us now take up, point by point, the manner in which western civilization has affected this *gemeinschaftliche* and processual form of authority.

Conflicting norms. To begin with, rapid change has, as we saw, given old and young a different social content, so that they possess conflicting norms. There is a loss of mutual identification, and the parent will not "catch up" with the child's point of view, because he is supposed to dominate rather than follow. More than this, social complexity has confused the standards *within* the generation. Faced with conflicting goals, parents become inconsistent and confused in their own minds in rearing their chil-

[12]House slaves, for example, are generally treated much better than field slaves. Authority over the former is of a personal type, while that over the latter (often in the form of a foreman-gang organization) is of a more impersonal or economic type.

[13]Sometimes compensated for by an interest in the grandchildren, which permits them partially to recover the role of the vigorous parent.

dren. The children, for example, acquire an argument against discipline by being able to point to some family wherein discipline is less severe, while the parent can retaliate by pointing to still other families wherein it is firmer. The acceptance of parental attitudes is less complete than formerly.

COMPETING AUTHORITIES. We took it for granted, when discussing rapid social change, that youth acquires new ideas, but we did not ask how. The truth is that, in a specialized and complex culture, they learn from competing authorities. Today, for example, education is largely in the hands of professional specialists, some of whom, as college professors, resemble the sophists of ancient Athens by virtue of their work of accumulating and purveying knowledge, and who consequently have ideas in advance of the populace at large (i.e., the parents). By giving the younger generation these advanced ideas, they (and many other extrafamilial agencies, including youth's contemporaries) widen the intellectual gap between parent and child.[14]

LITTLE EXPLICIT INSTITUTIONALIZATION OF STEPS IN PARENTAL AUTHORITY. Our society provides little explicit institutionalization of the progressive readjustments of authority as between parent and child. We are intermediate between the extreme of virtually permanent parental authority and the extreme of very early emancipation, because we encourage release in late adolescence. Unfortunately, this is a time of enhanced sexual desire, so that the problem of sex and the problem of emancipation occur simultaneously and complicate each other. Yet even this would doubtless be satisfactory if it were not for the fact that among us the exact time when authority is relinquished, the exact amount, and the proper ceremonial behavior are not clearly defined. Not only do different groups and families have conflicting patterns, and new situations arise to which old definitions will not apply, but the different spheres of life (legal, economic, religious, intellectual (do not synchronize, maturity in one sphere and immaturity in another often coexisting. The readjustment of authority between individuals is always a ticklish process, and when it is a matter of such close authority as that between parent and child it is apt to be still more ticklish. The failure of our culture to institutionalize this readjustment by a series of well-defined, well-publicized steps is undoubtedly a cause of much parent–youth dissension. The adolescent's sociological exit from his family, via education, work, marriage, and change of residence, is fraught with potential conflicts of interest which only a definite system of institutional controls can neutralize. The parents have a vital stake in what the offspring will do. Because his acquisition of independence will free the parents of many obligations, they are willing to relinquish their authority; yet, precisely because their own status is socially identified with that of their offspring, they wish to insure satisfactory conduct on the latter's part and are tempted to prolong their

[14]The essential point is not that there are other authorities—in every society there are extrafamilial influences in socialization—but that, because of specialization and individualistic enterprise, they are *competing* authorities. Because they make a living by their work and are specialists in socialization, some authorities have a competitive advantage over parents who are amateurs or at best merely general practitioners.

authority by making the decisions themselves. In the absence of institutional prescriptions, the conflict of interest may lead to a struggle for power, the parents fighting to keep control in matters of importance to themselves, the son or daughter clinging to personally indispensable family services while seeking to evade the concomitant control.

CONCENTRATION WITHIN THE SMALL FAMILY. Our family system is peculiar in that it manifests a paradoxical combination of concentration and dispersion. On the one hand, the unusual smallness of the family unit makes for a strange intensity of family feeling, while on the other, the fact that most pursuits take place outside the home makes for a dispersion of activities. Though apparently contradictory, the two phenomena are really interrelated and traceable ultimately to the same factors in our social structure. Since the first refers to that type of affection and antagonism found between relatives, and the second to activities, it can be seen that the second (dispersion) isolates and increases the intensity of the affectional element by sheering away common activities and the extended kin. Whereas ordinarily the sentiments of kinship are organically related to a number of common activities and spread over a wide circle of relatives, in our mobile society they are associated with only a few common activities and concentrated within only the immediate family. This makes them at once more instable (because ungrounded) and more intense. With the diminishing birth rate, our family is the world's smallest kinship unit, a tiny closed circle. Consequently, a great deal of family sentiment is directed toward a few individuals, who are so important to the emotional life that complexes easily develop. This emotional intensity and situational instability increase both the probability and severity of conflict.

In a familistic society, where there are several adult male and female relatives within the effective kinship group to whom the child turns for affection and aid, and many members of the younger generation in whom the parents have a paternal interest, there appears to be less intensity of emotion for any particular kinsman and consequently less chance for severe conflict.[15] Also, if conflict between any two relatives does arise, it may be handled by shifting mutual rights and obligations to another relative.[16]

OPEN COMPETITION FOR SOCIOECONOMIC POSITION. Our emphasis upon individual initiative and vertical mobility, in contrast to rural-stable regimes, means that one's future occupation and destiny are determined more at adolescence than at birth, the adolescent himself (as well as the parents) having some part in the decision. Before him spread a panorama of possible occupations and avenues of advancement, all of them fraught with the uncertainties of competitive vicissitude. The youth is ignorant of most of the

[15]Margaret Mead, "Social Organization of Manua," 84, Honolulu, Bernice P. Bishop Museum Bulletin 76, 1930. Large heterogeneous households early accustom the child to expect emotional rewards from many different persons, D. M. Spencer, "The Composition of the Family as a Factor in the Behavior of Children in Fijian Society," *Sociometry* (1939) 2:47–55.

[16]The principle of substitution is widespread in familism, as shown by the wide distribution of adoption, leviate, sororate, and classificatory kinship nomenclature.

facts. So is the parent, but less so. Both attempt to collaborate on the future, but because of previously mentioned sources of friction, the collaboration is frequently stormy. They evaluate future possibilities differently, and since the decision is uncertain yet important, a clash of wills results. The necessity of choice at adolescence extends beyond the occupational field to practically every phase of life, the parents having an interest in each decision. A culture in which more of the choices of life were settled beforehand by ascription, where the possibilities were fewer and the responsibilities of choice less urgent, would have much less parent–youth conflict.[17]

SEX TENSION. If until now we have ignored sex taboos, the omission has represented a deliberate attempt to place them in their proper context with other factors, rather than in the unduly prominent place usually given them.[18] Undoubtedly, because of a constellation of cultural conditions, sex looms as an important bone of parent–youth contention. Our morality, for instance, demands both premarital chastity and postponement of marriage, thus creating a long period of desperate eagerness when young persons practically at the peak of their sexual capacity are forbidden to enjoy it. Naturally, tensions arise—tensions which adolescents try to relieve, and adults hope they will relieve, in some socially acceptable form. Such tensions not only make the adolescent intractable and capricious, but create a genuine conflict of interest between the two generations. The parent, with respect to the child's behavior represents morality, while the offspring reflects morality *plus* his organic cravings. The stage is thereby set for conflict, evasion, and deceit. For the mass of parents, toleration is never possible. For the mass of adolescents, sublimation is never sufficient. Given our system of morality, conflict seems well nigh inevitable.

Yet it is not sex itself but the way it is handled that causes conflict. If sex patterns were carefully, definitely, and uniformly geared with nonsexual patterns in the social structure, there would be no parent–youth conflict over sex. As it is, rapid change has opposed the sex standards of different groups and generations, leaving impulse only chaotically controlled.

The extraordinary preoccupation of modern parents with the sex life of their adolescent offspring is easily understandable. First, our morality is sex-centered. The strength of the impulse which it seeks to control, the consequent stringency of its rules, and the importance of reproductive institutions for society, make sex so morally important that being moral and being sexually discreet are synonymous. Small wonder, then, that parents, charged with responsibility for their children and fearful of their own status in the eyes of the moral community, are preoccupied with what their offspring will do in this matter. Moreover, sex is intrinsically involved in the family structure and is therefore of unusual significance to family members *qua* family members. Offspring and parent are not simply two persons who happen to live together; they are two persons who happen to live together because of

[17]M. Mead, *Coming of Age in Samoa,* 200ff.

[18]Cf. L. K. Frank, "The Management of Tensions," *American Journal of Sociology,* March 1928, 33:706–22; M. Mead, *op. cit.,* 216–17, 222–23.

past sex relations between the parents. Also, between parent and child there stand strong incest taboos, and doubtless the unvoiced possibility of violating these unconsciously intensifies the interest of each in the other's sexual conduct. In addition, since sexual behavior is connected with the offspring's formation of a new family of his own, it is naturally of concern to the parent. Finally, these factors taken in combination with the delicacy of the authoritarian relation, the emotional intensity within the small family, and the confusion of sex standards, make it easy to explain the parental interest in adolescent sexuality. Yet because sex is a tabooed topic between parent and child,[19] parental control must be indirect and devious, which creates additional possibilities of conflict.

SUMMARY AND CONCLUSION. Our parent–youth conflict thus results from the interaction of certain universals of the parent–child relation and certain variables the values of which are peculiar to modern culture. The universals are (1) the basic age or birth-cycle differential between parent and child, (2) the decelerating rate of socialization with advancing age, and (3) the resulting intrinsic differences between old and young on the physiological, psychosocial, and sociological planes.

Though these universal factors *tend* to produce conflict between parent and child, whether or not they do so depends upon the variables. We have seen that the distinctive general features of our society are responsible for our excessive parent–adolescent friction. Indeed, they are the same features which are affecting *all* family relations. The delineation of these variables has not been systematic, because the scientific classification of whole societies has not yet been accomplished, and it has been difficult, in view of the interrelated character of societal traits, to seize upon certain features and ignore others. Yet certainly the following four complex variables are important: (1) the rate of social change; (2) the extent of complexity in the social structure; (3) the degree of integration in the culture; and (4) the velocity of movement (e.g., vertical mobility) within the structure and its relation to the cultural values.

Our rapid social change, for example, has crowded historical meaning into the family time-span, has thereby given the offspring a different social content from that which the parent acquired, and consequently has added to the already existent intrinsic differences between parent and youth, a set of extrinsic ones which double the chance of alienation. Moreover, our great societal complexity, our evident cultural conflict, and our emphasis upon open competition for socioeconomic status have all added to this initial effect. We have seen, for instance, that they have disorganized the important relation of parental authority by confusing the goals of child control, setting up competing authorities, creating a small family system, making necessary certain significant choices at the time of adolescence, and leading to

[19] "Even among the essentially 'unrepressed' Trobrianders the parent is never the confidant in matters of sex." Bronislaw Malinowski, *Sex and Reproduction in Savage Society*, 36*n*, London. Cf. the interesting article "Intrusive Parents," *The Commentator*, September 1938, which opposes frank sex discussion between parents and children.

an absence of definite institutional mechanisms to symbolize and enforce the progressively changing stages of parental power.

If ours were a simple rural-stable society, mainly familistic, the emancipation from parental authority being gradual and marked by definite institutionalized steps, with no great postponement of marriage, sex taboo, or open competition for status, parents and youth would not be in conflict. Hence, the presence of parent–youth conflict in our civilization is, one more specific manifestation of the incompatibility between an urban–industrial–mobile social system and the familial type of reproductive institutions.[20]

[20]For further evidence of this incompatibility, see the writer's "Reproductive Institutions and the Pressure for Population," *British Sociological Review,* July 1937, 29: 289–306.

*Permissiveness and Sex Roles**

David Riesman

Cross-generational misunderstandings are, of course, no new thing in America, nor are conflicts about permissiveness and sex. Indeed, foreign observers visiting this country a hundred years ago commented about the tolerance shown children, and, while some admired the children's poise and independence, others were horrified by their insolence or bad manners. Tocqueville was greatly impressed by the fact that American young women went around what was still a rude country without chaperones, and he and his fellow traveller, Beaumont, wrote home that American girls, while very attentive and appealing, were protected, not as on the continent by ignorance, but by what we might today call know-how. He was not quite sure how he felt about these emancipated women, with whom gallantry was no longer a sport for passing the time and asserting one's superiority.

Something like his complaint is echoed in the tendency for men of my

Reprinted by permission of the author and the publisher, The National Council on Family Relations, from *The Journal of Marriage and the Family* 21 (August 1959):211–17.

*This paper was originally presented at the Annual Symposium of the Committee on Human Development, University of Chicago, February, 1958, and was expanded in a talk at Kenyon College, October, 1958. Work on matters discussed herein has been facilitated by a grant from the Carnegie Corporation for the study of higher education.

own generation and older to look with dismay on the practice of going steady among young people in high school and college. This older generation compares going steady unfavorably with its own romantic and nostalgic images of "playing the field"; correspondingly, it sees young marriages as a too early captivity avoiding frivolity and flirtation.[1]

We should note at the outset that early dating and early sex life in general is characteristic of the working class, as Kinsey documented, and of the rural population in many peasant countries. What seems to have happened in this as in so many other ways, is that the middle class has been losing its traditional orientation towards the future and inhibitions in the present, and that the permissiveness which arises from inconsistency and indifference in the lower strata has now become a matter of principle and only an occasionally unprincipled tolerance in the educated strata. Thus, even debutantes and students at the elite colleges go steady, whereas they would once have thought such practices common.

In a recent article in *Science,* Margaret Mead and Rhoda Metraux have called attention to a hitherto unnoticed consequence of this change in values.[2] They were investigating (not by means of a national sample, but rather by careful selections here and there) the attitude of high school students towards science and scientists and they made the discovery that the career choice of boys was being increasingly influenced by the judgments of girls as to what were good careers for their boyfriends to be in. That is, if girls thought scientists would make poor husbands, this helped shape the image of the scientist that prevailed in high school—and helped, perhaps imperceptibly, to push boys towards careers that were considered compatible with decent domesticity. Of course girls were not wholly responsible for the image of the scientist which the researchers discovered: a person who is remote and sexless, who has too much or too little hair, wrapped up in the laboratory and not quite human—indeed, sometimes quite inhuman like a science fiction monster. But their article suggests that in an earlier day, when boys in the upper strata became aware of girls at a later point in life, when the boys were already themselves committed to a career, the judgment by girls would be less influential: the girls would have to take the men as they had become.

Now, however, both boys and girls are talking with each other about such serious matters as career choice, and not merely handing out a "line" with which to impress each other in the rating-dating game. The very fact that boys as well as girls are willing to go steady and to marry earlier indicates a general cultural change of emphasis towards the affective and nonwork side of life, and makes it possible for boys and girls together to decide

[1]Some critics, however, speak from the point of view of an older morality. Thus, Catholic priests at some parochial schools and colleges have forbidden steady dating on the ground that it is an occasion for sin. In this they reveal the protective bias the Church has always had towards women, but it could be argued that steady dating, while slightly increasing sin among young women, substantially reduces it among young men.

[2]"The Image of the Scientist among High-School Students: A Pilot Study," *Science*, 126 (August 30, 1957), pp. 384–90.

the kind of domestic life they will jointly seek and the sorts of careers that will further and not interfere with that ideal.

In these developments, we see reflected the greater prosperity of society; the situation of virtually full employment for the well-educated; the understandable growth, not so much of an irresponsible hedonism (although this is often charged and certainly does occur) as of a more relaxed view of what has to be done to get along—and of how much has to be sacrificed in order to get only marginally ahead. Here what might be termed "social permissiveness" cooperates with parental facilitation; thus Marvin B. Sussman showed in an article in the *American Sociological Review* a few years ago that middle class parents in New Haven were willing to stake their children to various sorts of help in the early years of marriage (even though they may not always have been pleased with the particular marriage or with its early consummation).[3]

If one talks to the faculties of medical schools, one finds them sometimes quite concerned with these developments. For one thing, there is evidence of a general decline of applications to medical school in the last several years, and it has been suggested that this is partly due to dislike of the postponement medical education requires. At the University of Kansas Medical School, three-quarters of the students are married, and this affects how they conduct themselves as students.[4] The married students are not eager for night duty, for example, or for the surgical residencies that involve night duty; nor do they yearn to sit around talking about science, ethics, and women with their fellow students. Rather, they are quickly off after their stint in the hospital to give their spouses a hand with the children and to relax with them in the evening. Faculties of medical schools under these altered conditions tend to recall their own student days as those of bachelor asceticism (modulated by an occasional binge), and readily feel out of touch with these new men who are on the one hand so mature (in being well started on family life and choice of specialty), and on the other hand, so "mature" as not to care to talk shop. And the students, in turn, eager to end the long period in which they must be supported by their wives and families, resent the protracted training necessary for certain specialties and the arduous isolation which, if not inherently "necessary," has traditionally been considered part of the folkways of that specialty.

What men have lost in willingness to undertake arduous and highly specialized careers have not, of course, marked any commensurate gain for women. Thus, although it is a good deal easier today than a generation ago for women to enter medical school, and although they probably suffer less hazing in school from their professors and from male students, they are still a tiny proportion of the students—10 per cent or less. (The situation is very different in many countries in Europe and in the Soviet Union where

[3]Marvin B. Sussman, "The Help Pattern in the Middle Class Family," *American Sociological Review,* 18 (February, 1953), no. 1, pp. 22–28.

[4]I am drawing here on unpublished materials prepared by Howard S. Becker and Blanche Geer of Community Studies, Inc., in Kansas City under the direction of Professor Everett C. Hughes of the University of Chicago.

women play a dominant role in medicine.) The same emphasis on the affective side of life, on the family as the most important element in the good life, which has influenced the career decisions of men, has also led even the most brilliant and energetic college women to decide that they do not want to undertake long preparation for careers which might cut them off from the chance of marriage or in some subtle way defeminize them. And while that has always been true of American women, college women today seem both more universally ready to hold a job than they once were (there are fewer playgirls) and less ready to risk, on behalf of greatly ambitious career aims, the possibility of a stable marriage.

These developments are occurring at the same time that there has been a great hue and cry, stimulated by Sputnik, that we need more doctors, more scientists, more engineers, more highly trained people generally. Most of this hue and cry is based on what I regard as an exploitative concern for the state of the national labor force in the Cold War; it assumes that it is inconceivable that we might end the Cold War, and that, in a society of abundance, we might regard the talents of our young people as an opportunity to develop new sorts of careers and new relations towards work. Among some of the most sensitive and gifted young people, there has developed the tendency to withdraw altogether from the great and overriding political concerns of their elders, sometimes by choosing fields such as the humanities or the ministry which could not have a conceivable Cold War or big-project relevance, and sometimes by withdrawing any deep involvement from work in large organizations even while going through the motions.[5] As a result of these developments, there would seem to be building up an often irrational reaction against permissiveness—sometimes in the mild forms in which we see it in the cartoons of *The New Yorker,* and sometimes in the intemperate attacks on the schools by such men as Admiral Rickover.

What is left out in this cross-generational bickering is any understanding of what is happening, of some of the positive values that are emerging, and of some of the problems for the individual as well as for society that these new emancipations bring. There can be no doubt that what many educated young men and women today are looking for in each other is not the rating-dating game of twenty years ago.[6] To be sure, there are still fraternities and sororities on the campus and still an interest in good looks, popularity, good grooming, and smoothness. But all this is more subdued and the relationships increasingly sought for are more searching, more profound, more sincere. There is more desire to share; less desire to impress. There is less desire to dazzle members of one's own sex and more to come to

[5]Compare the interesting article, "Beatniks in Business," *Mademoiselle* (March, 1959), pp. 74–75 and 142–45, and see more generally, my article, "Work and Leisure in the Post-industrial World," in Eric Larrabee and Rolf Meyersohn, Editors, *Mass Leisure,* Glencoe, Illinois: The Free Press, 1958.

[6]Compare the study by Robert Blood, Jr., "Uniformities and Diversities in Campus Dating Preferences," *Marriage and Family Living,* 18 (February, 1956), pp. 37–45.

some sort of humane terms with the opposite sex. Moreover, it seems to me that young people are increasingly preoccupied with their capacity to love as well as to be loved. And I have the impression that sexual relations themselves when they do occur come about less frequently from a desire on the part of the boys to present trophies to their own male vanity than to secure themselves against the anxiety that they may not be truly and deeply loved, or capable of love.

Moreover, the increase in going steady that has brought about some diminution of the search for those careers which require arduous preparation has not brought about a lessened level of seriousness among students either in high school or college. In fact, it could even be argued that young people who have made themselves secure in a vital area through the practice of going steady can consequently afford to commit themselves more fully to their studies, becoming more equable if sometimes less frantic students than were many in an earlier day who were constantly preoccupied as to whether or not they had a date or should have a date or what they might be missing if they did not.

At some of the more academically oriented colleges, the rise in the level of demands on students has made many students doubt their own intellectual adequacy—and then seek to prove that they are after all good for something in their relations with the opposite sex. They do not choose to go on dates rather than to study; rather they do both—and if something has to give way under this pressure, it is their sleep. (There is some evidence that students are staying up later and later and, if evidence from various student health services could be compared, it might shed interesting light on some of these problems.)

The seriousness and depth of some of these steady relationships in high school and college is such as to give young people the feeling that they really know members of the opposite sex well enough to choose a marriage partner much earlier in life than people of equivalent sensitivity would have dared to do with their eyes open in an earlier day. Talcott Parsons argues in his writings that romantic love allows a kind of leap of faith across the impossibility of making a rational choice (much as advertising encourages a similar leap of faith among equally available brand-name items). But in fact many of the young people are not "romantic" in the nineteenth century sense; they believe in love, but not in a starry-eyed way. Indeed, the danger of some of these steady relationships may be exactly like that of some marriages; that a plateau of routinization is too quickly reached, with stability quickly achieved as a platform for competent but unexciting family life and serious, if not totally demanding, work.

In our society, whatever becomes a fashion puts pressure on those whom the fashion does not readily fit. In an earlier day, when it was thought sober in the upper strata to postpone marriage, it took a certain hardihood or impulsivity to marry early, and to have more than two or three children. Today, in contrast, things are often hard on those who do not feel ready to "grow up," to date, to marry young, and to have a sizeable family. Girls, of course, are not chaperoned anymore, either in the Latin way or in the more characteristic Calvinist way in which they carried their invisible chaperone inside. Boys are, therefore, not protected from having to make advances to girls by the latters' obvious unavailability. Indeed, the availability of girls in America is an omnipresent and inescapable part of our visual esthetic—built into the widths of our cars, the reels of our movies, into the pages of our advertisements, and built into the girls themselves, I might add, in the way they carry themselves and dress. The greater, but still not sufficiently psychological awareness has produced the phenomenon I have occasionally seen as a teacher: that students feel under pressure from adults to have "experiences" and are ashamed to be thought dull and not to have any.

Likewise, boys and girls have a new fear, one which a generation earlier was not conscious for most men no matter how sheltered, nor for most women—that is, the fear that they might be homosexual. In talking with Dr. John Spiegel about some of the men's colleges in the Ivy League, we agreed that this fear is one factor which haunts the campus, putting pressure on many young men to be guarded in their relations with each other, and also with their male teachers, while at the same time putting pressure on them to seek out relations with girls in order to convince themselves and perhaps each other that they are not.

As a concomitant development, the ribbing of sissies, at least in the middle class, is much less strong now than it once was, and in that sense, greater "femininity" is being increasingly permitted to educated men in this country. While one can still find colleges where men define themselves as men by being athletic and going in for engineering, there are many institutions throughout the country where men can without embarrassment be interested in art, in English, in dance, and in music. But this very openness, which permits men to do things which they would once (and in many parts of the country today would still) reject, has also had the curious consequence that they cannot clearly and unequivocably define themselves as men by their roles. They have to define themselves as men, therefore, in other ways, and especially in the one physiological way which appears irrefutable; and the girls are under somewhat analogous pressure, possibly less out of a fear of homosexuality, but hardly less out of a fear of not being really a woman and responding to men as a woman should. Whereas, in the days of the double standard, nice boys would not molest good girls, that is college girls, now they often use Freud to persuade the latter, and their steady dates, that to be inhibited is bad, likely to harm the boy, if not produce or symbolize frigidity in the girl. Thus, we see that permissiveness in some areas, like any movement of liberation, produces unpermissiveness in others. Boys and girls, for instance, have *less* permission than they once did to proceed in their relations to each other and to themselves at idiosyncratic rates.

We can see what this means when we look at high schools in the way that my former colleague at Chicago, James Coleman, has recently been doing. He has asked high school students what they are interested in; and when boys are asked this question they volunteer a great many concerns;

they are interested in automobiles, in high-fi, in sports and ham radios, and even occasionally in the curriculum. They are interested in girls, too, but in rather a secondary way. In contrast, and here I interpret from his data which is still being coded and tabulated, the girls are interested in boys and in each other, and even their interest in each other I suspect is sometimes secondary or resonant to their interest in boys. Girls in high school are natural sociometrists; even in the fourth grade this is true. The boys have many defenses against being interested in girls, but the girls have very few comparable defenses against an interest in boys, and this is a pressure on boys as well as on girls. We know something of what this means in terms of age disparities. At Vassar the entering freshman girl is already date-conscious and is likely to be picked up, let us say at Yale, by upper classmen.[7] But the senior girl in high school is too old for the comparable boys now and is perhaps cut off by physical or psychological distance from college boys, whereas the freshman and sophomore boys in high school are thrown with girls who are not able to respond to them, or they to the girls, as our popular culture tells them that they should. If William James were to look at this situation, he would say that girls need a moral substitute for boys; and, indeed, for their own development, I think they need an alternative to sociometry as their major field of research in high school and college.

One reason why it seems to me that some people can profit from non-coeducation at some stages in their lives is that girls can be given in this way an alternative—at least a partial one—that allows them to cultivate, free from the pressure of boys and boy-minded girls, including the boy-minded parts of themselves, interests that might otherwise be thought of as unfeminine. And, by the same token, it may allow boys to cultivate an interest in such things as the student newspaper, or ballet, which are occasionally monopolized by girls in a co-ed school (to be sure, as I have already mentioned, most girls in a co-ed school will be less active and pluralistic in their interests than boys of similar background, but there may be a few who will take over certain artistic activities and thus define them in such a way that boys will feel excluded). We see here a paradox: the influence of girls on boys in high school and college can be a broadening one in that it saves the boys from a narrow vocationalism and over-intellectual or over-ambitious or over-technocratic occupation with getting ahead in conventional terms. So, too, girls can be saved by the presence of boys from the kinds of artful stuffiness and female "accomplishment" that some of the more fashionable and less intellectual junior colleges for women still advertise as their stock in trade. But at the margin, the presence of each limits rather than expands the potentialities of the other—and again permissiveness imposes subtle restraints of its own.[8]

[7]Compare, on the general developmental sequence of college girls at Vassar, Nevitt Sanford, *et al.*, "Personality Development in the College Years," *Journal of Social Issues,* 12, No. 4 (1956), pp. 1–72.

[8]Compare, for further discussion, Riesman, *Some Continuities and Discontinuities in the Education of Women,* John Dewey Memorial Lecture, Bennington College, 1956.

These changes in the awareness each sex has of the role of the other have a bearing on our ways of handling education of both sexes in the social sciences and in the other sciences. Every curriculum contains many implicit statements about ideas as "feminine" or "masculine"—statements which are carried in the language or texture of the discipline, and in the tone and attitudes of its professors. For instance, there are many teachers of psychology in college who resent the fact that women who are "interested in people" come into their courses, and these teachers react by turning their subject into a branch of engineering—an aggressively "male" subject from which all concrete and humane concerns of both men and women are excluded in the name of rigor, and in which precisely such considerations as we are here today discussing would not be called "psychology." Then, too, as already indicated, in many good colleges, the more sensitive students of both sexes feel themselves shut out from mathematics, physics, chemistry, and technology generally. This may, in a few cases, be because they associate these fields, understandably enough in our time, with missiles and war maneuvers, with all that they find oppressive and intractable in the modern world. But it is also because these subjects are often taught in such a way that the subtlety of their ideas is not conveyed, but only the "hardware." As I think of the great physicists and mathematicians of recent times, it seems to me that their ideas (consider Einstein, Oppenheimer, Bohr) have a quality which should not alienate sensitive and very feminine women or sensitive and very intraceptive men. But both in high school and college, these fields are often taught mainly by men, for whom the text is a kind of cook book—an old-style cook book at that. Conversely, English and art are taught in many secondary schools and some colleges as very much prissy, traditionally female and snob-tainted subjects.

As a result, certain compartmentalizations remain very important in our culture in spite of greater freedom and permissiveness. Women, for instance, remain shut out, by one set of snobberies and self-imposed restrictions, from college and university teaching, while men remain shut out by another set of constrictions from elementary school teaching and from the teaching of music in secondary school. Women in this country are decreasingly charged with carrying the burdens of culture alone, including the burden of human and humane understanding, but there is still much that needs to be done before men are permitted to share more equally in these tasks, and women in the tasks of the outside world of politics and work.[9] Our ideal here would be a culture in which the interests of each would be developed on behalf of the interests of all, on the no doubt utopian assumption that the work of the world would get done through genuine relatedness (in Erich Fromm's sense) and not through the captivity of either sex or the psychological compulsions of a class.

[9]I suppose some social scientists would argue that the division of labor here is both a good and a necessary thing. One could draw such an implication from the work of Parsons and Bales, linking the division of labor in small laboratory groups to the division of labor in the family. See Talcott Parsons and R. F. Bales, *Family, Socialization and Interaction Process,* Glencoe, Ill.: The Free Press, 1955.

In a way, this is already happening: the liberation of women from traditional and conventional bondages both accompanies industrialization and brings it in its wake. In these respects American women are the envy of the whole world, so that American movies, for instance, are a force for radical emancipation in Moslem countries, and men try to prevent their womenfolk from seeing them lest they become restless and dissatisfied.[10] Women in America are not as some people claim to think, the dominant sex, but having escaped from traditional bondages they are beginning to face the problems of freedom.

More generally, what I am trying to say is that permissiveness, liberating in its earlier installments, creates unanticipated problems as it spreads. I am inclined to think that the more privileged young people need today some permission to resist permissiveness, that is, some form of adult protection for those who at the moment do not want to pursue each other or to feel that, if they are not doing so, they are missing what not only matters most in life, but what would define them in an ultimate way as men or women. Let me recall in this connection Bruno Bettelheim's book, *Symbolic Wounds.* He argues there that the initiation rites are a way of reducing the identity crisis for the initiates, a way of telling them with severity enough to make it stick, literally so, that they are a young man or a young woman now, as the case may be: they are that, and no other—how shall I say it?—no other selves can come in. Our society, because it is more permissive, does not countenance such impositions, but the problem remains of providing young people with what Erik Erikson calls a moratorium in which their identity can be at large and open and various, without worry that for all of life what happens in high school or college will freeze the pattern.

[10]Compare Daniel Lerner, with the collaboration of Lucille W. Pevsner, *The Passing of Traditional Society: Modernizing the Middle East,* Glencoe, Ill.: The Free Press, 1958.

Communes

Rosabeth Moss Kanter

"Life together" is the experience of communal living expressed by one founder of a new 30-member commune in Vermont. Like others, she is participating in a renewed search for utopia and community, brotherhood and sharing, warmth and intimacy, participation and involvement, purpose and meaning. Today's utopians want to return to fundamentals. They want to put people back in touch with each other, nature and themselves.

This quest for togetherness is behind the proliferation of communal-living experiments. The ventures vary widely. There are small urban groups that share living quarters and raise their families together but hold outside jobs, and there are rural farming communes that combine work and living. Some are formal organizations with their own business enterprises, such as the Bruderhof communities, which manufacture Community Playthings. Others are loose aggregates without chosen names.

They have been started by political radicals, return-to-the-land homesteaders, intellectuals, pacifists, hippies and drop-outs, ex-drug addicts, behavioral psychologists following B. F. Skinner's *Walden Two,* humanistic psychologists interested in environments for self-actualization, Quakers in South America, ex-monks in New Hampshire, and Hasidic Jews in Boston. Estimates of the number of communal experiments today run to the hundreds. There are inter-community magazines, newsletters, information clearinghouses and conferences to share experiences, help build new utopias and bring potential communards together.

Now. Today's communal movement is a reawakening of the search for utopia in America that started as early as 1680, when religious sects first retreated to the wilderness to live in community. While experiments in communal living have always been part of the American landscape, only a few dozen survived for more than a few years. Building community has been difficult, and today's communes are heirs to the problems.

I have studied 19th-Century American communities, comparing 21

Reprinted by permission from *Psychology Today* 4 (July 1970):53–57, 58.

that lasted with nine that didn't, and have gathered information from 20 contemporary communes and from growth-and-learning communities. I then compared successful 19th-Century utopias with today's anarchist communes and growth-center communities and found that while the growth centers tend to incorporate important features of the 19th-Century groups that were successful, many of the anarchist communes do not.

FAMILY. Today's communes seek a family warmth and intimacy, to become extended families. A 50-person hippie commune in California, for example, called itself "the Lynch family"; a New Mexico commune "The Chosen Family"; a New York City group simply "The Family."

For some communes becoming a family means collective child-rearing, shared responsibility for raising children. Children and adults in a Vermont commune have their own separate rooms, and the children consider all the adults in the community their "parents." Other communes experiment sexually to change the man–woman relationship from monogamy to group marriage.

The desire is to create intense involvement in the group—feelings of connectedness, belonging and the warmth of many attachments. How did the successful utopias of the past achieve this?

Intimacy was a daily fact of life for successful 19th-Century communities. The group was an ever-present part of the member's day, for his fellows were his work-mates as well as his neighbors, and people ate and slept together in central buildings. Many successful communities saw themselves as families and addressed leaders in parental terms—Father Noyes in Oneida, Father Rapp in Harmony.

Exclusive couples and biological families were discouraged through celibacy, free love or group marriage. In Oneida's system of complex marriage, for example, each member had sexual access to every other member, with his or her consent and under the general supervision of community leaders. A man interested in a liaison would approach a woman through a third party; she had the right to refuse his attentions. Couples showing an excess of special love would be broken up or forced into relationships with others.

Successful 19th-Century communities tended to separate biological families and place children in dwelling units apart from their parents, creating instead a "family of the whole." In Oneida children were raised communally from soon after weaning. The heads of the children's department raised the children; they were called "papa" and "mother." Children visited their own parents individually once or twice a week but accepted the community's family life as the focus of their existence.

They also celebrated their togetherness joyfully in group rituals such as singing, religious services and observance of anniversaries, holidays and other festive occasions.

GROUP. Many members look to today's communities for personal growth through small-group processes in which members honestly and openly criticize and support one another. T-group interaction or mutual criticism in its various forms can be a primary and essential part of a community's goals. In the Synanon groups, community was first embodied in self-help group sessions for drug addicts and only later grew into the desire to establish a total way of life.

Other communes use group process to work out disagreements, to regenerate commitment, and to create a sense of intimate involvement. A Vermont commune reached a crisis when so many problems accumulated that people asked: *Just what are we doing here anyway?* An extended encounter group was held and the sense of common purpose reaffirmed.

Successful 19th-Century communities used a variety of group techniques, including confession, self-criticism, and mutual-criticism sessions, to solidify the group and deal with deviance and discontent before they became disruptive. The individual could bare his soul to the group, express his weaknesses, failings, doubts, problems, inner secrets. Disagreements between members could be discussed openly. These T-group-like sessions also showed that the content of each person's inner world was important to the community. Oneidans periodically submitted themselves for criticism by a committee of six to 12 judges and were expected to receive the criticism in silence and acquiesce to it in writing. Excessive introspection was considered a sin, and no matter was too private for mutual criticism.

The Llano Colony, a 20th-Century, socialist utopia, had a weekly "psychology" meeting that one observer described as a combination of "revival, pep meeting, and confessional."

Possibly because they developed such strong group ties, successful 19th-Century groups stayed together in the face of outside persecution, financial shakiness, and natural disasters. Unsuccessful utopias of the past, on the other hand, did not tend to build these kinds of group relations.

Property. The desire for sharing, participation and cooperation in today's communes extends to property and work. One ideal is to create economically self-sufficient communities, with all property owned in common. The desire for self-sufficiency and control over their own financial destinies leads many communes to form around farms, to attempt to provide for their maintenance needs themselves, to live in simple dwellings and to work the land.

Many of today's communards believe that money and private property create barriers between people. Money should be thrown into a common pot and property should belong to anyone who uses it. This acceptance of common ownership is reflected in the answer of a small child in a Cambridge commune, questioned about who owned a cat. He said, *The cat is everyone's.*

Many urban communes where members work at outside jobs try to operate with common exchequers. The commune has the responsibility to provide for everyone economically. In Synanon's new Tomales Bay city, as in all Synanon houses, goods and facilities are community-owned. Members receive small amounts of "walking-around money."

A common-work community is another important goal of today's groups. Some have their own businesses—agriculture, crafts, toy manufacturing (the Bruderhof), advertising specialties and gas stations (Synanon), schools, film and other media. In the Bruderhof groups, members work at assigned jobs in the household or school or factory, sharing kitchen and dining-room chores. Other communes without money-making enterprises may still expect strong participation in community upkeep.

In most successful 19th-Century utopias, property was jointly owned and shared, goods equally distributed to all members, and private property abolished. The successful groups all required members to sign over their property and financial holdings to the community on admission. At one point in Harmony's history the leader, George Rapp, even burned the contribution record book.

The successful groups tended to have their own means of support. Generally all members worked within the community. Oneidans, for example, first supported themselves by farming. Because of financial difficulties, they later engaged in manufacturing enterprises ranging from steel traps to silverware. A business board of individual department heads and other interested members regulated the industries. Work was a community-wide affair where possible, and jobs were rotated among members.

Such work arrangements required central coordination; how a member spent his time was a matter of community policy. In unsuccessful communities like Brook Farm, individual members made their own decisions about when and how long to work. The Shakers, on the other hand, instituted a minute-by-minute routine with bells ringing to mark the time.

These property and work arrangements were conducive to a strong community commitment and help account for the successful groups' longevity.

BELIEVERS. Often today's communities are founded to implement elaborate philosophies or world views communicated through charismatic leaders. Synanon coalesced 11 years ago around the visions of Chuck Dederich, who formed the community (now numbering in the thousands) on a $33 unemployment check. His personal example and teachings continue to guide the community. Mel Lyman is the central presence for Fort Hill. A number of communes consider their leaders manifestations of Christ, great prophets, or seers.

Many successful 19th-Century communities had charismatic figures; they were considered godlike, if not actually manifestations of God, and were viewed with awe by members, treated with deference and respect, and accorded special privileges and immunities. In successful communities when the charismatic died his teachings lived on. The Shakers continued to coalesce around Mother Ann Lee after her death, and today the Bruderhof still are translating the teachings of their founder from the German.

The emphasis on a value-based and value-oriented life required an ideological commitment or a set of vows for admission, a striking contrast with some of the unsuccessful communities. New Harmony, for example, merely advertised for anyone interested in joining a communal experiment.

TWO KINDS. Today's communities differ as widely in structure, values and ideology among themselves as the 19th-Century ones did. One set of present-day utopias, religious communities such as the Bruderhof and the

Hutterian Brethren, have their roots in the traditional communities of the past. But two distinct kinds of groups are emerging as the *now* forms: small anarchistic communes and communities formed around growth centers, of which Esalen, Kairos, Cumbres are examples.

Some of today's communes are small and anarchistic, consisting of 12, 20, to 30 persons. They seek intimacy and involvement, but refuse to structure community life. Everyone does his own thing at his own time. They are concerned with flexibility and mobility, not with permanence. They reject the control of other groups. Many tend to share living arrangements in which members continue to work outside instead of developing self-sufficient communities. Their lack of solid financial bases is a great problem. In addition they report that many jobs within the commune remain undone, many conflicts never get ironed out, and "family feeling" develops only with difficulty.

I find little definable pattern, rule, or group structure in many of today's anarchist communes. In a Maryland commune of 12, one pays nothing to join. Private property remains private, although members report that it is shared freely. Most members have outside jobs and contribute $30 a month each for food and utilities. All work within the community is voluntary. There are no leadership positions. Decisions are made individually.

Some of these communes do try to develop the intimate, T-group-like sessions of the 19th-Century utopias. But the anarchist groups have a tendency not to do this on a regular or formal basis.

Today's anarchist communes tend to lack integrating philosophies. Many begin with only a vague desire for closer personal relationships and group living in the most general sense.

A member of one short-lived commune talked about its failure: "We weren't ready to define who we were; we certainly weren't prepared to define who we weren't—it was still just a matter of intuition. We had come together for various reasons—not overtly for a common idea or ideal. . . . The different people managed to work together side by side for awhile, but there really was no shared vision."

Anarchist communes tend to be open to all comers at the start. In strong contrast with the successful 19th-Century communities, some anarchist communes do not make a member/non-member distinction. A member of a rural California commune that dissolved after a year saw this as one of their problems: "We were entirely open. We did not say no—we felt that this would make a more dynamic group. But we got a lot of sick people. . . . Most people came here just to get out of the city. . . . they had no commitment."

The prospects for most of today's anarchistic communes are dim; they lack the commitment-building practices of the successful communities of the 19th Century.

Today's growth-and-learning centers on the other hand offer greater prospects for success in longevity, economic viability and personal fulfillment. These groups tend to be highly organized, by comparison with their anarchistic cousins. In their own ways they implement many of the practices of successful 19th-Century groups.

These 100 or so growth centers—many of them outgrowths of the encounter-group movement—provide temporary communities in which their guests find intimacy and expressive involvement. For their staffs they are permanent communities of total involvement.

Growth-and-learning communities are centered around small-group interaction that generates strong group ties and family feeling. Encounter groups are part of the community life. Lama, in New Mexico, has a group meeting every evening for personal growth and the release of interpersonal tensions. The Synanon game is in many ways the Synanon community's most central activity.

At some communities, family feeling is extended; the community en-

Comparison of Nine Successful and 21 Unsuccessful Communities

	Successful:	Unsuccessful:
	Percentage that adhered to the practice	
GROUP RELATIONS		
Communal family structure:		
Free love or celibacy	100%	29%
Parent-child separation	48%	15%
Biological families not living together	33%	5%
Ritual:		
Songs about the community	63%	14%
Group singing	100%	73%
Special community occasions celebrated	83%	50%
Mutual criticism:		
Regular confession	44%	0
Mutual-criticism sessions	44%	26%
Daily group meetings	56%	6%
PROPERTY & WORK		
Communistic sharing:		
Property signed over to community at admission	100%	45%
Community-as-whole owned land	89%	76%
Community-owned buildings	89%	71%
Community-owned furniture, tools	100%	79%
Community-owned clothing, personal effects	67%	28%
Communal labor:		
No compensation for labor	100%	41%
No charge for community services	100%	47%
Job rotation	50%	44%
Communal work efforts	100%	50%
Fixed daily routine	100%	54%
Detailed specification of routine	67%	13%

courages sexual experimentation and acting on physical feelings. While some members may be married, they are not bound by monogamy. Finally, in these communities there is often an abundance of group rituals—from Tai Chi exercises (a Chinese moving meditation that resembles dance) to mixed-media celebrations of important events.

The growth-and-learning communities also tend to have explicit sets of values, integrating philosophies that members must share—from the principles of zazen to humanistic psychology. Members are expected to grow in the community spirit and, as at Synanon, character is the only status.

Some communities have communal living arrangements with minimum privacy. They tend to have stringent entrance requirements: potential members must meet community standards and often must serve long apprenticeships to be accepted.

In the growth-and-learning communities work tends to be communal; a member may lead a workshop then clean the kitchen, sharing responsibility as a growth experience. Discipline through work is a theme at Zen learning centers; a new Synanon member's first job often is to scrub toilets.

These communities also tend to have fixed daily routines and schedules with tasks assigned in advance.

Like the successful utopias of the past the growth communities have their charismatic figures, from the late Fritz Perls and William Schutz at Esalen to Cesareo Pelaez at Cumbres in New Hampshire.

Growth-and-learning communities, in short, tend to create family-like feeling, to use mutual criticism, to provide a strong sense of participation and responsibility, to affirm their bonds through ritual, to organize work communally, to have stringent entrance requirements, and to develop strong values symbolized by charismatic leaders.

In the light of history, the small anarchistic commune does not seem to be stable or enduring, while the growth-and-learning community appears to have much greater prospects. Yet in today's world—a mobile, change-oriented society that is increasingly wary of long-range commitments—there may be room for both kinds of groups. The small, dissolvable, unstructured commune may meet its members' needs for a temporary home and family. The more permanent growth-and-learning center is a place for enduring commitment for those who want a rooted way of life in community.

Roots of Black Manhood

Ulf Hannerz

Some 5.7 million people were simply not counted in the 1960 census, and most of them, it now appears, were Negro men living in northern cities. This statistical oversight, if that is what it was, is not unique to the government's census takers. Ever since the beginnings of the scholarly study of black people in the Americas, there has been an interesting fascination with the differences between the family life of Negroes and that of their white counterparts, the chief difference being seen as the dominant, not to say dominating, role of women in black families.

From E. Franklin Frazier's pioneering 1932 study of *The Negro Family in Chicago* through Melville Herskovits' *The Myth of the Negro Past* in 1941 to the so-called Moynihan Report of 1965, social scientists have been repeatedly rediscovering, analyzing and worrying over the crucial role of the mother (or grandmother) in the family structure of blacks in the New World. Herskovits saw the centrality of the mother as an African vestige, typical of the polygynous marriage in which every woman, with her offspring, formed a separate unit. Frazier is generally regarded as the first to ascribe to the institution of slavery itself the strongest influence in undermining the stability of marriage, an influence that was later reinforced when blacks encountered what Frazier perceived as the peculiarly urban evils of anonymity, disorganization and the lack of social support and controls. Moynihan, like Frazier, sees the matriarchal family as being practically without strengths, at least in the context of the larger American society, but his Report emphasizes the ways in which employer discrimination and, more recently, welfare policies have contributed to the breaking up (or foreclosure) of the male-dominated family unit among blacks.

In all of these studies, however, the black *man*—as son, lover, husband, father, grandfather—is a distant and "shadowy figure out there somewhere" . . . if only because his major characteristic as far as the household is concerned is his marginality or absence.

I do not mean to suggest that the black man is undiscovered territory.

Obviously he is not. His popular image was fixed for one (long) era in *Uncle Tom's Cabin* and prophetically fashioned for our own time in Norman Mailer's essay, "The White Negro." Here is Mailer's Hipster, modeled on the Negro: "Sharing a collective disbelief in the words of men who had too much money and controlled too many things, they knew almost as powerful a disbelief in the socially monolithic ideas of the single mate, the solid family and the respectable love life." And here is Mailer's black man:

> Knowing in the cells of his existence that life was war, nothing but war, the Negro (all exceptions admitted) could rarely afford the sophisticated inhibitions of civilization, and so he kept for his survival the art of the primitive, he lived in the enormous present, he subsisted for his Saturday night kicks, relinquishing the pleasures of the mind for the more obligatory pleasures of the body, and in his music he gave voice to the character and quality of his existence, to his rage and the infinite variations of joy, lust, languor, growl, cramp, pinch, scream and despair of his orgasm.

Certainly there is poetic exaggeration in Mailer's description, and perhaps a conscious effort to mythicize his subject; and certainly too there is a great deal of stereotyping in the general public's imagery of the people of the black ghetto. But hardly anyone acquainted with life in the ghetto can fail to see that Mailer's portrait captures much of the reality as well. Lee Rainwater's sketch of the "expressive life-style" of the black male shows a trained social scientist's analysis that is remarkably similar to Mailer's. And undoubtedly there *is* a sizable segment of the black male population that is strongly concerned with sex, drinking, sharp clothes and "trouble"; and among these men one finds many of those who are only marginally involved with married life. Of course, ghetto life styles are heterogeneous, and there are many men who live according to "mainstream" values; but it is to the ones who do not that we should turn our attention if we want to understand what kinds of masculinity go with the female-dominated family.

This essay is an attempt to outline the social processes within the ghetto communities of the northern United States whereby the identity of street-corner males is established and maintained. To set the stage and state the issues involved in this essay, I'd like to look at the views of two other observers of the ghetto male. One is Charles Keil, whose *Urban Blues* (1966) is a study of the bluesman as a "culture hero." According to Keil, the urban blues singer, with his emphasis on sexuality, "trouble" and flashy clothes, manifests a cultural model of maleness that is highly valued by ghetto dwellers and relatively independent of the mainstream cultural tradition. Keil criticizes a number of authors who, without cavilling at this description of the male role, tend to see it as rooted in the individual's anxiety about his masculinity. This, Keil finds, is unacceptably ethnocentric:

> Any sound analysis of Negro masculinity should first deal with the statements and responses of Negro women, the conscious motives of the men themselves and the Negro cultural tradition. Applied in this setting, psychological theory may then be able to provide important new insights in place of basic and unfortunate distortions.

Keil, then, comes out clearly for a cultural interpretation of the male role we are interested in here. But Elliot Liebow in *Tally's Corner* (1967), a study resulting from the author's participation in a research project that definitely considered ghetto life more in terms of social problems than as a culture, reaches conclusions which, in some of their most succinct formulations, quite clearly contradict Keil's:

> Similarities between the lower-class Negro father and son . . . do not result from "cultural transmission" but from the fact that the son goes out and independently experiences the same failures, in the same areas, and for much the same reasons as his father.

Thus father and son are "independently produced look-alikes." With this goes the view that the emphasis on sexual ability, drinking and so forth is a set of compensatory self-deceptions which can only unsuccessfully veil the streetcorner male's awareness of his failure.

Keil and Liebow, as reviewed here, may be taken as representatives of two significantly different opinions on why black people in the ghettos, and in particular the males, behave differently than other Americans. One emphasizes a cultural determinism internal to the ghetto, the other an economic determinism in the relationship between the ghetto and the wider society. It is easy to see how the two views relate to one's perspective on the determinants of the domestic structure of ghetto dwellers. And it is also easy to see how these perspectives have considerable bearing on public policy, especially if it is believed that the ghetto family structure somehow prevents full participation by its members in the larger American society and economy. If it is held, for example, that broad social and economic factors, and particularly poverty, make ghetto families the way they are—and this seems to be the majority opinion among social scientists concerned with this area—then public policy should concentrate on mitigating or removing those elements that distort the lives of black people. But if the style of life in the ghetto is culturally determined and more or less independent of other "outside" factors, then public policy will have to take a different course or drop the problem altogether qua problem.

Admittedly, the present opportunity structure places serious obstacles in the way of many ghetto dwellers, making a mainstream life-style difficult to accomplish. And if research is to influence public policy, it is particularly important to point to the wider structural influences that *can* be changed in order to give equal opportunity to ghetto dwellers. Yet some of the studies emphasizing such macrostructural determinants have resulted in somewhat crude conceptualizations that are hardly warranted by the facts and which in the light of anthropological theory appear very oversimplified.

First of all, let us dispose of some of the apparent opposition between the two points of view represented by Keil and Liebow. There is not necessarily any direct conflict between ecological-economic and cultural explanations; the tendency to create such a conflict in much of the current literature on poverty involves a false dichotomy. In anthropology, it is a commonplace that culture is usually both inherited and influenced by the community's relationship to its environment. Economic determinism and cultural determinism can go hand in hand in a stable environment. Since the ecological niche of ghetto dwellers has long remained relatively unchanged, there seems to be no reason why their adaptation should not have become in some ways cultural. It is possible, of course, that the first stage in the evolution of the specifically ghetto life-style consisted of a multiplicity of identical but largely independent adaptations from the existing cultural background—mainstream or otherwise—to the given opportunity structure, as Liebow suggests. But the second stage of adaptation—by the following generations—involves a perception of the first-stage adaptation as a normal condition, a state of affairs which from then on can be expected. What was at first independent adaptation becomes transformed into a ghetto heritage of assumptions about the nature of man and society.

Yet Liebow implies that father and son are independently produced as streetcorner men, and that transmission of a ghetto-specific culture has a negligible influence. To those adhering to this belief, strong evidence in its favor is seen in the fact that ghetto dwellers—both men and women—often express conventional sentiments about sex and other matters. Most ghetto dwellers would certainly agree, at times at least, that education is a good thing, that gambling and drinking are bad, if not sinful, and that a man and a woman should be true to each other. Finding such opinions, and heeding Keil's admonition to listen to the statements and responses of the black people themselves, one may be led to doubt that there is much of a specific ghetto culture. But then, after having observed behavior among these same people that often and clearly contradicts their stated values, one has to ask two questions: Is there any reason to believe that ghetto-specific behavior is cultural? And, if it *is* cultural, what is the nature of the coexistence of mainstream culture and ghetto-specific culture in the black ghetto?

To answer the first question, one might look at the kinds of communications that are passed around in the ghetto relating to notions of maleness. One set of relationships in which such communications occur frequently is the family; another is the male peer group.

Deficient Masculinity?

Much has been made of the notion that young boys in the ghetto, growing up in matrifocal households, are somehow deficient in or uncertain about their masculinity, because their fathers are absent or peripheral in household affairs. It is said that they lack the role models necessary for learning male behavior; there is a lack of the kind of information about the nature of masculinity which a father would transmit unintentionally merely by going about his life at home. The boys therefore supposedly experience a great deal of sex-role anxiety as a result of this cultural vacuum. It is possible that such a view contains more than a grain of truth in the case of some quite isolated female-headed households. Generally speaking, however, there may be less to it than meets the eye. First of all, a female-headed household without an adult male in residence but where young children are growing up—and where, therefore, it is likely that the mother is still rather young—is seldom one where adult males are totally absent. More or less steady boyfriends (sometimes including the separated father) go in and out. Even if these men do not assume a central household role, the boys can obviously use them as source material for the identification of male behavior. To be sure, the model is not a conventional middle-class one, but it still shows what males are like.

Furthermore, men are not the only ones who teach boys about masculinity. Although role-modeling is probably essential, other social processes can contribute to identity formation. Mothers, grandmothers, aunts and sisters who have observed men at close range have formed expectations about the typical behavior of men which they express and which influence the boys in the household. The boys will come to share in the women's imagery of men, and often they will find that men who are not regarded as good household partners (that is, "good" in the conventional sense) are still held to be attractive company. Thus the view is easily imparted that the hard men, good talkers, clothes-horses and all, are not altogether unsuccessful as men. The women also act more directly toward the boys in these terms—they have expectations of what men will do, and whether they wish the boys to live up (or down) to the expectations, they instruct them in the model. Boys are advised not to "mess with" girls, but at the same time it is emphasized that messing around is the natural thing they will otherwise go out and do—and when the boys start their early adventures with the other sex, the older women may scold them but at the same time point out, not without satisfaction, that "boys will be boys." This kind of maternal (or at least adult female) instruction of young males is obviously a kind of altercasting, or more exactly, socialization to an alter role—that is, women cast boys in the role complementary to their own according to their experience of man–woman relationships. One single mother to three boys and two girls put it this way:

> You know, you just got to act a little bit tougher with boys than with girls, 'cause they just ain't the same. Girls do what you tell them to do and don't get into no trouble, but you just can't be sure about the boys. I mean, you think they're OK and next thing you find out they're playing hookey and drinking wine and maybe stealing things from cars and what not. There's just something bad about boys here, you know. But what can you say when many of them are just like their daddies? That's the man in them coming out. You can't really fight it, you know that's the way it is. They know, too. But you just got to be tougher.

This is in some ways an antagonistic socialization, but it is built upon an expectation that it would be unnatural for men not to turn out to be in some ways bad—that is fighters, drinkers, lady killers and so forth. There is one thing worse than a no-good man—the sissy, who is his opposite. A boy who seems weak is often reprimanded and ridiculed not only by his peers but also by adults, including his mother and older sisters. The combination of role-modeling by peripheral fathers or temporary boyfriends with altercasting by adult women certainly provides for a measure of male role socialization within the family.

And yet, when I said that the view of the lack of models in the family was too narrow, I was not referring to the observers' lack of insight into many matrifocal ghetto families as much as I was to the emphasis they placed on the family as *the* information storage unit of a community's culture. I believe it is an ethnocentrism on the part of middle-class commentators to take it for granted that if information about sex roles is not transmitted from father to son within the family, it is not transmitted from generation to generation at all. In American sociology, no less than in the popular mind, there is what Ray Birdwhistell has termed a "sentimental model" of family life, according to which the family is an inward-turning isolated unit, meeting most of the needs of its members, and certainly their needs for sociability and affection. The "sentimental model" is hardly ever realistic even as far as middle-class American families are concerned, and it has even less relevance for black ghetto life. Ghetto children live and learn out on the streets just about as much as within the confines of the home. Even if mothers, aunts and sisters do not have street-corner men as partners, there is an ample supply of them on the front stoop or down at the corner. Many of these men have such a regular attendance record as to become quite familiar to children and are frequently very friendly with them. Again, therefore, there is no lack of adult men to show a young boy what men are like. It seems rather unlikely that one can deny all role-modeling effect of these men on their young neighbors. They may be missing in the United States census records, but they are not missing in the ghetto community.

Much of the information gained about sex roles outside the family comes not from adult to child, however, but from persons in the same age-grade or only slightly higher. The idea of culture being stored in lower age-grades must be taken seriously. Many ghetto children start participating in the peer groups of the neighborhood at an early age, often under the watchful eye of an elder brother or sister. In this way they are initiated into the culture of the peer group by interacting with children—predominantly of the same sex—who are only a little older than they are. And in the peer-group culture of the boys, the male sex role is a fairly constant topic of concern. Some observers have felt that this is another consequence of the alleged sex role anxiety of ghetto boys. This may be true, of course, at least in that it may have had an important part in the development of male peer-group life as a dominant element of ghetto social structure. Today, however, such a simple psychosocial explanation will not do. Most ghetto boys can hardly avoid associating with other boys, and once they are in the group, they are efficiently socialized into a high degree of concern with their sex role. Much of the joking, the verbal contests and the more or less obscene songs among small ghetto boys, serve to alienate them from dependence on mother figures and train them to the exploitative, somewhat antagonistic attitude toward women which is typical of streetcorner men.

"Mother!"

This is not to say that the cultural messages are always very neat and clear-cut. In the case of the kind of insult contest called "playing the dozens," "sounding" or (in Washington, D.C.) "joining," a form of ritualized interaction which is particularly common among boys in the early teens, the communication is highly ambiguous. When one boy says something unfavorable about another's mother, the other boy is expected either to answer in kind or to fight in defense of his honor (on which apparently that of his mother reflects). But the lasting impression is that there is something wrong about mothers—they are not as good as they ought to be ("Anybody can get pussy from your mother"), they take over male items of behavior and by implication too much of the male role ("Your mother smokes a pipe"). If standing up for one's family is the manifest expected consequence of "the dozens," then a latent function is a strengthening of the belief that ghetto women are not what they ought to be. The other point of significance is that the criteria of judgment about what a good woman should be like are apparently like those of the larger society. She should not be promiscuous, and she should stick to the mainstream female role and not be too dominant.

The boys, then, are learning and strengthening a cultural ambivalence involving contradictions between ideal and reality in female behavior. I will return to a discussion of such cultural ambivalence later. But the point remains that even this game involves continuous learning and strengthening of a cultural definition of what women are like that is in some ways complementary to the definition of what men are like. And much of the songs, the talk and the action—fighting, sneaking away with girls into a park or an alley or drinking out of half empty wine bottles stolen from or given away by adult men—are quite clearly preparations for the streetcorner male role. If boys and men show anxiety about their masculinity, one may suspect that this is induced as much by existing cultural standards as by the alleged nonexistence of models.

This socialization within the male peer group is a continuing process; the talk that goes on, continuously or intermittently, at the street corner or on the front steps may deal occasionally with a football game or a human-interest story from the afternoon newspaper, but more often there are tales from personal experience about adventures of drinking (often involving the police), about women won and lost, about feminine fickleness and the masculine guile (which sometimes triumphs over it), about clothing, or there may simply be comments on the women passing down the street. "Hi ugly . . . don't try to swing what you ain't got."

This sociability among the men seems to be a culture-building process. Shared definitions of reality are created out of the selected experiences of the participants. Women are nagging and hypocritical; you can't expect a union with one of them to last forever. Men are dogs; they have to run after many women. There is something about being a man and drinking liquor;

booze makes hair grow on your chest. The regularity with which the same topics appear in conversation indicates that they have been established as the expected and appropriate subjects in this situation, to the exclusion of other topics.

Mack asked me did I screw his daughter, so I asked: "I don't know, what's her name?" And then when I heard that gal was his daughter all right, I says, "Well, Mack, I didn't really have to take it 'cause it was given to me." I thought Mack sounded like his daughter was some goddam white gal. But Mack says, "Well, I just wanted to hear it from you." Of course, I didn't know that was Mack's gal, 'cause she was married and had a kid, and so she had a different name. But then you know the day after when I was out there a car drove by, and somebody called my name from it, you know, "hi darling," and that was her right there. So the fellow I was with says, "Watch out, Buddy will shoot your ass off." Buddy, that's her husband. So I says, "Yeah, but he got to find me first!"

Let me tell you fellows, I've been arrested for drunkenness more than two hundred times over the last few years, and I've used every name in the book. I remember once I told them I was Jasper Gonzales, and then I forgot what I had told them, you know. So I was sitting there waiting, and they came in and called "Jasper Gonzales," and nobody answered. I had forgotten that's what I said, and to tell you the truth, I didn't know how to spell it. So anyway, nobody answered, and there they were calling "Jasper Gonzales. Jasper Gonzales!" So I thought that must be me, so I answered. But they had been calling a lot of times before that. So the judge said, "Mr. Gonzales, are you of Spanish descent?" And I said, "Yes, your honor, I came to this country thirty-four years ago." And of course I was only thirty-five, but you see I had this beard then, and I looked pretty bad, dirty and everything, you know, so I looked like sixty. And so he said, "We don't have a record on you. This is the first time you have been arrested?" So I said, "Yes, your honor, nothing like this happened to me before. But my wife was sick, and then I lost my job you know, and I felt kind of bad. But it's the first time I ever got drunk." So he said, "Well, Mr. Gonzales, I'll let you go, 'cause you are not like the rest of them here. But let this be a warning to you." So I said, "Yes, your honor." And then I went out, and so I said to myself, "I'll have to celebrate this." So I went across the street from the court, and you know there are four liquor stores there, and I got a pint of wine and next thing I was drunk as a pig.

Were you here that time a couple of weeks ago when these three chicks from North Carolina were up here visiting Miss Gladys? They were really gorgeous, about 30–35. So Charlie says why don't we step by the house and he and Jimmy and Deekay can go out and buy them a drink. So they say they have to go and see this cousin first, but then they'll be back. But then Brenda (Charlie's wife) comes back before they do, and so these girls walk back and forth in front of the house, and Charlie can't do a thing about it, except hope they won't knock on his door. And then Jimmy and Deekay come and pick them up, and Fats is also there, and the three of them go off with these chicks, and there is Charlie looking through his window, and there is Brenda looking at them too, and asking Charlie does he know who the chicks are.

Groups of one's friends give some stability and social sanction to the meanings that streetcorner men attach to their experiences—meanings that may themselves have been learned in the same or preceding peer groups. They, probably more than families, are information storage units for the ghetto-specific male role. At the same time, they are self-perpetuating because they provide the most satisfactory contexts for legitimizing the realities involved. In other words, they suggest a program for maleness, but they also offer a haven of understanding for those who follow that program and are criticized for it or feel doubts about it. For of course all streetcorner males are more or less constantly exposed to the definitions and values of the mainstream cultural apparatus, and so some cultural ambivalence can hardly be avoided. Thus, if a man is a dog for running after women—as he is often said to be among ghetto dwellers—he wants to talk about it with other dogs who appreciate that this is a fact of life. If it is natural for men to drink, let it happen among other people who understand the nature of masculinity. In this way the group maintains constructions of reality, and life according to this reality maintains the group.

It is hard to avoid the conclusion, then, that there is a cultural element involved in the sex roles of streetcorner males, because expectations about sex are manifestly shared and transmitted rather than individually evolved. (If the latter had been the case, of course, it would have been less accurate to speak of these as roles, since roles are by definition cultural.) This takes us to the second question stated above, about the coexistence of conventional and ghetto-specific cultures. Streetcorner men certainly are aware of the male ideal of mainstream America—providing well for one's family, remaining faithful to one's spouse, staying out of trouble, etc.—and now and then every one of them states it as his own ideal. What we find here, then, may be seen as a bicultural situation. Mainstream culture and ghetto-specific culture provide different models for living, models familiar to everyone in the ghetto. Actual behavior may lean more toward one model or more toward the other, or it may be some kind of mixture, at one point or over time. The ghetto-specific culture, including the street-corner male role, is adapted to the situation and the experience of the ghetto dweller; it tends to involve relatively little idealization but offers shared expectations concerning self, others and the environment. The mainstream culture, from the ghetto dweller's point of view, often involves idealization, but there is less real expectation that life will actually follow the paths suggested by those ideals. This is not to say that the ghetto-specific culture offers no values of its own at all, or that nothing of mainstream culture ever appears realistic in the ghetto; but in those areas of life where the two cultures exist side by side as alternative guides to action (for naturally, the ghetto-specific culture, as distinct from mainstream culture, is not a "complete" culture covering all areas of life), the ghetto-specific culture is often taken to forecast what one can actually expect from life, while the mainstream norms are held up as perhaps ultimately more valid but less attainable under the given situational constraints. "Sure it would be good to have a good job and a good home and your kids in college and all that, but you got to be yourself and do what you know." Of course, this often makes the ghetto-specific cultural expectations into self-fulfilling prophecies, as ghetto dwellers try to attain what they believe they can attain; but, to be sure, self-fulfilling prophecies and realistic assessments may well coincide.

"Be Yourself"

On the whole, one may say that both mainstream culture and ghetto-specific culture are transmitted within many ghetto families. I have noted how socialization into the ghetto male role within the household is largely an informal process, in which young boys may pick up bits and pieces of information about masculinity from the women in the house as well as from males who may make their entrances and exits. On the other hand, when adult women—usually mothers or grandmothers—really "tell the boys how to behave," they often try to instill in them mainstream, not to say puritanical norms—drinking is bad, sex is dirty and so forth. The male peer groups, as we have seen, are the strongholds of streetcorner maleness, although there are times when men cuss each other out for being "no good." Finally, of course, mainstream culture is transmitted in contacts with the outside world, such as in school or through the mass media. It should be added, though, that the latter may be used selectively to strengthen some elements of the streetcorner male role; ghetto men are drawn to Westerns, war movies and crime stories both in the movie house and on their TV sets.

Yet, even if the nature of men's allegiance to the two cultures makes it reasonably possible to adhere, after a fashion, to both at the same time, the bicultural situation of streetcorner males involves some ambivalence. The rejection of mainstream culture as a guide to action rather than only a lofty ideal is usually less than complete. Of course, acting according to one or the other of the two cultures to a great extent involves bowing to the demands of the social context, and so a man whose concerns in the peer-group milieu are drinking and philandering will try to be "good" in the company of his mother or his wife and children, even if a complete switch is hard to bring about. There are also peer groups, of course, that are more mainstream-oriented than others, although even the members of these groups are affected by streetcorner definitions of maleness. To some extent, then, the varying allegiance of different peer groups to the two cultures is largely a difference of degree, as the following statement by a young man implies.

> Those fellows down at the corner there just keep drinking and drinking. You know, I think it's pretty natural for a man to drink, but they don't try to do nothing about it, they just drink every hour of the day, every day of the week. My crowd, we drink during the weekend, but we can be on our jobs again when Monday comes.

However, although where one is or who one is with does bring some order into this picture of bicultural ambivalence, it is still one of less than perfect stability. The drift between contexts is itself not something to which men are committed by demands somehow inherent in the social structure. Ghetto men may spend more time with the family, or more time with the peer group, and the extent to which they choose one or the other, and make a concomitant cultural selection, still appears to depend much on personal attachment to roles, and to changes in them. The social alignments of a few men may illustrate this. One man, Norman Hawkins, a construction laborer, spends practically all his leisure time at home with his family, only occasionally joining in the streetcorner conversations and behavior of the peer group to which his neighbor, Harry Jones, belongs. Harry Jones, also a construction worker, is also married and has a family but stays on the periphery of household life, although he lives with his wife and children. Some of the other men in the group are unmarried or separated and so seldom play the "family man" role which Harry Jones takes on now and then. Harry's younger brother, Carl, also with a family, used to participate intensively in peer group life until his drinking led to a serious ailment, and after he recuperated from this he started spending much less time with his male friends and more with his family. Bee Jay, a middle-aged bachelor who was raised by his grandmother, had a job at the post office and had little to do with street life until she died. Since then, he has become deeply involved with a tough, hard-drinking group and now suffers from chronic health problems connected with his alcoholism. Thus we can see how the life careers of some ghetto men take them through many and partly unpredictable shifts and drifts between mainstream and ghetto-specific cultures, while others remain quite stable in one allegiance or another.

Two Cultures

The sociocultural situation in the black ghetto is clearly complicated. The community shows a great heterogeneity of life-styles; individuals become committed in some degree to different ways of being by the impersonally-enforced structural arrangements to which they are subjected, but unpredictable contingencies have an influence, and their personal attachments to life-styles also vary. The socioeconomic conditions impose limits on the kinds of life ghetto dwellers may have, but these kinds of life are culturally transmitted and shared as many individuals in the present, and many in the past, live or have lived under the same premises. When the latter is the case, it is hardly possible to invent new adaptations again and again, as men are always observing each other and interacting with each other. The implication of some of Frazier's writings, that ghetto dwellers create their way of life in a cultural limbo—an idea which has had more modern expressions—appears as unacceptable in this case as in any other situation where people live together, and in particular where generations live together. The behavior of the street corner male is a natural pattern of masculinity with which ghetto dwellers grow up and which to some extent they grow into. To see it only as a complex of unsuccessful attempts at hiding failures by self-deception seems, for many of the men involved, to be too much psychologizing and too little sociology. But this does not mean that the attachment to the ghetto-specific culture is very strong among its bearers.

The question whether streetcorner males have mainstream culture or a specific ghetto culture, then, is best answered by saying that they have both, in different ways. There can be little doubt that this is the understanding most in line with that contemporary trend in anthropological thought which emphasizes the sharing of cultural imagery, of expectations and definitions of reality, as the medium whereby individuals in a community interact. It is noteworthy that many of the commentators who have been most skeptical of the idea of a ghetto-specific culture, or more generally a "culture of poverty," have been those who have taken a more narrow view of culture as a set of values about which an older generation consciously instructs the younger ones in the community.

Obviously, the answer to whether there is a ghetto-specific culture or not will depend to some extent on what we shall mean by culture. Perhaps this is too important a question to be affected by a mere terminological quibble, and perhaps social policy, in some areas, may well proceed unaffected by the questions raised by a ghetto-specific culture. On the other hand, in an anthropological study of community life, the wider view of cultural sharing and transmission which has been used here will have to play a part in our picture of the ghetto, including that of what ghetto males are like.

4 Stratification and Youth

As far as we can determine, all societies have evolved some means for allocating responsibilities and duties to their members (Lenski 1966). Since these activities are differentially evaluated, a ranking system is also found in all societies. *Social stratification* is the generic term for such ranking systems. A continuing debate has raged over the "inevitability" of stratification, but that issue is not our focus in this section. (See Bendix and Lipset, eds. 1966.)

The introduction of the young into adult social roles is accomplished in a variety of ways. In American society, there is no ritualized passage from youth to adulthood. However, as Parsons shows in his article, "Age and Sex in the Social Structure of the United States," the categories of age and sex are not as strong an influence on adult social roles in our society as they are in simpler, more traditional societies. Neither age nor sex alone determines the patterning of adult roles; they are determined by the interaction of age and kinship, formal education, occupation, and community participation. Parsons analyzes how society attempts to make people like what they have to do. Although the sexes are in many fundamental aspects treated alike in youth, at the point of adolescence, the youth culture differentiates two polar roles: the male social animal and the "glamour girl." This polarized treatment continues, with the male being expected to go into an occupational role and the female deprived of this fundamental source of integration and participation in the community. Parsons provides a clear sociological analysis of the conditions under which women's movements arise (women's liberation); the strains created by this asymmetrical role assignment for women are not easily resolved in the marketplace. Women are not permitted equal opportunities to compete, are discriminated against in occupations, and are traditionally "hired" by default to the role of raising children (because our society does not provide adequate alternative means for childrearing, such as day care centers, nurseries, or after-school entertainment centers). As Parsons points out, women are encouraged to rely on their sexual appeal, to participate in community affairs, or to become the "good companions" who must create roles that are parallel and complementary to their husbands.

The point at which the differentiation is least clear, but at which the strains in both male and female roles begin to appear, is adolescence. The youth culture, according to Parsons, eases the transition, but the transitional state is characterized by an unwillingness to take responsibility, an emphasis on good time and fun, and an element of romanticism. It is clear from previous articles in this book that the American youth culture derives its character from a number of social facts in American society and is not historically unique in form or content.

Parsons's general overview of age and sex roles as they pattern the transitions to adulthood is complemented by the research done by Psathas on parental control of adolescents. Psathas theorized that the class and ethnic backgrounds of a sample of high school boys would reveal the kind of parental control that was exerted on them. Although there were suggestions that Jewish families might tend to grant more independence than Italian families, Psathas did not predict which group would grant more independence to adolescents but instead hypothesied no differences (the null hypothesis). With regard to class, the same null hypothesis was advanced for test.

First a set of meaningful clusters of associated questions were identified. These were called (1) "permissiveness in outside activities," (2) "parental regard for judgment," (3) "activities with status implications," and (4) "permissiveness in age-related activities." Although the ethnic groups differed in how much the boys felt their parents controlled them, the differences were shown to be largely a function of class. Most of the Italians in the sample were of the lower and lower middle classes, while most of the Jewish boys were from the upper middle class. Two of the factors showed differences by class, with the higher classes showing less permissiveness on factors 1 and 4, and higher scores in parents' perceived regard for the judgment of their children. The middle classes strive to create anxiety by involving children in family interaction and by permitting them a degree of decision making which might test the rules—responsibility training. The lower classes, on the other hand, tend to create independence by permissiveness, or few controls over adolescents. Why is this the case?

Goode's analysis of love suggests the conditions under which Psathas's results might come about. Love is potentially disruptive because it is a universal psychological fact and does not necessarily follow the class, kin, or age lines that societies rest on. Goode demonstrates that because of its universality and potential for disrupting established social structure, love must be controlled. The most important sources of social continuity are probably class and lineage (kinship) in most societies; love can bind a variety of persons, not necessarily those of similar class or sharing arbitrary kin divisions. The kinds of controls evolved in societies range from child marriage, which binds couples to each other prior to interaction with peers, to "formally free choice" as in American society. Formally free choice is, however, constrained by the actions of peers and by the informal intervention of parents. This system of control is associated in most societies, as it is in ours, with a highly developed peer group.

Goode marshals a variety of evidence to demonstrate that the peer group in American society has a profound effect on the patterning of marriage choices; that is, marriage partners are chosen from homogeneous class, religious, racial, and educational groups. Research on dating practices before marriage illuminates the processes which determine the outcome Goode describes. It is reasonably clear from numerous studies of collegiate dating that a hierarchy of social groups exists on campus—fraternities and sororities—by which dating relationships may be predicted. If we know a girl's sorority, we can often pick out the fraternities from which her next date might come. It is also likely that as the relationship becomes more serious, we will find an even stronger correlation between the status of the groups to which the two persons belong. Women, as Goode suggests, are more closely controlled by their sororities than men by their fraternities (Scott 1965). Sororities have probably matched more men and women than computer dating services. The more serious the relationship, the more we may suppose that peer and parental pressures are increased, especially by parents of middle- and upper-middle-class girls.

The degree of control is greatest, as we have seen in Psathas's research, among the upper classes and status groups, in part because they have the most to lose by marriage with members of the lower classes. This loss may be roughly measured as a decrease in wealth, prestige, and continuity of access to other social resources. The upper classes seek to control love because they have the greatest stake in the maintenance of the status quo. The patterning of college dating is a concrete illustration of the theoretical importance of love: since love represents a potential threat to the existing stratification, it is always associated with a variety of social means for controlling this threat.

Age and Sex in the Social Structure of the United States

Talcott Parsons

In our society age grading does not to any great extent, except for the educational system, involve formal age categorization, but is interwoven with other structural elements. In relation to these, however, it constitutes an important connecting link and organizing point of reference in many respects. The most important of these for present purposes are kinship structure, formal education, occupation and community participation. In most cases the age lines are not rigidly specific, but approximate; this does not, however, necessarily lessen their structural significance.[1]

In all societies the initial status of every normal individual is that of child in a given kinship unit. In our society, however, this universal starting point is used in distinctive ways. Although in early childhood the sexes are not usually sharply differentiated, in many kinship systems a relatively sharp segregation of children begins very early. Our own society is conspicuous for the extent to which children of both sexes are in many fundamental respects treated alike. This is particularly true of both privileges and responsibilities. The primary distinctions within the group of dependent siblings are those of age. Birth order as such is notably neglected as a basis of discrimination; a child of eight and a child of five have essentially the privileges and responsibilities appropriate to their respective age levels without regard to what older, intermediate, or younger siblings there may be. The preferential treatment of an older child is not to any significant extent differentiated if and because he happens to be the first born.

Reprinted by permission of the author and the publisher, The American Sociological Association, from *American Sociological Review* 7 (October 1942):604–16.

[1]The problem of organization of this material for systematic presentation is, in view of this fact, particularly difficult. It would be possible to discuss the subject in terms of the above four principal structures with which age and sex are most closely interwoven, but there are serious disadvantages involved in this procedure. Age and sex categories constitute one of the main links of structural continuity in terms of which structures which are differentiated in other respects are articulated with each other; and in isolating the treatment of these categories there is danger that this extremely important aspect of the problem will be lost sight of. The least objectionable method, at least within the limits of space of such a paper, seems to be to follow the sequence of the life cycle.

There are, of course, important sex differences in dress and in approved play interest and the like, but if anything, it may be surmised that in the urban upper middle classes these are tending to diminish. Thus, for instance, play overalls are essentially similar for both sexes. What is perhaps the most important sex discrimination is more than anything else a reflection of the differentiation of adult sex roles. It seems to be a definite fact that girls are more apt to be relatively docile, to conform in general according to adult expectations, to be "good," whereas boys are more apt to be recalcitrant to discipline and defiant of adult authority and expectations. There is really no feminine equivalent of the expression "bad boy." It may be suggested that this is at least partially explained by the fact that it is possible from an early age to initiate girls directly into many important aspects of the adult feminine role. Their mothers are continually about the house and the meaning of many of the things they are doing is relatively tangible and easily understandable to a child. It is also possible for the daughter to participate actively and usefully in many of these activities. Especially in the urban middle classes, however, the father does not work in the home and his son is not able to observe his work or to participate in it from an early age. Furthermore many of the masculine functions are of a relatively abstract and intangible character, such that their meaning must remain almost wholly inaccessible to a child. This leaves the boy without a tangible meaningful model to emulate and without the possibility of a gradual initiation into the activities of the adult male role. An important verification of this analysis could be provided through the study in our own society of the rural situation. It is my impression that farm boys tend to be "good" in a sense in which that is not typical of their urban brothers.

The equality of privileges and responsibilities, graded only by age but not by birth order, is extended to a certain degree throughout the whole range of the life cycle. In full adult status, however, it is seriously modified by the asymmetrical relation of the sexes to the occupational structure. One of the most conspicuous expressions and symbols of the underlying equality, however, is the lack of sex differentiation in the process of formal education, so far, at least, as it is not explicitly vocational. Up through college, differentiation seems to be primarily a matter on the one hand of individual ability, on the other hand of class status, and only to a secondary degree of sex differentiation. One can certainly speak of a strongly established pattern that all children of the family have a "right" to a good education, rights which are graduated according to the class status of the family but also to individual ability. It is only in post-graduate professional education, with its direct connection with future occupational careers, that sex discrimination becomes conspicuous. It is particularly important that this equality of treatment exists in the sphere of liberal education since throughout the social structure of our society there is a strong tendency to segregate the occupational sphere from one in which certain more generally human patterns and values are dominant, particularly in informal social life and the realm of what will here be called community participation.

Although this pattern of equality of treatment is present in certain fundamental respects at all age levels, at the transition from childhood to adolescence new features appear which disturb the symmetry of sex roles, while still a second set of factors appears with marriage and the acquisition of full adult status and responsibilities.

An indication of the change is the practice of chaperonage, through which girls are given a kind of protection and supervision by adults to which boys of the same age group are not subjected. Boys, that is, are chaperoned only in their relations with girls of their own class. This modification of equality of treatment has been extended to the control of the private lives of women students in boarding schools and colleges. Of undoubted significance is the fact that it has been rapidly declining not only in actual effectiveness but as an ideal pattern. Its prominence in our recent past, however, is an important manifestation of the importance of sex role differentiation. Important light might be thrown upon its functions by systematic comparison with the related phenomena in Latin countries where this type of asymmetry has been far more accentuated than in this country in the more modern period.

It is at the point of emergence into adolescence that there first begins to develop a set of patterns and behavior phenomena which involve a highly complex combination of age grading and sex role elements. These may be referred to together as the phenomena of the "youth culture." Certain of its elements are present in pre-adolescence and others in the adult culture. But the peculiar combination in connection with this particular age level is unique and highly distinctive for American society.

Perhaps the best single point of reference for characterizing the youth culture lies in its contrast with the dominant pattern of the adult male role. By contrast with the emphasis on responsibility in this role, the orientation of the youth culture is more or less specifically irresponsible. One of its dominant features themes is "having a good time" in relation to which there is a particularly strong emphasis on social activities in company with the opposite sex. A second predominant characteristic on the male side lies in the prominence of athletics, which is an avenue of achievement and competition which stands in sharp contrast to the primary standards of adult achievement in professional and executive capacities. Negatively, there is a strong tendency to repudiate interest in adult things and to feel at least a certain recalcitrance to the pressure of adult expectations and discipline. In addition to, but including, athletic prowess the typical pattern of the male youth culture seems to lay emphasis on the value of certain qualities of attractiveness, especially in relation to the opposite sex. It is very definitely a rounded humanistic pattern rather than one of competence in the performance of specified functions. Such stereotypes as the "swell guy" are significant of this. On the feminine side there is correspondingly a strong tendency to accentuate sexual attractiveness in terms of various versions of what may be called the "glamor girl" pattern.[2] Although these patterns defining

[2]Perhaps the most dramatic manifestation of this tendency lies in the prominence of the patterns of "dating," for instance among college women. As shown by an unpublished participant-observer study made at one of the Eastern women's colleges, perhaps the

roles tend to polarize sexually—for instance, as between star athlete and socially popular girl—yet on a certain level they are complementary, both emphasizing certain features of a total personality in terms of the direct expression of certain values rather than of instrumental significance.

One further feature of this situation is the extent to which it is crystallized about the system of formal education.[3] One might say that the principal centers of prestige dissemination are the colleges, but that many of the most distinctive phenomena are to be found in high schools throughout the country. It is of course of great importance that liberal education is not primarily a matter of vocational training in the United States. The individual status on the curricular side of formal education is, however, in fundamental ways linked up with adult expectations, and doing "good work" is one of the most important sources of parental approval. Because of secondary institutionalization this approval is extended into various spheres distinctive of the youth culture. But it is notable that the youth culture has a strong tendency to develop in directions which are either on the borderline of parental approval or beyond the pale, in such matters as sex behavior, drinking, and various forms of frivolous and irresponsible behavior. The fact that adults have attitudes toward these things which are often deeply ambivalent and that on such occasions as college reunions they may outdo the younger generation, in drinking, for instance, is of great significance, but probably structurally secondary to the youth-versus-adult differential aspect. Thus the youth culture is not only, as is true of the curricular aspect of formal education, a matter of age status as such but also shows strong signs of being a product of tensions in the relationship of younger people and adults.

From the point of view of age grading, perhaps the most notable fact about this situation is the existence of definite pattern distinctions from the periods coming both before and after. At the line between childhood and

---

most important single basis of informal prestige rating among the residents of a dormitory lies in their relative dating success—though this is by no means the only basis. One of the most striking features of the pattern is the high publicity given to the "achievements" of the individual in a sphere where traditionally in the culture a rather high level of privacy is sanctioned—it is interesting that once an engagement has occurred a far greater amount of privacy is granted. The standards of rating cannot be said to be well integrated, though there is an underlying consistency in that being in demand by what the group regards as desirable men is perhaps the main standard.

It is true that the "dating" complex need not be exclusively bound up with the "glamor girl" stereotype of ideal feminine personality—the "good companion" type may also have a place. Precisely, however, where the competitive aspect of dating is most prominent the glamor pattern seems heavily to predominate, as does, on the masculine side, a somewhat comparable glamorous type. On each side at the same time there is room for considerable differences as to just where the emphasis is placed—for example as between "voluptuous" sexuality and more decorous "charm."

[3]A central aspect of this focus of crystallization lies in the element of tension, sometimes of direct conflict, between the youth culture patterns of college and school life, and the "serious" interests in and obligations toward curricular work. It is of course the latter which defines some at least of the most important foci of expectations of doing "good" work and justifying the privileges granted. It is not possible here to attempt to analyze the interesting ambivalent attitudes of youth toward curricular work and achievement.

adolescence "growing up" consists precisely in ability to participate in youth culture patterns, which are not, for either sex, the same as the adult patterns practiced by the parental generation. In both sexes the transition to full adulthood means loss of a certain "glamorous" element. From being the athletic hero or the lion of college dances, the young man becomes a prosaic business executive or lawyer. The more successful adults participate in an important order of prestige symbols but these are of a very different order from those of the youth culture. The contrast in the case of the feminine role is perhaps equally sharp, with at least a strong tendency to take on a "domestic" pattern with marriage and the arrival of young children.

The symmetry in this respect must, however, not be exaggerated. It is of fundamental significance to the sex role structure of the adult age levels that the normal man has a "job," which is fundamental to his social status in general. It is perhaps not too much to say that only in very exceptional cases can an adult man be genuinely self-respecting and enjoy a respected status in the eyes of others if he does not "earn a living" in an approved occupational role. Not only is this a matter of his own economic support but, generally speaking, his occupational status is the primary source of the income and class status of his wife and children.

In the case of the feminine role the situation is radically different. The majority of married women, of course, are not employed, but even of those that are a very large proportion do not have jobs which are in basic competition for status with those of their husbands.[4] The majority of "career" women whose occupational status is comparable with that of men in their own class, at least in the upper middle and upper classes, are unmarried, and in the small proportion of cases where they are married the result is a profound alteration in family structure.

This pattern, which is central to the urban middle classes, should not be misunderstood. In rural society, for instance, the operation of the farm and the attendant status in the community may be said to be a matter of the joint status of both parties to a marriage. Whereas a farm is operated by a family, an urban job is held by an individual and does not involve other members of the family in a comparable sense. One convenient expression of the difference lies in the question of what would happen in case of death. In the case of a farm it would at least be not at all unusual for the widow to continue operating the farm with the help of a son or even of hired men. In the urban situation the widow would cease to have any connection with

[4]The above statement, even more than most in the present paper, needs to be qualified in relation to the problem of class. It is above all to the upper middle class that it applies. Here probably the great majority of "working wives" are engaged in some form of secretarial work which would, on an independent basis, generally be classed as a lower middle class occupation. The situation at lower levels of the class structure is quite different since the prestige of the jobs of husband and wife is then much more likely to be nearly equivalent. It is quite possible that this fact is closely related to the relative instability of marriage which Davis and Gardner (*Deep South*) find, at least for the community they studied, to be typical of lower class groups. The relation is one which deserves careful study.

the organization which had employed her husband and he would be replaced by another man without reference to family affiliations.

In this urban situation the primary status-carrying role is in a sense that of housewife. The woman's fundamental status is that of her husband's wife, the mother of his children, and traditionally the person responsible for a complex of activities in connection with the management of the household, care of children, etc.

For the structuring of sex roles in the adult phase the most fundamental considerations seem to be those involved in the interrelations of the occupational system and the conjugal family. In a certain sense the most fundamental basis of the family's status is the occupational status of the husband and father. As has been pointed out, this is a status occupied by an individual by virtue of his individual qualities and achievements. But both directly and indirectly, more than any other single factor, it determines the status of the family in the social structure, directly because of the symbolic significance of the office or occupation as a symbol of prestige, indirectly because as the principal source of family income it determines the standard of living of the family. From one point of view the emergence of occupational status into this primary position can be regarded as the principal source of strain in the sex role structure of our society since it deprives the wife of her role as a partner in a common enterprise. The common enterprise is reduced to the life of the family itself and to the informal social activities in which husband and wife participate together. This leaves the wife a set of utilitarian functions in the management of the household which may be considered a kind of "pseudo-" occupation. Since the present interest is primarily in the middle classes, the relatively unstable character of the role of housewife as the principal content of the feminine role is strongly illustrated by the tendency to employ domestic servants whenever financially possible. It is true that there is an American tendency to accept tasks of drudgery with relative willingness, but it is notable that in middle class families there tends to be a dissociation of the essential personality from the performance of these tasks. Thus, advertising continually appeals to such desires as to have hands which one could never tell had washed dishes or scrubbed floors.[5] Organization about the function of housewife, however, with the addition of strong affectional devotion to husband and children, is the primary focus of one of the principal patterns governing the adult feminine role—what may be called the "domestic" pattern. It is, however, a conspicuous fact that strict adherence to this pattern has become progressively less common and has a strong tendency to a residual status—

[5]This type of advertising appeal undoubtedly contains an element of "snob appeal" in the sense of an invitation to the individual by her appearance and ways to identify herself with a higher social class than that of her actual status. But it is almost certainly not wholly explained by this element. A glamorously feminine appearance which is specifically dissociated from physical work is undoubtedly a genuine part of an authentic personality ideal of the middle class, and not only evidence of a desire to belong to the upper class.

that is, to be followed most closely by those who are unsuccessful in competition for prestige in other directions.

It is, of course, possible for the adult woman to follow the masculine pattern and seek a career in fields of occupational achievement in direct competition with men of her own class. It is, however, notable that in spite of the very great progress of the emancipation of women from the traditional domestic pattern only a very small fraction have gone very far in this direction. It is also clear that its generalization would only be possible with profound alterations in the structure of the family.

Hence it seems that concomitant with the alteration in the basic masculine role in the direction of occupation there have appeared two important tendencies in the feminine role which are alternative to that of simple domesticity on the one hand, and to a full-fledged career on the other. In the older situation there tended to be a very rigid distinction between respectable married women and those who were "no better than they should be." The rigidity of this line has progressively broken down through the infiltration into the respectable sphere of elements of what may be called again the glamor pattern, with the emphasis on a specifically feminine form of attractiveness which on occasion involves directly sexual patterns of appeal. One important expression of this trend lies in the fact that many of the symbols of feminine attractiveness have been taken over directly from the practices of social types previously beyond the pale of respectable society. This would seem to be substantially true of the practice of women smoking and of at least the modern version of the use of cosmetics. The same would seem to be true of many of the modern versions of women's dress. "Emancipation" in this connection means primarily emancipation from traditional and conventional restrictions on the free expression of sexual attraction and impulses, but in a direction which tends to segregate the elements of sexual interest and attraction from the total personality and in so doing tends to emphasize the segregation of sex roles. It is particularly notable that there has been no corresponding tendency to emphasize masculine attraction in terms of dress and other such aids. One might perhaps say that in a situation which strongly inhibits competition between the sexes on the same plane the feminine glamor pattern has appeared as an offset to masculine occupational status and to its attendant symbols of prestige. It is perhaps significant that there is a common stereotype of the association of physically beautiful, expensively and elaborately dressed women with physically unattractive but rich and powerful men.

The other principal direction of emancipation from domesticity seems to lie in emphasis on what has been called the common humanistic element. This takes a wide variety of forms. One of them lies in a relatively mature appreciation and systematic cultivation of cultural interests and educated tastes, extending all the way from the intellectual sphere to matters of art, music, and house furnishings. A second consists in cultivation of serious interests and humanitarian obligations in community welfare situations and the like. It is understandable that many of these orientations are most conspicuous in fields where through some kind of tradition there is an element of particular suitability for feminine participation. Thus, a woman who takes obligations to social welfare particularly seriously will find opportunities in various forms of activity which traditionally tie up with women's relation to children, to sickness and so on. But this may be regarded as secondary to the underlying orientation which would seek an outlet in work useful to the community following the most favorable opportunities which happen to be available.

This pattern, which with reference to the character of relationship to men may be called that of the "good companion," is distinguished from the others in that it lays far less stress on the exploitation of sex role as such and more on that which is essentially common to both sexes. There are reasons, however, why cultural interests, interest in social welfare and community activities are particularly prominent in the activities of women in our urban communities. On the one side the masculine occupational role tends to absorb a very large proportion of the man's time and energy and to leave him relatively little for other interests. Furthermore, unless his position is such as to make him particularly prominent his primary orientation is to those elements of the social structure which divide the community into occupational groups rather than those which unite it in common interests and activities. The utilitarian aspect of the role of housewife, on the other hand, has declined in importance to the point where it scarcely approaches a full-time occupation for a vigorous person. Hence the resort to other interests to fill up the gap. In addition, women, being more closely tied to the local residential community, are more apt to be involved in matters of common concern to the members of that community. This peculiar role of women becomes particularly conspicuous in middle age. The younger married woman is apt to be relatively highly absorbed in the care of young children. With their growing up, however, her absorption in the household is greatly lessened, often just at the time when the husband is approaching the apex of his career and is most heavily involved in its obligations. Since to a high degree this humanistic aspect of the feminine role is only partially institutionalized it is not surprising that its patterns often bear the marks of strain and insecurity, as perhaps has been classically depicted by Helen Hokinson's cartoons of women's clubs.

The adult roles of both sexes involve important elements of strain which are involved in certain dynamic relationships, especially to the youth culture. In the case of the feminine role, marriage is the single event toward which a selective process, in which personal qualities and effort can play a decisive part, has pointed. That determines a woman's fundamental status, and after that her role patterning is not so much status determining as a matter of living up to expectations and finding satisfying interests and activities. In a society where such strong emphasis is placed upon individual achievement it is not surprising that there should be a certain romantic nostalgia for the time when the fundamental choices were still open. This element of strain is added to by the lack of clear-cut definition of the adult feminine role. Once the possibility of a career has been eliminated there still tends to be a rather unstable oscillation between emphasis in the direction of domesticity or glamor or good companionship. According to situational pressures and individual character the tendency will be to emphasize one or another of these more strongly. But it is a situation likely to produce a rather high level of insecurity. In this state the pattern of domesticity must be ranked lowest in terms of prestige but also, because of the strong emphasis in community sentiment on the virtues of fidelity and devotion to husband and children, it offers perhaps the highest level of a certain kind of security. It is no wonder that such an important symbol as Whistler's mother concentrates primarily on this pattern.

The glamor pattern has certain obvious attractions since to the woman who is excluded from the struggle for power and prestige in the occupational sphere it is the most direct path to a sense of superiority and importance. It has, however, two obvious limitations. In the first place, many of its manifestations encounter the resistance of patterns of moral conduct and engender conflicts not only with community opinion but also with the individual's own moral standards. In the second place, it is a pattern the highest manifestations of which are inevitably associated with a rather early age level—in fact, overwhelmingly with the courtship period. Hence, if strongly entered upon, serious strains result from the problem of adaptation to increasing age.

The one pattern which would seem to offer the greatest possibilities for able, intelligent, and emotionally mature women is the third—the good companion pattern. This, however, suffers from a lack of fully institutionalized status and from the multiplicity of choices of channels of expression. It is only those with the strongest initiative and intelligence who achieve fully satisfactory adaptations in this direction. It is quite clear that in the adult feminine role there is quite sufficient strain and insecurity so that widespread manifestations are to be expected in the form of neurotic behavior.

The masculine role at the same time is itself by no means devoid of corresponding elements of strain. It carries with it to be sure the primary prestige of achievement, responsibility and authority. By comparison with the role of the youth culture, however, there are at least two important types of limitations. In the first place, the modern occupational system has led to increasing specialization of the role. The job absorbs an extraordinarily large proportion of the individual's energy and emotional interests in a role the content of which is often relatively narrow. This in particular restricts the area within which he can share common interests and experiences with others not in the same occupational specialty. It is perhaps of considerable significance that so many of the highest prestige statuses of our society are of the specialized character. There is in the definition of roles little to bind the individual to others in his community on a comparable status level. By contrast with this situation, it is notable that in the youth culture common human elements are far more strongly emphasized. Leadership and eminence are more in the role of total individuals and less of competent specialists. This perhaps has something to do with the significant tendency in our society for all age levels to idealize youth and for the older age groups to attempt to imitate the patterns of youth behavior.

It is perhaps as one phase of this situation that the relation of the adult man to persons of the opposite sex should be treated. The effect of the specialization of occupational role is to narrow the range in which the sharing of common human interests can play a large part. In relation to his wife the tendency of this narrowness would seem to be to encourage on her part either the domestic or the glamorous role, or community participation somewhat unrelated to the marriage relationship. This relationship between sex roles presumably introduces a certain amount of strain into the marriage relationship itself since this is of such overwhelming importance to the family and hence to a woman's status and yet so relatively difficult to maintain on a level of human companionship. Outside the marriage relationship, however, there seems to be a notable inhibition against easy social intercourse, particularly in mixed company.[6] The man's close personal intimacy with other women is checked by the danger of the situation being defined as one of rivalry with the wife, and easy friendship without sexual-emotional involvement seems to be inhibited by the specialization of interests in the occupational sphere. It is notable that brilliance of conversation of the "salon" type seems to be associated with aristocratic society and is not prominent in ours.

Along with all this goes a certain tendency for middle-aged men, as symbolized by the "bald-headed row," to be interested in the physical aspects of sex—that is, in women precisely as dissociated from those personal considerations which are important to relationships of companionship or friendship, to say nothing of marriage. In so far as it does not take this physical form, however, there seems to be a strong tendency for middle-aged men to idealize youth patterns—that is, to think of the ideal inter-sex friendship as that of their pre-marital period.[7]

In so far as the idealization of the youth culture by adults is an expression of elements of strain and insecurity in the adult roles it would be expected that the patterns thus idealized would contain an element of romantic unrealism. The patterns of youthful behavior thus idealized are not those of actual youth so much as those which older people wish their own youth might have been. This romantic element seems to coalesce with a similar element derived from certain strains in the situation of young people themselves.

The period of youth in our society is one of considerable strain and insecurity. Above all, it means turning one's back on the security both of status and of emotional attachment which is engaged in the family of orientation. It is structurally essential to transfer one's primary emotional attachment to a marriage partner who is entirely unrelated to the previous family situation. In a system of free marriage choice this applies to women as well as men. For the man there is in addition the necessity to face the hazards of

[6]In the informal social life of academic circles with which the writer is familiar there seems to be a strong tendency in mixed gatherings—as after dinner—for the sexes to segregate. In such groups the men are apt to talk either shop subjects or politics whereas the women are apt to talk about domestic affairs, schools, their children, etc., or personalities. It is perhaps on personalities that mixed conversation is apt to flow most freely.

[7]This, to be sure, often contains an element of romanticization. It is more nearly what he wishes these relations had been than what they actually were.

occupational competition in the determination of a career. There is reason to believe that the youth culture has important positive functions in easing the transition from the security of childhood in the family of orientation to that of full adult in marriage and occupational status. But precisely because the transition is a period of strain it is to be expected that it involves elements of unrealistic romanticism. Thus significant features of youth patterns in our society would seem to derive from the coincidence of the emotional needs of adolescents with those derived from the strains of the situation of adults.

A tendency to the romantic idealization of youth patterns seems in different ways to be characteristic of modern Western society as a whole.[8] It is not possible in the present context to enter into any extended comparative analysis, but it may be illuminating to call attention to a striking difference between the patterns associated with this phenomenon in Germany and in the United States. The German "youth movement," starting before the First World War, has occasioned a great deal of comment and has in various respects been treated as the most notable instance of the revolt of youth. It is generally believed that the youth movement has an important relation to the background of National Socialism, and this fact as much as any suggests the important difference. While in Germany as everywhere there has been a generalized revolt against convention and restrictions on individual freedom as embodied in the traditional adult culture, in Germany particular emphasis has appeared on the community of male youth. "Comradeship" in a sense which strongly suggests that of soldiers in the field has from the beginning been strongly emphasized as the ideal social relationship. By contrast with this, in the American youth culture and its adult romanticization a much stronger emphasis has been placed on the cross-sex relationship. It would seem that this fact, with the structural factors which underlie it, have much to do with the failure of the youth culture to develop any considerable political significance in this country. Its predominant pattern has been that of the idealization of the isolated couple in romantic love. There have, to be sure, been certain tendencies among radical youth to a political orientation but in this case there has been a notable absence of emphasis on the solidarity of the members of one sex. The tendency has been rather to ignore the relevance of sex difference in the interest of common ideals.

The importance of youth patterns in contemporary American culture throws into particularly strong relief the status in our social structure of the most advanced age groups. By comparison with other societies the United States assumes an extreme position in the isolation of old age from participation in the most important social structures and interests. Structurally speaking, there seem to be two primary bases of this situation. In the first place, the most important single distinctive feature of our family structure is the isolation of the individual conjugal family. It is impossible to say

[8] *Cf.* E. Y. Hartshorne, "German Youth and the Nazi Dream of Victory," *America in a World at War,* Pamphlet, No. 12, New York, 1941.

that with us it is "natural" for any other group than husband and wife and their dependent children to maintain a common household. Hence, when the children of a couple have become independent through marriage and occupational status the parental couple is left without attachment to any continuous kinship group. It is, of course, common for other relatives to share a household with the conjugal family but this scarcely ever occurs without some important elements of strain. For independence is certainly the preferred pattern for an elderly couple, particularly from the point of view of the children.

The second basis of the situation lies in the occupational structure. In such fields as farming and maintenance of small independent enterprises there is frequently no such thing as abrupt "retirement," rather a gradual relinquishment of the main responsibilities and functions with advancing age. So far, however, as an individual's occupational status centers in a specific "job," he either holds the job or does not, and the tendency is to maintain the full level of functions up to a given point and then abruptly to retire. In view of the very great significance of occupational status and its psychological correlates, retirement leaves the older man in a peculiarly functionless situation, cut off from participation in the most important interests and activities of the society. There is a further important aspect of this situation. Not only status in the community but actual place of residence is to a very high degree a function of the specific job held. Retirement not only cuts the ties to the job itself but also greatly loosens those to the community of residence. Perhaps in no other society is there observable a phenomenon corresponding to the accumulation of retired elderly people in such areas as Florida and Southern California in the winter. It may be surmised that this structural isolation from kinship, occupational, and community ties is the fundamental basis of the recent political agitation for help to the old. It is suggested that it is far less the financial hardship[9] of the position of elderly people than their social isolation which makes old age a "problem." As in other connections we are very prone to rationalize generalized insecurity in financial and economic terms. The problem is obviously of particularly great significance in view of the changing age distribution of the population with the prospect of a far greater proportion in the older age groups than in previous generations. It may also be suggested that, through well-known psychosomatic mechanisms, the increased incidence of the disabilities of older people, such as heart disease, cancer, etc., may be at least in part attributed to this structural situation.

[9]That the financial difficulties of older people in a very large proportion of cases are real is not to be doubted. This, however, is at least to a very large extent a consequence rather than a determinant of the structural situation. Except where it is fully taken care of by pension schemes, the income of older people is apt to be seriously reduced, but, even more important, the younger conjugal family does not feel an obligation to contribute to the support of aged parents. Where as a matter of course both generations shared a common household, this problem did not exist.

*Ethnicity, Social Class, and Adolescent Independence from Parental Control**

George Psathas

During the years of adolescence the individual moves toward independence from parental control. In a society characterized by rapid social change and the lack of explicit norms regarding this transition, there are likely to be variations in the handling of the adolescent. Some families may grant a great degree of independence to the adolescent. Others may continue to supervise and restrict the adolescent much as they do younger children.

In this study the differences between certain ethnic groups and between social classes are investigated with regard to the degree of independence from parental control granted the adolescent. Members of Southern Italian and Eastern European Jewish ethnic groups in New Haven, Connecticut were selected for study. These groups were similar in their time of arrival and place of settlement in this country but had different cultural backgrounds. Differences could reasonably be attributed to ethnicity only if the groups compared had an approximately equal time in which to become acculturated and assimilated.

No research is reported in the literature contrasting these two ethnic groups with regard to adolescent independence. Studies describing the cultural background of these two groups indicate that both Italian and Jewish children were traditionally subordinated to their parents.[1] Patriarchal au-

Reprinted by permission of the author and the publisher, The American Sociological Association, from *American Sociological Review* 22 (August 1957):415–23.

*Expanded version of paper read at the annual meeting of the American Sociological Society, September, 1956, and based on the author's unpublished doctoral dissertation, Yale University, 1956. The writer is indebted to Theodore Anderson, Leo W. Simmons, and August B. Hollingshead of Yale University and to Karl F. Schuessler and Albert K. Cohen of Indiana University for their valuable advice and suggestions.

[1]The following sources were helpful in describing Southern Italian culture: Paul J. Campisi, "Ethnic Family Patterns: The Italian Family in the United States," *American Journal of Sociology,* 53 (January, 1948) , pp. 443–46; Irving L. Child, *Italian or American? The Second Generation in Conflict,* New Haven: Yale University Press, 1943; Caroline Ware, *Greenwich Village, 1920–1930,* Boston: Houghton Mifflin, 1935; and Phyllis H. Williams, *South Italian Folkways in Europe and America,* New Haven: Yale University

thority stressed the duties rather than the rights of the child in Italy. So long as the father lived, the sons owed him a great measure of respect and obedience, whether they were married or not.

This subordination also characterized Jewish culture, but in intellectual matters individuality and independence were highly valued. The contrast between physical and intellectual matters was great in the life of the boy. As soon as he started his studies, sometimes at the age of three, he was treated as an adult in matters of the intellect. But even when physically mature, he was still a "baby" to his mother who never stopped worrying about his health, warmth and safety. The child was taught to respect authority not because of the person who embodied it but because of the matter it pertained to. He was taught to question authority in his schooling, since even the Divine Law is subject to interpretation. Thus, in intellectual matters independence was encouraged while in other activities the Jewish son appears to have received no strikingly different treatment than the Italian boy. The greater encouragement in intellectual matters given the Jewish boy might carry over to other activities, but in Italian culture this possibility did not exist. At any rate, no inference concerning the direction of differences between Italian and Jewish adolescents with regard to independence from parental control seems possible from available evidence.

With regard to social class variations there is little explicit concern in the literature with adolescent independence. An early study by Dimock,[2] using a crude measure labelled "emancipation from parents," found no correlation between socio-economic status and this measure. Nye found that adolescent–parent adjustment is "better" in the higher socio-economic levels where adolescents scored higher on "feeling of being loved and secure, feeling that parents trust and have confidence in them, socialization including disciplinary relationships, attitudes toward the parents' personality, and relationships in interaction affecting the adolescent's contact with groups outside the family."[3] Landis and Stone[4] report that social classes do not differ in terms of whether parental authority patterns are democratic, authoritarian, or intermediate. The democratic authority pattern resembles the definition of independence from parental control used in this study.

Press, 1938. For Eastern European Jewish culture: Theodore Bienenstock, "Anti-Authoritarian Attitudes in the Eastern European 'Shtetl' Community," *American Journal of Sociology,* 57 (September, 1951), pp. 150–58; I. Graeber and S. H. Britt, (Eds.), *Jews in a Gentile World,* New York: Macmillan, 1942; Ruth Landes and Mark Zborowski, "Hypotheses Concerning the Eastern European Jewish Family," *Psychiatry,* 13 (November, 1950), pp. 447–64; and Mark Zborowski and Elizabeth Herzog, *Life Is With People,* New York: International Universities Press, 1952.

[2]Helen S. Dimock, *Rediscovering the Adolescent,* New York: Association Press, 1937, pp. 144–45.

[3]Ivan Nye, "Adolescent-Parent Adjustment—Socio-Economic Level as a Variable," *American Sociological Review,* 16 (June 1951), p. 344.

[4]Paul H. Landis and Carol L. Stone, "The Relationship of Parental Authority Patterns to Teen-Age Adjustments," Bulletin No. 538, Washington Agricultural Experiment Station, Pullman: State College of Washington, 1952.

Procedure

Twenty-five questionnaire items were compiled, some drawn from studies of adolescents by Nye[5] and Landis and Stone,[6] the others constructed by the writer. Each item was stated in multiple choice form with the answer categories ranging from "high" independence to "low" independence. Some areas of activity such as driving the family car, parties in the home, or holding a job were deliberately omitted since some boys might not engage in them. The numbers assigned to the items, which are somewhat abbreviated for presentation here, do not represent the order in which they appeared in the original questionnaire but are arbitrarily assigned for purposes of clarity.

Questionnaire Items

1. Before I go out on dates, parents ask me where I am going: never; seldom; half the time; usually; always
2. Before I go out on dates, parents ask me with whom I am going: never; seldom; half the time; usually; always
3. Do you have to account to parents for way you spend your money: not at all; for some of spending; for almost all spending
4. Are you allowed trips out of town without parents: whenever I want; almost everytime I want; sometimes; rarely; never
5. Do parents check on whether you do your homework: never; seldom; half the time; most of the time; almost always
6. In family discussions do parents encourage your opinion: always; usually; half the time; seldom; never
7. With regard to family problems, parents discuss them with me: always; usually; half the time; seldom; never
8. Do parents give opportunities to share responsibilities: as much as I like; almost as much as I like; yes, but not as much as I like; no, only rarely; no, never
9. Parents respect my opinion and judgment: all of the time; most of the time; half the time; seldom; never
10. In family discussions, parents take my opinion seriously: almost always; usually; sometimes; seldom; never
11. When requiring me to do something, parents explain the reason: always; usually; half the time; seldom; never
12. With regard to whom I go on dates with parents criticize: never; seldom; half the time; usually; always
13. With regard to where I go on dates, parents criticize: never; seldom; half the time; usually; always
14. When invited to relative's home, parents insist you go with them: never; seldom; half the time; usually; always

[5]Nye, *op. cit.*

[6]Landis and Stone, *op. cit.*

15. Do parents try to influence choice of occupation: never; hardly at all; try slightly; try moderately; try very hard
16. Does (Do) parent(s) help you buy your clothes: hardly ever; sometimes; usually; always
17. With regard to evenings out, parents allow: every evening if I wish; all week-end, some school nights; week-end, not school nights; only occasional evening; almost never allowed out
18. Who makes final decision on buying clothes: I do, without parents' advice; I do with parents' advice; parents with my advice; parents without my advice
19. Who makes your doctor or dentist appointments: I do myself; I do with parents' agreement; parents do with my agreement; parents without asking me
20. When parents don't approve of a boy you spend a lot of time with what do they do: they never disapprove; tell me but leave it up to me; tell me to stop seeing him but don't insist; insist I stop seeing him
21. What do parents think of boys you spend a lot of time with: approve all; most; some; very few; none
22. Where do you get most of your spending money: money I earn; a regular allowance; money given as needed but no regular allowance; money earned plus regular allowance; money earned plus money given as needed
23. Considering the family income, my parents, if I need money, are: very generous; fairly generous; average; rather stingy; very stingy
24. Is father unreasonable in his commands: frequently; occasionally; only rarely; never
25. Is mother unreasonable in her commands: frequently; occasionally; only rarely; never

The questionnaire was administered to sophomore boys in public and private high schools in New Haven during regularly scheduled classroom periods.[7] A number of background items were included in the questionnaire to determine the boy's ethnic background and his parents' social class. Persons were classified in the Italian ethnic group if both parents were Italian by country of birth or nationality, and at least three of four grandparents Italian. Jews were so defined if both parents had Jewish religious affiliation. The country of birth of the parents or grandparents was used to distinguish Jews from Eastern Europe (Russia, Poland, Hungary or Rumania) from other Jews. Although it was not possible to distinguish between Northern and Southern Italians, most Italians in New Haven are from Southern Italy and Sicily.[8] The group labelled Other Ethnics is a residual category.

The following additional controls were applied: cases of homes broken by death, separation, or divorce were excluded; only members of the Cau-

[7]Ninety-four per cent of the regularly enrolled sophomore boys in these schools completed the questionnaire.

[8]Jerome K. Meyers, "The Differential Time Factor in Assimilation" (unpublished Ph.D. dissertation, Yale University, 1949), p. 26.

casian race were included; and, from the Italian and Jewish groups, cases of mixed ethnic marriages in the parental generation were excluded.

Almost all boys (92 per cent) were between the ages of 15 and 17, the median age being 15 years and 10 months. In the case of both the Italian and Jewish groups, 56 per cent of the boys were third generation Americans, i.e., parents born in the U.S., and approximately one-third[9] were second generation. Thus, these two groups are roughly comparable in terms of their length of residence in America.

However, they differ considerably when classified according to Hollingshead's Index of Social Position,[10] a measure of social class based on the father's occupation, education, and ecological area of residence. Table 1 presents a breakdown of the Italian, Jewish and Other Ethnic groups by social class. It will be observed that 88 per cent of the Jews are found in the three highest social classes in contrast to 10 per cent of the Italians.

CONSTRUCTING A MEASURE OF INDEPENDENCE. Twenty of the original twenty-five items were first submitted to Guttman scale analysis to determine whether the content area was uni-dimensional.[11] The response categories for items included in the scale analysis were dichotomized by determining where a "logical" split could be made between the categories.[12] Scale analysis revealed that more than one dimension existed; the coefficient of reproducibility on the second approximation reached only .84.

In order to establish the number of major dimensions involved in this content area, factor analysis was then employed. For each pair of items a tetrachoric correlation coefficient was computed based on all 476 cases.[13]

[9]The actual figures are 37 per cent for the Italians and 34 per cent for the Jews. The group labelled Other Ethnic showed a smaller proportion of second generation boys, 15 per cent, approximately the same proportion of third generation, 51 per cent, but a larger proportion of fourth generation, 31 per cent. Thus, the Other Ethnic group includes more of the earlier immigrants.

[10]August B. Hollingshead and Fritz C. Redlich, "Social Stratification and Psychiatric Disorders," *American Sociological Review,* 18 (April, 1953), pp. 163–69, present a detailed description of the five classes in the New Haven community this index describes.

The social class distribution of all boys in the present sample was found to compare favorably with the 5 per cent Random Sample of Households in the New Haven community reported by Hollingshead and Redlich. A chi-square test of significance comparing the two samples revealed a p value greater than .05.

[11]Of the five excluded, one item revealed no spread of responses (No. 21), one had been designed merely as an introduction to another item which was included (No. 22), and three were judged by inspection to be unrelated to the variable independence from parental control (Nos. 23, 24, and 25). One additional item (No. 20) was included in the scale analysis but eliminated from the factor analysis when it was later discovered that 17 per cent of the respondents had either left it unanswered or checked it as inapplicable.

[12]For example, for No. 9, it seems reasonable to group categories (1) all of the time and (2) most of the time; to also group (4) seldom and (5) never; and to place category (3) half the time, with either of these groups depending on the distribution of responses. Categories (1) and (2) contained 64 per cent of the responses and if category (3) were included with these the percentage would rise to 90. In order to avoid as extreme a split as this, category (3) was placed with the bottom two categories.

[13]It should be cautioned that factor analysis results based on the tetrachoric correlation coefficient are likely to have greater variability than those based on the Pearsonian r. See Raymond B. Cattell, *Factor Analysis,* New York: Harper and Brothers, 1952, pp. 326–27.

Table 1. Ethnic Groups by Social Class

	Italians		Jews		Other Ethnics		Total	
Social Class	N	Per Cent	N	Per Cent	N	Per Cent	N	Per Cent
I and II[a]	2	1.1	23	33.8	40	17.7	65	13.7
III	17	9.3	37	54.4	57	25.2	111	23.3
IV	110	60.4	7	10.3	107	47.3	224	47.0
V	48	26.4	—	—	13	5.8	61	12.8
Unknown[b]	5	2.7	1	1.5	9	4.0	15	3.2
	182	99.9	68	100.0	226	100.0	476	100.0

[a]Because of the small number of cases in Class I, Classes I and II are combined.

[b]Unknown cases are those in which the respondent did not provide sufficient information to permit class assignment.

The matrix of tetrachoric correlations is set out in Table 2. Thurstone's centroid method for factor analysis was then applied.[14] Four factors were extracted and after four orthogonal and five oblique rotations of the axes, a simple structure solution was achieved. Table 3 presents the oblique rotated factor matrix. The factor loadings for items included in a particular factor are in bold face type in the column labelled with the name of the factor. Interpretations of the four factors are based on the factor loadings in Table 3 considering only those loadings above .200 as significant.

Interpretations of the Factors

Factor 1, defined by Items 1–5, is concerned with a number of activities that involve parental supervision. These items involve activities that occur outside the home with the possible exception of Item 5 concerning checking on homework. The parents may supervise these activities directly or indirectly and punish the son by withholding permission for his participating or by exercising close supervision of his performance. The adolescent who scores high on this cluster of items may be said to be relatively free from parental supervision in his activities outside the home. For this reason the factor has been labelled Permissiveness in Outside Activities.

Factor 2 includes seven items (Nos. 4 and 6–11) concerning family discussions and decisions made in the home. Each of these items involves verbal interaction between parents and son and, with the exception of Item 4, concern no specific issue but rather seem to reflect the general regard that the parents have for the son's opinion or judgment. Consequently, this factor is labelled Parental Regard for Judgment.

Factor 3 is a little more heterogeneous. It includes five items (Nos. 9 and 12–15). The activities involved here seem to be those which affect the

[14]L. L. Thurstone, *Multiple Factor Analysis,* Chicago: University of Chicago Press, 1947.

Table 2. Original Tetrachoric Correlation Matrix for 19 Questionnaire Items[a]

Item Number	1	2	3	4	5	6	7	8	9	10	11	12	13	14	15	16	17	18	19
1		742	518	194	280	–172	–115	–168	–207	–104	–156	072	144	246	007	420	347	178	037
2		–	455	106	169	–020	–142	–054	–063	–099	–212	195	208	267	–056	439	338	212	072
3			–	374	265	–162	–135	–021	–085	–084	088	308	217	262	045	137	249	154	–042
4				–	151	001	097	171	183	168	–029	006	063	115	–058	201	348	027	171
5					–	–156	–264	–163	–171	–142	–153	094	–019	200	010	149	315	081	–003
6						–	517	444	474	456	251	–027	–035	–268	021	–002	–132	–037	024
7							–	561	358	374	314	–061	–109	–031	–024	115	–141	–027	014
8								–	510	345	220	152	096	024	073	058	–202	038	041
9									–	548	268	340	118	119	177	023	–008	013	037
10										–	238	006	–087	041	049	069	000	–035	091
11											–	–020	–075	043	–068	083	–084	040	061
12												–	634	226	205	210	246	078	109
13													–	383	195	259	237	117	008
14														–	052	187	330	291	054
15															–	–107	026	–039	–057
16																–	489	646	231
17																	–	295	148
18																		–	142
19																			–

[a]Decimals, properly preceding each entry, have been omitted for purposes of clarity.

son's "reputation" or "character." Each of the activities has implications for how others will regard him. His choice of an occupation, his visiting relatives, whom he dates and where he goes on dates may be the object of his parents' concern that he "do the right thing" so that others will have a "good opinion" of him. This factor is labelled Activities with Status Implications.

The activities in Factor 4 (Nos. 14 and 16–19) refer to matters related to the age of the boy. Buying clothes, making doctor and dentist appointments, evenings out, and visiting relatives probably vary more with the age of the boy than the activities in Factor 3. At his present age, making such choices is an indication of his greater freedom from parental control and this factor is called Permissiveness in Age-Related Activities.

Intercorrelations of the Factors

Table 4 presents the intercorrelations of the four factors after the five oblique rotations. Primary Factors 1, 3, and 4 show positive intercorrelations with the highest correlation existing between 1 and 4, Permissiveness in Outside Activities and Permissiveness in Age-Related Activities respectively.

Table 3. Factor Loadings[a] of 19 Items Grouped by Each of the Four Factors; Oblique Rotated Factor Matrix V

Item No.	Permissiveness in Outside Activities	Parental Regard for Judgment	Activities with Status Implications	Permissiveness in Age-Related Activities	Communality h^2
1	**.644**	−.041	−.071	.032	.650
2	**.617**	−.012	.066	−.015	.611
3	**.550**	.042	.088	−.036	.464
4	**.284**	**.231**	−.090	.183	.218
5	**.210**	−.187	−.086	.130	.186
6	.071	**.698**	−.071	−.015	.520
7	.071	**.688**	−.056	.005	.500
8	.149	**.688**	.171	−.100	.506
9	−.103	**.621**	**.426**	.027	.623
10	−.057	**.603**	.083	.130	.161
11	−.124	**.345**	.038	.119	.177
12	.003	.015	**.704**	.013	.584
13	.016	−.091	**.668**	.003	.550
14	.051	−.074	**.350**	**.209**	.313
15	−.024	.033	**.338**	−.149	.123
16	.004	.061	−.042	**.724**	.702
17	.064	−.132	.021	**.542**	.517
18	−.089	−.029	.055	**.522**	.349
19	−.094	.046	−.038	**.320**	.110

[a]The factor loadings represent the correlation between each item and the factor in question.

Table 4. Correlations Between the Primary Factors after Oblique Rotation

Factors	Permissiveness in Outside Activities 1	Parental Regard for Judgment 2	Activities with Status Implications 3	Permissiveness in Age-Related Activities 4
1	1.000	−.307	.325	.499
2		1.000	−.007	−.095
3			1.000	.321
4				1.000

Factor 2, Parental Regard for Judgment, is negatively correlated with Factor 1 and shows low negative correlations with Factors 3 and 4.

An examination of the original tetrachoric correlation between items (Table 2) leads to comparable results. For example, the mean (which is here used for summarizing purposes) of the correlation coefficients for every item in Factor 1 with every item in Factor 4 is .197, which is larger than the mean of the inter-item correlations between Factors 1 and 3 (.067), and Factors 3 and 4 (.072). The mean of the coefficients between items in Factors 1 and 2 is negative (−.123), while for Factors 2 and 3 and Factors 2 and 4 it is positive and low (.072 and .033 respectively). The foregoing computations exclude any common items found in the two factors being compared.

By comparison, the intra-factor item by item correlations, i.e., the mean of the coefficients for items within a particular factor, are all positive and larger than the abovementioned means of the inter-factor item by item coefficients. For Factors 1, 2, 3, and 4 these are .325, .308, .245, and .281 respectively. Computations exclude the correlation between an item and itself which is unity.

We conclude that the factors determined by the factor analysis represent different dimensions of independence from parental control and are only moderately intercorrelated. Factors 1 and 4 come closest to representing a general independence factor. The negative correlation found between Factors 1 and 2 (in Table 4) and also in the inter-factor item by item comparison (in Table 2) indicates that Factor 2 bears a qualitatively different relation to the other dimensions of independence. An interpretation of this relation will be advanced below.

Ethnic Groups

The first hypothesis to be tested was stated in null form: There are no differences between Italian and Jewish ethnic groups with regard to the degree of independence from parental control granted the adolescent boy.

A scale score for each individual on each of the four dimensions of independence was computed,[15] and there are thus four tests of the hypothesis. Because of the different social class composition of the two ethnic groups, the analysis of variance[16] was chosen as the most suitable statistical test since it would permit controlling for social class when testing for ethnic differences. Four separate analysis of variance tests were made testing for the difference between ethnic groups holding class constant and four tests of class differences holding ethnicity constant. The latter findings will be discussed below under social class.

Table 5 presents the mean scores for Italians and Jews by social class for each of the scales.[17] No statistically significant differences (at the .05 level) are found between Italian and Jewish adolescents when social class is held constant for any of the four dimensions of independence. Interaction, when tested, was not significant.

It is interesting to note, however, that when a simple *t*-test is used to compare the means for Italians and Jews on each dimension and social class is not controlled, Jewish boys have significantly higher scores ($p<.05$) on Parental Regard for Judgment and Italian boys are higher on Permissiveness in Age-Related Activities.

Thus, differences exist between the two ethnic groups (using *t*-test) with regard to two dimensions of independence but the differences do not exist when social class is controlled. The differential social class distribution of the two groups accounts for this result. It appears, then, that both groups have become assimilated into the class cultures of American society, corroborating Davis' hypothesis that "class cultures are (so strong) that they tend to obliterate differences in the national cultures of foreign-born white groups in this country."[18] To say that there are no cultural differences between the two groups would, however, be erroneous. The differential class distribution of Italians and Jews undoubtedly reflects differences in their

[15]The procedure used to compute individual scores for each dimension required the calculation of normalized standard scores for the response categories in each questionnaire item. A weight was assigned to each response category in a particular item, this weight being a normalized standard score derived in the manner described by Allen L. Edwards, *Statistical Methods for the Behavioral Sciences*, New York: Rinehart, 1954, pp. 107–11. In order to take into account the factor loading that was determined from the factor analysis, each response category weight was multiplied by the factor loading for the particular item and divided by the standard deviation of the distribution of responses to the particular item. To eliminate negative scores an arbitrary constant of 100 was added to all scores.

[16]In order to correct for disproportionality in the number of Italian and Jewish cases within each class and the absence of any Jewish cases in Class V, the analysis of variance method used in that described by George W. Snedecor, *Statistical Methods*, Ames: Iowa State College Press, 1946, pp. 189–290. This method takes into account disproportionate numbers and requires subtraction of one degree of freedom for the cell with no entry.

[17]Although it would be desirable in the interests of reliability to have more items included in each of the factors, given the design of the research this was not possible. Caution should be exercised in interpreting the results of the *F* tests reported below since individual scale scores for each factor are based on only a few items.

[18]Allison Davis, "Socialization and Adolescent Personality," in Guy E. Swanson, Theodore M. Newcomb, and Eugene L. Hartley (Eds.), *Readings in Social Psychology*, New York: Henry Holt, 1952, p. 522.

Table 5. Mean of Scale Scores for Italian and Jewish Adolescents for each Dimension of Independence by Social Class

Social Class	Permissiveness in Outside Activities Ital.	Jews	$\bar{Y}$	Parental Regard for Judgment Ital.	Jews	$\bar{Y}$	Activities with Status Implications Ital.	Jews	$\bar{Y}$	Permissiveness in Age-Related Activities Ital.	Jews	$\bar{Y}$	*N* Ital.	Jews
I and II	80	97	95	137	119	120	134	104	106	89	88	88	2	23
III	103	97	99	113	117	116	101	115	111	92	91	91	17	37
IV	102	90	101	88	107	89	103	102	103	106	96	105	110	7
V	110	—	110	95	—	95	105	—	105	120	—	120	48	—
$\bar{X}$	104	96		93	117		104	110		108	91		177	67
F between ethnics *df* 1,236	.80			.47			.59			.35				
F between classes *df* 3,236	1.09			1.73			.37			5.06[a]				

[a]Indicates a statistically significant difference, $p < .05$.

cultural backgrounds that operated to produce greater class achievement for Jews. The investigation of such factors is another research problem but the present findings suggest that independence from parental control does not distinguish the two groups. It is probably not capable of explaining the continuation of differences in social class achievement if the Jewish boys follow their fathers' pattern and outstrip Italian boys in class achievement.

Social Classes

The second hypothesis to be tested was stated in the null form: There are no differences between social classes with regard to the degree of independence from parental control granted the adolescent boy.

This hypothesis was tested using all cases, Italian, Jewish and Other Ethnics. The category Other Ethnics was not analyzed by specific ethnic background of the subjects.[19] The analysis of variance, single variable of classification was used to test the differences between social classes. Once again, four separate tests were made, one for each dimension of independence.

Table 6 presents the mean scores for each social class for each scale measuring the dimensions of independence. Significant differences are observed as follows: the *lower* social classes have *higher* scores on Permissiveness in Outside Activities (Factor 1) and Permissiveness in Age-Related Activities (Factor 4). For both of these dimensions there is a gradual progression from low to high mean scores. The *higher* social classes have significantly *higher* scores on Parental Regard for Judgment (Factor 2).

It is of importance to note that the analysis of variance tests based on data in Table 5 comparing social classes while controlling for Italian and Jewish ethnic background reveal no significant differences for any of the dimensions of independence except Permissiveness in Age-Related Activi-

Table 6. Mean of Scale Scores for All Ethnics Combined for each Dimension of Independence by Social Class

Social Class	Permissiveness in Outside Activities	Parental Regard for Judgment	Activities with Status Implications	Permissiveness in Age-Related Activities	*N*[b]
I and II	90	121	102	86	65
III	98	112	104	92	111
IV	100	91	97	103	224
V	108	94	104	108	61
F between classes *df* 3,457	4.21[a]	9.51[a]	1.06	16.89[a]	461

[a]Indicates a statistically significant difference, $p < .05$.

[b]A total of 15 cases of unknown social class, 1 Jewish, 5 Italian, and 9 Other Ethnics, are omitted from analysis.

[19]Since ethnic background was not determined, cases of mixed ethnic marriages involving persons other than Jews or Italians, are included. Other controls are similar.

ties. When ethnic groups are combined and ethnicity is not controlled, differences between social classes then appear for Permissiveness in Outside Activities and Parental Regard for Judgment as well as for Permissiveness in Age-Related Activities. This finding suggests that comparisons of social classes based on only two ethnic groups, which differ as greatly as do the ones studied here, are not reliable indicators of the true range of class differences in the total population. In addition, it is indicated that ethnic comparisons must always take into account class differences.

Although the findings from research on adolescents have been inconclusive, the present findings with regard to social classes do seem to be comparable to the conclusions of many studies of child rearing practices.[20] Such studies have found that the middle classes are more positively concerned with fostering independence in their children but are less permissive than lower-class parents. They expect the child to assume responsibilities at an earlier age than do lower-class parents. Life in lower-class families, on the other hand, is reportedly "less strictly organized and fewer demands are made upon (the children)," according to Ericson.[21] Our findings show that the less rigid standards in the lower classes lead to a greater independence, that is, the adolescent boy scores higher on Permissiveness in Outside Activities and Permissiveness in Age-Related Activities. These dimensions of independence seem to reflect the relaxation of controls rather than a positive training for independence.

The lower amount of independence granted by middle-class families in these two dimensions seems to reflect their deliberate attempts to socialize anxiety[22] into the adolescent. The maintenance of supervision and the withdrawal of approval serve to make the adolescent more aware of the importance of "proper" behavior, i.e., conformity to class standards. In addition, discussing family problems, explaining the reasons for parental commands, and asking for his opinion (items included in Parental Regard for Judgment), may also be instrumental in socializing anxiety. By encouraging, listening to and respecting the son's opinions in discussions parents not only have the opportunity to establish rules of conduct but also to test and check the degree of acceptance of these standards by the son. The higher scores on Parental Regard for Judgment in the middle classes may indicate that the adolescent son has become sufficiently socialized to be able to discuss the pros and cons of various decisions with his parents even though the relaxation of controls over his behavior has not yet occurred to the same extent

[20]Allison Davis and Robert Havighurst, "Social Class and Color Differences in Child Rearing," *American Sociological Review,* 11 (December 1946) pp. 698–710; Davis, "Socialization and Adolescent Personality," *op. cit.,* pp. 520–31; Martha C. Ericson, "Social Status and Child Rearing Practices," in Theodore Newcomb and Eugene L. Hartley (Eds.), *Readings in Social Psychology,* New York: Henry Holt, 1947, pp. 494–501; and Arnold Green, "The Middle Class Male Child and Neurosis," *American Sociological Review,* 11 (February, 1946), pp. 31–41.

[21]Ericson, *op. cit.,* p. 501.

[22]Davis, "Socialization and Adolescent Personality," *op. cit.,* describes this process.

that it has in the lower classes. Parental Regard for Judgment is part of the training for independence and provides continuing opportunities for the parents to establish and reinforce rules of conduct. It is perhaps this dimension of independence that is referred to when it is noted that the middle classes train for independence.

An additional interpretation is that family discussions serve the function of inducing greater conformity to family norms. In discussions the son has a chance to voice his opinions and to test his ideas *vis-à-vis* those of his parents. After discussions are concluded, greater conformity (i.e., less permissiveness) may result in that the son, by sharing in the decision, has incorporated it as his own and is more willing to abide by it.

An analogous process has been observed in small group studies. Given the existence of democratic values in our society, an effective method of motivating conformity in individuals is to provide them with the opportunity to participate in decisions concerning their activities. The group dynamics and the human relations in industry approaches stress the idea that high member participation in decision making leads to high morale and greater conformity to group norms by individual members.[23]

The present finding may thus be a specific case of a more general group process. The group in this case is the family and not a work group or laboratory group. High participation on the part of the members, especially the son, leads to greater conformity to family norms. The price for high "independence" in the sense of inclusion in family decisions is having to abide by those family decisions, which may then result in low "independence" in the sense of less permissiveness.

One suggestion that can be made on the basis of the interpretations advanced here is that a revision of the concept of independence is indicated. Independence may involve either permissiveness stemming from few controls being exerted over a person's behavior—or responsibility. Responsibility refers to the individual's inclusion in the decision making process. These two aspects of independence may be negatively correlated in the area of adolescent–parent relationships and either, but perhaps not both, should be used as a measure of "independence from parental control."

Summary

A questionnaire was used to obtain information from a sample of adolescent boys in the New Haven high schools. The Southern Italian and Eastern European Jewish ethnic groups were selected for study.

Factor analysis of 19 questionnaire items revealed four dimensions of

[23]Representative of this approach are Ronald Lippitt, *Training in Community Relations,* New York: Harper and Brothers, 1949; Kurt Lewin, "Group Decision and Social Change," in Swanson, Newcomb and Hartley, *op. cit.,* pp. 459–73; and Lester Coch and John R. P. French, "Overcoming Resistance to Change," *Human Relations,* 1 (August 1948), pp. 512–32.

the variable independence from parental control, which were not all positively intercorrelated.

When social class was controlled, no significant differences between the scores of Italian and Jewish adolescents on any of the dimensions of independence were observed.

When social classes were compared, adding other ethnic groups to the comparison, significant differences were observed for three of the four dimensions of independence. Lower class families appear to be more permissive as evidenced by the adolescents' higher scores on Permissiveness in Outside Activities and Permissiveness in Age-Related Activities. Adolescents in the middle classes score higher on Parental Regard for Judgment but are nevertheless carefully supervised in other activities.

*The Theoretical Importance of Love**

William J. Goode

Because love often determines the intensity of an attraction[1] toward or away from an intimate relationship with another person, it can become one element in a decision or action.[2] Nevertheless, serious sociological attention has only infrequently been given to love. Moreover, analyses of love generally have been confined to mate choice in the Western World, while the structural importance of love has been for the most part ignored. The present paper views love in a broad perspective, focusing on the structural patterns by which societies keep in check the potentially disruptive effect of love relationships on mate choice and stratification systems.

Reprinted by permission of the author and the publisher, The American Sociological Association, from *American Sociological Review* 24 (February 1959):38–47.

*This paper was completed under a grant (No. M–2526–S) by the National Institute of Mental Health.

[1]On the psychological level, the motivational power of both love and sex is intensified by this curious fact (which I have not seen remarked on elsewhere): Love is the most projective of emotions, as sex is the most projective of drives; only with great difficulty can the attracted person believe that the object of his love or passion does not and will not reciprocate the feeling at all. Thus, the person may carry his action quite far, before accepting a rejection as genuine.

[2]I have treated decision analysis extensively in an unpublished paper by that title.

Types of Literature on Love

For obvious reasons, the printed material on love is immense. For our present purposes, it may be classified as follows:

1. Poetic, humanistic, literary, erotic, pornographic: By far the largest body of all literature on love views it as a sweeping experience. The poet arouses our sympathy and empathy. The essayist enjoys, and asks the reader to enjoy, the interplay of people in love. The storyteller—Boccaccio, Chaucer, Dante—pulls back the curtain of human souls and lets the reader watch the intimate lives of others caught in an emotion we all know. Others—Vatsyayana, Ovid, William IX Count of Poitiers and Duke of Aquitaine, Marie de France, Andreas Capellanus—have written how-to-do-it books, that is, how to conduct oneself in love relations, to persuade others to succumb to one's love wishes, or to excite and satisfy one's sex partner.[3]

2. Marital counseling: Many modern sociologists have commented on the importance of romantic love in America and its lesser importance in other societies, and have disparaged it as a poor basis for marriage, or as immaturity. Perhaps the best known of these arguments are those of Ernest R. Mowrer, Ernest W. Burgess, Mabel A. Elliott, Andrew G. Truxal, Francis E. Merrill, and Ernest R. Groves.[4] The antithesis of romantic love, in such analyses, is "conjugal" love; the love between a settled, domestic couple.

A few sociologists, remaining within this same evaluative context, have instead claimed that love also has salutary effects in our society. Thus, for example, William L. Kolb[5] has tried to demonstrate that the marital counselors who attack romantic love are really attacking some fundamental values of our larger society, such as individualism, freedom, and personality growth. Beigel[6] has argued that if the female is sexually repressed, only the

[3]Vatsyayana, *The Kama Sutra,* Delhi: Rajkamal, 1948; Ovid, "The Loves," and "Remedies of Love," in *The Art of Love,* Cambridge, Mass.: Harvard University Press, 1939; Andreas Capellanus, *The Art of Courtly Love,* translated by John J. Parry, New York: Columbia University Press, 1941; Paul Tuffrau, editor, *Marie de France: Les Lais de Marie de France,* Paris L'edition d'art, 1925; see also Julian Harris, *Marie de France,* New York: Institute of French Studies, 1930, esp. Chapter 3. All authors but the first *also* had the goal of writing literature.

[4]Ernest R. Mowrer, *Family Disorganization,* Chicago: The University of Chicago Press, 1927, pp. 158–65; Ernest W. Burgess and Harvey J. Locke, *The Family,* New York: American Book, 1953, pp. 436–37; Mabel A. Elliott and Francis E. Merrill, *Social Disorganization,* New York: Harper, 1950, pp. 366–84; Andrew G. Truxal and Francis E. Merrill, *The Family in American Culture,* New York: Prentice-Hall, 1947, pp. 120–24, 507–9; Ernest R. Groves and Gladys Hoagland Groves, *The Contemporary American Family,* New York: Lippincott, 1947, pp. 321–24.

[5]William L. Kolb, "Sociologically Established Norms and Democratic Values," *Social Forces,* 26 (May, 1948), pp. 451–56.

[6]Hugo G. Beigel, "Romantic Love," *American Sociological Review,* 16 (June, 1951), pp. 326–34.

psychotherapist or love can help her overcome her inhibitions. He claims further that one influence of love in our society is that it extenuates illicit sexual relations; he goes on to assert: "Seen in proper perspective, [love] has not only done no harm as a prerequisite to marriage, but it has mitigated the impact that a too-fast-moving and unorganized conversion to new socio-economic constellations has had upon our whole culture and it has saved monogamous marriage from complete disorganization."

In addition, there is widespread comment among marriage analysts, that in a rootless society, with few common bases for companionship, romantic love holds a couple together long enough to allow them to begin marriage. That is, it functions to attract people powerfully together, and to hold them through the difficult first months of the marriage, when their different backgrounds would otherwise make an adjustment troublesome.

3. Although the writers cited above concede the structural importance of love implicitly, since they are arguing that it is either harmful or helpful to various values and goals of our society, a third group has given explicit if unsystematic attention to its structural importance. Here, most of the available propositions point to the functions of love, but a few deal with the conditions under which love relationships occur. They include:

(1) An implicit or assumed descriptive proposition is that love as a common prelude to and basis of marriage is rare, perhaps to be found as a pattern only in the United States.

(2) Most explanations of the conditions which create love are psychological, stemming from Freud's notion that love is "aim-inhibited sex."[7] This idea is expressed, for example, by Waller who says that love is an idealized passion which develops from the frustration of sex.[8] This proposition, although rather crudely stated and incorrect as a general explanation, is widely accepted.

(3) Of course, a predisposition to love is created by the socialization experience. Thus some textbooks on the family devote extended discussion to the ways in which our society socializes for love. The child, for example, is told that he or she will grow up to fall in love with someone, and early attempts are made to pair the child with children of the opposite sex. There is much joshing of children about falling in love; myths and stories about love and courtship are heard by children; and so on.

(4) A further proposition (the source of which I have not been able to locate) is that, in a society in which a very close attachment between parent and child prevails, a love complex is necessary in order to motivate the child to free him from his attachment to his parents.

(5) Love is also described as one final or crystallizing element in the decision to marry, which is otherwise structured by factors such as class, ethnic origin, religion, education, and residence.

(6) Parsons has suggested three factors which "underlie the prominence of the romantic context in our culture": (a) the youth culture frees the in-

[7]Sigmund Freud, *Group Psychology and the Analysis of the Ego,* London: Hogarth, 1922, p. 72.

[8]Willard Waller, *The Family,* New York: Dryden, 1938, pp. 189–92.

dividual from family attachments, thus permitting him to fall in love; (b) love is a substitute for the interlocking of kinship roles found in other societies, and thus motivates the individual to conform to proper marital role behavior; and (c) the structural isolation of the family so frees the married partners' affective inclinations that they are able to love one another.[9]

(7) Robert F. Winch has developed a theory of "complementary needs" which essentially states that the underlying dynamic in the process of falling in love is an interaction between (a) the perceived psychological attributes of one individual and (b) the complementary psychological attributes of the person falling in love, such that the needs of the latter are felt to be met by the perceived attributes of the former and *vice versa.* These needs are derived from Murray's list of personality characteristics. Winch thus does not attempt to solve the problem of why our society has a love complex, but how it is that specific individuals fall in love with each other rather than with someone else.[10]

(8) Winch and others have also analyzed the effect of love upon various institutions or social patterns: Love themes are prominently displayed in the media of entertainment and communication, in consumption patterns, and so on.[11]

4. Finally, there is the cross-cultural work of anthropologists, who in the main have ignored love as a factor of importance in kinship patterns. The implicit understanding seems to be that love as a pattern is found only in the United States, although of course individual cases of love are sometimes recorded. The term "love" is practically never found in indexes of anthropological monographs on specific societies or in general anthropology textbooks. It is perhaps not an exaggeration to say that Lowie's comment of a generation ago would still be accepted by a substantial number of anthropologists:

> But of love among savages? . . . Passion, of course, is taken for granted; affection, which many travelers vouch for, might be conceded; but Love? Well, the romantic sentiment occurs in simpler conditions, as with us—in fiction. . . . So Love exists for the savage as it does for ourselves—in adolescence, in fiction, among the poetically minded.[12]

A still more skeptical opinion is Linton's scathing sneer:

> All societies recognize that there are occasional violent, emotional attachments between persons of opposite sex, but our present American culture is practically the only one which has attempted to capitalize these, and make

[9]Talcott Parsons, *Essays in Sociological Theory,* Glencoe, Ill.: Free Press, 1949, pp. 187–89.

[10]Robert F. Winch, *Mate Selection,* New York: Harper, 1958.

[11]See, e.g., Robert F. Winch, *The Modern Family,* New York: Holt, 1952, Chapter 14.

[12]Robert H. Lowie, "Sex and Marriage," in John F. McDermott, editor, *The Sex Problem in Modern Society,* New York: Modern Library, 1931, p. 146.

them the basis for marriage. . . . The hero of the modern American movie is always a romantic lover, just as the hero of the old Arab epic is always an epileptic. A cynic may suspect that in any ordinary population the percentage of individuals with a capacity for romantic love of the Hollywood type was about as large as that of persons able to throw genuine epileptic fits.[13]

In Murdock's book on kinship and marriage there is almost no mention, if any, of love.[14] Should we therefore conclude that, cross-culturally, love is not important, and thus cannot be of great importance structurally? If there is only one significant case, perhaps it is safe to view love as generally unimportant in social structure and to concentrate rather on the nature and functions of romantic love within the Western societies in which love is obviously prevalent. As brought out below, however, many anthropologists have in fact described love *patterns*. And one of them, Max Gluckman,[15] has recently subsumed a wide range of observations under the broad principle that love relationships between husband and wife estrange the couple from their kin, who therefore try in various ways to undermine that love. This principle is applicable to many more societies (for example, China and India) than Gluckman himself discusses.

The Problem and its Conceptual Clarification

The preceding propositions (except those denying that love is distributed widely) can be grouped under two main questions: What are the consequences of romantic love in the United States? How is the emotion of love aroused or created in our society? The present paper deals with the first question. For theoretical purposes both questions must be reformulated, however, since they implicitly refer only to our peculiar system of romantic love. Thus: (1) In what ways do various love patterns fit into the social structure, especially into the systems of mate choice and stratification? (2) What are the structural conditions under which a range of love patterns occurs in various societies? These are overlapping questions, but their starting point and assumptions are different. The first assumes that love relationships are a universal psychosocial possibility, and that different social systems make different adjustments to their potential disruptiveness. The second does not take love for granted, and supposes rather that such relationships will be rare unless certain structural factors are present. Since in both cases the analysis need not depend upon the correctness of the assumption, the problem may be chosen arbitrarily. Let us begin with the first.[16]

We face at once the problem of defining "love." Here, love is defined

[13]Ralph Linton, *The Study of Man,* New York: Appleton-Century, 1936, p. 175.

[14]George Peter Murdock, *Social Structure,* New York: Macmillan, 1949.

[15]Max Gluckman, *Custom and Conflict in Africa,* Oxford: Basil Blackwell, 1955, Chapter 3.

[16]I hope to deal with the second problem in another paper.

as a strong emotional attachment, a cathexis, between adolescents or adults of opposite sexes, with at least the components of sex desire and tenderness. Verbal definitions of this emotional relationship are notoriously open to attack; this one is no more likely to satisfy critics than others. Agreement is made difficult by value judgments: one critic would exclude anything but "true" love, another casts out "infatuation," another objects to "puppy love," while others would separate sex desire from love because sex presumably is degrading. Nevertheless, most of us have had the experience of love, just as we have been greedy, or melancholy, or moved by hate (defining "true" hate seems not to be a problem). The experience can be referred to without great ambiguity, and a refined measure of various degrees of intensity or purity of love is unnecessary for the aims of the present analysis.

Since love may be related in diverse ways to the social structure, it is necessary to forego the dichotomy of "romantic love—no romantic love" in favor of a continuum or range between polar types. At one pole, a strong love attraction is socially viewed as a laughable or tragic aberration; at the other, it is mildly shameful to marry without being in love with one's intended spouse. This is a graduation from negative sanction to positive approval ranging at the same time from low or almost nonexistent institutionalization of love to high institutionalization.

The urban middle classes of contemporary Western society, especially in the United States, are found toward the latter pole. Japan and China, in spite of the important movement toward European patterns, fall toward the pole of low institutionalization. Village and urban India is farther toward the center, for there the ideal relationship has been one which at least generated love after marriage, and sometimes after betrothal, in contrast with the mere respect owed between Japanese and Chinese spouses.[17] Greece after Alexander, Rome of the Empire, and perhaps the later period of the Roman Republic as well, are near the center, but somewhat toward the pole of institutionalization, for love matches appear to have increased in frequency—a trend denounced by moralists.[18]

This conceptual continuum helps to clarify our problem and to interpret the propositions reviewed above. Thus it may be noted, first, that individual love relationships may occur even in societies in which love is viewed as irrelevant to mate choice and excluded from the decision to marry. As Linton conceded, some violent love attachments may be found in any society. In our own, the Song of Solomon, Jacob's love of Rachel, and

[17]Tribal India, of course, is too heterogeneous to place in any one position on such a continuum. The question would have to be answered for each tribe. Obviously it is of less importance here whether China and Japan, in recent decades, have moved "two points over" toward the opposite pole of high approval of love relationships as a basis for marriage than that both systems as classically described viewed love as generally a tragedy; and love was supposed to be irrelevant to marriage, i.e., noninstitutionalized. The continuum permits us to place a system at some position, once we have the descriptive data.

[18]See Ludwig Friedländer, *Roman Life and Manners under the Early Empire* (Seventh Edition), translated by A. Magnus, New York: Dutton, 1908, Vol. 1, Chapter 5, "The Position of Women."

Michal's love for David are classic tales. The Mahabharata, the great Indian epic, includes love themes. Romantic love appears early in Japanese literature, and the use of Mt. Fuji as a locale for the suicide of star crossed lovers is not a myth invented by editors of tabloids. There is the familiar tragic Chinese story to be found on the traditional "willowplate," with its lovers transformed into doves. And so it goes—individual love relationships seem to occur everywhere. But this fact does not change the position of a society on the continuum.

Second, reading both Linton's and Lowie's comments in this new conceptual context reduces their theoretical importance, for they are both merely saying that people do not *live by* the romantic complex, here or anywhere else. Some few couples in love will brave social pressures, physical dangers, or the gods themselves, but nowhere is this usual. Violent, self-sufficient love is not common anywhere. In this respect, of course, the U.S. is not set apart from other systems.

Third, we can separate a *love pattern* from the romantic love *complex*. Under the former, love is a permissible, expected prelude to marriage, and a usual element of courtship—thus, at about the center of the continuum, but toward the pole of institutionalization. The romantic love complex (one pole of the continuum) includes, in addition, an ideological prescription that falling in love is a highly desirable basis of courtship and marriage; love is strongly institutionalized.[19] In contemporary United States, many individuals would even claim that entering marriage without being in love requires some such rationalization as asserting that one is too old for such romances or that one must "think of practical matters like money." To be sure, both anthropologists and sociologists often exaggerate the American commitment to romance;[20] nevertheless, a behavioral and value complex of this type is found here.

But this complex is rare. Perhaps only the following cultures possess the romantic love value complex: modern urban United States, Northwestern Europe, Polynesia, and the European nobility of the eleventh and twelfth centuries.[21] Certainly, it is to be found in no other major civiliza-

[19]For a discussion of the relation between behavior patterns and the process of institutionalization, see my *After Divorce,* Glencoe, Ill.: Free Press, 1956, Chapter 15.

[20]See Ernest W. Burgess and Paul W. Wallin, *Engagement and Marriage,* New York: Lippincott, 1953, Chapter 7 for the extent to which even the engaged are not blind to the defects of their beloveds. No one has ascertained the degree to which various age and sex groups in our society actually believe in some form of the ideology.

Similarly, Margaret Mead in *Coming of Age in Samoa,* New York: Modern Library, 1953, rates Manu'an love as shallow, and though these Samoans give much attention to love-making, she asserts that they laughed with incredulous contempt at Romeo and Juliet (pp. 155–56). Though the individual sufferer showed jealousy and anger, the Manu'ans believed that a new love would quickly cure a betrayed lover (pp. 105–8). It is possible that Mead failed to understand the shallowness of love in our own society: Romantic love is, "in our civilization, inextricably bound up with ideas of monogamy, exclusiveness, jealousy, and undeviating fidelity" (p. 105). But these are *ideas* and ideology; *behavior* is rather different.

[21]I am preparing an analysis of this case. The relation of "courtly love" to social structure is complicated.

tion. On the other hand, the *love pattern,* which views love as a basis for the final decision to marry, may be relatively common.

Why Love Must Be Controlled

Since strong love attachments apparently can occur in any society and since (as we shall show) love is frequently a basis for and prelude to marriage, it must be controlled or channeled in some way. More specifically, the stratification and lineage patterns would be weakened greatly if love's potentially disruptive effects were not kept in check. The importance of this situation may be seen most clearly by considering one of the major functions of the family, status placement, which in every society links the structures of stratification, kinship lines, and mate choice. (To show how the very similar comments which have been made about sex are not quite correct would take us too far afield; in any event, to the extent that they are correct, the succeeding analysis applies equally to the control of sex.)

Both the child's placement in the social structure and choice of mates are socially important because both placement and choice link two kinship lines together. Courtship or mate choice, therefore, cannot be ignored by either family or society. To permit random mating would mean radical change in the existing social structure. If the family as a unit of society is important, then mate choice is too.

Kinfolk or immediate family can disregard the question of who marries whom, only if a marriage is not seen as a link between kin lines, only if no property, power, lineage honor, totemic relationships, and the like are believed to flow from the kin lines through the spouses to their offspring. Universally, however, these are believed to follow kin lines. Mate choice thus has consequences for the social structure. But love may affect mate choice. Both mate choice and love, therefore, are too important to be left to children.

The Control of Love

Since considerable energy and resources may be required to push youngsters who are in love into proper role behavior, love must be controlled *before* it appears. Love relationships must either be kept to a small number or they must be so directed that they do not run counter to the approved kinship linkages. There are only a few institutional patterns by which this control is achieved.

1. Certainly the simplest, and perhaps the most widely used, structural pattern for coping with this problem is child marriage. If the child is betrothed, married, or both before he has had any opportunity to interact intimately as an adolescent with other children, then he has no resources with which to oppose the marriage. He cannot earn a living, he is physically weak and is socially dominated by his elders. Moreover, strong love attach-

ments occur only rarely before puberty. An example of this pattern was to be found in India, where the young bride went to live with her husband in a marriage which was not physically consummated until much later, within his father's household.[22]

2. Often, child marriage is linked with a second structural pattern, in which the kinship rules define rather closely a class of eligible future spouses. The marriage is determined by birth within narrow limits. Here, the major decision, which is made by elders, is *when* the marriage is to occur. Thus, among the Murngin, *galle,* the father's sister's child, is scheduled to marry *due,* the mother's brother's child.[23] In the case of the "four-class" double descent system, each individual is a member of *both* a matri-moiety and a patri-moiety and must marry someone who belongs to neither; the four-classes are (1) ego's own class, (2) those whose matri-moiety is the same as ego's but whose patri-moiety is different, (3) those who are in ego's patri-moiety but not in his matri-moiety, and (4) those who are in neither of ego's moieties, that is, who are in the cell diagonally from his own.[24] Problems arise at times under these systems if the appropriate kinship cell—for example, parallel cousin or cross-cousin—is empty.[25] But nowhere, apparently, is the definition so rigid as to exclude some choice and, therefore, some dickering, wrangling, and haggling between the elders of the two families.

3. A society can prevent widespread development of adolescent love relationships by socially isolating young people from potential mates, whether eligible or ineligible as spouses. Under such a pattern, elders can arrange the marriages of either children or adolescents with little likelihood that their plans will be disrupted by love attachments. Obviously, this arrangement cannot operate effectively in most primitive societies, where youngsters see one another rather frequently.[26]

[22]Frieda M. Das, *Purdah,* New York: Vanguard, 1932; Kingsley Davis, *The Population of India and Pakistan,* Princeton: Princeton University Press, 1951, p. 112. There was a widespread custom of taking one's bride from a village other than one's own.

[23]W. Lloyd Warner, *Black Civilization,* New York: Harper, 1937, pp. 82–84. They may also become "sweethearts" at puberty; see pp. 86–89.

[24]See Murdock, *op. cit.,* pp. 53 ff. *et passim* for discussions of double-descent.

[25]One adjustment in Australia was for the individuals to leave the tribe for a while, usually eloping, and then to return "reborn" under a different and now appropriate kinship designation. In any event, these marital prescriptions did not prevent love entirely. As Malinowski shows in his early summary of the Australian family systems, although every one of the tribes used the technique of infant betrothal (and close prescription of mate), no tribe was free of elopements, between either the unmarried or the married, and the "motive of sexual love" was always to be found in marriages by elopement. B. Malinowski, *The Family Among the Australian Aborigines,* London: University of London Press, 1913, p. 83.

[26]This pattern was apparently achieved in Manus, where on first menstruation the girl was removed from her playmates and kept at "home"—on stilts over a lagoon—under the close supervision of elders. The Manus were prudish, and love occurred rarely or never. Margaret Mead, "Growing Up in New Guinea," in *From the South Seas,* New York: Morrow, 1939, pp. 163–66, 208.

Not only is this pattern more common in civilizations than in primitive societies, but is found more frequently in the upper social strata. *Social* segregation is difficult unless it is supported by physical segregation—the harem of Islam, the zenana of India[27] or by a large household system with individuals whose duty it is to supervise nubile girls. Social segregation is thus expensive. Perhaps the best known example of simple social segregation was found in China, where youthful marriages took place between young people who had not previously met because they lived in different villages; they could not marry fellow-villagers since ideally almost all inhabitants belonged to the same *tsu*.[28]

It should be emphasized that the primary function of physical or social isolation in these cases is to minimize informal or intimate social interaction. Limited social contacts of a highly ritualized or formal type in the presence of elders, as in Japan, have a similar, if less extreme, result.[29]

4. A fourth type of pattern seems to exist, although it is not clear cut; and specific cases shade off toward types three and five. Here, there is close supervision by duennas or close relatives, but not actual social segregation. A high value is placed on female chastity (which perhaps is the case in every major civilization until its "decadence") viewed either as the product of self-restraint, as among the 17th Century Puritans, or as a marketable commodity. Thus love as play is not developed; marriage is supposed to be considered by the young as a duty and a possible family alliance. This pattern falls between types three and five because love is permitted before marriage, but only between eligibles. Ideally, it occurs only between a betrothed couple, and, except as marital love, there is no encouragement for it to appear at all. Family elders largely make the specific choice of mate, whether or not intermediaries carry out the arrangements. In the preliminary stages youngsters engage in courtship under supervision, with the understanding that this will permit the development of affection prior to marriage.

I do not believe that the empirical data show where this pattern is prevalent, outside of Western Civilization. The West is a special case, be-

[27]See Das, *op. cit.*

[28]For the activities of the *tsu*, see Hsien Chin Hu, *The Common Descent Group in China and Its Functions,* New York: Viking Fund Studies in Anthropology, 10 (1948). For the marriage process, see Marion J. Levy, *The Family Revolution in Modern China,* Cambridge: Harvard University Press, 1949, pp. 87–107. See also Olga Lang, *Chinese Family and Society,* New Haven: Yale University Press, 1946, for comparisons between the old and new systems. In one-half of 62 villages in Ting Hsien Experimental District in Hopei, the largest clan included 50 per cent of the families; in 25 per cent of the villages, the two largest clans held over 90 per cent of the families; I am indebted to Robert M. Marsh who has been carrying out a study of Ching mobility partly under my direction for this reference: F. C. H. Lee, *Ting Hsien, She-hui K'ai-K'uang t'iao-ch'a,* Peiping: Chung-hua p'ing-min Chiao-yu ts'u-chin hui, 1932, p. 54. See also Sidney Gamble, *Ting Hsien: A North China Rural Community,* New York: International Secretariat of the Institute of Pacific Relations, 1954.

[29]For Japan, see Shidzué Ishimoto, *Facing Two Ways,* New York: Farrar and Rinehart, 1935, Chapters 6, 8; John F. Embree, *Suye Mura,* Chicago: University of Chicago Press, 1950, Chapters 3, 6.

cause of its peculiar relationship to Christianity, in which from its earliest days in Rome there has been a complex tension between asceticism and love. This type of limited love marked French, English, and Italian upper class family life from the 11th to the 14th Centuries, as well as 17th Century Puritanism in England and New England.[30]

5. The fifth type of pattern permits or actually encourages love relationships, and love is a commonly expected element in mate choice. Choice in this system is *formally* free. In their 'teens youngsters begin their love play, with or without consummating sexual intercourse, within a group of peers. They may at times choose love partners whom they and others do not consider suitable spouses. Gradually, however, their range of choice is narrowed and eventually their affections center on one individual. This person is likely to be more eligible as a mate according to general social norms, and as judged by peers and parents, than the average individual with whom the youngster formerly indulged in love play.

For reasons that are not yet clear, this pattern is nearly always associated with a strong development of an adolescent peer group system, although the latter may occur without the love pattern. One source of social control, then, is the individual's own 'teen age companions, who persistently rate the present and probable future accomplishments of each individual.[31]

Another source of control lies with the parents of both boy and girl. In our society, parents threaten, cajole, wheedle, bribe, and persuade their children to "go with the right people," during both the early love play and later courtship phases.[32] Primarily, they seek to control love relationships by influencing the informal social contacts of their children: moving to appropriate neighborhoods and schools, giving parties and helping to make out invitation lists, by making their children aware that certain individuals have ineligibility traits (race, religion, manners, tastes, clothing, and so on).

[30]I do not mean, of course, to restrict this pattern to these times and places, but I am more certain of these. For the Puritans, see Edmund S. Morgan, *The Puritan Family*, Boston: Public Library, 1944. For the somewhat different practices in New York, see Charles E. Ironside, *The Family in Colonial New York*, New York: Columbia University Press, 1942. See also: A. Abram, *English Life and Manners in the Later Middle Ages*, New York: Dutton, 1913, Chapters 4, 10; Emily J. Putnam, *The Lady*, New York: Sturgis and Walton, 1910, Chapter 4; James Gairdner, editor, *The Paston Letters, 1422–1509*, 4 vols., London: Arber, 1872–1875; Eileen Power, "The Position of Women," in C. G. Crump and E. F. Jacobs, editors, *The Legacy of the Middle Ages*, Oxford: Clarendon, 1926, pp. 414–16.

[31]For those who believe that the young in the United States are totally deluded by love, or believe that love outranks every other consideration, see: Ernest W. Burgess and Paul W. Wallin, *Engagement and Marriage*, New York: Lippincott, 1953, pp. 217–238. Note Karl Robert V. Wikman, *Die Einleitung Der Ehe. Acta Academiae Aboensis* (*Humaniora*), 11 (1937), pp. 127 ff. Not only are reputations known because of close association among peers, but songs and poetry are sometimes composed about the girl or boy. Cf., for the Tikopia, Raymond Firth, *We, the Tikopia*, New York: American Book, 1936, pp. 468 ff.; for the Siuai, Douglas L. Oliver, *Solomon Island Society*, Cambridge: Harvard University Press, 1955, pp. 146 ff. The manu'ans made love in groups of three or four couples; cf. Mead, *Coming of Age in Samoa*, *op. cit.*, p. 92.

[32]Marvin B. Sussman, "Parental Participation in Mate Selection and Its Effect upon Family Continuity," *Social Forces*, 32 (October, 1953), pp. 76–81.

Since youngsters fall in love with those with whom they associate, control over informal relationships also controls substantially the focus of affection. The results of such control are well known and are documented in the more than one hundred studies of homogamy in this country: most marriages take place between couples in the same class, religious, and educational levels.

As Robert Wikman has shown in a generally unfamiliar (in the United States) but superb investigation, this pattern was found among 18th Century Swedish farmer adolescents, was widely distributed in other Germanic areas, and extends in time from the 19th Century back to almost certainly the late Middle Ages.[33] In these cases, sexual intercourse was taken for granted, social contact was closely supervised by the peer group, and final consent to marriage was withheld or granted by the parents who owned the land.

Such cases are not confined to Western society. Polynesia exhibits a similar pattern, with some variation from society to society, the best known examples of which are perhaps Mead's Manu'ans and Firth's Tikopia.[34] Probably the most familiar Melanesian cases are the Trobriands and Dobu,[35] where the systems resemble those of the Kiwai Papuans of the Trans-Fly and the Siuai Papuans of the Solomon Islands.[36] Linton found this pattern among the Tanala.[37] Although Radcliffe-Brown holds that the pattern is not common in Africa, it is clearly found among the Nuer, the Kgatla (Tswana-speaking), and the Bavenda (here, without sanctioned sexual intercourse).[38]

A more complete classification, making use of the distinctions suggested in this paper, would show, I believe, that a large minority of known societies exhibit this pattern. I would suggest, moreover, that such a study would reveal that the degree to which love is a usual, expected prelude to marriage is correlated with (1) the degree of free choice of mate permitted

[33]Wikman, *op. cit.*

[34]Mead, *Coming of Age in Samoa, op. cit.*, pp. 97–108; and Firth, *op. cit.*, pp. 520 ff.

[35]Thus Malinowski notes in his "Introduction" to Reo F. Fortune's *The Sorcerers of Dobu,* London: Routledge, 1932, p. xxiii, that the Dobu have similar patterns, the same type of courtship by trial and error, with a gradually tightening union.

[36]Gunnar Landtman, *Kiwai Papuans of the Trans-Fly,* London: Macmillan, 1927, pp. 243 ff.; Oliver, *op. cit.*, pp. 153 ff.

[37]The pattern apparently existed among the Marquesans as well, but since Linton never published a complete description of this Polynesian society, I omit it here. His fullest analysis, cluttered with secondary interpretations, is in Abram Kardiner, *Psychological Frontiers of Society,* New York: Columbia University Press, 1945. For the Tanala, see Ralph Linton, *The Tanala,* Chicago: Field Museum, 1933, pp. 300–303.

[38]Thus, Radcliffe-Brown: "The African does not think of marriage as a union based on romantic love, although beauty as well as character and health are sought in the choice of a wife," in his "Introduction" to A. R. Radcliffe-Brown and W. C. Daryll Ford, editors, *African Systems of Kinship and Marriage,* London: Oxford University Press, 1950, p. 46. For the Nuer, see E. E. Evans-Pritchard, *Kinship and Marriage Among the Nuer,* Oxford: Clarendon, 1951, pp. 49–58. For the Kgatla, see I. Schapera, *Married Life in an African Tribe,* New York: Sheridan, 1941, pp. 55 ff. For the Bavenda, although the report seems incomplete, see Hugh A. Stayt, *The Bavenda,* London: Oxford University Press, 1931, pp. 111 ff., 145 ff., 154.

in the society and (2) the degree to which husband–wife solidarity is the strategic solidarity of the kinship structure.[39]

Love Control and Class

These sociostructural explanations of how love is controlled lead to a subsidiary but important hypothesis: From one society to another, and from one *class* to another within the same society, the sociostructural importance of maintaining kinship lines according to rule will be rated differently by the families within them. Consequently, the degree to which control over mate choice, and therefore over the prevalence of a love pattern among adolescents, will also vary. Since, within any stratified society, this concern with the maintenance of intact and acceptable kin lines will be greater in the upper strata, it follows that noble or upper strata will maintain stricter control over love and courtship behavior than lower strata. The two correlations suggested in the preceding paragraph also apply: husband–wife solidarity is less strategic relative to clan solidarity in the upper than in the lower strata, and there is less free choice of mate.

Thus it is that, although in Polynesia generally most youngsters indulged in considerable love play, princesses were supervised strictly.[40] Similarly, in China lower class youngsters often met their spouses before marriage.[41] In our own society, the "upper upper" class maintains much greater control than the lower strata over the informal social contacts of their nubile young. Even among the Dobu, where there are few controls and little stratification, differences in control exist at the extremes: a child betrothal may be arranged between outstanding gardening families, who try to prevent their youngsters from being entangled with wastrel families.[42] In an-

[39]The second correlation is developed from Marion J. Levy, *The Family Revolution in China,* Cambridge: Harvard University Press, 1949, p. 179. Levy's formulation ties "romantic love" to that solidarity, and is of little use because there is only one case, the Western culture complex. As he states it, it is almost so by definition.

[40]E.g., Mead, *Coming of Age in Samoa, op. cit.,* pp. 79, 92, 97–109. Cf. also Firth, *op. cit.,* pp. 520 ff.

[41]Although one must be cautious about China, this inference seems to be allowable from such comments as the following: "But the old men of China did not succeed in eliminating love from the life of the young women. . . . Poor and middle-class families could not afford to keep men and women in separate quarters, and Chinese also met their cousins. . . . Girls . . . sometimes even served customers in their parents' shops." Olga Lang, *op. cit.,* p. 33. According to Fried, farm girls would work in the fields, and farm girls of ten years and older were sent to the market to sell produce. They were also sent to towns and cities as servants. The peasant or pauper woman was not confined to the home and its immediate environs. Morton H. Fried, *Fabric of Chinese Society,* New York: Praeger, 1953, pp. 59–60. Also, Levy (*op. cit.,* p. 111): "Among peasant girls and among servant girls in gentry households some premarital experience was not uncommon, though certainly frowned upon. The methods of preventing such contact were isolation and chaperonage, both of which, in the 'traditional' picture, were more likely to break down in the two cases named than elsewhere."

[42]Fortune, *op. cit.,* p. 30.

swer to my query about this pattern among the Nuer, Evans-Pritchard writes:

> You are probably right that a wealthy man has more control over his son's affairs than a poor man. A man with several wives has a more authoritarian position in his home. Also, a man with many cattle is in a position to permit or refuse a son to marry, whereas a lad whose father is poor may have to depend on the support of kinsmen. In general, I would say that a Nuer father is not interested in the personal side of things. His son is free to marry any girl he likes and the father does not consider the selection to be his affair until the point is reached when cattle have to be discussed.[43]

The upper strata have much more at stake in the maintenance of the social structure and thus are more strongly motivated to control the courtship and marriage decisions of their young. Correspondingly, their young have much more to lose than lower strata youth, so that upper strata elders *can* wield more power.

Conclusion

In this analysis I have attempted to show the integration of love with various types of social structures. As against considerable contemporary opinion among both sociologists and anthropologists, I suggest that love is a universal psychological potential, which is controlled by a range of five structural patterns, all of which are attempts to see to it that youngsters do not make entirely free choices of their future spouses. Only if kin lines are unimportant, and this condition is found in no society as a whole, will entirely free choice be permitted. Some structural arrangements seek to prevent entirely the outbreak of love, while others harness it. Since the kin lines of the upper strata are of greater social importance to them than those of lower strata are to the lower strata members, the former exercise a more effective control over this choice. Even where there is almost a formally free choice of mate—and I have suggested that this pattern is widespread, to be found among a substantial segment of the earth's societies—this choice is guided by peer group and parents toward a mate who will be acceptable to the kin and friend groupings. The theoretical importance of love is thus to be seen in the sociostructural patterns which are developed to keep it from disrupting existing social arrangements.

[43]Personal letter, dated January 9, 1958. However, the Nuer father can still refuse if he believes the demands of the girl's people are unreasonable. In turn, the girl can cajole her parents to demand less.

5 Deviance and Collective Behavior

Deviance involves rule breaking and rule breakers; collective behavior involves the emergence of new forms of social relationships. In the extreme the two categories are clearly distinguished: criminals and most deviants do not seek to change the social order or to innovate social arrangements; people involved in most social movements, cults, sects, and crowds do not engage in criminal activities. However, because change-oriented activities generate resistance, legal or informal, which leads to legal charges and enforcement against innovators, and because criminal activity is also used to create sociopolitical change (for example, bombings and terrorism), the line between deviance and collective behavior is rather blurred.

Violating some standard of behavior in a complex society is almost inevitable. The normative standards are vague; the expected degree of response, if specified at all, is uncertain; and response is based on the situation in which the violation occurs. We may, in fact, agree with David Matza (1969) that to deviate is natural. The implication of the above is that an act or behavior itself may be less important than people's response to it. For example, a suit was brought during fall 1970 to halt the Michigan–Michigan State football game. A large rock festival had been held in central Michigan in the late summer, and the usual huge crowd of musicians, drug freaks (both buyers and sellers), teeny-boppers, and travelers scandalized the local citizenry. A second hard-rock festival was planned for September 6, but it was cancelled when the county prosecutor obtained a restraining order against it. The suit against the football game was brought by a janitor at the University of Michigan, formerly a student there and an ex-sports editor for the student paper. He stated, "I've decided to file this suit because Governor Millikin and other so-called law and order political figures in this state have selectively applied the law to repress one form of mass culture while allowing another to exist" (quoted in the *Detroit Free Press,* October 9, 1970). After the August rock festival, the governor of the state had said that if drugs and rock festivals were to be synonymous, there would be no more rock festivals in Michigan. Many localities passed ordinances strictly controlling gatherings of 5,000 or more people.

The suit filer charged that college football games were also synonymous with illegal possession of drugs (for example, alcohol); based on affidavits signed by ten people at the previous week's game, the suit charged:

> Adults and minors drank so much beer, wine, and liquor that it required two pickup trucks to haul the bottles away after the game.
>
> Grade school children picked up and drank from discarded half-filled bottles of liquor.
>
> Youths in stands used marijuana and other drugs.
>
> City and county policemen in the stands for the game did not enforce the alcohol and drug laws.
>
> Traffic congestion, complicated by insufficient parking spaces and inebriated drivers, tied up a two-square-mile area before and after the game.
>
> Fans in the stands on several occasions became disorderly and also physically handed both male and female spectators up and down the rows of spectators.

The point of the challenge to the legal system is clear: the behavior of the spectators included many illegal acts at both "festivals." However, one was associated with hippie culture, youth, and immorality, while the other event was characterized as mature, adult, clean fun. A hearing dismissed the suit on the afternoon before the game.

The same is true of a wide variety of illegal acts, something not overlooked by the residents of prisons:

> Most of the guys here have been ditch diggers, assembly-line workers, farm workers, waiters, dock workers, such like that. That's the old filtering process at work. . . . The higher the socio-economic class, the greater the education, and the less it's going to be represented in prison. Most upper- and middle-class criminals are white collar. And the vast majority of white collar criminals don't even get into a courtroom. Out of those who do get hauled into court, a large percentage don't get convicted, and out of those that get convicted, a large percentage get put on probation. That leaves the slobs. . . . We're crude enough to use a crowbar or a pistol, or sleight of hand, instead of more refined

book juggling, misrepresentation, and under the table pay-offs for services rendered. (Griswold et al. 1970, p. 265)

Many sorts of behaviors that might be labeled criminal are not, for the political process operates in the creation of the law as well as in its application. By creating and applying rules, society produces deviants and deviance (socially disapproved categories of behavior).

In the process of labeling deviants, the mass media play an important role. The creation of images and stereotypes clarifies and isolates segments of behavior and certain groups for special attention. Turner and Surace (1956) studied the distribution of negative and positive themes dealing with Mexican-Americans in the *Los Angeles Times* prior to a series of sporadic episodes of violence primarily involving servicemen and Mexican-Americans dressed in "zoot suits," baggy suits with narrow pegged legs and wide padded shoulders. There was no negative shift in the presentation of the symbolic Mexican, but there was development of the "Zooter" symbol, which came to be regarded apart from the positive features of the Mexican culture and heritage of Los Angeles. The Zooter symbol was an omnibus crisis symbol suggesting draft-dodgers, gang attacks, sex crimes, and delinquency. Once established, the Zooter theme allowed the magnification and interpretation of other events; for example, a gang attack would have been described as a zoot-suit attack. As Turner and Surace summarize, ". . . the 'Zooter' symbol was a recasting of many of the elements formerly present and sometimes associated with Mexicans in a new and instantly recognizable guise. This new association of ideas relieved the community of ambivalence and moral obligations and gave sanction to making Mexicans the victims of widespread hostile crowd behavior."

The press is able to allocate space to a given story, to alter placement and size of headlines, to determine how much publicity to give each news story and related feature stories, and to choose the nature and types of emotional words used. Newspapers, as Davis (1952) had shown, can create "crime waves" independently of the actual events. Further, Wilde (1968) investigated the procedures used by one Chicago newspaper to process the news and found that the basic operating assumption of newsmen and the public was that news was made by "officials." A crime story was written from information gathered from the police, not from criminals; a story on disruption was portrayed by interviews with the police and firemen involved, not with rioters. News was made by officials, and attacks, disruptions, and other news were seen through official eyes.

Michael Brown, in an article sympathetic to the plight of the hippies, argues that the media played an important role in sharpening and directing social scorn of the hippies. The media-created image of drug-crazed freaks coalesced the engines of repression; this in turn altered the hippies' own self-image:

> When people are attacked as a group, they change. Individuals in the group may or may not change, but the organization and expression of their collective

> life will be transformed. When the members of a gathering believe that there is grave danger imminent and that opportunities for escape are rapidly diminishing, the group loses its organizational quality. It becomes transformed in panic. This type of change can also occur outside a situation of extreme urgency. When opportunities for mobility or access to needed resources are cut off, people may engage in desperate collective actions. In both cases, the conversion of social form occurs when members of a collectivity are about to be hopelessly locked into undesired and undesirable positions.

In other words, the response of the hippies appears both reasonable and understandable once we realize the repression leveled at them. That which people fear about youth in general is also true of hippies—they are free, or at least they make much of their attempt to be free. Their search for intimacy and spontaneity contrasts with the norm of industrialized societies. Perhaps it is more what they symbolize or express than what they do that leads to the reaction Brown describes in detail. In this sense, the "Hippie" has been subjected to a widespread national campaign that precisely parallels the one that created the negative image of the "Zoot-suiter."

The hippie subculture developed because there were enough resources, ideological materials (symbols and ideologies), and exchanges to permit the development of group consciousness. Other kinds of deviant behavior are not adopted by a group; they are individualistic in nature. Others take a group form but lack an organized ideology. Juvenile gangs are one example. They seem to arise in rapidly changing urban areas where norms and values are in transition and where social controls are relatively weak. Fighting is a means of structuring the group, of giving it a temporary order. The most binding and obligatory norms in a gang are those of fighting and defense of territory and self. The important investment of the person is not in the larger social order, from which he is largely isolated, but in the fighting gang. Keiser discusses a black gang in Chicago (although ganging and gang organization are by no means limited to blacks or to other minorities), which provided self-esteem, identity, and a sense of community and power for young men. Rather than embodying a response to frustration, or to blocked opportunities, these gangs, as Suttles (1969) shows, are the minimal social organization that creates a positive, supportive social base for marginal young. In this sense, do gangs differ greatly from fraternities and sororities in structure, roles, symbols, and activities? Perhaps for this fundamental reason the most effective means of dealing with juvenile gangs has been the detached worker program (in which Keiser, the author of the selection, worked). This program supports young men who associate themselves with gangs in an attempt to forestall gang battles, to provide advice, and to redirect some of the gangs into political or social welfare activity. This effort has been somewhat successful in the Woodlawn area of Chicago.

The Condemnation and Persecution of Hippies

Michael E. Brown

This article is about persecution and terror. It speaks of the Hippie and the temptations of intimacy that the myth of Hippie has made poignant, and it does this to discuss the institutionalization of repression in the United States.

When people are attacked as a group, they change. Individuals in the group may or may not change, but the organization and expression of their collective life will be transformed. When the members of a gathering believe that there is a grave danger imminent and that opportunities for escape are rapidly diminishing, the group loses its organizational quality. It becomes transformed in panic. This type of change can also occur outside a situation of strict urgency: When opportunities for mobility or access to needed resources are cut off, people may engage in desperate collective actions. In both cases, the conversion of social form occurs when members of a collectivity are about to be hopelessly locked into undesired and undesirable positions.

The process is not, however, automatic. The essential ingredient for conversion is social control exercised by external agents on the collectivity itself. The result can be benign, as a panic mob can be converted into a crowd that makes an orderly exit from danger. Or it can be cruel.

The transformation of groups under pressure is of general interest; but there are special cases that are morally critical to any epoch. Such critical cases occur when pressure is persecution, and transformation is destruction. The growth of repressive mechanisms and institutions is a key concern in this time of administrative cruelty. Such is the justification for the present study.

Social Control as Terror

Four aspects of repressive social control such as that experienced by Hippies are important. First, the administration of control is suspicious. It projects a dangerous future and guards against it. It also refuses the risk of inadequate coverage by enlarging the controlled population to include all who might be active in any capacity. Control may or may not be administered with a heavy hand, but it is always a generalization applied to specific instances. It is a rule and thus ends by pulling many fringe innocents into its bailiwick; it creates as it destroys.

Second, the administration of control is a technical problem which depending on its site and object, requires the bringing together of many different agencies that are ordinarily dissociated or mutually hostile. A conglomerate of educational, legal, social welfare, and police organization is highly efficient. The German case demonstrates that. Even more important, it is virtually impossible to oppose control administered under the auspices of such a conglomerate since it includes the countervailing institutions ordinarily available. When this happens control is not only efficient and widespread, but also legitimate, commanding a practical, moral and ideological realm that is truly "one-dimensional."

Third, as time passes, control is applied to a wider and wider range of details, ultimately blanketing its objects' lives. At that point, as Hilberg suggests in his *The Destruction of the European Jews,* the extermination of the forms of lives leads easily to the extermination of the lives themselves. The line between persecution and terror is thin. For the oppressed, life is purged of personal style as every act becomes inexpressive, part of the struggle for survival. The options of a life-style are eliminated at the same time that its proponents are locked into it.

Fourth, control is relentless. It develops momentum as organization accumulates, as audiences develop, and as unofficial collaborators assume the definition of tasks, expression and ideology. This, according to W.A. Westley's "The Escalation of Violence Through Legitimation," is the culture of control. It not only limits the behaviors, styles, individuals and groups toward whom it is directed, it suppresses all unsanctioned efforts. As struggle itself is destroyed, motivation vanishes or is turned inward.

These are the effects of repressive control. We may contrast them with the criminal law, which merely prohibits the performance of specific acts (with the exception, of course, of the "crime without victims"—homosexuality, abortion, and drug use). Repression converts or destroys an entire social form, whether that form is embodied in a group, a style or an idea. In this sense, it is terror.

These general principles are especially relevant to our understanding of tendencies that are ripening in the United States day by day. Stated in terms that magnify it so that it can be seen despite ourselves, this is the persecution of the Hippies, a particularly vulnerable group of people who are the cultural wing of a way of life recently emerged from its quiet and individualistic quarters. Theodore Roszak, describing the Hippies in terms of their relationship to the culture and politics of dissent, notes that "the underlying unity of youthful dissent consists . . . in the effort of beat-hip bohemianism to work out the personality structure, the total life-style that follows from New Left social criticism." This life-style is currently bearing the brunt of the assault on what Roszak calls a "counter-culture"; it is an assault that is becoming more concentrated and savage every day. There are lessons for the American future to be drawn from this story.

Persecution

Near Boulder, Colorado, a restaurant sign says "Hippies not served here." Large billboards in upstate New York carry slogans like "Keep America Clean: Take a Bath," and "Keep America Clean: Get a Haircut." These would be as amusing as ethnic jokes if they did not represent a more systematic repression.

The street sweeps so common in San Francisco and Berkeley in 1968 and 1969 were one of the first lines of attack. People were brutally scattered by club-wielding policemen who first closed exits from the assaulted area and then began systematically to beat and arrest those who were trapped. This form of place terror, like surveillance in Negro areas and defoliation in Vietnam, curbs freedom and forces people to fight or submit to minute inspection by hostile forces. There have also been one-shot neighborhood pogroms, such as the police assault on the Tompkins Square Park gathering in New York's Lower East Side on Memorial Day, 1967: "Sadistic glee was written on the faces of several officers," wrote the *East Village Other*. Some women became hysterical. The police slugged Frank Wise, and dragged him off, handcuffed and bloody, crying, "My God, my God, where is this happening? Is this America?" The police also plowed into a group of Hippies, Yippies, and straights at the April, 1968, "Yip-in" at Grand Central Station. The brutality was as clear in this action as it had been in the Tompkins Square bust. In both cases, the major newspapers editorialized against the police tactics, and in the first the Mayor apologized for the "free wielding of nightsticks." But by the summer of 1968, street sweeps and busts and the continuous presence of New York's Tactical Police Force had given the Lower East Side an ominous atmosphere. Arrests were regularly accompanied by beatings and charges of "resistance to arrest." It became clear that arrests rather than subsequent procedures were the way in which control was to be exercised. The summer lost its street theaters, the relaxed circulation of people in the neighborhood and the easy park gatherings.

Official action legitimizes nonofficial action. Private citizens take up the cudgel of law and order newly freed from the boundaries of due process and respect. After Tompkins Square, rapes and assaults became common as local toughs assumed the role, with the police, of defender of the faith. In Cambridge, Massachusetts, following a virulent attack on Hippies by the Mayor, *Newsweek* reported that vigilantes attacked Hippie neighborhoods in force.

Ultimately more damaging are the attacks on centers of security. Police raids on "Hippie pads," crash pads, churches and movement centers have become daily occurrences in New York and California over the past two and a half years. The usual excuses for raids are drugs, runaways and housing violations, but many incidents of unlawful entry by police and the expressions of a more generalized hostility by the responsible officials suggests that something deeper is involved. The Chief of Police in San Francisco put it bluntly; quoted in *The New York Times Magazine* in May, 1967, he said:

> Hippies are no asset to the community. These people do not have the courage to face the reality of life. They are trying to escape. Nobody should let their young children take part in this hippy thing.

The Director of Health for San Francisco gave teeth to this counsel when he sent a task force of inspectors on a door-to-door sweep of the Haight-Ashbury—"a two-day blitz" that ended with a strange result, again according to *The Times:* Very few of the Hippies were guilty of housing violations.

Harassment arrests and calculated degradation have been two of the most effective devices for introducing uncertainty to the day-to-day lives of the Hippies. Cambridge's Mayor's attack on the "hipbos" (the suffix stands for body odor) included, said *Newsweek* of Oct. 30, 1967, a raid on a "hippie pad" by the Mayor and "a platoon of television cameramen." They "seized a pile of diaries and personal letters and flushed a partially clad girl from the closet." In Wyoming, *The Times* reported that two "pacifists" were "jailed and shaved" for hitchhiking. This is a fairly common hazard, though Wyoming officials are perhaps more sadistic than most. A young couple whom I interviewed were also arrested in Wyoming during the summer of 1968. They were placed in solitary confinement for a week during which they were not permitted to place phone calls and were not told when or whether they would be charged or released. These are not exceptional cases. During the summer of 1968, I interviewed young hitchhikers throughout the country; most of them had similar stories to tell.

In the East Village of New York, one hears countless stories of apartment destruction by police (occasionally reported in the newspapers), insults from the police when rapes or robberies are reported, and cruel speeches and even crueler bails set by judges for arrested Hippies.

In the light of this, San Francisco writer Mark Harris' indictment of the Hippies as paranoid seems peculiar. In the September 1967 issue of *The Atlantic,* he wrote,

> The most obvious failure of perception was the hippies failure to discriminate among elements of the Establishment, whether in the Haight-Ashbury or in San Francisco in general. Their paranoia was the paranoia of all youthful heretics. . . .

This is like the demand of some white liberals that Negroes acknowledge that they (the liberals) are not the power structure, or that black people must distinguish between the good and the bad whites despite the fact that the black experience of white people in the United States has been, as the President's Commission on Civil Disorder suggested, fairly monolithic and racist.

Most journalists reviewing the "Hippie scene" with any sympathy at all seem to agree with *Newsweek* that "the hippies do seem natural prey for publicity-hungry politicians—if not overzealous police," and that they have been subjected to varieties of cruelty that ought to be intolerable. This tactic was later elaborated in the massive para-military assault on Berkeley residents and students during a demonstration in support of Telegraph Avenue's street people and their People's Park. The terror of police violence, a constant in the lives of street people everywhere, in California carries the additional threat of martial law under a still-active state of extreme emergency. The whole structure of repression was given legitimacy and reluctant support by University of California officials. Step by step, they became allies of Reagan's "dogs of war." Roger W. Heyns, chancellor of the Berkeley campus, found himself belatedly reasserting the university's property in the lot. It was the law and the rights of university that trapped the chancellor in the network of control and performed the vital function of providing justification and legitimacy for Sheriff Madigan and the National Guard. Heyns said: "We will have to put up a fence to re-establish the conveniently forgotten fact that this field is indeed the university's and to exclude unauthorized personnel from the site. . . . The fence will give us time to plan and consult. We tried to get this time some other way and failed—hence the fence." And hence "Bloody Thursday" and the new regime.

And what of the Hippies? They have come far since those balmy days of 1966–67, days of flowers, street-cleaning, free stores, decoration and love. Many have fled to the hills of Northern California to join their brethren who had set up camps there several years ago. Others have fled to communes outside the large cities and in the Middle West. After the Tompkins Square assault, many of the East Village Hippies refused to follow the lead of those who were more political. They refused to develop organizations of defense and to accept a hostile relationship with the police and neighborhood. Instead, they discussed at meeting after meeting, how they could show their attackers love. Many of those spirits have fled; others have been beaten or jailed too many times; and still others have modified their outlook in ways that reflect the struggle. Guerrilla theater, Up Against the Wall Mother Fucker, the Yippies, the urban communes; these are some of the more recent manifestations of the alternative culture. One could see these trends growing in the demonstrations mounted by Hippies against arrests of runaways or pot smokers, the community organizations, such as grew in Berkeley for self-defense and politics, and the beginnings of the will to fight back when trapped in street sweeps.

It is my impression that the Hippie culture is growing as it recedes from the eye of the media. As a consequence of the destruction of their urban places, there has been a redistribution of types. The flower people have left for the hills and become more communal; those who remained in the city were better adapted to terror, secretive or confrontative. The Hippie culture is one of the forms radicalism can take in this society. The youngsters, 5,000 of them, who came to Washington to counter-demonstrate against the Nixon inaugural showed the growing amalgamation of the New

Left and its cultural wing. The Yippies who went to Chicago for guerrilla theater and learned about "pigs" were the multi-generational expression of the new wave. A UAWMF (Up Against the Wall Mother Fucker) drama, played at Lincoln Center during the New York City garbage strike—they carted garbage from the neglected Lower East Side and dumped it at the spic 'n' span cultural center—reflected another interpretation of the struggle, one that could include the politically militant as well as the culturally defiant. Many Hippies have gone underground—in an older sense of the word. They have shaved their beards, cut their hair, and taken straight jobs, like the secret Jews of Spain; but unlike those Jews, they are consciously an underground, a resistance.

What is most interesting and, I believe, a direct effect of the persecution, is the enormous divergence of forms that are still recognizable by the outsider as Hippie and are still experienced as a shared identity. "The Yippies," says Abbie Hoffman, "are like Hippies, only fiercer and more fun." The "hippie types" described in newspaper accounts of drug raids on colleges turn out, in many cases, to be New Leftists.

The dimensions by which these various forms are classified are quite conventional: religious-political, visible-secret, urban-hill, communal-individualistic. As their struggle intensifies, there will be more efforts for unity and more militant approaches to the society that gave birth to a real alternative only to turn against it with a mindless savagery. Yippie leader Jerry Rubin, in an "emergency letter to my brothers and sisters in the movement" summed up:

> Huey Newton is in prison.
> Eldridge Cleaver is in exile.
> Oakland Seven are accused of conspiracy.
> Tim Leary is up for 30 years and how many of our brothers are in court and jail for getting high?
> . . .
> Camp activists are expelled and arrested.
> War resisters are behind bars.
> Add it up!

Rubin preambles his summary with:

> From the Bay Area to New York, we are suffering the greatest depression in our history. People are taking bitterness in their coffee instead of sugar. The hippie-yippie-SDS movement is a "white nigger" movement. The American economy no longer needs young whites and blacks. We are waste material. We fulfill our destiny in life by rejecting a system which rejects us.

He advocates organizing "massive mobilizations for the spring, nationally coordinated and very theatrical, taking place near courts, jails, and military stockades."

An article published in a Black Panther magazine is entitled "The Hippies Are Not Our Enemies." White radicals have also overcome their initial rejection of cultural radicals. Something clearly is happening, and it is being fed, finally, by youth, the artists, the politicos and the realization, through struggle, that America is not beautiful.

Some Historical Analogies

The persecution of the Jews destroyed both a particular social form and the individuals who qualified for the Jewish fate by reason of birth. Looking at the process in the aggregate, Hilberg describes it as a gradual coming together of a multitude of loose laws, institutions, and intentions, rather than a program born mature. The control conglomerate that resulted was a refined engine "whose devices," Hilbert writes, "not only trap a larger number of victims; they also require a greater degree of specialization, and with that division of labor, the moral burden too is fragmented among the participants. The perpetrator can now kill his victims without touching them, without hearing them, without seeing them. . . . This ever growing capacity for destruction cannot be arrested anywhere." Ultimately, the persecution of the Jews was a mixture of piety, repression and mobilization directed against those who were in the society but suddenly not of it.

The early Christians were also faced with a refined and elaborate administrative structure whose harsh measures were ultimately directed at their ways of life: their social forms and their spiritual claims. The rationale was, and is, that certain deviant behaviors endanger society. Therefore, officials are obligated to use whatever means of control or persuasion they consider necessary to strike these forms from the list of human possibilities. This is the classical administrative rationale for the suppression of alternative values and world views.

As options closed and Christians found the opportunities to lead and explore Christian lives rapidly struck down, Christian life itself had to become rigid, prematurely closed and obsessed with survival.

The persecution of the early Christians presents analogies to the persecution of European Jews. The German assault affected the quality of Jewish organizations no less than it affected the lives of individual Jews, distorting communities long before it destroyed them. Hilberg documents some of the ways in which efforts to escape the oppression led on occasion to a subordination of energies to the problem of simply staying alive—of finding some social options within the racial castle. The escapist mentality that dominated the response to oppression and distorted relationships can be seen in some Jewish leaders in Vienna. They exchanged individuals for promises. This is what persecution and terror do. As options close and all parts of the life of the oppressed are touched by procedure, surveillance and control, behavior is transformed. The oppressed rarely retaliate (especially where they have internalized the very ethic that rejects them), simply because nothing is left untouched by the persecution. No energy is available for hostility, and, in any case, it is impossible to know where to begin. Bravery is stoicism. One sings to the cell or gas chamber.

The persecution of Hippies in the United States involves, regardless of the original intentions of the agencies concerned, an assault on a way of life, an assault no less concentrated for its immaturity and occasional ambivalence. Social, cultural and political resources have been mobilized to bring a group of individuals into line and to prevent others from refusing to toe the line.

The attractiveness of the Hippie forms and the pathos of their persecution have together brought into being an impressive array of defenders. Nevertheless theirs has been a defense of gestures, outside the realm of politics and social action essential to any real protection. It has been verbal, scholarly and appreciative, with occasional expressions of horror at official actions and attitudes. But unfortunately the arena of conflict within which the Hippies, willy-nilly, must try to survive is dominated not by the likes of Susan Sontag, but by the likes of Daniel Patrick Moynihan whose apparent compassion for the Hippies will probably never be translated into action. For even as he writes (in the *American Scholar,* Autumn, 1967) that these youths are "trying to tell us something" and that they are one test of our "ability to survive," he rejects them firmly, and not a little *ex cathedra,* as a "truth gone astray." The Hippie remains helpless and more affected by the repressive forces (who will probably quote Moynihan) than by his own creative capacity or the sympathizers who support him in the journals. As John Kifner reported in *The Times,* " 'This scene is not the same anymore,' said the tall, thin Negro called Gypsy. '. . . There are some very bad vibrations.' "

Social Form and Cultural Heresy

> But it's just another murder. A hippie being killed is just like a housewife being killed or a career girl being killed or a hoodlum being killed. None of these people, notice, are persons; they're labels. Who cares who Groovy was; if you know he was a 'hippie,' then already you know more about him than he did about himself.
>
> See, it's hard to explain to a lot of you what a hippie is because a lot of you really think a hippie IS something. You don't realize that the word is just a convenience picked up by the press to personify a social change thing beginning to happen to young people. (Paul William, in an article entitled "Label Dies—But Not Philosophy," *Open City,* Los Angeles, November 17–23, 1967.)

Because the mass media have publicized the growth of a fairly well-articulated Hippie culture, it now bears the status of a social form. Variously identified as "counter-culture," "Hippie-dom," "Youth" or "Underground," the phenomenon centers on a philosophy of the present and takes the personal and public forms appropriate to that philosophy. Its values constitute a heresy in a society that consecrates the values of competition, social manipulation and functionalism, a society that defines ethical quality by long-range and general consequences, and that honors only those attitudes and institutions that affirm the primacy of the future and large-scale over the local and immediately present. It is a heresy in a society that eschews the primary value of intimacy for the sake of impersonal service to large and enduring organizations, a society that is essentialist rather than existentialist, a society that prizes biography over interactive quality. It is a heresy in a country whose President could be praised for crying, "Ask not what your country can do for you, but what you can do for your country!" Most important, however, it is heresy in a society whose official values, principles of operation and officials themselves are threatened domestically and abroad.

For these reasons the Hippie is available for persecution. When official authority is threatened, social and political deviants are readily conjured up as demons requiring collective exorcism and thus a reaffirmation of that authority. Where exorcism is the exclusive province of government, the government's power is reinforced by the adoption of a scapegoat. Deviant style and ideals make a group vulnerable to exploitation as a scapegoat, but it is official action which translates vulnerability into actionable heresy.

By contrast, recent political developments within black communities and the accommodations reached through bargaining with various official agencies have placed the blacks alongside the Viet Cong as an official enemy, but not as a scapegoat. As an enemy, the black is not a symbol but a source of society's troubles. It is a preferable position. The Hippie's threat lies in the lure of his way of life rather than in his political potential. His vulnerability as well as his proven capacity to develop a real alternative life permits his selection as scapegoat. A threatened officialdom is all too likely to take the final step that "brings on the judge." At the same time, by defining its attack as moderate, it reaffirms its moral superiority in the very field of hate it cultivates.

A Plausible Force

We are speaking of that which claims the lives, totally or in part, of perhaps hundreds of thousands of people of all ages throughout the United States and elsewhere. The number is not inconsiderable.

The plausibility of the Hippie culture and its charisma can be argued on several grounds. Their outlook derives from a profound mobilizing idea: Quality resides in the present. Therefore, one seeks the local in all its social detail—not indulgently and alone, but openly and creatively. Vulnerability and improvisation are principles of action, repudiating the "rational" hierarchy of plans and stages that defines, for the grounded culture, all events as incidents of passage and means to an indefinitely postponable end—as transition. The allocation of reality to the past and the future is rejected in favor of the present, and a present that is known and felt immediately, not judged by external standards. The long run is the result rather than the goal of the present. "Psychical distance," the orientation of the insulated tourist to whom the environment is something forever foreign or of the administrator for whom the world is an object of administration, is repudiated as a relational principle. It is replaced by a principle of absorption. In this, relationships are more like play, dance or jazz. Intimacy derives from absorption, from spontaneous involvement, to use Erving Goffman's phrase, rather than from frequent contact or attraction, as social psychologists have long argued.

This vision of social reality makes assumptions about human nature. It sees man as only a part of a present that depends on all its parts. To be a "part" is not to play a stereotyped role or to plan one's behavior prior to entering the scene. It is to be of a momentum. Collaboration, the overt manifestation of absorption, is critical to any social arrangement because the present, as experience, is essentially social. Love and charisma are the reflected properties of the plausible whole that results from mutual absorption. "To swing" or "to groove" is to be of the scene rather than simply at or in the scene. "Rapping," an improvised, expansive, and collaborative conversational form, is an active embodiment of the more general ethos. Its craft is humor, devotion, trust, openness to events in the process of formation, and the capacity to be relevant. Identity is neither strictly personal nor something to be maintained, but something always to be discovered. The individual body is the origin of sounds and motions, but behavior, ideas, images, and reflective thought stem from interaction itself. Development is not of personalities but of situations that include many bodies but, in effect, one mind. Various activities, such as smoking marijuana, are disciplines that serve the function of bringing people together and making them deeply interesting to each other.

The development of an authentic "counter-culture," or, better, "alternative culture," has some striking implications. For one, information and stress are processed through what amounts to a new conceptual system—a culture that replaces, in the committed, the intrapersonal structures that Western personality theories have assumed to account for intrapersonal order. For example, in 1966, young Hippies often turned against their friends and their experience after a bad acid trip. But that was the year during which "the Hippie thing" was merely one constructive expression of dissent. It was not, at that point, an alternative culture. As a result, the imagery cued in by the trauma was the imagery of the superego, the distant and punitive authority of the Western family and its macrocosmic social system. Guilt, self-hatred and the rejection of experience was the result. Many youngsters returned home filled with a humiliation that could be forgotten, or converted to a seedy and defensive hatred of the dangerously deviant. By 1968 the bad trip, while still an occasion for reconversion for some, had for others become something to be guarded against and coped with in a context of care and experienced guidance. The atmosphere of trust and new language of stress-inspired dependence rather than recoil as the initial stage of cure. One could "get high with a little help from my friends." Conscience was purged of "authority."

Although the ethos depends on personal contact, it is carried by underground media (hundreds of newspapers claiming hundreds of thousands of readers), rock music, and collective activities, artistic and political, which deliver and duplicate the message; and it is processed through a generational flow. It is no longer simply a constructive expression of dissent and thus attractive because it is a vital answer to a system that destroys vitality; it is culture, and the young are growing up under the wisdom of its older generations. The ethos is realized most fully in the small communes that dot the American urbscape and constitute an important counter-institution of the Hippies.

This complex of population, culture, social form, and ideology is both a reinforcing environment for individuals and a context for the growth and elaboration of the complex itself. In it, life not only begins, it goes on; and, indeed, it must go on for those who are committed to it. Abbie Hoffman's *Revolution for the Hell of It* assumes the autonomy of this cultural frame of reference. It assumes that the individual has entered and has burned his bridges.

As the heresy takes an official definition and as the institutions of persecution form, a they-mentality emerges in the language which expresses the relationship between the oppressor and the oppressed. For the oppressed, it distinguishes life from nonlife so that living can go on. The they-mentality of the oppressed temporarily relieves them of the struggle by acknowledging the threat, identifying its agent, and compressing both into a quasi-poetic image, a cliché that can accommodate absurdity. One young man said, while coming down from an amphetamine high: "I'm simply going to continue to do what I want until they stop me."

But persecution is also structured by the they-mentality of the persecutors. This mentality draws lines around its objects as it fits them conceptually for full-scale social action. The particular uses of the term "hippie" in the mass media—like "Jew," "Communist," "Black Muslim," or "Black Panther"—cultivates not only disapproval and rejection but a climate of opinion capable of excluding Hippies from the moral order altogether. This is one phase of a subtle process that begins by locating and isolating a group, tying it to the criminal, sinful or obscene, developing and displaying referential symbols at a high level of abstraction which depersonalize and objectify the group, defining the stigmata by which members are to be known and placing the symbols in the context of ideology and readiness for action.

At this point, the symbols come to define public issues and are, consequently, sources of strength. The maintenance of power—the next phase of the story—depends less on the instruction of reading and viewing publics than on the elaboration of the persecutory institutions which demonstrate and justify power. The relationship between institution and public ceases to be one of expression or extension (of a public to an institution) and becomes one of transaction or dominance (of a public with or by an institution). The total dynamic is similar to advertising or the growth of the military as domestic powers in America.

An explosion of Hippie stories appeared in the mass media during the summer of 1967. Almost every large-circulation magazine featured articles on the Hippie "fad" or "subculture." *Life's* "The Other Culture" set the tone. The theme was repeated in *The New York Times Magazine,* May 14, 1967, where Hunter Thompson wrote that "The 'Hashbury' (Haight-Ashbury in San Francisco) is the new capital of what is rapidly becoming a drug culture." *Time's* "wholly new subculture" was "a cult whose mystique derives essentially from the influences of hallucinogenic drugs." By fall, while maintaining the emphasis on drugs as the cornerstone of the culture, the articles had shifted from the culturological to a "national character" approach, reminiscent of the World War II anti-Japanese propaganda, as personal traits were piled into the body of the symbol and objectification began. The Hippies were "acid heads," "generally dirty," and "visible, audible and sometimes smellable young rebels."

As "hippie" and its associated terms ("long-haired," "bearded") accumulated pejorative connotation, they began to be useful concepts and were featured regularly in news headlines: for example, "Hippie Mother Held in Slaying of Son, 2" (*The New York Times,* Nov. 22, 1967); "S Squad Hits Four Pads" (*San Francisco Chronicle,* July 27, 1967). The articles themselves solidified usage by dwelling on "hippie types," "wild drug parties" and "long-haired, bearded" youths (see, for example, *The New York Times* of Feb. 13, 1968, Sept. 16, 1968 and Nov. 3, 1967).

This is a phenomenon that R. H. Turner and S. J. Surace described in 1956 in order to account for the role of media in the development of hostile consciousness toward Mexicans. The presentation of certain symbols can remove their referents from the constraints of the conventional moral order so that extralegal and extramoral action can be used against them. Political cartoonists have used the same device with less powerful results. To call Mexican-Americans "zootsuiters" in Los Angeles, in 1943, was to free hostility from the limits of the conventional, though fragile, antiracism required by liberal ideology. The result was a wave of brutal anti-Mexican assaults. Turner and Surace hypothesized that:

> To the degree, then, to which any symbol evokes only one consistent set of connotations throughout the community, only one general course of action with respect to that object will be indicated, and the union of diverse members of the community into an acting crowd will be facilitated . . . or it will be an audience prepared to accept novel forms of official action.

First the symbol, then the accumulation of hostile connotations, and finally the action-issue: Such a sequence appears in the news coverage of Hippies from the beginning of 1967 to the present. The amount of coverage has decreased in the past year, but this seems less a result of sympathy or sophistication and more one of certainty: The issue is decided and certain truths can be taken for granted. As this public consciousness finds official representation in the formation of a control conglomerate, it heralds the final and institutional stage in the growth of repressive force, persecution and terror.

The growth of this control conglomerate, the mark of any repressive system, depends on the development of new techniques and organizations.

But its momentum requires an ideological head of steam. In the case of the Hippie life the ideological condemnation is based on several counts: that it is dangerous and irresponsible, subversive to authority, immoral, and psychopathological.

Commenting on the relationship between beliefs and the development of the persecutory institutions for witch-control in the 16th century, Trevor-Roper, in an essay on "Witches and Witchcraft," states:

> In a climate of fear, it is easy to see how this process could happen: how individual deviations could be associated with a central pattern. We have seen it happen in our own time. The "McCarthyite" experience of the United States in the 1950's was exactly comparable: Social fear, the fear of an incompatible system of society, was given intellectual form as a heretical ideology and suspect individuals were persecuted by reference to that heresy.

The same fear finds its ideological expression against the Hippies in the statement of Dr. Stanley F. Yolles, director of the National Institute of Mental Health, that "alienation," which he called a major underlying cause of drug abuse, "was wider, deeper and more diffuse now than it has been in any other period in American history." The rejection of dissent in the name of mental health rather than moral values or social or political interest is a modern characteristic. Dr. Yolles suggested that if urgent attention is not given the problem:

> there are serious dangers that large proportions of current and future generations will reach adulthood embittered towards the larger society, unequipped to take on parental, vocational and other citizen roles, and involved in some form of socially deviant behavior. . . .

Dr. Seymour L. Halleck, director of student psychiatry at the University of Wisconsin, also tied the heresy to various sources of sin: affluence, lack of contact with adults, and an excess of freedom. Dr. Henry Brill, director of Pilgrim State Hospital on Long Island and a consultant on drug use to federal and state agencies, is quoted in *The New York Times,* Sept. 26, 1967:

> It is my opinion that the unrestricted use of marijuana type substances produces a significant amount of vagabondage, dependency, and psychiatric disability.

Drs. Yolles, Halleck, and Brill are probably fairly representative of psychiatric opinion. Psychiatry has long defined normality and health in terms of each other in a "scientific" avoidance of serious value questions. Psychiatrists agree in principle on several related points which could constitute a medical rational foundation for the persecution of Hippies: They define the normal and healthy individual as patient and instrumental. He plans for the long range and pursues his goals temperately and economically. He is an individual with a need for privacy and his contacts are moderate and respectful. He is stable in style and identity, reasonably competitive and optimistic. Finally, he accepts reality and participates in the social forms which constitute the givens of his life. Drug use, sexual pleasure, a repudiation of clear long-range goals, the insistence on intimacy and self-affirmation, distrust of official authority and radical dissent are all part of the abnormality that colors the Hippies "alienated" or "disturbed" or "neurotic."

This ideology characterizes the heresy in technical terms. Mental illness is a scientific and medical problem, and isolation and treatment are recommended. Youth, alienation and drug use are the discrediting characteristics of those who are unqualified for due process, discussion or conflict. The genius of the ideology has been to separate the phenomenon under review from consideration of law and value. In this way the mutual hostilities that ordinarily divide the various agencies of control are bypassed and the issue endowed with ethical and political neutrality. Haurek and Clark, in their "Variants of Integration of Social Control Agencies," described two opposing orientations among social control agencies, the authoritarian-punitive (the police, the courts) and the humanitarian-welfare (private agencies, social workers), with the latter holding the former in low esteem. The Hippies have brought them together.

The designation of the Hippie impulse as heresy on the grounds of psychopathology not only bypasses traditional enmity among various agencies of social control, but its corollaries activate each agency. It is the eventual coordination of their efforts that constitutes the control conglomerate. We will briefly discuss several of these corollaries before examining the impact of the conglomerate. Youth, danger and disobedience are the major themes.

Dominating the study of adolescence is a general theory which holds that the adolescent is a psychosexual type. Due to an awakening of the instincts after a time of relative quiescence, he is readily overwhelmed by them. Consequently, his behavior may be viewed as the working out of intense intrapsychic conflict—it is symptomatic or expressive rather than rational and realistic. He is idealistic, easily influenced, and magical. The idealism is the expression of a threatened superego; the susceptibility to influence is an attempt to find support for an identity in danger of diffusion; the magic, reflected in adolescent romance and its rituals, is an attempt to get a grip on a reality that shifts and turns too much for comfort. By virtue of his entrance into the youth culture, he joins in the collective expression of emotional immaturity. At heart, he is the youth of Golding's *Lord of the Flies,* a fledgling adult living out a transitional status. His idealism may be sentimentally touching, but in truth he is morally irresponsible and dangerous.

Youth

As the idealism of the young is processed through the youth culture, it becomes radical ideology, and even radical practice. The attempts by parents and educators to break the youth culture by rejecting its symbols and limiting the opportunities for its expression (ranging from dress regulations in school to the censorship of youth music on the air) are justified as a response to the dangerous political implications of the ideology of developed and ingrown immaturity. That these same parents and educators find their efforts to conventionalize the youth culture (through moderate imitations of youthful dress and attempts to "get together with the kids") rejected encourages them further to see the young as hostile, unreasonable and intransigent. The danger of extremism (the New Left and the Hippies) animates their criticism, and all intrusions on the normal are read as pointing in that direction. The ensuing conflict between the wise and the unreasonable is called (largely by the wise) the "generation gap."

From this it follows that radicalism is the peculiar propensity of the young and, as Christopher Jencks and David Riesman have pointed out in *The Academic Revolution,* of those who identify with the young. At its best it is not considered serious; at its worst it is the "counter-culture." The myth of the generation gap, a myth that is all the more strongly held as we find less and less evidence for it, reinforces this view by holding that radicalism ends, or should end, when the gap is bridged—when the young grow older and wiser. While this lays the groundwork for tolerance or more likely, forbearance, it is a tolerance limited to youthful radicalism. It also lays the groundwork for a more thorough rejection of the radicalism of the not-so-young and the "extreme."

Thus, the theory of youth classifies radicalism as immature and, when cultivated, dangerous or pathological. Alienation is the explanation used to account for the extension of youthful idealism and paranoia into the realm of the politically and culturally adult. Its wrongness is temporary and trivial. If it persists, it becomes a structural defect requiring capture and treatment rather than due process and argument.

Danger

Once a life-style and its practices are declared illegal, its proponents are by definition criminal and subversive. On the one hand, the very dangers presupposed by the legal proscriptions immediately become clear and present. The illegal life-style becomes the living demonstration of its alleged dangers. The ragged vagabondage of the Hippie is proof that drugs and promiscuity are alienating, and the attempts to sleep in parks, gather and roam are the new "violence" of which we have been reading. Crime certainly is crime, and the Hippies commit crime by their very existence. The dangers are: (1) crime and the temptation to commit crime; (2) alienation and the temptation to drop out. The behaviors that, if unchecked, become imbedded in the personality of the suspectible are, among others, drug use (in particular marijuana), apparel deviance, dropping out (usually of school), sexual promiscuity, communal living, nudity, hair deviance, draft resistance, demonstrating against the feudal oligarchies in cites and colleges, gathering, roaming, doing strange art and being psychedelic. Many of these are defused by campaigns of definition; they become topical and in fashion. To wear bell-bottom pants, long side-burns, flowers on your car and beads, is, if done with taste and among the right people, stylish and eccentric rather than another step toward the brink or a way of lending aid and comfort to the enemy. The disintegration of a form by co-opting only its parts is a familiar phenomenon. It is tearing an argument apart by confronting each proposition as if it had no context, treating a message like an intellectual game.

Drugs, communalism, gathering, roaming, resisting and demonstrating, and certain styles of hair have not been defused. In fact, the drug scene is the site of the greatest concentration of justificatory energy and the banner under which the agencies of the control conglomerate unite. That their use is so widespread through the straight society indicates the role of drugs as temptation. That drugs have been pinned so clearly (despite the fact that many Hippies are nonusers) and so gladly to the Hippies, engages the institutions of persecution in the task of destroying the Hippie thing.

The antimarijuana lobby has postulated a complex of violence, mental illness, genetic damage, apathy and alienation, all arising out of the ashes of smoked pot. The hypothesis justifies a set of laws and practices of great harshness and discrimination, and the President recently recommended that they be made even more so. The number of arrests for use, possession or sale of marijuana has soared in recent years: Between 1964 and 1966 yearly arrests doubled, from 7,000 to 15,000. The United States Narcotics Commissioner attributed the problem to "certain groups" which give marijuana to young people, and to "false information" about the danger of the drug.

Drug raids ordinarily net "hippie-type youths" although lately news reports refer to "youths from good homes." The use of spies on campuses, one of the bases for the original protest demonstrations at Nanterre prior to the May revolution, has become common, with all its socially destructive implications. Extensive spy operations were behind many of the police raids of college campuses during 1967, 1968 and 1969. Among those hit were Long Island University's Southampton College (twice), State University College at Oswego, New York, the Hun School of Princeton, Bard College, Syracuse University, Stony Brook College and Franconia College in New Hampshire; the list could go on.

It is the "certain groups" that the Commissioner spoke of who bear the brunt of the condemnation and the harshest penalties. The laws themselves are peculiar enough, having been strengthened largely since the Hippies became visible, but they are enforced with obvious discrimination. Teenagers arrested in a "good residential section" of Naugatuck, Connecticut, were treated gently by the circuit court judge:

> I suspect that many of these youngters should not have been arrested. . . . I'm not going to have these youngsters bouncing around with these charges hanging over them.

They were later released and the charges dismissed. In contrast, after a "mass arrest" in which 15 of the 25 arrested were charged with being in a place where they knew that others were smoking marijuana, Washington's

Judge Halleck underscored his determination "to show these long-haired ne'er-do-wells that society will not tolerate their conduct" (*Washington Post,* May 21, 1967).

The incidents of arrest and the exuberance with which the laws are discriminatorily enforced are justified, although not explained, by the magnifying judgment of "danger." At a meeting of agents from 74 police departments in Connecticut and New York, Westchester County Sheriff John E. Hoy, "in a dramatic stage whisper," said, "It is a frightening situation, my friends . . . marijuana is creeping up on us."

One assistant district attorney stated that "the problem is staggering." A county executive agreed that "the use of marijuana is vicious," while a school superintendent argued that "marijuana is a plaguelike disease, slowly but surely strangling our young people." Harvard freshmen were warned against the "social influences" that surround drugs and one chief of police attributed drug use and social deviance to permissiveness in a slogan which has since become more common (*St. Louis Post-Dispatch,* Aug. 22, 1968).

Bennett Berger has pointed out that the issue of danger is an ideological ploy (*Denver Post,* April 19, 1968): "The real issue of marijuana is ethical and political, touching the 'core of cultural values.' " *The New York Times* of Jan. 11, 1968, reports, "Students and high school and college officials agree that 'drug use has increased sharply since the intensive coverage given to drugs and the Hippies last summer by the mass media.' " It is also supported by other attempts to tie drugs to heresy: *The New York Times* of Nov. 17, 1968, notes a Veterans Administration course for doctors on the Hippies which ties Hippies, drugs, and alienation together and suggests that the search for potential victims might begin in the seventh or eighth grades.

The dynamic relationship between ideology, organization and practice is revealed both in President Johnson's "Message on Crime to Insure Public Safety" (delivered to Congress on February 7, 1968) and in the gradual internationalizing of the persecution. The President recommended "strong new laws," an increase in the number of enforcement agents, and the centralization of federal enforcement machinery. At the same time, the United Nations Economic and Social Council considered a resolution asking that governments "deal effectively with publicity which advocates legalization or tolerance of the non-medical use of cannabis as a harmless drug." The resolution was consistent with President Johnson's plan to have the Federal Government of the United States "maintain world-wide operations . . . to suppress the trade in illicit narcotics and marijuana." The reasons for the international campaign were clarified by a World Health Organization panel's affirmation of its intent to prevent the use or sale of marijuana because it is "a drug of dependence, producing health and social problems." At the same time that scientific researchers at Harvard and Boston University were exonerating the substance, the penalties increased and the efforts to proscribe it reached international proportions. A number of countries, including Laos and Thailand, have barred Hippies, and Mexico has made it difficult for those with long hair and serious eyes to cross its border.

Disobedience

The assumption that society is held together by formal law and authority implies in principle that the habit of obedience must be reinforced. The details of the Hippie culture are, in relation to the grounded culture, disobedient. From that perspective, too, their values and ideology are also explicitly disobedient. The disobedience goes far beyond the forms of social organization and personal presentation to the conventional systems of healing, dietary practice and environmental use. There is virtually no system of authority that is not thrown into question. Methodologically, the situationalism of pornography, guerrilla theater and place conversion is not only profoundly subversive in itself; it turns the grounded culture around. By coating conventional behavioral norms with ridicule and obscenity, by tying radically different meanings to old routines, it challenges our sentiments. By raising the level of our self-consciousness it allows us to become moral in the areas we had allowed to degenerate into habit (apathy or gluttony). When the rock group, the Fugs, sings and dances "Group Grope" or any of their other songs devoted brutally to "love" and "taste," they pin our tender routines to a humiliating obscenity. We can no longer take our behavior and our intentions for granted. The confrontation enables us to disobey or to reconsider or to choose simply by forcing into consciousness the patterns of behavior and belief of which we have become victims. The confrontation is manly because it exposes both sides in an arena of conflict.

When questions are posed in ways that permit us to disengage ourselves from their meaning to our lives, we tolerate the questions as a moderate and decent form of dissent. And we congratulate ourselves for our tolerance. But when people refuse to know their place, and, what is worse, our place, and they insist on themselves openly and demand that we redecide our own lives, we are willing to have them knocked down. Consciousness permits disobedience. As a result, systems threatened from within often begin the work of reassertion by an attack on consciousness and chosen forms of life.

Youth, danger and disobedience define the heresy in terms that activate the host of agencies that, together, comprise the control conglomerate. Each agency, wrote Trevor-Roper, was ready: "The engine of persecution was set up before its future victims were legally subject to it." The conglomerate has its target. But it is a potential of the social system as much as it is an actor. Trevor-Roper comments further that:

> once we see the persecution of heresy as social intolerance, the intellectual difference between one heresy and another becomes less significant.

And the difference, one might add, between one persecutor and another becomes less significant. Someone, it does not matter who, tells Mr. Blue (in Tom Paxton's song): "What will it take to whip you into line?"

How have I ended here? The article is an analysis of the institutionalization of persecution and the relationship between the control conglomerate which is the advanced form of official persecution and the Hippies as an alternative culture, the target of control. But an analysis must work within a vision if it is to move beyond analysis into action. The tragedy of America may be that it completed the technology of control before it developed compassion and tolerance. It never learned to tolerate history, and now it is finally capable of ending history by ending the change that political sociologists and undergroups understand. The struggle has always gone on in the mind. Only now, for this society, is it going on in the open among people. Only now is it beginning to shape lives rather than simply shaping individuals. Whether it is too late or not will be worked out in the attempts to transcend the one-dimensionality that Marcuse described. That the alternative culture is here seems difficult to doubt. Whether it becomes revolutionary fast enough to supersede an officialdom bent on its destruction may be an important part of the story of America.

As an exercise in over-estimation, this essay proposes a methodological tool for going from analysis to action in areas which are too easily absorbed by a larger picture but which are at the same time too critical to be viewed outside the context of political action.

The analysis suggests several conclusions:

Control usually transcends itself both in its selection of targets and in its organization.

At some point in its development, control is readily institutionalized and finally institutional. The control conglomerate represents a new stage in social organization and is an authentic change-inducing force for social systems.

The hallmark of an advanced system of control (and the key to its beginning) is an ideology that unites otherwise highly differing agencies.

Persecution and terror go in our society. The Hippies, as a genuine heresy, have engaged official opposition to a growing cultural-social-political tendency. The organization of control has both eliminated countervailing official forces and begun to place all deviance in the category of heresy. This pattern may soon become endemic to the society.

The Teen-Age Gang: An Introduction

R. Lincoln Keiser

The streets, alleys and gangways of Chicago's West Side form the natural habitat of an alarming, bizarre and yet fascinating organization—The Teen-Age Gang. Much has been written in the mass media concerning these organizations. Every few months one reads of pitched battles, beatings and shootings which are the essence of the internecine conflicts between various rival groups. The police, the courts and the various social agencies in the community have all become involved in combating these organizations. Yet if the effort to stamp out—or more realistically to alter—these organizations to fit what is considered acceptable behavior in the community is to be successful a thorough knowledge of the nature of these groups and of the social and cultural factors that produce them is needed.

Before going further it would be helpful to delineate more carefully the subject matter. The word "gang" as it is popularly used covers a variety of delinquent youth organizations. James F. Short, in his introduction to the abridged version of Thrasher's classic study, *The Gang,* distinguishes three kinds of delinquent groups each organized for different purposes. The first may be called the hustling gang. The hustling gang is organized for the purpose of economic gain through non-legitimate means. Such things as automobile stripping rings, burglary rings, etc., are examples of this kind of organization. Membership in the hustling gang is small. It varies between three and ten. There is no formal power structure. The roles are not institutionalized into any formal organization. One could draw an analogy between the hustling gang and a sandlot football team to illustrate this.

Whereas in an organized football club leadership functions are institutionalized in the roles of "captain," "quarterback" and "coach" in a sandlot game leadership falls to the individual with the most natural leadership regardless of the role, i.e., "quarterback," "end," "center," that he happens to be playing. So it is with the hustling gang. Decision making falls to that

Reprinted by permission of the publisher from *Briefs* of the Social Service Department of the Municipal Court of Chicago, vols. 6, 7, and 8 (March, June, and September 1965): 3–4, 1–4, 1–4.

person with the greatest amount of leadership ability without the leadership role being institutionalized into the group structure.

Status in the hustling gang is determined by two things, skill in hustling and what is called "heart." "Heart" can best be translated as the ratio between bravery and hustling ability.

The second kind of delinquent gang is organized for the purpose of illegal drug use. Membership in these groups is more diffuse than in hustling gangs. The use of drugs legitimatizes the individual throughout the sub-culture of drug users. Status is determined by the "kick" one gets from the use of drugs and the quality of the drug one possesses. For example, boys talk in glowing terms of how they "turned on to pot" and what "mellow stuff" they had "coming in."

The third kind of delinquent gang may be called the warrior gang. It is this type of organization that will be the subject of this series. Warrior gangs are organized for the purpose of gaining prestige, rights to women and territory through fighting. The ideology of violence is dominant in the value system.

The word "gang" as it is generally used covers all three of these delinquent organizations. However, the boys in the warrior groups resent the use of "gang" to refer to their organization. They refer to their groups as clubs. Therefore, this is the word that will be used in these articles.

It is not possible to quote an exact figure on the size of these groups without taking an actual census. So far as it is known this has not been done. However, in talking with members of various clubs several estimates have been given. The Vice Lord Nation has been estimated as having one thousand to three thousand members. The same estimate was given for the Egyptian Cobra Nation. The Racketeers were estimated at about three hundred, and the Roman Saints between five hundred and eight hundred. The large clubs are divided into branches which are organized in a pyramidal structure.

Leadership in the Warrior Club is highly institutionalized. Although leaders are chosen on the basis of their leadership ability, they are chosen to occupy an institutionalized role, i.e., president, vice-president, supreme war councilor, etc. The next article will give a detailed analysis of the structure of one of these groups, the Vice Lord Nation.

Of all the clubs on the West Side the Conservative Vice Lord Nation is at present the largest, best organized and, without doubt, the most notorious. Newspaper accounts have made it nationally known. One member, acting unofficially as club historian, collects newspaper clippings involving the club. He has already filled one scrapbook and has just begun working on clippings for 1962!

The content of this analysis is not based on actual observation of the gangs in their natural habitat. Rather it is derived primarily from tape recorded interviews with club members. Eleven boys ranging in age from 17 to 21 years were interviewed. Two held the office of secretary-treasurer, three of war councilor, one of vice-president and five held no office. Actual observation as well as interviews would have been preferable. Nevertheless the ideal models that exist in the minds of the Vice Lord members are significant as they affect behavior. Individuals who perceive their social world in terms of specific models tend to act in predictable ways within given situations. It should be stressed that this article is not presented as a "piece of research." Rather it gives a picture of street corner gangs as seen by members of the Vice Lord Nation and as interpreted by the interviewer. It is hoped that the reader will gain some insight into the phenomenon of teen-age gangs and especially of the Vice Lord Nation.

History

The Vice Lord Nation is said to have originated in what is called "Charlie Town," the Illinois State Training School for Boys at St. Charles, Illinois. According to one of the original members who was present when the Lords was formed, the club began in Harding Cottage as a small social group of six who prior to commitment had belonged to a club known as the Imperial Chaplains. At that time the Imperials was a federation of teen-age street corner gangs existing on the West Side. When the boys were released and returned to Chicago they decided to start their own branch of the Imperials and call it the Imperial Vice Lords. The Imperial Vice Lords did not remain a branch of the Imperials. Friction developed between the Imperial Vice Lords and the Imperial Chaplains and fighting broke out at a party at which both groups were present. Although the Lords were outnumbered they won the fight and in the process injured several Imperials. This fight established the Vice Lords as a group completely independent of the Imperials. From then on the group was known as the Conservative Vice Lords.

The Vice Lords added to their strength and size by breaking up a branch of the Imperials called the Imperial Knights. Although no actual war occurred the Vice Lords pressured the Imperial Knights to such an extent that they disbanded and were incorporated into the Vice Lord Nation. One of the original Lords who is now a college student gives the following account of this:

> Now we had broke up the Imperial Knights back in '59. See, the Lords were from about Pulaski to Homan, and the only other group that was there in that neighborhood was the Imperial Knights. So we felt that they had to go. But we knew them all! In fact, we grew up with most of them, so I guess we didn't actually fight. There was always incidents, but we never did actually come out and fight. This is only one incident, but it helped do it. They had a dance one night, and we came down there—about twelve of us. I was leading this particular group. Now we didn't actually fight, but we just squared them up so bad—kind of roughed them up in front of their girls—and turned the party out! And they left without a fight.
>
> Then at another dance, Ring put a cigarette out in Polecat's eye. Polecat was one of their leaders who later became one of the top Lords. And a lot of things happened like this, so all of them, they broke up their club and became Vice Lords.

As the reputation of the Vice Lords continued to grow, branch organizations were formed. The original group became known as Vice Lord City. Other branches developed in several ways. One was through conquest and alliance. For example, the Monroe Lords was formed in this way. A club known as the Ambassadors started fighting a club called the Imperial Burpies. The Ambassadors lost to the Burpies and were incorporated into that club. When the Vice Lords fought the Burpies, the old Ambassadors withdrew and made an alliance with the Vice Lords. After the Burpies were defeated the old Ambassadors and the remnants of the Burpies became the Monroe Branch of the Vice Lords.

Other branches were formed by groups of boys who decided to start a Vice Lord branch in their own neighborhood. After "hanging" with the City Lords and proving themselves to be "regular fellows" they were allowed to set up their own branch and to use the Vice Lord name.

However, new branches usually were formed as a result of the high rate of spatial mobility found in the ghetto. As members of the various branches moved out of the neighborhood they would start new branches in their own neighborhood. Since they were already known as Vice Lords it was not necessary for them to prove themselves.

Membership

In the previous article the size of the Vice Lord Nation was given as being somewhere between one thousand and three thousand. This is an astounding figure. However, there are not one to three thousand hard dedicated members all engaged in gang fighting. Rather, there are different degrees of membership. The "heavy" members—to use the jargon of the club—are those who actively participate in all the club activities. There are also peripheral members. These include: 1. boys belonging to the club who participate to a lesser degree than the "heavy" members and 2. the older boys who once were "heavy," but whose present participation is slight. For instance, some have married, become employed or simply lost interest in gang fighting. In addition to these peripheral members there are also those who have never actually joined the club but are connected to it by certain ties of alliance. They have friends or relatives in the club, they attend club parties, and fight with club members if threatened or "jumped on" by members of another gang.

The Vice Lords have no standard initiation for new members. Initiation varies both among the different sub-organizations in the club and among the various individuals involved. In some cases a boy simply moves into a neighborhood which has a Vice Lord organization and hangs with members of the club. He participates in certain activities with them, "runs" with them on the streets and gradually takes part in more and more of their activities until finally he is considered a member.

Sometimes a boy will commit some act that gives him prestige in the eyes of the club members and he will be asked to join. An example of this is a boy nicknamed "Mad Dog." Mad Dog moved into the neighborhood of the City Lords. His first day in the neighborhood he was challenged by two younger brothers of one of the club's "heavy" members. In the fight that followed he not only whipped the two younger brothers but the older brother as well! He was then asked to join the Vice Lords. To do so he was required to "box" with "Stomp Daddy," the president of the branch. After the fight between them Stomp Daddy and Mad Dog stood back to back and fought off the other members of the club who came at them from all sides in a "free-for-all." Mad Dog fought until his jaw was put out of joint. Since he had won the respect of the club members he was taken into the group.

Branch Structure

The Vice Lord Nation is divided into distinct groups which are loosely allied in a federation. Each group has its own name. Several of the more powerful are: Vice Lord City, centered at the corner of 16th and Lawndale; the Monroe Lords on Monroe Street; the Maypole Lords on Maypole Avenue; the California Lords; and the Sacramento Lords; the West Side War Lords; and the Albany Vice Lords. Vice Lord City is the original branch and is probably the most important powerful group in the entire federation. It is considered the center of the Vice Lord Nation and the Vice Lord Social Center is located in its territory. All the Lords in the Nation have access to the center. Although autonomous each branch generally acknowledges the seniority of the City Lords. When the entire Nation meets (there have been several such meetings), the leaders of the City Lords conduct the meeting and the members of the City are responsible for maintaining order. Although some branches may be feuding, no fighting is allowed during these meetings.

The branches of the Vice Lord Nation are organized on the principle of segmentary opposition as illustrated in Diagram 1. In the diagram, 1 is antagonistic towards 2 but will unite in opposition to 3 and 4. Likewise 1 through 4 will form an alliance against 5 through 8. Finally, all of A and B will unite against any force attacking from outside the system. Whereas, in most documented segmentary opposition systems the links between units are based on biological relationships, within the Vice Lord Nation the links are based on the origin of the particular branches. The linkage of branches into

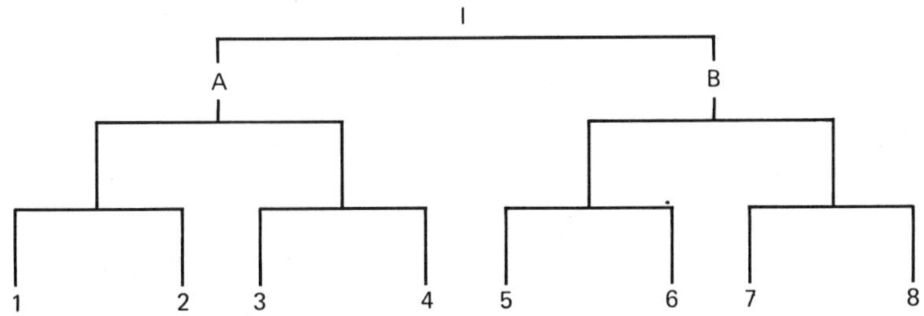

wider and wider alliance blocks is based on the fact that Vice Lords who move out of their neighborhood and either form new branches or join existing branches in their new neighborhood still feel ties of loyalty to the branch from which they came.

Diagram 2 shows the order of origin. The City Lords is the original group. From the City Lords came the Maypole Lords and the Albany Lords. The Albany Lords was in turn the parent group of the Sacramento Lords. The Monroe Lords had a prior existence as a separate club before joining the federation. They "gave birth" to the California Lords from which came the West Side War Lords.

Segmentary opposition is illustrated by the feud between the Monroe Lords and the Maypole Lords. The first actual fighting occurred when a group of Monroe Lords ambushed some Maypole Lords in their hangout. The Maypole Lords retaliated at a dance. Two distinct alliance blocks then formed. The City Lords joined the Maypole Lords since many Maypole Lords originally belonged to "The City." Monroe Lords were supported by the California Lords who had branched off from the Monroe Lords.

Segmentary opposition is further illustrated by the reaction of the Monroe and Maypole branches to the invasion of Vice Lord territory by a "foreign" club. A Monroe Lord gives the following account of this occurrence:

> Now while this [the feud between the Monroe and Maypole branches] was going on, the Racketeers was steady coming over . . . and they were throwing gas bombs, and they had got pretty good at it. But we united with the Maypole Lords and trapped them over in Douglas Park . . . which they weren't expecting us. They had done wrong, and they knew they had done wrong. Before they knew it, we were on them! This was both us and the Maypole Lords. This was about two days after we had got the Maypole Lords in the restaurant. But the fight between us was still going on. We were still mad with them, and they were still mad because we had beat up a lot of them and tore up their "hangout."

In feuds between branches fighting is generally limited to fists although bottles and sticks are sometimes used. In wars between clubs, however, shot-guns, pistols and knives are used. This use of weapons is similar

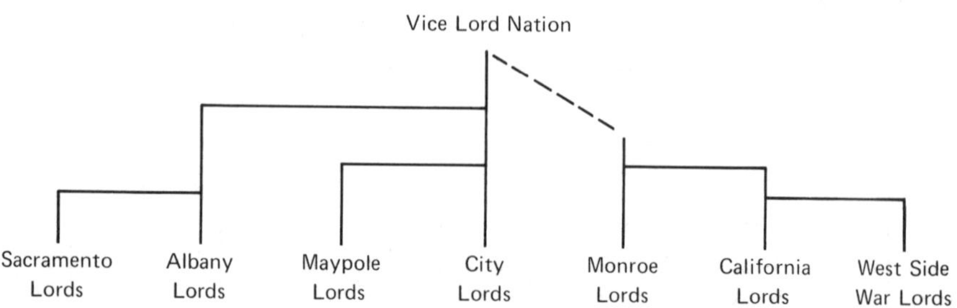

to non-Western societies organized on the principle of segmentary opposition. Weapons are limited in feuds between units of a tribe but are unlimited between tribes.

Sub-branch Organization—Sets

Each branch of the Vice Lord Nation is divided into three sets: The Seniors, the Juniors and the Midgets. Some branches even have Pee Wee Vice Lords. Each set has its own officers and conducts its own meetings. There are, therefore, not only as many presidents, vice-presidents, etc., as there are branches but within each branch there are three separate groups of officers as well. Counting the seven branches in the diagram there are twenty-one separate groups of officers.

Criterion for membership in a particular set varies with each branch. The criterion in Vice Lord City is a combination of "heart," size and age, in that order. ("Heart" is defined as the ratio between bravery in warfare and fighting skill.) The Midgets are usually 14 and 15 years of age, the Juniors are 16 and 17 and the Seniors are 18 and over.

Set membership in the City Lords is controlled by the leaders of the Seniors. A boy's reputation generally determines the set to which he is assigned. It also determines whether or not he will be allowed to change his membership from one set to another. Thus, the Midgets and the Juniors are most actively involved in gang fighting since they lack prestige and are determined to move up in the hierarchy. To do this they must spread the fame of their name by committing "brave deeds." The Seniors, on the other hand, already occupy a prestigious position in the status system and have less to gain by taking part in violent activities since they risk losing the advantages of their position by either being injured or killed or arrested and sent to jail.

Set membership is determined somewhat differently by the Monroe Lords. Generally the Midgets are boys 16 years of age and older who are small in size, the Seniors are boys 16 and older who are large and the Juniors are all those under 16 regardless of size. However, individual choice is the most important consideration in set membership. Usually a boy is free to join whatever set he chooses as long as the boys will accept him in that set. If at a later time he wishes to change his set membership he is free to do so provided the boys in the other set will accept him as a member.

Formal Political Organization

Formal political organization is well developed in the various branches of the Vice Lord Nation. There are seven distinct offices although all of them are not found in every branch. These are president, vice-president, secretary-treasurer, supreme war councilor, war councilor, gunkeeper and sergeant-at-arms.

The president is responsible for conducting meetings and is in charge of the branch delegation sent to meetings of the entire Nation. He is the symbolic head of the branch and in feuding and warfare his injury is the prime objective of enemy forces.

The vice-president is the president's assistant. He has little power except when the president is in jail or otherwise out of the picture, at which time he takes over the responsibilities of the president.

Specific information about the war council is available only for the Midgets of the Albany branch. In this group the war council is comprised of the supreme war councilor, the president and vice-president and a number of members. When one of its members has been attacked by individuals outside the group the war council decides whether or not the group will fight. All decisions have to be approved by a majority of the council. If it decides to fight the war council organizes and leads the planned battles. Actually much of the fighting which occurs results from accidental encounters between enemy peer groups, in which case the war councilors have no particular function.

The secretary-treasurer handles any money the group may have. This is usually an insignificant amount which is spent for social events and on rare occasions for bailing members out of jail.

The gunkeeper is responsible for the group's weapons. In some branches this responsibility falls to one of the war councilors. The sergeant-at-arms maintains order during meetings.

Territory

The territorial boundaries of the various branches are not clearly defined. Although Douglas Boulevard is the strongly defined boundary between the City Lords and a club known as the Roman Saints the eastern boundary of "The City" is not commonly agreed upon. Some say it is Homan Avenue while others say it is Kedzie. Although it is true that Douglas and Pulaski are thought to form definite southern and western boundary lines, it is misleading to view Vice Lord territory simply as connecting boundary lines on a map. Focal points of strategic territory are also important in the way the club members actually see their "map." Vice Lord members view their map not only in terms of specifically bounded territory but also in terms of certain street corners that have strategic importance to them; i.e., the statue that stands on the corner of Independence and Douglas. The possession of this statue has been the cause of many battles between the Vice Lords and their enemies.

The Peer Group

The Vice Lord Nation is divided into distinct groups called branches. These are further divided into sets usually based on age. Crosscutting the set organization of the branch is a system of peer groups which form the basic units in the Vice Lord social structure. These groups are the focus for warfare, political power struggles and social activities. Their structure is rather amorphous since membership is not strictly defined and leadership is not institutionalized into a set of formal political officers. In one of the peer groups in the City Lords, for example, one of the leaders was secretary-treasurer of the Seniors while another was president of the Juniors. Within the peer group itself neither was considered to out-rank the other. Because of this loose structure peer groups are similar in organization to the hustling gangs. . . . . In the jargon of the streets a group of boys in a peer group are referred to as "running partners."

Many peer groups have their own name and most have a definite position in a ranked hierarchy. In Vice Lord City a few years ago "The Magnificent Seven" was the most powerful. Another powerful group was known as "The Rat Pack." At present there is a group known as "The Brothers of the Spear." In the Sacramento Lords the most important of these groups is called "The Gallant Men."

Peer groups play a crucial role in deciding the outcome of power struggles within the branch organization. Peer groups fight one another in support of rival leaders vying for positions of power within the branch. In some clubs these power struggles have ended in the fission of the branch. For example, the "K" Town Egyptian Cobras split into the Spanish Cobras and the Impala Cobras. However, the Vice Lord branches have remained intact mainly because of the diplomatic ability of the president of the City Lords.

The Status System

As a club member one's status on the streets is based on what is known as "rep." A boy's "rep" is determined not only by his own reputation but also by the reputation of his peer group, his set, his branch and his club. The first step in gaining a "rep" is to have a nickname. This is usually bestowed upon an individual by the other members of the peer group. Some of the more colorful names are: Stomp Daddy, Pony Soldier, Goliath, Mighty Katanga, Attila the Hun, King Main, Cave Man and Blue Goose. Once a nickname is acquired the next step is to establish the fame of the name by committing "brave deeds." The deeds of Big Pep, a leader of the original group of the Vice Lords, have become legend on the streets of Lawndale. The story of how he and the other members of The Magnificent Seven "squared" the entire Imperial Chaplain Nation was related by a boy who has never even spoken to Big Pep.

Warfare

Gangfighting generally falls into three categories. The first is a planned battle commonly known as a rumble, a term which is not part of club jargon but has been popularized by Hollywood and the press. In this kind of gang warfare the decision to fight is made by the rival clubs, and the time and place for a battle is set in advance. Before fighting actually begins the opposing war councilors meet in the center of the battlefield with their supporting forces drawn up behind them. In some instances the war councilors recount the "reps" of the various "warriors" present with the hope of "squaring," i.e. facing down, the enemy without having to fight. Following is a Vice Lord's account of this kind of gangfight:

> Now a fight like this really looks funny when it starts, but it turns out to be terrifying! When it's just coming night is when most of the fighting occurs so if the police come, then everybody can get away.
>
> You got a stick, or maybe a knife, or a chain and some fools got shotguns. What you really do, you stand there and the councilors are the first ones up. You stand back and you wait and see if they come to an agreement and talk. Now everybody standing there watching everybody else to see what's going to happen. And all of a sudden maybe a blow will be passed, and if it is a fight starts right there. Let's say this is what happened. Now nine out of ten you know everybody in your club, or everybody who came with you. You standing just like you'd met in a crowd and you were talking. It's really almost a semicircle. You just standing there and you're looking—you're watching the councilor. And if a blow pass automatically the first thing you do is hit the man closest to you. After that if things get too tight for you then you get out of there. If it look like you getting whupped you get out. It's all according to your nerve. The first who runs, that's it right there. Naturally if you're standing there and you're fighting, and you see half the club starting to run, you know the other half going to run soon. All it takes is one to run and the whole crowd breaks up. That's how a club gets its "rep"—by not running, by standing its ground.

It should be noted, however, that incidents such as these are infrequent. Much more common is the second type of gangfighting called "wolf packing." Wolf packing is usually carried out by peer groups. It consists of raids into enemy or neutral territory with the object of ambushing enemy forces.

Finally, many gangfights result from the accidental confrontation of groups from rival clubs. The Vice Lords themselves refer to all kinds of fights as "humbugs." While "wolf packing" designates raiding activity, the author has not heard any special terms used to designate accidental confrontations and the "classic" rumble.

Collective Representations

Every social group has its own body of customs, rituals, symbols and beliefs called collective representations. The function of these cultural elements is to reinforce the unity of the group. In a way these elements symbolize the group's unity in the face of the outside hostile world. The Vice Lord Nation is no different in this respect from other social groups for it has a well-developed body of collective representations. The insignia or "coat-of-arms" of the Vice Lord Nation devised by one of the original founders of the club consists of a top hat, cane and white gloves. The uniform of the Lords is a cape in the Vice Lord colors of red and black. Red symbolizes blood while black stands for strength, heroism and evil. The letters CVL (Conservative Vice Lords) are on the back and the individual's name is on the side. Police pressure has stopped the wearing of these capes in public but many Lords still own them and sometimes wear them at Vice Lord functions.

The essence of language is its symbolic nature. The idiomatic element of a particular group's language not only conveys the obvious meaning assigned to specific words but also symbolizes the unity of the group itself. Slang and argot especially have this dual symbolism. The Vice Lords and other predominantly Negro clubs have developed their own argot system which symbolizes the group's unity. Since human interaction is mainly through language, it also legitimatizes one's participation in the interaction of the group. For example, in the argot of the Vice Lords "burn" means shoot, "boss" means good or wonderful, and "The Man" means the police.

Perhaps the most colorful of all Vice Lord customs is the wine ritual. It is a Vice Lord rule that prior to drinking a bottle of wine a small portion must be poured on the ground in the form of the letter V. This portion is for every Vice Lord dead or in jail. At large social gatherings where many Lords are present the rite is usually performed with the group standing in a circle while the wine is poured in the middle. As the wine is poured from the first bottle someone speaks the names of members of the particular group giving the party who are dead or in jail. Sometimes, however, all that is said is something like, "This is for all the fellows that can't be here."

The wine ritual makes a strong impression on those participating in it. A boy knows that if he is killed or sent to jail he will not be forgotten. This knowledge has a definite integrating effect on group cohesion.

Discussion

The social and cultural system of the Vice Lord Nation poses many questions to those interested in understanding the warrior gang phenomenon. Four stand out in this author's mind. Why do warrior clubs form? Why is fighting such an important part of the club's activities? What is the source for the behavioral models? And how does warrior club delinquency relate to other forms of delinquency? As yet there have been no completely satisfactory answers to these questions although it is possible to isolate certain factors and find certain clues that throw light on the problems.

1. Why do warrior clubs form? Certainly it is no coincidence that groups similar to the Vice Lords are found in cities from London to Tokyo in areas settled by the culturally deprived. Such conditions as low level of education, economic deprivation, family disorganization, and limited opportunity for advancement are found in slums throughout the world. All

are important in providing an environment conducive to the development of warrior gangs.

It should be noted, however, that warrior gangs fall into a more comprehensive category of social systems—the warrior society—which is not limited to slum areas in urban settlements, but is found throughout history in most parts of the world. Plains Indian societies such as the Blackfeet and the Sioux are well-known examples from our own heritage. Looking at the Vice Lord phenomenon from this wider perspective, our emphasis is now focused on those factors important in the development of the Vice Lords and also common to warrior societies in general.

Although undoubtedly there are many common denominators, we will be concerned mainly with the following factor: Warrior societies often form where there is a rapid breakdown of social organization, where patterns of interaction and values are weakly institutionalized into a unitary social and cultural system, and where existing mechanisms for social control are relatively undeveloped. A look at the area in which the Vice Lords were formed illustrates this.

The West Side of Chicago, the area in which the Vice Lords and other warrior clubs developed, is one of rapid social transformation. In a short time the neighborhoods of this area changed from predominantly white to predominantly Negro. The majority of those flooding the West Side came from two sources—directly from the rural South and from older ghettos razed by urban renewal.

While the new inhabitants from these areas were no more politically minded than many other groups in Chicago, they experienced a greater alienation from the formal political system in their new neighborhoods due to racial antagonisms. Whereas the people living in the more established ghetto areas generally felt that the neighborhood political organization was controlled by Negro politicians, their feelings changed when they moved to the West Side. There, to a greater extent, they identified the formal political system with a white-controlled organization. This led to a greater antagonism towards the police. Since the police force was considered an arm of the formal political system and the formal political system was identified with an alien—even enemy—group, the legitimacy of the police to enforce social controls was more strongly questioned.

Immigrants from the South have always felt alienated from the formal political system. But in the rural South there was an established social organization with effective mechanisms for social control. When every one in a community—or for that matter any social group—knows one another, ridicule and approval are effective ways of controlling deviancy. Life in the West Side ghetto is much different. Such conditions as high spatial mobility, high population density and the accompanying anonymity reduce the effectiveness of ridicule and approval as social control mechanisms. Therefore, in the new ghetto neighborhoods of the West Side the mechanisms of ridicule and approval were more or less inoperative, and the effectiveness of the police force as a control was nominal. It is not surprising that in this relative socio-cultural vacuum, youth has created its own social organization.

With such warrior societies as the Tusi (Watusi) of Africa, the Blackfeet and Sioux of the Plains and the Swat Pathans of Pakistan urbanization was not the catalytic agent, but these groups were formed in a similar sociocultural environment. Each of these societies formed in the wake of disrupting migrations which resulted in a breakdown in the operation of the established mechanisms for social control and therefore necessitated the revamping of the social structure to fit changed conditions. As we have seen, in the case of the Vice Lords this social and cultural disorganization can be traced to the processes of urbanization. With other societies there undoubtedly are other reasons. In any case the resulting breakdown was the same and warrior groups were formed.

2. The question arises, what is this principle of political organization which forms the basis for placing various groups in the category of warrior societies? The answer lies in the second question posed above: Why is fighting such an important part of the club's activities.

Fighting is an important element in the life of many peoples. It is essential in warrior societies like the Vice Lords, where politics is based on the principle of self-help. The principle works like this: Human beings cannot exist in an atmosphere of uncontrolled violence. Unlike complex political systems where violence is controlled by a specialized group (a police force, for example), in systems organized on self-help violence is controlled both by retaliation and by the threat of retaliation. If, for example, it is known that violence to a Vice Lord will bring instant retaliation against either the offender or any member of the offender's group, then both individuals and groups will think twice before injuring a Vice Lord. In the case of warrior gangs the greater the reputation of both the individual members and the club, the greater the fear of retaliation will be. Therefore, it is usually safer to belong to a club with a famous reputation. Herein lies the crux of the matter. For groups to become so feared that others will feel restrained from using violence against them it is first necessary to commit acts of violence and in this way establish a reputation as a gang to be feared. Then periodic acts of violence are necessary to maintain the reputation and to prove to outsiders that a group is both willing and able to retaliate if its members are injured. Thus, in order for social systems organized on the principle of self-help to operate with a minimum of stability, a certain amount of violence is necessary to keep violence under control. Self-help operates in the same manner whether the opposing groups are rival peer groups, feuding branches, or enemy clubs.

3. What is the source of the Vice Lords' behavioral models? The models for behavior, and the underlying values in the Vice Lord social system were not created by pure innovation, but were borrowed. Much of the idealized behavior of the Lords is modeled after that found in comic books, epic historical movies, and TV adventure programs. The Vice Lords idealize the man of action, the warrior, and think of fighting in terms of epic adventure. For example, a boy testifying in Boys' Court about a gangfight said that during the battle one of the boys yelled, "I am Dough Belly, the Mighty Gladiator!"

4. The final question has to do with the nature of warrior club delinquency. It is apparent that the Vice Lords have their own values and their own behavioral norms like all other societies. Individuals behaving in a manner considered unacceptable to the group are subject to negative sanctions. One will probably find within the Vice Lords, as within other societies, a normal range of personality types. The prevalence of delinquency within these gangs is not the result of an unusually large number of boys with personality defects. Rather it stems from the internalization of a "blue print for behavior" which, although functional in the streets of the ghetto, is aberrant and even dysfunctional relative to the more powerful middle class which controls the community. Thus, it is different in kind from the delinquency of those individuals whose "criminal" behavior stems from emotional problems. This is important to remember in dealing with gang boys.

This paper has dealt with the phenomenon of warrior clubs with special emphasis on the social and cultural system of the Vice Lord Nation. One is inclined to condemn warrior clubs and other similarly organized societies, and perhaps rightly so, but a look at today's headlines shows that modern nations organize their interrelationships in the same manner. The warrior club offers its members a functional solution to many problems that ghetto life poses. In this context observe the members of warrior clubs who appear in Boys' Court. In many cases the boy stands before the court apparently with little or no support. A grandmother, aunt or mother may be present but most of the family is too scattered or unconcerned to come. Then, after his case is heard, one notices six . . . ten . . . or even more youths leave the courtroom. These are his "partners," his fellow club members. They care what happens to him. They care enough to spend a day sitting in a courtroom located in a police station. They care enough to risk injury fighting in his behalf. To a boy who must face life in the ghetto, the club offers him a way of coping with the problems he faces. Until the community can provide a better solution to these problems gang boys will remain fearsome warriors prowling their urban battlefields.

6 Ecology and Demography

Ecology is the study of the principles governing the interrelationships of organisms and their environments. Human ecology is the study of man's interrelation with his social, physical, and symbolic environment. Social environment is the other beings, in varying numbers, who interact with each other; physical environment is the material and natural nonsocial objects; and symbolic environment is that which man creates for himself through his symbols, things that stand for other things.

Demography deals with the growth rate, size, distribution, and special consequences of human populations.

Ecology and demography study the social consequences of given rates of population growth, size, and density. The social psychology of population includes attitudes and values of population growth and control. It is possible to analyze a growth curve demographically without reference to the social meanings growth may create or alter; it is also possible to take both into account, as the Moller article argues. Moller carefully points out that the number of young, rate of growth, and ratio of the young to the remainder of the population are social facts, but they may or may not be psychologically relevant to a given group. In other words, sheer numbers of young people will not automatically, or even necessarily, provide a political power base.

Moller argues that the coincidence of large numbers of youth inadequately absorbed into the society, rapid and disruptive change, and development of youth leaders will make youth a potent political force. He provides numerous fascinating historical examples of the power of youth in Germany, Italy, Russia, and France.

Lofland's analysis of age segregation and the creation of the "youth ghetto" is a socio-psychological complement to Moller's historical, structural, and demographic analysis. Whereas Moller begins with historical facts, Lofland begins with man's symbolic environment, with the categories he uses to sort reality. Lofland documents the arbitrariness of our construction of reality, in that nearly all our rules and norms are both imagined and open to question. Societal complexity, from this perspective, arises from the perceived clustering of categories in everyday life, for example, the combining of age, sex, and kinship to create families. Paradoxically, the very complexity that results requires some practical solution, some simplifying formula. Lofland argues that people tend to focus on one simple category as pivotal, or most significant, among all these simplifying categories.

When age is associated with a specific territory, crowding, low income, and little identification with local institutions, a matter of population and ecology is converted into a social problem. Special definitions and perceptions result in a special social-control apparatus directed toward the problem group (see Brown), a special literature explaining the nature of the outgroup, and attribution of moral failings to that group. Once such a definition of youth is developed, and the low income of the objects of attention (the young) continues, there is little chance of eliminating the negative labels.

Moller argues that societies that can absorb the demands of the young, or of other minorities, can meet the challenge to the social order often symbolized by youth.

The potential for prolonged conflict, particularly in university towns, is certainly apparent. Lofland suggests that it occurs whenever there is low ingroup–outgroup contact, little flow of information between groups, and exploitation of the minority by the majority. The image, as Friedenberg pointed out, is used to reduce and dehumanize people to mere objects, to isolate and stereotype them even further. Will population growth in the United States have these consequences for a variety of yet to be identified minorities?

Youth as a Force in the Modern World

Herbert Moller

I

The unprecedented number of young people in the world today can be isolated as one of the crucial reality factors conditioning political and cultural developments. Age distribution is only one demographic variable in the complex of social and political life, but the tremendous growth of world population in the twentieth century has magnified its dynamic potentialities. To gain perspective, it will be useful to briefly consider the role of youth in the light of historical experience.

Throughout the centuries, spontaneous youth organizations have had a continuous existence, but a ferment among the young with its subsequent departure from cultural or political tradition can be observed only at certain times and in certain geographical areas. As a rule, young people become conspicuous in public life in periods of rapid demographic growth. Of the numerous historical examples only a few can be referred to in this essay. Moreover, in view of the predominantly narrative nature of historiography and its low level of generality, these illustrations serve only to suggest plausible agreements between contemporary events of demographic and general history.

The Protestant Reformation in west-central Europe provides an example of one of the outstanding youth movements in history. Luther himself published the Ninety-five Theses at the age of 34; he wrote his three great Reformation tracts in 1520 at the age of 37. In the 1520's, Wittenberg University, which had been founded in 1502, boasted probably the youngest faculty in the history of German universities, a teaching staff of uncommon brilliance and ideological cohesion. A number of men younger than Luther received professorships: Aurogallus was appointed at the age of 30, Justin Jonas and Augustin Schiff at 27, Johannes Hainpol and Melanchthon at 21; the latter was quickly acknowledged the leader of the philosophical faculty though he was younger than many of his students.

Reprinted by permission of the author and the publisher, The Cambridge University Press, from *Comparative Studies in Society and History* 10 (April 1968):237–60.

The younger scholars became Luther's earliest adherents, while most of the older ones condemned his ideas. Some of them, together with members of the local clergy, left Wittenberg or were discharged; others held out as best they could until they died. One, a canon at the *Schlosskirche,* who opposed all ritual innovation, was forced to change his attitude when Luther's youthful followers smashed his windows.

The growing reputation of the Wittenberg reformers attracted a reserve of young scholars ready and able to fill posts that fell vacant, or indeed any intellectual gap. Such a man as Agricola, for example, came to Wittenberg at 22 and remained until he had found an effective function in the reform movement. During the early years of the Reformation, the number of university students leapt from about 1,500 to 2,000 and more. Since Wittenberg was a small town of only 2,500 regular inhabitants, the influx of students gave it an exceptionally youthful population.[1] The devotion of these students to their leaders was shown as early as 1519, when Luther, Carlstadt, and Melanchthon set out for the Leipzig disputation in two open wagons "surrounded by nearly two thousand armed students and other supporters."[2] Students flocked to the lectures of Melanchthon and increasingly rejected the Thomists and Scotists entrenched in the older German universities like Leipzig, Frankfurt on the Oder, Greifswald, Rostock, Basel, and others. These institutions, firmly opposing the Reformation for two decades, lost first their students and then their scholarly reputations. Some time after 1535 every one of them had to be reconstituted.

Although Luther complained that the evangelical message did not find acceptance among the old, he was forced to hold the students in check to prevent them from going too far in their protests against Pope and Emperor. Melanchthon, also, fought an inclination to primitivism among students. Some of them carried their opposition to Aristotle and scholasticism to the point of rejecting all scholarship, and advocated the innocent simplicity of the Apostles. Luther's early followers outside Wittenberg (Bugenhagen, Bucer, *et al.*) were, almost to a man, younger than he, whereas, with the exception of Eck, all his more important opponents were older. Some well-known humanists like Erasmus of Rotterdam, at first sympathized with Luther's ideas of reform, then broke with him. But Erasmus was already 50 in 1517 when the Theses were promulgated.[3]

It is imperative to distinguish between precocious individuals and actual youth movements. For instance, in 1531, the Spaniard Michel Servetus published his famous *De Trinitatis Erroribus* at 19 years of age. Sixteenth-century Spain, however, experienced no trace of a youth movement, a fact which, viewed quantitatively, relates to the depletion of its cohorts of late adolescents and young adults through emigration to the Spanish overseas

[1] Herbert Schöffler, *Die Reformation* (Bochum-Langendreer, Pöppinghaus, 1936), pp. 33–98; reprint, *Wirkungen der Reformation* (Frankfurt a.M., Klostermann, 1960), pp. 126–66.

[2] George H. Williams, *The Radical Reformation* (Philadelphia, Westminster Press, 1962), p. 39.

[3] Schöffler, *Wirkungen,* pp. 130–31, 141–74.

empire and through naval, military, and government service abroad. In Germany, by contrast, in the years immediately preceding the Lutheran Reformation, there existed an intellectual proletariat. Priests, in particular—either impoverished or unattached to a parish—vagrant preachers, prophets, and demagogues went about haranguing the populace. But among the craftsmen too, younger people experienced protracted vocational insecurity, and many saw no hope of ever escaping the condition of a dependent and often unemployed journeyman. Tax records of some German cities attest to a downward mobility of middle-income groups in the later fifteenth or early sixteenth centuries. The early years of the sixteenth century brought numerous local revolts of peasants, knights, and city people, culminating in the great Peasants' War of 1524–25, which in northern Germany was a conflict actually more urban than rural.[4]

These events were connected with a demographic upturn beginning in the mid-fifteenth century, reversing the downward trend that had been caused by the Black Death and succeeding epidemics. There were considerable regional differences. In England and most of France between 1470 and 1550, an increasing prosperity served the needs of the growing population. Conditions differed, however, in northern Italy, Switzerland, eastern France (Burgundy), and the entire area of the old German Empire where the upsurge, begun slowly after 1450, rose sharply about 1500, threatening to shake the existing social order. Demographic information, inadequate with reference to entire countries during this period, nevertheless suggest a long-term growth trend. Research on smaller areas, however, yields more specific data. On the basis of the number of houses in thousands of towns and villages in a compact region of central Germany, Koerner found that the construction of dwelling units increased rapidly in the second quarter of the sixteenth century, then slowed down consistently from a growth rate of 7.1% in the 1520's, 6.8% in the 1530's, 6.5% in the 1540's to 3.3% in the 1590's. Although no figures for the first two decades of the sixteenth century are available, the natural increase of the population had most likely reached its greatest momentum some time before the year 1500. In the 1520's, despite depression and turmoil, more people were setting up homes of their own than in any later decade. This information agrees with the assumption of large cohorts of young adults in the first several decades of the sixteenth century.[5]

The youth movement of the first half of the sixteenth century was not limited to the Lutheran Reformation. Zwingli at 32 first challenged the old faith; Calvin at 26 had the temerity to dedicate his *Institutes of the Chris-*

[4]Willy Andreas, *Deutschland vor der Reformation* (Stuttgart, Deutsche Verlags-Anstalt, 1932). Will-Erich Peuckert, *Die grosse Wende* (Hamburg, Claassen & Goverts, 1948). Günther Franz, *Der deutsche Bauernkrieg* (München & Berlin, Oldenbourg, 1933).

[5]Fritz Koerner, "Die Bevölkerungszahl und -dichte in Mitteleuropa zum Beginn der Neuzeit," *Forschungen und Fortschritte,* XXXIII (1959), Heft 11, pp. 325–31. For other than German demographic data, Josiah C. Russell, *Late Ancient and Medieval Population* (= *Transactions American Philosophical Society,* N.S., Vol. 48, Part 3) (Philadelphia, American Philosophical Society, 1958), pp. 113–27.

tian Religion to Francis I, inviting him to reform himself and his Kingdom of France. Theodor Beza and Sebastian Franck both joined the Reformation in their twenties. Those going over to the radical wing of the Reformation were remarkably young. Hans Denck, expelled from Nuremberg at 25, died at 27; Louis Haetzer, banished from Augsburg at 25, died at 30; Felix Mantz, leader of the Zurich radicals at 25, was executed at 27; Conrad Grebel, the founder of the Swiss Brethren, experienced conversion at 23, died at 28; Melchior Hoffmann became a Lutheran at 27, an Anabaptist at 30; Menno Simons, ordained a priest at 28, felt his first dogmatic doubts at 29, but laid down his priestly office only at the age of 40.

The Reformation period has been treated here at some length in order to emphasize the fact that the demographic factor operates independently of the industrial, modern, or "anti-imperialist" social context. To be sure, not all important movements in history are characterized by a youthful leadership and youthful supporters. Neither the Catholic Counter-Reformation nor the Enlightenment can be considered a youth movement in this sense, as opposed to early seventeenth-century English puritanism which apparently can.

There can be no doubt about the surge of youthful activism in several European countries in roughly the last 30 years of the eighteenth century. Child mortality declined in western and central Europe after 1750, while the life expectancy of older people did not noticeably improve.[6] As a consequence the number of young people increased considerably. In the 1770's and 1780's France had a higher proportion of late adolescents and young adults under 30 than at any time thereafter.[7] In 1789, those over 40 years of age constituted only 24 percent of the French population, while those between 20 and 40 years constituted 40 percent, and those under 20 made up 36 percent. Exposed to the economic hardships that prevailed between 1785 and 1794, the numerous under-employed young people formed an explosive population group. Their presence contributed decisively to the revolutionary unrest in city and country, and also to the military ventures of the Revolutionary and Napoleonic wars.[8] Brinton pointed out the large number of unemployed young intellectuals: "One is struck in studying French society in the years just preceding the Revolution with a kind of jam in the stream of bright young men descending on Paris to write and talk their way to fortune. Mercier in his *Tableau de Paris* tells how every sunny day young men might be seen on the Quays, washing and drying their only shirts, ruffled and lacy symbols of high social status."[9]

[6]D. V. Glass and D. E. C. Eversley, eds., *Population in History* (London, Edward Arnold, 1965), pp. 404, 447. William L. Langer, "Europe's Initial Population Explosion," *Amer. Hist. Rev.*, LXIX (1963–64), 1–17.

[7]See Table 3, p. 230.

[8]Jacques Godechot, *Les révolutions (1770–1779)* (Paris, Presses Universitaires de France, 1963), p. 86.

[9]Crane Brinton, *The Anatomy of Revolution*, Rev. ed. (1952. Reprint, New York, Vintage Books, 1957), p. 66.

Outside of France, unrest, resistance to authorities, and vagrancy became a major problem among working class youth; discontent and excitability spread among the younger generation of the educated classes. Nationalistic enthusiasm appeared for the first time as a potent emotional theme, originally in France, then, with a strong anti-French note, in other countries. The explosion of revolutionary, warlike, nationalist, and anti-imperialist (i.e., anti-French) activity toward the end of the eighteenth and in the early nineteenth centuries received its social fuel from the large youth cohorts of "Europe's initial population explosion."[10]

Most countries of Europe experienced a more or less rapid demographic growth in the course of the nineteenth century, and revolutionary agitators like Mazzini put their faith in the activism of the young. Persons over 40 were excluded from Mazzini's organization, Young Italy. He wrote: "Place the young at the head of the insurgent masses; you do not know what strength is latent in those young bands, what magic influence the voices of the young have on the crowd; you will find them a host of apostles for the new religion. But youth lives on movement, grows great in enthusiasm and faith. Consecrate them with a lofty mission; inflame them with emulation and praise; spread through their ranks the word of fire, the word of inspiration; speak to them of country, of glory, of power, of great memories."[11] Mazzini became the revered leader of young militants, who in turn became the teachers of other national youth movements.

In societies undergoing disruptive change, adolescents and young adults are eminently attracted by direct action as well as by ideologies promising perfection in a hurry. It was said of Garibaldi that he could at any time gather an army of young volunteers for a patriotic cause. For the development of Italy, however, it was decisive that the Piedmontese government prevented the young idealists led by Mazzini and Garibaldi from taking over power. In fact, outside Italy also, "movement governments," which have become the promise and the terror of the twentieth century, were generally averted in the nineteenth century.

Compared with Italy, nineteenth-century Germany, whose population grew much more rapidly, had a smaller share of impulsive activism. This may be attributed to Germany's more forceful industrialization and to its social advance, both of which facilitated the economic integration of young people. An important aspect of the German development was the internal migration of young people to cities and industrial areas in response to increasing job opportunities, not only—as in many underdeveloped countries—because of rural misery and hopelessness. The discontent as well as the enthusiasm of the German working class flowed into a purposeful socialist labor move-

[10]Godechot, *op. cit.* Henri Brunschwig, *La crise de l'état prussien à la fin du XVIIIe siècle et la genèse de la mentalité romantique* (Paris, Presses Universitaires de France, 1947). Fritz Valjavec, *Die Entstehung der politischen Strömungen in Deutschland 1770–1815 (Munich,* Oldenbourg, 1951), pp. 185–86, 214–24, 235–37, 321.

[11]Quoted by Frederick Hertz, *Nationality in History and Politics* (London, Routledge & Kegan Paul, 1944), p. 388.

ment. Middle-class youth had good reasons to adjust to available vocational prospects; many did so with a single-mindedness deeply deplored by German authors of a romantic bent. Aggressive fantasies found fertile fields in the increasingly strident nationalism; nevertheless, nihilism had no place in German society before the First World War.

The opposite extreme characterized nineteenth-century Russia: economic development lagged far behind the tremendous surge of population growth. Despair and violence among the Russian peasantry was paralleled in the upper and middle classes by "successive waves of angry young men."[12] For instance, the three major intellectual leaders of "Young Russia" in the early 1860's were all young. Chernyshevsky's political activity was ended at 34, in 1862, when he was arrested and, two years later, condemned to forced labor. Dobrolyubov died at 25; Pisarev at 28.[13]

In the nineteenth century, when the nations of Europe were growing on an unprecedented scale, they possessed larger cohorts of adolescents and young adults than those of today; yet the proportions of these age groups never loomed as large as they do in the developing countries of the present; furthermore, Europe's "population explosion" was attenuated by the availability of outlets for emigration, of which especially the younger people availed themselves. Much of the restless energy and adventuresomeness of youth was thus transferred to overseas colonies and to the United States.

The proportion of young people began to fall early in the twentieth century in most nations of western Europe, owing to the decline in the fertility rate which had started around 1880. This process, more pronounced in the British Isles, France, Belgium, German-speaking Austria, and Sweden than in Germany and Italy, could be regarded as a demographic slope descending from Russia, Rumania, and Bulgaria in the east to Ireland and France in the west. The Habsburg Monarchy, attempting as it did to resist the national-revolutionary movements of the Serbs and Croats, was politically the most exposed area of this slope. The South-Slavic peoples of the Habsburg Monarchy had a higher fertility rate than did the Austro-Germans and Hungarians; and in the great assault on the cohesion of the Habsburg Empire, which ended in its destruction, teen-agers and young adults played a notable role.

Gavrilo Princip, who had just finished high school when he assassinated Archduke Francis Ferdinand, belonged to the circle of young intellectuals and high school students called Young Bosnia. Although this small group of conspirators received weapons and technical help from the Serbian Black Hand society, they acted independently and, in the days immediately before the assassination, refused to desist from their plan. The assassination of the Archduke, in June 1914, cannot be counted as a major cause but rather as the spark that set off the conflagration; yet to a considerable extent it forced the hand of the Serbian government, and thereby determined

[12] The phrase is Adam B. Ulam's. See his *The Bolsheviks* (New York, Macmillan, 1965).

[13] E. Lampert, *Sons Against Fathers: Studies in Russian Radicalism and Revolution* (Oxford, Clarendon Press, 1965); on youth activities esp. pp. 85–92, 125, 236–42.

the timing and conditions of the outbreak of the war. The Young Bosnians despised the Serbian bourgeoisie who cooperated with the Austrians "for the sake of material gain." Gavrilo Princip is reported to have said, shortly before the assassination, that if he could force the entire business community of Sarajevo into a matchbox, he would set it alight.[14] In prison, Princip said to the psychiatrist, Dr. Pappenheim: "Our generation was mostly conservative, but in the people as a whole there existed the wish for national liberation. The older generation was of a different opinion from the younger one as to how to bring it about . . . The older generation wanted to secure liberty from Austria in a legal way; we do not believe in such liberty." Dedijer writes that many youths were involved in the national-revolutionary struggle, and that "in almost every family there was a revolt of the younger generation against the older." High school boys, in particular, highly politicized and deeply dedicated, remained uncorrupted by the lure of money, alcohol, love, family, and vocational interests.[15]

The political significance of the Young Bosnians is seen in their opposition to the cautious policy of the Serbian government of the Old Radicals under Pašić and in their plan to use violence to force those leaders to abandon their slow-moving policy and risk a military showdown with the Habsburgs. In this they succeeded; after the assassination, many diplomats felt that the government of Serbia would be unable to maintain itself against internal opposition if it acceded to all the demands of the Austrian ultimatum and thus permitted Serbian sovereignty to be impaired.[16]

After the end of the First World War, political turbulence remained high in eastern Europe where populations were both younger and poorer. In Germany, as in all of Europe, birth rates declined rapidly in the 1920's; about 1930 Germany's population was no longer reproducing itself. However, the proportion of young adults remained very high in Germany as a result of high rates of natural increase twenty to thirty years earlier. The cohorts of 1900 to 1914, more numerous than any earlier ones, had not been decimated by the war. When they entered the labor market, between 1918 and 1932, their ranks were swelled by immigrants from the ceded territories of Alsace-Lorraine, Poznan, Polish Upper Silesia, etc., and by German nationals from abroad, mostly from eastern and southeastern Europe. Altogether close to one and a half million entered Germany between 1918 and 1925. At the same time, emigration to the United States was reduced by the quota system; and by 1930, under the impact of the depression, it ceased altogether and was replaced by a reverse movement of impoverished former emigrants back to Germany.[17]

[14]Vladimir Dedijer, *The Road to Sarajevo* (New York, Simon & Schuster, 1966), p. 207.

[15]*Ibid.*, pp. 207–8, 222, 262–63.

[16]Imanuel Geiss, *Juli 1914: Die europäische Krise und der Ausbruch des Ersten Weltkrieges* (Munich, Deutscher Taschenbuch Verlag, 1965), pp. 25–26 and documents Nos. 56, 67, 100.

[17]Eugene M. Kulischer, *Europe on the Move: War and Population Changes, 1917–1947* (New York, Columbia, 1948), pp. 160–88.

Table 1. Age Group 20–45 in Percent of Total Population of Germany[18]

1871	35.3
1880	34.9
1890	34.4
1900	35.6
1911	35.9
1925	38.8
1933	41.5
1950	35.8
1959	33.7

As a result of these developments the labor market became glutted. When the depression hit the German economy, the age group from 20 to 45, the core of the working force, was the largest in German history. Even during the relatively prosperous years of the Weimar Republic, young people of the large youth cohorts were marching and rallying. Never before had German youth formed so many organizations, each of which combined comradeship among members with intense hatred of opponents.[19]

In the elections of 1930, 4,600,000 first-time voters went to the polls, mainly young people who had begun their adult life without either work or hope. They brought Hitler his first great electoral success. From a demographic viewpoint the economic depression hit Germany at the worst possible time: employment was shrinking precisely at a time when the employable population reached its postwar peak. In 1933, the year Hitler came to power, the influx of youth had already begun to taper off. The number of cohorts born during the First World War and the postwar period and entering the labor market after 1932 was so small that German politicians and population experts were greatly concerned about the future of the white race.[20] Despite an upturn of the birth rate under Hitler, it never reached the level of 1925. The Second World War further thinned out the ranks of the young adults, and, to the extent that age composition conditions social life, Germany has become a different nation. By 1960, 60 percent of German adolescents professed to be "politically indifferent," 30 percent were "interested," and only 10 percent "politically engaged."[21]

The most important change was the thoughtful and liberal attitude of

[18]Walther G. Hoffmann, *Das Wachstum der deutschen Wirtschaft seit der Mitte des 19. Jahrhunderts* (Berlin, Springer, 1965), p. 177.

[19]The politicized youth of the 1920's differed completely from the romantic, anti-urban *Jugendbewegung* of the pre-war decade. Helmut Schelsky, *Die skeptische Generation* (1957; Sonderausgabe: Düsseldorf Köln, Diederichs, 1963), Chap. 4, section on "Die Generation der politischen Jugend."

[20]Kulischer *op. cit.*, pp. 161, 187. Rudolf Heberle, *From Democracy to Nazism: A Regional Case Study of Political Parties in Germany* (Baton Rouge, Louisiana State University, 1945), p. 123. Marcel Dutheil, *La population allemande* (Paris, Payot, 1937), Chaps. II, XV.

[21]Walter Jaide, *Das Verhältnis der Jugend zur Politik* (Berlin-Spandau, Luchterhand, 1963).

the majority of the last-named group. German postwar youth, "the skeptical generation," is interested in vocational advancement, early marriage, and a comfortable and pleasurable life; as Schelsky has pointed out, emotional attitudes of young and middle-aged people are less differentiated today than formerly. Since the mid-fifties, when prosperity returned to Europe, aggressive anti-social conduct of teen-agers has become a problem in all industrialized countries; but nowhere in Europe have teen-age cliques hardened into stable organizations; nowhere has adolescent rebellion generated political postures. In all industrialized countries of Europe, the non-alienated are setting the style of life.

In the United States, by contrast, political demonstrations and civil rights projects began about 1960 and gathered momentum each successive year, as violence increasingly replaced mere verbal protests. The most active civil rights workers were under thirty. On the college scene, the change from the "silent generation" to the mass rallies and truculent oratory of the sixties, although led by an avant-garde of atypical students, was backed by a surprisingly large following of sympathizers.[22] The yearning for "participatory democracy" and the new mood of social activism coincided with the rise of the more numerous cohorts of the 1940's and 1950's reaching late adolescence and college age in the 1960's. In actuality, the most vociferous radicalism expresses the hopelessness of a young counter-elite. They sense the futility of their aggressive aspirations in a prosperous and flexible society that offers attractive rewards for achievers, tames large numbers of young people through early marriage and parenthood, and in time absorbs even most of its alienated youth, a minority in any case.

Negroes face a different situation. Living in a society that incites in all of its members the expectation of a high consumption level, they remain economically depressed. Because their fertility has been higher for all years for which relevant data are available, Negroes show a higher proportion of adolescents and young adults than does the white population. In addition, postwar fertility rose somewhat more rapidly for the non-white population.[23] The increase in Negro youth has been most pronounced in the big cities. Almost all of the American Negroes who migrated, during the past half century, from the Deep South to the northern and western cities were teen-agers and young adults; their average age was 20–24. Consequently their high fertility rate, in the new urban environment, aggravated economic and housing problems. Although the 1960 census reported that the majority of Negroes living in northern and western cities had been born in them, surprisingly enough this home-grown urban Negro population had an

[22]Jacob R. Fishman and Frederick Solomon, "Youth and Social Action," and "Youth and Peace: A Psychological Study of Student Peace Demonstrators in Washington," *Journal of Social Issues*, XX, No. 4 (Oct. 1964), pp. 1–28, 54–73.

[23]U.S. Department of Health, Education, and Welfare: Public Health Service, *Natality Statistics Analysis: United States—1964 (National Center for Health Statistics, Ser.* 21, No. 11) (Washington, D.C., U.S. Government Printing Office, Feb. 1967), pp. 11–13. "In 1964, the excess of the fertility rate (births per 1,000 women 15–44 years of age) for non-whites over that of whites was 42 percent." *Ibid.*, p. 11.

average age of only about 12 years.[24] The youthfulness of the American Negro population accounts for much of the impetus and vitality of the civil rights movement. On the other hand, it has also led to a growth of uncontrolled aggressiveness, costing the older and more moderate leaders their popularity and leading toward a rejection of integration and, possibly, the development of a separate anti-white Negro sub-culture.

In non-western nations, the outlook for young revolutionaries appears brightest where the poverty and insecurity of an underdeveloped but changing economy coincides with a high proportion of adolescents and young adults. This situation is aggravated by the accelerated urbanization of the developing countries, which must certainly be considered as a major source of floating discontent and activism. Millions of the rural distressed are invading the cities and looking for employment, which too often is not available. In Greater Bombay, according to the 1961 census, about 65 percent of the population were immigrants. Similar situations in other large Indian cities result from a corresponding increase in the rate of rural-urban migration in recent years. In Asia and Latin America almost all migrants to urban centers are young people between 10 and 35 years of age.[25]

The numerous revolts that have occurred since the Second World War coincide with the accelerated population growth. In several countries the first wave of revolutionary youth have already been opposed, defeated, and replaced by a younger movement of political activists. For instance, Egypt's first modern party composed of the youth who rioted in 1919 and became the driving force in the Wafd were, between 1946 and 1952, reproached by the young street fighters and guerrillas, especially students, who themselves were preparing the way for the *coup d'état* of the young military intelligentsia.[26]

The key dates of revolutionary activities are, of course, not connected with any particular year-cohorts but with a decade or more of young people, usually led by men in their thirties. In China the so-called "Student Movement" of 1919 and the 1920's was composed of students, professors, and returned students from abroad, most of whom were between the ages of 17 and 25, and most of whom enthusiastically joined the Kuomintang.[27] But by 1936 the Kuomintang had lost the support of educated youth, for Chiang, meeting increased pressure from the warlords and the Communists,

[24]C. Horace Hamilton, "The Negro Leaves the South," *Demography,* I (1964), p. 285.

[25]Jag Mohan Sehgal, "The Population Distribution in Greater Bombay," *Asian Economic Review,* VIII, No. 2 (Feb. 1966), pp. 185–97. Carmen A. Miró, "The Population of Latin America," *Demography,* I (1964), pp. 19–29. U Aung Thein, "Some Aspects of Urban Explosions in Developing Countries," *Population Index,* XXXII (1966), p. 349.

[26]P. J. Vatikiotis, *The Egyptian Army in Politics: Pattern for New Nations?* (Bloomington, Indiana University Press, 1961), pp. 40, 45–52, 79.

[27]Tsi C. Wang, *The Youth Movement in China* (New York, New Republic, 1928), pp. 2–3, 160–241. Dr. Hu Shih was born in 1891 and returned to China in 1917 to become professor of philosophy at the National University of Peking; *ibid.,* p. 11. John Israel, *Student Nationalism in China, 1927–1937* (Stanford, Cal., University Press, 1967).

was forced to buy time from the Japanese, a development that effectively dampened the revolutionary ardor of the students. More and more widely, thereafter, the Communists enlisted the support of middle-class youth against foreigners. Whatever the origins and the meaning of the "Great Cultural Revolution" of 1966–67, this frightful terroristic campaign testifies to the energies that can be generated from the organization of vast numbers of unsocialized teen-agers.

The recent history of Indonesia has also been characterized by successive waves of revolutionary youth. In the revolution of 1945–46, not only the Dutch but also most of the native aristocrats lost their positions and were replaced by nationalist politicians and by the *pemudas,* the "Generation of '45," or young revolutionary activists. The *pemuda* movement drew in young men from every social background, who "formed the most important of the new organizations to appear at the local level, the army, and the *badan perdjuangan* [the irregular *pemuda* organization] . . . It produced the majority both of those who committed atrocities and those who showed the highest and most self-sacrificing idealism."[28]

Again in 1965–66, after the Communist *coup* had been thwarted by the army and Sukarno thereupon tried to withdraw political power from the military, college students were first to revolt. After they had been subdued by Sukarno's forces, they called on the organized high school students, who responded with an uprising that brought about the downfall of Sukarno's government. In this case, Muslim and other non-Communist teenagers went into the streets with the approval and admiration of their families: the young people took risks which their parents themselves would not have taken, and in the following months they helped to identify and hunt down Communists or reputed Communists. Possibly close to half a million people were butchered by the young idealists and General Suharto's soldiers.[29] For over a year the university students and their allies, and the association of high school students continued to hold mass demonstrations and to press for further changes. An Indonesian intellectual, serving them as an informal mentor, explained, "They are very frustrated and very angry. In a critical moment of our history, these passionate, dedicated, immature, politically untutored students have taken over. Now they are getting their political education very quickly."[30]

II

It is generally recognized that the presence of a large number of adolescents and young adults influences social and political affairs; it is revealing, how-

[28]John R. W. Smail, *Bandung in the Early Revolution, 1945–1946: A Study in the Social History of the Indonesian Revolution* (Ithaca, N.Y., Cornell University, Department of Asian Studies, 1964), p. 156.

[29]Tarzie Vittachi, *The Fall of Sukarno* (London, A. Deutsch, 1967).

[30]Alfred Friendly, Jr., "Indonesian Youth Seeks New Order," *New York Times,* Sept. 11, 1966.

ever, to elucidate this aspect of the age composition by statistical comparisons of various countries in different stages of demographic development.

Table 2 presents the proportion of persons aged 15 to 29 per 100 persons of the total older population for selected countries. The omission of children under 15 gives prominence to the population group often referred to as "the young generation," who impress and modify the established society through their cultural, economic, and political activities.

The table shows widely differing ratios for the developed and the now-developing countries. While in Belgium there are three times as many people over 30 than between 15 and 29 years of age, in Morocco, the Philippines, and other countries there are over 90 adolescents and young adults for every hundred middle-aged and older persons. In many of the now-developing countries, the age-group from 15 to 29 is still growing absolutely as well as in proportion to the population over 30, since a much larger number of children over 15 are moving up into the 15 to 29 age bracket. If the figures for Senegal can be trusted, the number of children under 15 equals that of the entire older population. Unless emigration or an exceptional rise in mortality should reduce the younger population there and in several other now-developing countries, people aged 15 to 29 will soon equal or outnumber their compatriots aged 30 and over.

A comparison of the respective age groups in Japan and Egypt brings out the contrast between the developed and the now-developing countries. While the age ratios, as defined for Table 2, differ only by one point (64.1 *vs.* 65.1), the proportion of young people in Japan will decline rapidly in the near future, whereas in Egypt it is rising. Tropical Africa in particular, demographically a late-comer, is only now in the early phase of accelerating population growth; it will have a very large contingent of young adults in the coming decades.[31] For Mainland China, the age structure can only be estimated; the age ratio, as defined for Table 2, is probably over 80. The corresponding age ratio of the Soviet Union, like that of the U.S.A., had reached a low point around 1961, probably between 53 and 54.[32] At that time the 16- to 19-year-old cohorts were small owing to the birth deficit during the Second World War. Since then, larger cohorts have moved into the 15- to 29-year group and the ratio has probably gone up.

The age structure has been frequently investigated in regard to the dependent population, i.e. children and people over 65 years of age. In the under-developed countries, where children under 15 account for 36 to 48 percent of the population, capital formation and hence economic modernization is retarded by the need to support a large unproductive population. The high child-dependency load borne by those countries least able to afford it often becomes an unrecognized cause of discontent for the people and of frustration for political leaders and intellectuals whose visions of national accomplishment cannot be realized.

However, a large—and in many cases an unusually large—contingent of

[31]Ansley J. Coale, "Estimates of Fertility and Mortality in Tropical Africa," *Population Index,* XXXII (1966), pp. 173–81.

[32]United Nations, *Demographic Yearbook,* 17th issue, 1965.

Table 2. Ratios of 15–29 Year Group to 100 Persons 30 Years and Over, and Supporting Data in Thousands[a]

Year	Country	Ratio	Total Population	30 Years and over	15–29 Years	Under 15
1963	Belgium	34.1	9,290	5,279	1,799	2,212
1963	Sweden	36.6	7,604	4,386	1,605	1,613
1965	England & Wales	36.7	47,763	26,956	9,902	10,905
1964	France	38.0	48,411	26,378	10,026	12,008
1962	Italy	43.9	50,946	26,720	11,730	12,496
1965	U.S.A.	45.4	194,583	92,631	42,043	59,909
1964	Japan	64.1	97,186	43,635	27,961	25,590
1960	U.A.R. = Egypt	65.1	25,984	9,011	5,864	11,110
1960	Syria	73.7	4,565	1,413	1,041	2,111
1961	India	73.8	438,775	149,006	109,750	180,019
1960	Turkey	73.9	27,775	9,390	6,938	11,427
1961	Pakistan	74.4	90,283	28,726	21,378	40,179
1960	Senegal	75.4	3,110	1,020	769	1,789
1961	Indonesia	76.5	96,319	31,603	24,172	40,544
1963	Ceylon	79.4	10,625	3,515	2,790	4,320
1965	Venezuela	82.1	8,722	2,615	2,147	3,960
1961	Peru	84.0	9,907	3,053	2,563	4,290
1960	Ghana	85.3	6,727	2,013	1,717	2,997
1960	Brazil	85.4	70,119	21,676	18,512	29,931
1960	Mexico	85.7	34,923	10,484	8,987	15,452
1960	Dominican Rep.	88.9	3,047	850	756	1,441
1962	Kenya	90.3	8,636	2,449	2,212	3,976
1963	Morocco	90.3	12,665	3,605	3,254	5,806
1957	Tanzania	92.8	8,663	2,585	2,399	3,679
1965	Philippines	96.3	32,345	8,780	8,453	15,112

[a]Computed from United Nations, *Demographic Yearbook,* XVII (1965), Section 6. Data of Indonesia based on a 1% sample of census returns.

adolescents and young adults adds to the potential restlessness and instability in these societies. This situation is caused by the fact that a larger proportion of children now reach age 15 than did so before the present century. Especially since World War II, mortality rates have declined spectacularly in Asia, Africa, and Latin America. Contrary to common belief, a decline in the death rate does not mean that the number of old people substantially increases; in underdeveloped countries people 65 years and up account only for 2 to 4 percent of the population. A decline of the death rate involves above all the survival of children, since health improvements benefit greater numbers of young people than old. Even as late as the 1940's, 45 percent of the population of India died before reaching age 15.[33] The re-

[33]D. Gosh, *Pressure of Population and Economic Efficiency in India* (Indian Council of World Affairs, 1947).

duction in the mortality of infants, children, and young adults constitutes by far the most important aspect of demographic modernization. As a result of this process the proportion of older people actually shrinks.[34]

The survival of a greater number of children implies a disproportionately large population in the 15 to 29 age bracket, though only for a limited time, since with the aging of the larger cohorts the entire age structure tends to revert to its former shape. Two additional factors, however, must be considered. First, the arrival of larger year-cohorts at the age of fertility is likely to further increase the number of children, even though the fertility rate remains constant, because of the presence of a larger number of potential parents than in previous years. Thus, after 15 years, this secondary surge of births will again swell the age group of adolescents and young adults.

Second, if the fertility rate begins to decline, as it is now doing in several underdeveloped countries, the number of adolescents and young adults relative to the entire population will at first increase, but after 15 years will begin to decrease. Declines in fertility, however, will be moderate in the next twenty years or more, even though we can expect a steady dissemination of birth control information. Since Asia, Africa, and Latin America now have very young populations, the number of families will increase rapidly; and even if average families become smaller, the aggregate fertility of these populations will remain high for several decades. The demographic development of Japan serves as an example of what can be expected under the most favorable conditions. Japan's birth rate declined by approximately 50 per cent in the twenty years following World War II; yet its population grew in two decades from 73 million to 100 million, and the ratio of adolescents and young adults to persons over 29, though constantly declining, is still high.

Furthermore, with respect to age distribution for the entire world population, the proportion of adolescents and young adults cannot fail to increase, because the underdeveloped are growing faster than the developed nations. According to a United Nations forecast made in 1966, the former comprised 67 percent of the global population in 1960 but will amount to 76 percent by the year 2000. Various considerations, therefore, lead to the conclusion that young people represent an unusually large proportion of the world population at present and will continue to do so for the remainder of the twentieth century.

Since the "young nations" now going through the early stages of demographic modernization have collected no reliable historical census data on age composition, and since many of the data on age groups recorded in the *Demographic Yearbooks* of the United Nations are either patently erroneous or at least suspect, it will be instructive to tabulate historical series of age ratios for some nations of Europe and America for which good data are available.

[34]Ansley J. Coale, "How a Population Ages or Grows Younger," in *Population: The Vital Revolution,* ed. R. Freedman (Chicago, Aldine Publishing Co., 1964), Chap. 3.

Europe experienced its "population explosion" in the latter part of the eighteenth and nineteenth centuries. However, despite this demographic expansion, Table 3 shows that in Europe the 15 to 29 age group at no time amounted to 80 percent of the older population; in fact, in Sweden, France, Germany, and Hungary, for as far back as records go, it never reached even 70 percent.

The reasons for the lower age ratios of Europe are varied. First, in France as well as in certain other regions of Europe, farmers and other commoners are known to have limited the number of their progeny as early as the eighteenth century. Second, improvement in health, hygiene, and nutrition came only slowly in Europe in contrast to the rapid application of modern biochemical and other scientific knowledge in the now-developing countries. Third, the opportunities for emigration available to Europeans attracted predominantly young people. For instance, the sudden drop of the ratio for Greece after the census of 1890 is attributable to massive emigration of the young. Finally, a new movement to limit families began to make itself felt between the years of 1850 and 1880 in western and central Europe. With the coming of the small family ideal, the proportion of adolescents and young adults to the older population dropped in one country after another.

Greece, together with other Balkan countries and Russia for which no age data are available, showed a higher proportion of adolescents and young adults than did western and northern Europe, excepting the British Isles. Great Britain and Russia reported the highest rates of natural increase among the nations of Europe during the nineteenth century; and Ireland, prior to the great famine of 1845–46, anticipated some of the most unfortunate characteristics of present-day underdeveloped countries: in 1841, the ratio of the 16 to 30 age group to that of 31 and over was 96.2 to 100.[35] Yet apart from these exceptional cases, Europe's demographic growth was never as explosive as that of many of the now-developing countries.

The age composition of countries such as the United States and Argentina is differentiated from that of European countries by the massive immigration of predominantly young people with a consequently high proportion of women in the child-bearing period. The extreme youthfulness of these populations is therefore not the result of natural increase alone. Since the First World War, immigration has become a relatively minor factor in the demographic experience of the United States, and changes in the age composition are largely conditioned by fluctuations of natality, mortality, and the mean age at marriage. Table 4 presents the changes in the age composition of the United States since 1930 and projections to 1980.

In Table 4, the ratios of the 15 to 29 age group relative to the middle-aged and older population reflect the earlier fluctuations of the birth rate in the United States. The ratio declined between 1930 and 1960 due to the decrease of immigration during and after the First World War, as well as

[35]Computed from K. H. Connell, *The Population of Ireland 1750–1845* (Oxford, Clarendon Press, 1950), p. 192.

Table 3. Historical Series of Ratio of Youth 15–29 to 100 Persons 30 Years and Over, for Selected Countries*

Year	Sweden	France	Great Britain	Germany	Hungary	Greece	U.S.A.
1750	62.9						
1760	59.8						
1770	63.2						
1776		64.9					
1780	63.6						
1786		62.9					
1790–91	56.6	60.7					
1800–01	57.0	57.0					
1810–11	61.1	58.1					
1820–21	62.8	58.6					
1830–31	59.1	56.9					108.5[m]
1840–41	69.7	56.3	77.1[a]				103.7[m]
1850–51	69.5	54.3	73.8				101.0
1860–61	61.2	54.0	70.5			79.4	94.7
1870–71	58.0	50.3	69.9	63.6[b]	65.3[mc]	77.5	86.4
1880–81	61.3	48.5	72.5	64.5		78.6	84.1
1890–91	54.7	48.8	73.0	66.7		78.5	80.9
1900–01	57.4	48.5	72.1	67.9		74.7	73.1
1910–11	57.3	47.4	62.5	65.2	66.2	63.9	73.1
1920–21	57.1	44.9	54.7		67.2		62.9
1925				63.7			
1930–31	54.0	45.5	51.4		62.6	71.8	59.3
1933				49.5			
1936		38.0					
1940–41	47.6		43.4	42.5[e]	48.5	61.2	52.2
1946		37.1		33.4[f]			
1950–51	34.8	42.5	35.9		50.0[d]	65.6	45.4
1960	33.6	35.8	33.8	40.4[f]	45.5	52.1	39.4
1963				39.4[f]			
1964		38.0			39.8	49.1	
1965	37.9		36.9				45.4

a = approximate b = year 1871 c = year 1869 d = year 1949 e = year 1939 f = Federal Republic and W. Berlin m = males only. French and British data for odd-numbered years from 1791 to 1951; all others for even-numbered years, unless specifically indicated otherwise.

*Computed from Gustav Sundbärg, *Bevölkerungsgeschichte Schwedens 1750–1900* (Stockholm, Norstedt & Söner, 1907). Sweden: Statitiska Centralbyán, *Statistisk årsbok för Sverige 1950; 1956; 1966.* J. Bourgeois-Pichat, "The General Development of the Population of France since the Eighteenth Century," in *Population in History,* ed. D. V. Glass & D. E. C. Eversley (London, E. Arnold, 1965), pp. 474–506, App. II. Germany: *Statistik des Deutschen Reiches,* Vol. 451, 2: *Volkszählung: Die Bevölkerung des Deutschen Reiches nach den Ergebnissen der Volkszählung 1933,* Heft 2: *Geschlecht, Alter, und Familienstand* (Berlin, 1936). B. R. Mitchell, *Abstract of British Historical Statistics* (Cambridge, Eng., University Press, 1962), pp. 12–13. Lajos Thirring, "Magyarország népessége 1869–1949 között," in *Magyarország Történeti Demográfiája,* ed. József Kovacsics (Budapest, Közgazdasági és Jogi Könyvkiadó, 1963),

Table 4. Ratios of Persons 15–29 Years of Age to 100 Persons 30 Years and Over in the U.S.A., in Thousands, 1930–1980[a]

Year	Ratio	15–29 Years	30 Years and over
1930	59.3	32,381	54,614
1940	52.2	34,019	65,131
1945	50.9	35,250	69,202
1950	45.4	34,526	76,128
1955	40.7	33,696	82,759
1960	39.4	34,889	88,648
1965	45.4	42,043	92,631
1970	52.2	50,061	95,977
1975	56.7	57,367	101,142
1980	56.0	61,175	109,317

[a]Enumerated population based on *Statistical Abstracts of the United States* and U.N. *Demographic Yearbooks.* Estimated future population, 1970–1980, on the assumption of 400,000 immigrants per annum, based on *Statistical Abstract of the U.S., 1966,* p. 6, No. 3.

from the decreasing birth rate of the 1920's and 1930's; a third factor is the increase in the number of older people because of improved health conditions.

The American fertility rate climbed in the 1940's, especially following World War II, reaching its peak in 1957. The "baby boom," which necessitated the building of numerous elementary schools in the 1950's, reached the high schools, the labor market, and the colleges around 1960. Also the altar. With the increase in the number of potential mothers during the 1960's, plus a further increase during the 1970's, more children will be born; thus, after 1980 the proportion of adolescents and young adults will doubtless rise again. Almost certainly, therefore, the United States will have a high proportion of young people between 15 and 29 in comparison with other Western countries for the remainder of this century. However, even with a relatively high fertility rate, the United States will never approach the high proportions of teen-agers and young adults seen in most underdeveloped countries today and in the near future.

A rise in the rate of fertility, such as occurred in the United States in the 1940's and part of the 1950's, has nearly the same effect on the age structure as has a decline of mortality, the predominant cause for the increase in the number of young people in Asia, Africa, and Latin America. Regret-

pp. 282–83, Table 25. V. G. Valaoras, "A Reconstruction of the Demographic History of Modern Greece," *Milbank Memorial Fund Quarterly,* XXXVIII (1960), No. 2, pp. 138–39. U.S. Bureau of the Census, *Historical Statistics of the United States, Colonial Times to 1957* (Washington, D.C., 1960), Series A 71–85. *Statistical Abstract of the United States, 1966.* United Nations, *Demographic Yearbooks, 1948–1965.*

tably, the lack of reliable and regular censuses in the underdeveloped countries in previous decades precludes a presentation of their age ratios in historical perspective. Certainly, however, in most of the now-developing countries the large number of children, relative to the older population, combined with the large proportion of young adults with their high aggregate fertility potential, will perpetuate for several decades high ratios of adolescents and young adults.

III

In any community the presence of a large number of adolescents and young adults influences the temper of life; and the greater the proportion of young people the greater the likelihood of cultural and political change. "If poor aging peasants can be left to misery or even starvation without serious political consequences, the case is different with the young generation."[36] Age composition, to be sure, constitutes only one determinant in the functioning of society; therefore it cannot be assumed that a large proportion of young people makes the same implications for every nation, nor even for every poor and starving nation. Too often, however, a direct and exclusive correlation between the incidence of violence and of poverty is taken for granted. This impression is easily created by the observation that outbursts of violence are more frequent, nationally, in disadvantaged neighborhoods and, internationally, in underdeveloped and overpopulated countries. But since poor and crowded neighborhoods as well as underdeveloped countries have high proportions of young people, age composition must be considered as a major coefficient in the incidence of violent behavior.

For instance, the struggle of the American Negroes in the 1960's has been borne almost exclusively by Negro youth. Since the Second World War, American Negroes have not become poorer in absolute terms, especially not in the big northern cities where the greater part of the struggle against white society has taken place. But Negroes have become younger. The large contingent of Negro teen-agers cannot be accounted the only factor in the explosive discontent that led to riots, for the widening gap between white and Negro incomes and white and Negro unemployment played an important part. But the presence of youth in large numbers stood out as a factor of crucial importance: the attitudes of the young contrasted sharply with those of the older Negroes, who were, for the most part, too disspirited to bring themselves to go out and demonstrate, to vote in city elections, or even to meet suppression and violence with violence.[37]

Class antagonism is another factor whose importance in revolutionary change is deflated, once attention is directed to the role of youth. The

[36]Nathan Keyfitz, "Age Distribution as a Challenge to Development," *Amer. Journal of Sociology,* LXX (1964–65), p. 665.

[37]Lewis W. Jones, "The New World of Negro Youth," in *Problems of Youth,* ed. Muzafer Sherif and Carolyn W. Sherif (Chicago, Aldine Publishing Co., 1965), pp. 65–88.

widely held assumption that political revolutions are caused by class struggles or are synonymous with class struggles has been challenged in the past few years by historical research on the Puritan Revolution, the French Revolution, the rise of National Socialism in Germany, and other more recent governmental upheavals. Smail's unique study of the early Indonesian revolution, as it worked on the local level, led him to conclude that class factors were irrelevant and that "the main distinction between the radicals and the moderates of the Indonesian Revolution was one of generations. . . . The *pemuda* [youth] movement as a whole was the most characteristic expression of the times; it drew in young men of every kind of background—rural and urban, *santri* [devout Muslims] and secular, educated and illiterate."

At the national level, in Djakarta, the revolution was a struggle between the foreign Dutch and a domestic elite; but the sentiment of nationalism was not essential for the revolutionary activities and the replacement of officials. "In this period the revolutionary process worked with the same vigor in the rural areas, where the Dutch and the British did not appear at all and where nationalism as such was of little significance." In the Indonesian revolution the most decisive factors were the population pressure that had been growing ever stronger during the course of the twentieth century, the weakening of the traditional power structure through the events of the Pacific War, and the activism of youth stimulated during the Japanese occupation.[38] Similarly, the 1964 revolution in Zanzibar had for its official aim the replacement of an Arab by a Negro elite; but the rise of young adults—even though of Arab origin—to positions of power was an equally important, if less well-publicized aspect.

Historical evidence appears to indicate that the subversion of any established government, if not accomplished by *coup d'état,* requires a movement that cuts across social classes; and whether such a movement is directed against a native or a foreign elite, young people provide the driving force and often, to a large extent, the intellectual and organizational leadership. "Most of the nationalistic movements in the Middle East, Asia, and Africa have consisted of young people, students, or officers who rebelled against their elders. . . . At the same time there usually has developed a specific youth consciousness and ideology that intensifies the nationalistic movement to 'rejuvenate' the country."[39] As a result many of the newly formed nations have what Robert C. Tucker has called "movement-regimes," i.e., governments under single-party auspices and based on a revolutionary mass movement.[40]

Since the world population is bound to grow very rapidly in the coming decades, the absolute number of young people will increase tremen-

[38]Smail, *op. cit.,* pp. 10–13, 22–23, 156–57.

[39]S. N. Eisenstadt, "Archetypal Patterns of Youth," *Daedalus,* Winter 1962: *Youth: Change and Challenge,* p. 36.

[40]Robert C. Tucker, "Towards a Comparative Politics of Movement-Regimes," *Amer. Political Science Rev.,* LV (June 1961), 281–89.

dously. In many countries their proportion to the older age groups will rise, until finally declining birth rates and mass longevity will reverse the present trend. The social and economic consequences of large youth cohorts, of course, vary greatly among different societies. Broadly speaking, it can be said that developed and prosperous countries can cope best with the need for larger educational facilities, the effects on the labor market, and changes in consumption. These same countries can also profit more readily from the advantages of a young population, from their physical vigor, intellectual flexibility, and educability. A dynamic and developed society can best stimulate, utilize, and reward the creative originality that belongs to those under 35. A youthful population represents a great reservoir of inventiveness and potential accomplishment. However, most societies throughout history have been too poor in capital resources, too rigid and monopolistic in their social structure, and too limited in their educational facilities to avail themselves of these human potentials, a fact which still holds true of most societies today. The overwhelming majority of human talent remains unrecognized and goes to waste. Unfortunately underdeveloped societies produce underdeveloped personalities, both intellectually and emotionally.

Irrespective of social and economic conditions, an increase in the number of youth in any society involves an increase in social turbulence. Young people are conspicuously inclined to take risks, to expose themselves and others to danger, and tend to engage in socially disruptive behavior. Discounting the considerable variation from nation to nation, long-range statistics confirm the fact that everywhere in the Western world males between 15 and 29 years of age commit more crimes against property and more homicides than the older population.[41] As a rule they commit fewer suicides, with the notable exception of soldiers and, in recent decades, college students, who have higher suicide rates than the remainder of their coevals. But the aggressiveness of male adolescents and young adults is for the most part directed outwards, a finding which represents one of the most pronounced differences between younger and older men that are statistically measurable.[42] The impression that lawlessness is on the rise among the young population of the United States can to a considerable extent be attributed to the continually enlarging *proportion* of the younger age groups in recent years.[43]

An increase in social unrest as a result of a high proportion of youth in the age structure must be assumed also on the grounds that psychopathic

[41]For international historical data, Georg von Mayr, *Statistik und Gesellschaftslehre,* III: *Moralstatistik* (Tübingen, Mohr, 1917), pp. 760–801. *Crime in the United States: Uniform Crime Reports for the U.S.,* issued annually by J. E. Hoover, Fed. Bureau of Investigation, U.S. Department of Justice; see Tables on "Total Arrests by Age."

[42]Louis I. Dublin, *Suicide: A Sociological and Statistical Study* (New York, Ronald, 1963), Chap. 3. For historical international data, G. v. Mayr, *op. cit.,* pp. 309–15.

[43]Albert D. Biderman in *Social Indicators,* ed. Raymond Bauer (Cambridge, Mass., M.I.T. Press, 1966), pp. 122–29, convincingly criticizes on this score the F.B.I.'s *Crime in the United States* quoted above.

behavior is specific to youth. Many who commit acts of cruelty, brutality, or even crime as young men keep out of trouble after they reach the age of 25, 30, or 35. Although the individual "age curves" of psychopathy (or "sociopathy") assume a variety of shapes, all manifestations of this personality disorder—from "wild oats" behavior, excessive self-assertion and pugnacity to criminal acts—are predominantly related with youth. It follows that primitive tendencies and psychopathic behavior can be expected to increase in any population commensurately with its youthfulness. The increase will exceed proportion if the higher rate of natural increase involves a rise of illegitimacy or larger families or both, since the rate of juvenile delinquency is demonstrably higher for illegitimate children and for those with many siblings than for children who are less frequently the victims of neglect or rejection.

Psychopathy is episodic—in contrast with neurotic and psychotic states—and thus wears a "mask of sanity," as Hervey Clerkley felicitously put it. Psychopaths do not act out all the time. If they did, "society would have to destroy them at an early age in self-defense. They appear to be normal and even amiable people in between their psychopathic episodes."[44] For this reason they often become instrumental among their peers in the escalation of violence. Research in the symbiotic relationships of psychopaths with schizophrenic or paranoiac persons is a desideratum and may throw light on certain extraordinary interactions between two individuals or within groups.[45]

In the Western world, though youth may be in ferment, the majority are usually stabilized emotionally and socially within the context of the adult society. But in the now-developing countries, adults are also involved in the crisis of instability.[46] As a consequence, adolescents in these nations live more closely attuned to the temper of the whole society and to the aspirations of older men. Young people are more active politically, often playing a leading role in the overthrow of their governments. In countries dominated by the mentality of the young, political mythologies and eschatological beliefs take on a high degree of importance, and political reality is often perceived, in a Manichean frame of thought, as opposing forces of good and irredeemable evil. The extreme "ideological groups are well-nigh completely monopolized by young people." The leaders and prophets of the "Wretched of the Earth" are passionately opposed to "the myth of liberal tolerance"; and projecting their own desperate troubles onto the political scene, they preach the destruction of existing society as the only cure for a

[44]Dr. Milton S. Gurvitz, of Great Neck, New York, to whom I am indebted for pointing out the age-specific and episodic nature of psychopathy. Hulsey Cason, "The Concept of the Psychopath," *Amer. Jour. of Orthopsychiatry*, XVIII (1948), pp. 297–308.

[45]Ernest M. Gruenberg, "Socially Shared Psychopathology," in *Explorations in Social Psychology*, ed. Alexander H. Leighton *et al.* (New York, Basic Books, 1957), pp. 201–29, gives some suggestive ideas on this subject.

[46]Raoul Makarius, *La jeunesse intellectuelle d'Egypte au lendemain de la Deuxième Guerre Mondiale* (Paris and The Hague, Mouton, 1960), p. 75.

world so immoral as to have hurt them.[47] It is noteworthy that movements of consuming hatred are rising in the more youthful populations, while "the end of ideology" has arrived in the developed countries of the West.

Any judgment on the utility or disutility of the influence of the young and of youthful mass movements on society must consider an array of problems: Who are the elites with a mass appeal to youth? What percentage of the young population is alienated? What are the reasons for their alienation? To what extent are force and terrorism needed to effectuate or prevent certain changes? What are the social and human costs of change, and what are the costs of the preservation of the status quo? And so on.

Some general observations can be made regarding the methods of political action that have been employed by more or less revolutionary youth movements in the past and that are being used more frequently and more self-consciously in the latter half of the twentieth century. Since activist youth are facing established governments vastly superior in military power to their own, meeting them on equal terms, as in open battle, would be self-destructive. There remain two strategies suitable for the weak. The first attempts to disarm the opponent morally by a complete renunciation of force, subscribing to non-violence, allowing helpless members to be imprisoned, tortured, or martyred, turning the other cheek, and exposing themselves to abuse by the powerful. This moral campaign of asserting one's injured rights aims at eroding the conscience of the powerful and enlisting public support. As a contemporary exponent of this strategy explains: "It is up to the citizenry, those outside power, to engage in permanent combat with the state, short of violent escalatory revolution, but beyond the gentility of the ballot-box, to insure justice, freedom and well-being."[48] This "permanent combat" is of course effective only against a liberal state.

The second method of overcoming the powerful is insurgent or guerrilla warfare. To an even greater extent than the first method it is accessible almost exclusively to the young, since guerrilla fighters must endure incredible deprivations and discomforts and a life of permanent danger. Regular governments, and especially civilized governments, find it extremely difficult to cope with determined underground terrorism. For instance, General Grivas, of Cyprus fame, explained in his book the practice of his execution squads, whose task was to stalk their victims from the rear, shoot them and make off, after passing the gun to a child or young girl whom the British were not expected to charge with murder.[49]

[47]Vladimir C. Nahirny, "Some Observations on Ideological Groups," *Amer. Jour. of Sociology,* LXVII (1961–62), pp. 397–462. On Frantz Fanon, the author of *The Wretched of the Earth,* Irene L. Gendzier, "Frantz Fanon: In Search of Justice," *Middle East Jour.,* Autumn 1966, pp. 534–44.

[48]Howard Zinn, "The Healthful Use of Power," *Amer. Jour. of Orthopsychiatry,* XXXVI (1966), pp. 90–95.

[49]Régis Debray, *Révolution dans la révolution? Lutte armée et lutte politique en Amérique latine (Paris,* François Maspero, 1967) is an outstanding exposition of insurgent warfare. George Grivas, *General Grivas on Guerrilla Warfare.* Trans. by A. A. Pallis (New York, Praeger, 1965).

The two strategies may seem contradictory, and those who subscribe to one usually reject the other with sincere horror; but whenever in history a revolt was directed against well-established adversaries, typical youth-ideologies such as Anabaptism or anarchism manifested themselves in irenic and belligerent shapes at the same time, swinging easily and suddenly from one extreme to the other. Both strategies reject legal methods of parliamentary procedures, "electoral opium," compromise or slow progress. Both aim at the overthrow and humiliation of the enemy; and both are supported by the chiliastic hope that "the last shall be first."

The purpose and direction that young people find in movements of rebellion help many to overcome the insecurity and hopelessness of a futile existence. The feeling of being able to cope with hardship and danger, the enjoyment of comradeship, and the acceptance of their peers is basic to a sense of identity in the young. Even belonging to an anti-social and destructive movement can have a salutary effect on the personality formation of a boy or girl, especially in times of social dislocation.[50]

One of the most serious consequences of "liberation movements" is the inculcation of hostility in children. Basic political attitudes and beliefs are formed in adolescence, and even earlier in life. Prejudices learned in the first two decades of life are highly resistant to later experience. The orgies of hatred now indulged in by leaders of the young in various parts of the world greatly exceed in scope and intensity the teaching of nationalism to children and adults in the 150 years following the American and French revolutions. These hatreds will remain a long-lasting legacy of the age of the "population explosion."

Social change is not engineered by youth, but it is most manifest in youth. "The potential for change is concentrated in the cohorts of young adults who are old enough to participate directly in the movements impelled by change, but not old enough to have become committed to an occupation, a residence, a family of procreation, or a way of life."[51] The direction of social change results from the total situation in which the young find themselves, including the types of leaders with whom they interact and the traditions and institutions they have inherited. The presence of a large contingent of young people in a population may make for a cumulative process of innovation and social and cultural growth; it may lead to elemental, directionless acting-out behavior; it may destroy old institutions and elevate new elites to power; and the unemployed energies of the young may be organized and directed by totalitarian rulers. The dynamism of its large and youthful populations distinguishes the crowded history of the twentieth century.

[50]On the mental health aspects of youth movements, Fishman and Solomon, "Youth and Social Action," *loc. cit.*, pp. 16–20.

[51]Norman B. Ryder, "The Cohort as a Concept in the Study of Social Change," *Amer. Sociol. Rev.*, XXX (1965), p. 848.

The New Segregation: A Perspective on Age Categories in America

John Lofland

I want to analyze the dynamics of age and youth in America as instances of general processes of differentiation and stratification in complex societies. In order to do this, it is necessary, first, to introduce some rather abstract and seemingly remote conceptions. These seemingly remote conceptions involve the notions of social categories, of categorical clusterings, and of pivotal categories. Beyond sheer concepts, the tone and style of this first section are intended to promote in the reader an experience of distance, a perspective from which he can view the subsequent discussion. Not cuteness, then, but *epoché*. From within this first developed perspective, I want, second, to discuss age as a principle of stratification, and to analyze some features of contemporary age categories. Third, and finally, I will focus upon the emerging "youth ghetto" in America and discuss adult conceptions of and practices toward it, conduct within it, and interaction between it and categories of adults.[1]

I may begin with the observation that there exists a most peculiar species of animal whose most distinctive characteristics include, among other things, the following: it walks on its hind legs, uses symbols, and is extraordinarily sensitive to what the other animals of its kind think and feel about it. This animal is further distinguished by, and very peculiar in, the assiduousness with which it feels a need linguistically to designate objects in the world. So it is that this creature has a category with which it designates its general kind of object and which serves to set it off from all other objects in the world. The more esoterically inclined of these animals

Abridged from "The Youth Ghetto," *Journal of Higher Education* 39, No. 3 (March 1968), pp. 121–43. Reprinted by permission of the author and the publisher.

[1]I should like to express my indebtedness to the works of, and conversations with, Lyn H. Lofland, Gerald D. Suttles and Max Heirich. The seemingly unconnected, but actually parallel work of Suttles on an inner-city slum and Heirich on campus demonstrations provided the proximate stimulus for a more generalized statement. See Gerald D. Suttles, *The Social Order of the Slum* (Chicago: University of Chicago Press, 1968); Max Heirich, *Conflict on the Campus* (New York: Columbia University Press, 1971).

label the general category *homo sapiens;* while the more mundane dub the category merely "mankind," "human beings," "people," or—that vestige of male supremacy—"man."

This animal is not satisfied, however, with simply setting itself off from all the other kinds of objects in the world. Nor is it satisfied with the enterprise of making fine distinctions among and between all the objects that fall outside its own general category. This animal, which calls itself man, or mankind, engages also in making distinctions within the category of its most general kind.

One of the more popular subdivisions is based on differential place in what is identified as the reproductive cycle. The dimension of sex is thus divined and there arises a division between the categories of "male" and "female." A second very widespread division identifies the amount of time human objects have existed and divides mankind on the dimension of age. There are, thus, categories such as "child," "adolescent," "adult," and so forth, the specific terms depending upon who is doing the discriminating and designating.

Because it is possible for selected combinations of people to produce other people and to cooperate in managing their joint young products, and, moreover, to cooperate in the task of sheer survival, there exists yet another basis for further division of mankind, this time along the dimension of their biological relationships to one another. There are, thus, categories of family or kin position. Many units of kin occupying adjacent ground may come to see that particular territory as reasonably and legitimately "theirs," setting it off (at least symbolically) from all other pieces of ground on the planet. As some kin groups come to dominate other kin groups, the claimed area may grow quite large, relative to the total space on the planet. Or, it may be quite small, yet be seen as equally crucial, as, for example, with units such as neighborhoods or even city blocks. Our animal may even get to feel that the location of one's residence on the planet is a crucially important dimension along which to distinguish categories of territorial habitation.

Such a territorial category of mankind, settled in a place for a long period of time, may even come to feel that it has some special way of life that distinguishes "my kind of people" from all the rest of the people in the world. There can thus arise a dimension called "culture," and various categories of it.

In moving around on the planet, differences in specific definitions of sex, age, kinship, and territory may be seen as associated with differences in the color or form of the surface casing of the animal; and so another dimension along which to divide kinds of people in the world appears, one sometimes called "race" or "ethnicity."

The process of extracting sustenance from the surface of the planet (or from other people) may place these two-legged animals in relations to one another such that it is felt reasonable to divide the general category yet again, this time along the dimension of how the materials necessary for physical survival are assembled. Such designations may be called jobs or occupations and in some societies may run into thousands upon thousands of distinctive categories. Such categories, themselves, have differential capacity to assemble resources. Some seem able to command the obedience of many of the other animals. Thus there can grow up a dimension of difference, designated by this animal with categories such as the more wealthy and the less wealthy, or the rich and the poor.

This species of animal, then, is that kind of creature that is constantly dividing itself into categories of "kinds of people" along dimensions such as sex, age, kin, territory, culture, race, work, and material resources.

Having complicated its world by discriminating all these and other dimensions and designating numerous categories along them, humans then try to simplify the world again through the process of clustering selected categories of some of the dimensions. So it is that a significant proportion of the species feels, for example, that animals of a certain category of the dimension, race, should reside in certain categories of the dimension, territory, and should assemble sustenance by occupying themselves with certain categories of the dimension, work. More particularly, some of the species feel that what are called "whites" should reside in "nice" neighborhoods and make a living from some of the "cleaner" kinds of work; and correspondingly, other categories of race have their appropriate other places and other categories of work.

Or, some of the species may feel that certain categories of age are most appropriately clustered with certain kinship categories and with certain occupational categories. When these presumed proprieties of clustering are broached, comment and punishment are undertaken as a means of forcing these erroneously clustered instances of the species back into a proper or acceptable cluster of displayed categories. We see such a concern on those occasions when newspapers, for example, deem as newsworthy the fact that two married sixteen-year-olds are publisher-editors of a town newspaper.[2] Or, when it is deemed newsworthy—even to the extent of requiring an accompanying picture—when a sixteen-year-old girl marries a sixty-two-year-old man, thereby becoming "stepmother to five, grandmother to another five and a great-grandmother."[3]

When the categories of a set of dimensions begin, empirically, to pile upon one another—that is, to cluster—this peculiar animal not only perceives and comes to expect the clustering but introduces a further simplification. One of the categories of the dimensions so piled up is singled out and treated publicly as their most important and significant feature. It defines the character of those animals whose categories are so clustered. That is, there comes to be a pivotal category that defines "who those people are," socially speaking. Indeed, as we shall see, the singled out pivotal category may have ascribed to it a causal force; it may be seen as responsible for

[2]*Detroit Free Press,* March 15, 1965, p. 1.

[3]*Ibid.,* July 21, 1965, p. 2.

"making" the animals the way they are relative to their other clustered categories.

Through time and across societies, what particular categories have piled upon one another or have clustered seems to have varied considerably; and, therefore, so have the particular categories singled out as pivotally defining human animals to one another.

What category is defined as pivotal is, of course, a function of specific, defined situations and the social organizational units of reference within which human animals are encountering one another. A person momentarily situated within a work setting may be pivotally defined as a worker. The same person, shifted to a family, political, or religious setting, may, in them, be pivotally defined, respectively, as a father, politician, or believer. In these examples, the social organizational units of reference are organizations and the categories attributed as pivotal derive from the designative framework of the corresponding setting.

Under some conditions the unit of reference with which a large proportion of the population defines one another in specific encounters comes to be the society at large. Thus, in contemporary America, if the male just mentioned is, say, Negro, and in a racially mixed work setting, others are not likely to pivotally define him as worker but as a Negro who happens incidentally to be a worker as well.

Those pivotal categories which permeate a wide variety of concrete settings—are used by a very high proportion of the population as a basis upon which they pivotally identify—and which are in conflict with one another may be called nationally dividing dimensions and pivotal categories. In the short history of America there has already been a succession of different nationalized dimensions and pivotal categories around which division and conflict have been organized. Going back only to the middle of the last century, we see, in succession, the nationalized dimension of territory and its nationalized pivotal categories, northerner and southerner; the nationalized dimension of income or work and its nationalized pivotal categories, capitalist and worker; the nationalized dimension of nativity and its nationalized pivotal categories, immigrant and native-born; the nationalized dimension of sex and its nationalized pivotal categories, suffragette (female) and male; the nationalized dimension (more recently) of race and its nationalized pivotal categories, white and Negro.

Although a variety of nationalized dimensions of categorical conflict may be taking place at any given time, it would seem, from these examples, that one or another nationalized dimension becomes more or less primary in a given period and a variety of other dimensions of conflict are assimilated to the prime nationalized dimension. That is, alliances are formed for the purpose of a single basis of conflict. Thus, in the northerner–southerner case, the agricultural–industrial, slaver–nonslaver, states-rights–federalism categories became assimilated to a dimension of territory and its categories.

If one or another nationalized set of pivotal categories is likely to be a primary basis of conflict during a given period, there is raised the question of how one or another specific set comes to have this primacy. That is, one can assume there is always some prime dimension of conflict, some prime, nationalized, pivotal categories, and inquire into the conditions under which a particular dimension comes to the forefront.

While this is the most general question to pose, it is not my purpose here to explore a generalized answer. It is my purpose, rather, to take the question and its conceptual context as a framework within which to view some contemporary trends on the basis of which tentatively to suggest what might be the next nationalized dimension whose pivotal categories are, for Americans, the foremost bases of conflict.

At this time, I am inclined to think that the current piling up of categorical sharing suggests that the dimension of age (and the categories it provides) is becoming, or will become, our next identity and conflict equivalent of southerner and northerner, capitalist and worker, immigrant and "native stock," suffragette and male, white and Negro.

Let me point to some of the ways in which this new kind of piling up is occurring, referring first to the age category of youth.

1. If a dimension is to provide pivotal identities, it is highly facilitating to have it pile upon or coincide with territory. While territory itself may become the dimension of pivotal identification—as with northerner–southerner, USA–USSR—very often the sharing of territory will facilitate the public articulation of some other category that happens to coincide with a particular territory. One wonders, for example, whether the categories capitalist–worker, immigrant–native-born, Negro–white, would have been so nationally pivotal if they had not also been founded upon each opposing category having its own territory. In these terms, one might suggest, also, that the suffragettes, in contrast with the groups mentioned above, were never able to escalate sex categories as pivotal identities and bases of conflict to the extent that they might have wished because every major piece of territory they occupied was massively infiltrated by males.

Relative to age in American technological society, we may note that the coincidence between it and territory is proceeding apace and is most spectacular in the host communities of the ever-expanding multiversities. Into many of these communities in recent years, there have thronged literally tens of thousands of what we might call "youth"—human animals ranging in age from late teens to middle twenties. Because the political powers have opted for the model of a few large educational institutions, rather than many small ones, "cities of youth" are being created. The populations of some of them now approach or surpass forty thousand and the end is not yet in sight. Apparently some institutions even project enrollment figures of fifty to seventy-five thousand within the not too distant future.

Already, for example, 30 per cent of the population of Ann Arbor, Michigan, is composed of youth, or more precisely, students at the University of Michigan. They are not, however, distributed evenly throughout the city but are concentrated at its center, around the university. As apartment construction continues and as the university expands by about a thousand students a year, one can envision the day when the entire center city of Ann Arbor will be composed almost exclusively of human beings in their late teens to middle twenties. This trend is fostered in no small measure by the enormous rental rates in the center city which are likely to continue to rise and which force other age categories into the suburbs.

2. Thrust upon communities typically unprepared for their arrival, a significant proportion of the youth in these territories live crowded together in inadequate housing or equally crowded together in new but rent-gouging apartment buildings. Indeed the current circumstances of student living conditions—high density, crowding, bad housing, and rent gouging—remind one of the living conditions and exploitation of the immigrants in New York and Chicago in the early part of the century and of the Negroes in those (and other) cities somewhat later. Ghetto landowners come to think the ghetto area, as one owner of apartment buildings in Ann Arbor has put it, "a real estate paradise."

3. Also similar to early immigrants and later Negroes, the youth piled into these territories have low incomes, a fact which further serves to differentiate them from the surrounding population. Lacking the considerable amount of excess resources necessary to paint-up and fix-up their dwellings, youth, as did immigrants and as do Negroes, come to have publicly identifiable—that is, "sloppy and shoddy"—places of habitation. And, like other low income peoples, past and present, they rent rather than buy dwelling space.

4. Faced with uncertain employment and residence futures—actually a certainty that they will have to move—youth in these territories do not, to any significant degree, develop identification with local social institutions that precede their arrival—the pre-existing local political organizations, churches, business organizations, and so forth. As was said of the earlier ghetto dwellers, they "stay with their own kind" and participate in informal and formal social organization dominated by others of their own category.

Such piling up of categories makes for, I think, the possibility of ghettos very similar to those that the dominant population worried about in connection with Italian, Irish, and Polish immigrants some forty or more years ago and the kind that we still worry about today in connection with Negroes. Only now, instead of Italian, Irish, Polish, or Negro ghettos, the dominant sectors of the population may well become concerned about "youth ghettos" and all the social processes that surround concern over ghetto areas are likely to begin. Indeed, they have begun, as I shall suggest in a moment.

First, however, we must pursue the obvious implication that categories piling up in one kind of territory means that other kinds of categories are likely to be piling up in yet other territories. If youth are being territorially segregated, this means that they cannot be in some other places. These other places are of equal interest, for in them reside the sectors of the population who will be engaging in concern over youth ghettos.

Concomitant with the rise of youth ghettos has been a growth of rather age-homogeneous bands of territory ringing American cities. These are the well-known suburban tracts, many neighborhoods of which have a rather peculiar character. In some of them one finds a population composed almost exclusively of what we might call "early adults"—human animals ranging in age, roughly, from late twenties to late thirties; and children—human animals below the age of about twelve. "Middle adults"—humans in their early forties to late fifties; and "late-adults"—humans in their sixties and older; and teenagers are in a decided minority; in many cases, they are hardly present at all.

Piled upon this age category of early adult and its coincidence with a territory, one finds the employment and financial state known as "struggling" or "being on the way up." The neat row houses of early adults market in the fifteen to twenty-five thousand dollar range. Deep in installment debt, their lives are centered on the family unit. They are concerned that politicians treat them kindly, that is, that taxes be kept down. And they are likely to have voted for Goldwater.

In other suburban tracts, one finds a population composed almost exclusively of middle adults (forties and fifties) and teenagers. The neighborhood is largely undisgraced by the presence of children, early adults, or late adults and the neat row houses of the middle adults market in the twenty-five to fifty thousand dollar and up range. In large measure the middle adults have passed their "struggling." They have, in some sense, arrived.

Indeed, there would seem to be evolving a pattern wherein an age–sex unit of early adults establishes itself in an early-adult neighborhood, its members spawn their offspring and then, at the appropriate age, move to a middle-adult territory. In this way, age–sex units are always able to be with their "own kind," territorially protected from the contamination of contact with many other age categories. Teenagers, especially, are usually able to be with their corresponding age-category mates. They can be uncompromised by entanglements with children, early adults, or late adults.

Although all of this is only a tendency at present, it would seem to be a growing tendency and one which assumes additional significance in the light of the already more pronounced territorial segregation of late adults. We are all well aware that persons of sixty and over—often described with polite euphemisms such as "senior citizens"—have begun to assemble in special buildings in cities, in special neighborhoods within suburbs, and, indeed, in special areas of the nation. It is apparently the case that significant portions of Florida, Arizona, and Southern California are becoming something like the states of late adulthood. Piled upon these categories of age and territory are others, such as the marginal or unemployed state, often called "retirement." Special kinds of legislation have developed for this age group, defining their monetary rights and duties and relating even to the possibility of their marrying one another.

Among these six categories of age, two—youth and late adulthood—are already proceeding toward highly pronounced territorial segregation with the concomitant clustering of yet other categorical sharings around their respective ages and territories. The remaining four are already splitting into two sets of two each. Early adults are still territorially linked to children and middle adults are still territorially linked to teenagers.

However, the territorial link between middle adults and teenagers shows signs of weakening, given the absorption that teenagers have in the culture that centers on the high school. While teenagers must still share a household with middle adults and face school-and-other-specialized keepers of teenagers, they are achieving a rather well defined and dominated set of territories spread throughout communities. These include the school itself, drive-ins, and the like.[4] This separation is limited, however, in a way somewhat similar to the way in which the territorial integrity of the suffragettes was limited. While both had or have special territories, these were or are not large areas from which persons of other categories could or can be, at least formally, excluded.

Nonetheless, this partial territorial segregation exists and is deepening. Combined with the propensity of early adults to send their children to school at ever earlier ages, one can wonder if these remaining two sets of two categories (early adults and children; middle adults and teenagers) will not themselves territorially divide.

Perhaps it is not entirely unrealistic, fanciful, or whimsical to suggest that there may come a day when children are almost entirely segregated under the supervision of child-rearing specialists. Perhaps parts of, say, Nevada, Utah, Wyoming, or Montana, could be given over to the task and designated as Children's States. Under such circumstances, early adults could devote themselves exclusively to the struggle of making it to the next neighborhood. The increasing numbers of college-educated, female early adults who now mourn the disuse of their talents and the incompatability of children and career, would be free more actively to participate with their male partners in the climb up.

Likewise, the separation of teenagers into teen cities, very much like the developing youth ghettos, would free their middle-adult parents to participate more intensively in the social and political machinations of the occupations in which they have now come to power.

Segregation, after all, has its attractions as well as its limitations. Given the already strong tendency of children and teenagers (indeed, of all the age categories) to group together and to prefer one another's company, these youngest categories may well, in the future, come to demand the same kinds of territorial rights now enjoyed by youth and late adults. At present, of course, they are still rather dominated by their respective age-superiors in territories run by, and fundamentally belonging to, these superiors. Equal justice for all might well be construed in the future to mean that each age category, including children and teenagers, has a right to its own piece of ground.

At such a future time, arguments are also likely to arise for the efficiency and effectiveness of specialized age territories for children and teenagers. In the same way that the family-oriented cottage industry and the "putting-out system" of industrial manufacture collapsed in the face of competition by the superior effectiveness of a centralized, industrial process, so

[4]James S. Coleman, *The Adolescent Society* (New York: Free Press of Glencoe, 1961).

too, the last remaining cottage industry—that of producing persons—might well falter in the face of harsh criticism of its inefficiency, its widely variable standards of production, and excessive rate of rejects. Although they phrase them in different terms, many educators are, in fact, already making exactly these criticisms.

Let me shift, finally, to a direct focus on the youth ghetto. I will discuss, in order, relations of adults to this territory, conduct within it, and some aspects of interaction between the two.

These topics are appropriately conceived in terms that we might use in discussing other, more familiar, kinds of ghettos. The more familiar ones have, of course, historically been based upon religion, ethnicity, or race. However, certain kinds of social processes seem relatively common to almost all ghettos, age-category ones included.

A condition of territorial segregation wherein a variety of additional categories are piled up, promotes a situation of low information flow from the ghetto to the surrounding territories. When low information flow occurs in the context of a measure of suspicion, fear, and distrust, the information most likely to be noticed, remembered, and circulated by persons in extra-ghetto territories is that which is discrediting or defaming. Adopting the point of view of suspicious, fearful, and distrustful persons, it is altogether reasonable for them to be attuned to discrediting information from the ghetto; such information serves to put them further on guard to protect themselves.

One type of defamation takes the form of imputing to the pivotal category in question a wide range of personal failings, often felt to be caused by the pivotal category itself. Non-ghetto dwellers build up in their minds an imputed "personality" of sorts that is believed to be characteristic of the particular ghetto dwellers, the particular pivotal category.[5]

In recent years we have begun to see the development of the rudiments of an imputed ghetto personality of youth, or, more narrowly, of students. Adults, the superordinate category in this case, seem to have begun the process of noticing, remembering, and relating a variety of kinds of imputed personal features of this latest stigmatized category.

One hears it commented that "they" are boisterous, they have no respect for property, they work irregularly and drive recklessly. They throw garbage out of their windows, and break bottles in the streets and on the sidewalks. They lounge in an unseemly fashion on balconies, dangle out of windows, and congregate in public thoroughfares. They accost strangers on the street with arcane propositions. They gamble all night, fail to pay shopkeepers and landlords, shoplift, and engage in riotous drinking sprees. They hang around on the streets, jaywalk, talk in a loud and crude fashion in public places, and live in disorder and filth. They let their dwellings run down, living like "animals," crowded six and seven together in small apartments. They have loose sexual behavior and fail to keep their bodies and

[5]Cf. Suttles, *op. cit.*, and the literature cited therein.

clothes properly scrubbed and ordered. They engage in crime. Their women have no shame but dress scantily and recline suggestively on lawns or around buildings. They are residentially unstable, always moving, frequently leaving the landlord or even their own kind in the lurch.

Establishments which cater to their peculiar tastes are dimly lit and outfitted in outlandish decor. Obscene slogans and writings and pictures are likely to be found in the stores they frequent, especially the book shops.

While yet scattered and relatively uncrystallized as a personality portrait of youth ghetto residents, there would seem to be here already the elements of the classic portrait of failings attributed to ghetto dwellers throughout American history. This portrait has typically included—as it does here—the elements of laziness, irresponsibility, hedonism, lack of pride in property or personal appearance, promiscuousness, deviousness, and family and employment instability. We are currently most familiar with this portrait of imputations relative to Negro and Spanish-American ghetto dwellers, but essentially the same kinds of imputations were once made of, for example, the Italians and the Irish before their ghettos disintegrated. Indeed, where ghettos based on these latter pivotal categories persist, the process still goes on.[6] Such failings were imputed also to "laborers," or working men, during the struggle for unions in America.[7]

In addition to becoming objects of defaming imputations, ghetto dwellers find themselves, as well, the objects of specialized processes of social control and recognition. Such efforts are specialized because, while they are sometimes described as though they applied to the entire population, they are directed at the ghetto dwellers in particular.

Although they are relatively rudimentary as yet, we already see such specialized control and recognition efforts in, for example, the University of Michigan's attempt to regulate student operation of automobiles anywhere in an entire county without special registration. Laws regarding mufflers on motor vehicles have been adopted, and aimed, according to the public discussion, at the motorcycles of youth. (They are, it is said, terribly noisy.)

Within the context of ghettoization, already existing controls aimed especially at youth take on new significance. The military draft, which falls with special force on youth, comes to be defined as a special burden. Because of the uncertainty over whether any one of them is or is not twenty-one years of age, the purchase of alcoholic beverages becomes, typically, an occasion for an ID shakedown. In much the same way that Negroes in some parts of the country even today have to worry about obtaining public service, youth have to be concerned over producing a sufficient amount of "ID" even to ratify their minimal standing as persons. The treatment they receive at the hands of barmaids and bartenders and liquor store clerks serves well

[6]Suttles, *op. cit.*

[7]A similar kind of imputation of personal failings, of course, also takes place between regions of nations and nations themselves that are in conflict.

to communicate their special pivotal identity and to communicate others' assumption that youth are "likely to be liars." So, too, their credit may be a matter for suspicion and the obtaining of a telephone may require a special "security deposit," serving organizationally to impute to them an untrustworthy personal character.

And also parallel to Negroes, employers are willing to offer many youth only menial unskilled jobs and reluctant to proffer employment with career or developmental possibilities. That is, employers discriminate against youth in terms of whether they have made some kind of settlement with the military. If none has been made, reasonable employment is difficult to obtain. While employers are entirely rational in this, it constitutes, from the point of view of youth, a form of discrimination.

Youth become, too, objects of special recognition in the name of nondiscrimination. A few radio stations, for example, have demonstrated their democratic virtues not only by having ethnic and racial radio programs but by setting aside hours or even days for youth programs. Radio stations in Ann Arbor recognize that area's special German past with "old country" shows, and at least one station gives over Saturday to student "ethnic radio." The youthful announcer for that day refers to Ann Arbor as "Student City."[8]

Eventually most ghettos rouse the moral sentiments of the dominant population to the point that a special corps of helping and rehabilitative personnel are recruited and deployed into the areas. It is the mission of these personnel to reduce the number of horrendous things that go on there and to make the residents straighten up and be good citizens.

While this kind of missionary activity, on any significant scale, may lie far in the future in relation to youth ghettos, one can discern its beginnings in such enterprises as the "campus ministry" and in the expansion of psychological counseling for those youth who are students.

Informational inaccessibility and fear and suspicion of ghettos promote, in addition to defaming stereotypes of imputed personal features and specialized control, a special revelationary literature.

This literature is centrally oriented to the question, "What are X (the pivotal category) *really* like?" Whether the "X" has been southerners, workers, suffragettes, immigrants, or of late, Negroes, the popular press has frenzied itself with efforts to "inform" the dominant sectors of the society what is "really" going on, what, of late, is "happening." Such popular revelations promise us an "inside view" of the innermost sections and horrendous events of the ghetto. Complete with the most grim or most bizarre of photographs and drawings, such revelations often lead the reader to believe that not only are his worst suspicions true but things are even worse than he had thought.

[8]Like the separate entrances for whites and Negroes in southern states, Ann Arbor, Michigan's, YM–YWCA has a special side door neatly lettered with the words YOUTH ENTRANCE.

While we are most familiar with these popular revelations, historically, in connection with immigrants and Negroes, a similar kind of presentation is now being made about youth. One of these, published by *Look,* the contemporary master of the popular revelation, is called *Youth Quake.*[9] Retailing for one dollar, its cover features a blurred psychedelic-like photograph of youth on a dance floor in "wildly" colored dress, presumably wreathing under the sounds emitted by a musical group. The front page text promises to tell us "WHAT'S HAPPENING" in these terms:

> Turned on and Tuned in . . . Teeny-boppers, Hippies . . . Sunset Strip to Washington Square . . . Conversations parents never hear—Sex, Drugs, God, Morality, Success—Mod and Mini . . . Psychedelic Lights . . . and much much more.

It should be noted that popular revelations of ghetto life are not entirely negative in character. While there is a large element of indignation and "tut-tutting," it is perhaps most accurate to say that these revelations contain a mixture of horror and romantic fascination with "people who live that way." Evil, after all, must have its attractions—to be natural—otherwise it would not be so popular. Nor would the dominant categories of a society have to put so much energy into eliminating or holding it in check.

It is in part such romantic fascination that, in the past, made Harlem such a lure for white Manhattan residents and tourists. Indeed, historically, a variety of kinds of ghettos have come to service the vice needs of the population at large. Youth ghettos will perhaps also come to service the demand for vice.

The market for such popular revelations inevitably gives rise to the phenomenon of ghetto spies, persons who either are permitted openly to hang around in the ghetto or who actually pass as "one," whatever the "one" in question may be. The spies of popular revelations are often reporters on assignment, but quite often, also, free lancers, as was apparently the case with race-ghetto spy John Griffin, author of *Black Like Me.*[10] Paul Goodman is perhaps the leading youth ghetto spy among a wide range of persons who have tried to get in on this new kind of act.[11] Perhaps the ultimate in age-category spying has, however, already been achieved by that thirty-three-year-old lady who claims, "I Passed as a Teenager."[12]

And, as has occurred with respect to previous ghettos, some members of the dominant pivotal category defect to "the other side." In the same way that some of the economic elite, in Marxian terms, are said to see the "true" direction of history and defect to the workers, or that some whites defect to and take up the Negro cause, we are now beginning to have age-category de-

[9]Jack V. Fox, *Youth Quake* (New York: Cowles Educational Books, 1967).

[10]John H. Griffin, *Black Like Me* (Boston: Houghton Mifflin Company, 1961).

[11]Paul Goodman, *Growing Up Absurd* (New York: Vintage Books, Inc., 1956).

[12]Lyn Tornabene, "I Passed as a Teenager," *Ladies' Home Journal,* LXXIV (June, 1967), pp. 113–18, and a book of the same title.

fectors. Edgar Friedenberg is perhaps the leading exemplar of such defection.[13]

In attempting briefly to characterize what happens within ghettos themselves, we must keep in mind two previously discussed points. First, the piling up or clustering of devalued categories in a given territory is in fact taking place. Second, this factual clustering is perceived (however dimly) by the surrounding populace and becomes a basis upon which all manner of failings additionally are imputed. Taken together, factual clustering and the additional imputations form the situation of the ghettoite.

Two significant features of the situation of the ghettoite are: (1) extraordinary exposure to others of "his own kind," and correspondingly limited exposure to persons of "other kinds"; and (2) limited objective possibilities for establishing a stable life style, primarily because of low income, which is, in turn, a function of the imputations and practices of disreputability made of "his kind" by the surrounding populace.

The situation of the ghettoite is conducive to or "ready made for" familiar strategic lines of adaptation or response. I will mention two well-known strategies of adaptation appearing frequently in all ghettos which are now appearing in youth ghettos.

First, it is possible, and rather reasonable, for the ghettoite to accept the just-mentioned facts of his situation and to accommodate to them. He can come to believe that the imputations made and treatment accorded to his category by the dominant sectors of the society are in a significant measure true, reasonable, and justified. While he views these as sad facts, he nonetheless accepts them as valid. The imputations of the ways in which he displays personal failings become then a basis upon which actual and new items of "personal failure" are predicated. (The irony here, of course, is that such new personal failings are perceived by the dominant categories and become the basis upon which they, in their turn, predicate more intensive imputations and discriminatory practices. That treatment, in its turn, feeds back to the ghettoite, and so it goes on.)

Under conditions of low income and almost exclusive exposure to one's "own" stigmatized kind and an uncertain residential future, and indeed, an uncertain future generally, it becomes reasonable to relax one's efforts at a conventional personal appearance and to relax one's efforts, as well, to maintain a conventionally clean, well-kept, and orderly household.

We are, of course, familiar with the relaxation of personal and household standards in ghettos based on ethnic or racial pivotal categories. And we are familiar, too, with the imputations sometimes made as to why these standards are relaxed. Among the most popular has been the notion of a special "lower class" or "Negro personality" which causes personal and household disorder and dirt.

However, the same pattern of personal and household dirt occurs in youth ghettos. The youth found to display this pattern are drawn largely

[13]Edgar Z. Friedenberg, *Coming of Age in America* (New York: Random House, 1965).

from middle and upper middle class backgrounds, a setting which presumably trained them in high standards of personal and household order and cleanliness. In the youth ghetto, we find a portion of them living in a fashion very similar to that in which people in other ghettos live.[14] And presumably when they depart from the ghetto for early adult neighborhoods, they will maintain the very particular style of cleanliness and order so characteristic of those neighborhoods.

It can be suggested that the youth ghetto pattern of personal and household disorder and dirt is a very important "control" or contrast case which tells us that it is not ghetto people qua deep-lying personality patterns that conduce to this relaxation, but rather the ghetto situation. As has been said, the ghetto situation is one of high exposure to one's own kind, low income, and uncertainty of residential and general future. Exposure almost exclusively to one's own kind reduces the felt need for "respectable" presentation. Low income makes respectable presentation extremely difficult to accomplish. Middle class people are insufficiently appreciative of the very high total cost of the tools and machines, paint, repair materials, and furnishings necessary to the rehabilitation and maintenance of a "respectable" household. This is especially the case where one is attempting this in what is already a ghetto dwelling. And, of course, an uncertain residential and general future renders the entire effort unreasonable in the first place. If we are to understand this pattern of ghetto living, then, we are better advised to scrutinize the characteristics of the ghetto situation rather than the personal characteristics of whatever category of people happen to be found there.

Second, while the majority of ghetto residents seem to "take it" and a proportion drift into the first pattern, a minority refuse to accept their situation and project a more active strategy of response. Co-mingling in the intensive fashion now made possible and necessary, some ghetto dwellers begin to crystallize new and unusual ideologies which purport to explain and interpret their particular situation and, typically, also to describe and explain all the rest of the world. Members of the human species who live in the ghetto situation seem particularly likely to spawn and be attracted to new and unusual ideologies that are characterized by members of the dominant society as "radical," "bizarre," "peculiar," or "fantastic." Ghettoites are particularly likely to so occupy themselves because of a lack of exposure to the more moderate and modulating categories of persons who might convince them of other realities; because of the stigmatizing imputations they face; and because of the objective deprivation and social exclusion under which they labor.

The general class of active ideological responses to the ghetto situation itself divides into two types of directions, which even sometimes compete with one another for adherents. One type, which might be called the political response, defines the ghetto situation and other sectors of society in

[14]I refer here to the garden-variety, run-of-the-mill youth in such ghettos, not simply to the more spectacular patterns embodied in youthful radicals or hippies.

terms of relatively immediate measures that can be undertaken to better the lot of ghettoites and perhaps even the life of the entire society. We are, of course, quite familiar with this in regard to Negro ghettos and the variety of civil rights organizations that seek to make this or that concrete change in the social order. The suggestion here, however, is that we can best understand what is called "The New Left"—meaning, most prominently, Students for a Democratic Society—as a movement arising out of the youth ghetto in the same way political movements have, historically, risen out of other kinds of ghettos.

If the ghettoization of youth continues, we should expect to see the rise of a variety of kinds of other political responses, many of them more limited and moderate than Students for a Democratic Society. Already there are attempts to organize renters and to register student voters in order to increase their political power. There may come a day, indeed, when some cities will find that their politics revolve around the voting strength of various age-category ghettos, in the same way that Chicago politics has long revolved around ethnic and racial enclaves.

The other type of more active ideological response is considerably more sweeping in the scope of its projected change in the social order, but ironically more passive in the degree to which it seeks to make changes in that order. I refer to the various retreating and utopian—not untypically, religious—responses which involve withdrawing into highly distinctive residential enclaves, often within the ghetto, and living out therein a life that is considered perfect and ideal. The outside world is seen as sinful, demented, deluded, decadent, or otherwise in need of revolutionary change. Except for perhaps some efforts at making individual converts, such utopians do not directly attack the social order. The most famous instance of this type of response in connection with Negro ghettos has, of course, been Father Divine's Heavens.[15] We are witnessing, I think, an analytically identical strategy of response in the so-called "hippies" who have appropriated certain dwellings in youth ghettos as their utopian communities and who have even moved out to create their own ghettos, as was once the case in the Haight-Ashbury district of San Francisco. Although yet lacking a widely acknowledged messianic leader, their ideology is remarkably similar to that espoused by followers of Father Divine, especially in the emphasis upon love, good-will, and the decadence of the larger society.

One other pattern of response should be mentioned, although it has not as yet appeared in the youth ghetto, at least not in organized form. This is the militant revolutionary pattern, exemplified by the Black Nationalists, or at least those among the Black Nationalists who advocate guerrilla warfare and violent subversion. But perhaps this still lies in the future and will only appear if youth ghettoization becomes very extreme.

The possibility and viability of the militant revolutionary pattern, and all the other patterns of response, are, of course, crucially undercut by a

[15]Sara Harris, *Father Divine, Holy Husband* (Garden City, New York: Doubleday and Company, Inc., 1953).

fundamental feature peculiar to age itself. While people who are identified in terms of racial and ethnic pivotal categories will remain instances of those categories all their lives, youth as a category is impermanently occupied. It would seem to be enormously difficult to predicate any kind of enduring collective action upon a population of participants that is continually leaving the category while others are continually arriving. In the end, that feature must be recognized as fundamentally debilitating to organized age-category conflict.

Nonetheless, conflicts between the age categories of a more limited but highly spectacular character are still possible, and even likely, under conditions of youth ghettoization.

The prime meaning of ghettoization is, as mentioned, the piling up of all manner of categories of dimensions that are different from the categories of the rest of the society. A prime effect of this piling up of categories shared within a territory and little shared across territories, is the decline of routine, trustful relationships with individuals and organizations in extra-ghetto territories. Ghettoites are intensively and routinely exposed to other ghettoites, but only fractionally exposed in a routine fashion to non-ghettoites.

Such a situation of separation of categories of people serves to create distance, in both the physical and social senses, and, therefore, to engender relative ignorance or lack of information as to the intentions, plans, motives, and good or evil will of the other pivotal category.

If there comes to be an absence of cross-categorical interaction, joint-problem solving, routine negotiation, and the like, there is created within both pivotal categories a condition of distrust and fear of the opposite category. This situation of separation and therefore distrust and fear spawned by ignorance is to be contrasted with the kinds of relations between social categories that create trust and confidence and therefore social stability. Cross-categorical trust and confidence are most likely to prevail where there is a high rate of relatively free interaction, relatively large numbers of communication channels, and prompt attention to grievances which can easily be brought to the attention of persons who will act to settle disputes in a just manner. A large number of communication links between categories allows each reasonably to present its point of view, its motives, its plans, its intentions. While each category may not agree with the other on such matters, each side is at least relatively accurately informed and there is little or no necessity for making all manner of surmises, guesses, and imputations of the motives and plans of its opposite number. Equally as important, in preparing such cross-category revelations of its plans and intentions, each is induced to modify its perspective to order to make it more acceptable to the opposite category. Concomitant with such exchanges are personal friendships, informal ties, personalistic advantages and pay-offs, and other more diffuse inter-categorical modes of compromising the involvement of persons in their own category. A tradition of exchange of views and negotiated settlements makes it more likely that any action initiated by one side will be received in an atmosphere of trust. All these practices make it less likely that any action by either category will be defined as fundamentally threatening.

We find precisely the opposite obtaining between ghettos and the host society. The absence of effective communication, co-optation, and compromise breeds, as noted, fear, suspicion, and distrust. Such a situation is fertile ground for the spread of all manner of fearful and cynical rumors as to what "the other side" is "really" up to. In the absence of reasonable information, the most gross of cynical motives can be and are imputed.

It is in the situation of separation, fear, distrust, and negative imputations between categories that an action initiated by one category can be defined as fundamentally threatening to the basic interest of the opposite category.

If an action is defined as a fundamental threat, then it is reasonable to respond to this threat with a swift, decisive, strong defense. Of course, the opposite category which is the recipient of this defense thereupon feels itself grossly threatened. The recipient category, in order to protect its now felt-to-be-threatened fundamental interests, reciprocates with its own swift, decisive, strong defense. The opposite category is consequently even more threatened and responds in kind. We thus have what is called the escalation of conflict, a process that is the joint product of the two parties and a process that seems always to have an ambiguous beginning point, unless one traces the history of the relation all the way back to the beginnings of the original categorical separation.[16]

Where the swift, decisive, strong defense involves large numbers of ghetto persons acting in a nonroutine manner in public places, it is popularly labeled a demonstration, riot, or collective outburst.[17] We have seen a number of these in connection with Negro ghettos. It is in exactly the same terms of ghettoization—the terms of separation, of fear, of distrust, and of high probability of threat—that we can also best understand—similar events occurring on college campuses, that is, in youth ghettos.

If youth ghettos have already fired their shot heard round the world, it was probably the Berkeley "demonstrations," "disturbances," "revolt," or "revolution" of 1964–65. (Pick a label according to the preference of your age category.)

The well-known events at Berkeley were only a spectacular episode in the long history of decreasing categorical sharing and the growth of a relatively enclosed youth ghetto along the southern edge of the Berkeley campus. The relations between the two categories—university and youth—came finally to a confrontation where each category saw itself enormously threat-

[16]Excellent documentation and conceptualization of these situations and processes are presented in Suttles, *op. cit.*, and Heirich, *op. cit.* The process sketched in the foregoing passages may well be among the few that are found at all levels of social organization.

[17]When such defensive action involves merely individuals or small groups, it is labeled crime, delinquency, or deviance. When it involves nations it is labeled "war." Such differences in popular labels should not detract attention from the essential similarity of the social processes.

ened by the other category. Each category saw itself as rightly defending itself against the threats posed by the other category. It is indeed ironic that the growth of Berkeley's academic eminence in America closely corresponds to the growth of the conditions of separation between youth and the university. Berkeley's scholarly and research eminence was purchased at the price of relative indifference to, and separation from, its almost 28,000 charges. And, as the university learned, the price was much higher than it had been originally calculated. Although allowing at least one-quarter of the tenured faculty in many departments to be on leave for research (and a large "in residence" proportion on psychological leave) and allowing a large proportion of the teaching to be performed by youth called teaching assistants is conducive to a world-wide reputation for scholarship, these practices, when combined with a wide variety of other kinds of indifference and separation, are incompatible with linking the category of youth to the social order.[18]

And even more ironic, where there has been little communication, cooptation, and compromise between categories, it becomes all the more difficult to initiate them. Under conditions of separation, fear, threat, and defense, each category comes, indeed, rather fiercely to pronounce its refusal to compromise what are now well articulated and ideologized principles. That is, the existing separation tends to deepen and solidify into principled inter-categorical opposition.

I have suggested the possibility that we may be embarking upon a period in the American experience when age will become a nationalized pivotal dimension around which categories of persons are differentiated. I necessarily imply that a new kind of segregation may be afoot.

I am, of course, mindful of all those oft-printed remarks, running back at least to ancient Greece, which tell us that almost every generation has thought that new and unprecedented (and most often terrible) things were taking place among its youth. Such reprinted expressions of alarm are intended to tell us that the perception of the unprecedented—typically the decadent—is simply a generational illusion spawned by the fears of older persons. While I will make no judgment as to whether younger generations were or are decadent, one can say that very frequently there has in fact been an enormous change in generational views and practices, a change enshrined most recently in the transformation of Western societies into advanced, industrial, technological social orders.

We should be prepared to expect that the coming of this newest kind of social order might itself create a wide variety of likewise new types of categorical segregations, while yet other segregations disintegrate. So far as I have been able to determine, the current scale of the clustering of persons into territories on the basis of age is indeed a new phenomenon.

While the emerging primacy of the age dimension, and its categories,

[18]My characterization of the Berkeley events is drawn from Heirich's definitive study, especially Chap. I, "Structuring the Conflict."

seems to be new, the social processes it follows, and that follow from it, are very old and universal. While we may have to come to grips with a new content and substance of social conflict, we need not at all despair, because we do know something about the character of the formal and analytic processes involved, and the concepts and propositions appropriate to an understanding of it.

7 Youth and Education

Education is a formal means of socialization. Our society considers that education takes place within formal organizations devoted to learning; colleges and universities have now institutionalized and bureaucratized activities that the Greek students of Socrates undertook for fun or leisure. But socialization also occurs in a variety of other settings, with a number of groups large and small, throughout life. Besides the family, the most universal experience of youth is the school. In most states, the young must de jure be students until they are 16 to 18 years old.

Educational institutions must both pass on the revered traditions and beliefs of the past and at the same time train students for an increasingly uncertain future. As society has grown and as we have tried to realize our stated beliefs in equality, education has become mass education, and schools have become the most burdensome bureaucracies imaginable. Instead of making students autonomous, creative, and able to anticipate the future, schools have become the homes of the most hide-bound, timorous, and rule-oriented occupational groups, that is, teachers, principals, and administrators. The very means adopted to accomplish mass education have become the greatest enemy of attaining it.

Our democratic view of education assumes that it is like other processes in the mass society; greater "inputs" of money, staff, training, and equipment will yield greater "outputs" of equally trained children. Sociologists have studied the relative effects on socialization of certain identifiable aspects of the school system, including the structure of socializing institutions, the personnel, the entering characteristics of students (self-concept, I.Q., achievement orientation, social class position), and the emergent products of the experience (such as student roles, student culture, peer groups, and interaction between students and teachers). Each selection in this section deals with an aspect of education as socialization experience.

Campbell and Coleman were granted a federal government contract following passage of the Civil Rights Act of 1964 to survey schools and determine what might be done to define equality and to create a greater degree of equality among the nation's schools. They undertook a survey of 800 school systems, gathering data from 645,000 children and their teachers, principals, and counselors. Their data were gathered in various regions of the United States, in schools with differing ratios of black and white students. Campbell and Coleman measured the relative influence of facilities, curriculum, and student assignment policies on the students' test results. Their rationale was that test results were the most useful measure of students' capacity to compete for opportunities in society. In light of the selection by Becker included here, which shows the ritual aspects of education, and of the recent writings of Kozol (1968), Kohl (1967), and others, the selection of test results as a dependent variable may reflect the attitudes of teachers toward their students and the subtle repression in the classroom more than the actual capacity of the students to achieve. Campbell and Coleman may admit this possibility, but the survey technique they chose could never reveal it. Further, the very choice of a written, culture-bound test of achievement pre-judges what is "capacity to achieve" or "equality." Many educators have pointed out the inherent prejudice of standardized tests: white students have been taught to be accomplished test takers, whereas the skills of blacks may lie in other areas, and many never receive instruction in being "test-wise."

Other research findings suggest that the "learning environment" is socially and psychologically most critical to education. Campbell and Coleman show that if students enter school with a disadvantage, the school is unable to overcome it; students who enter with a disadvantage leave having fallen farther behind. The difficulty in assessing these results, aside from the culture- and class-bound nature of the indicators, is in determining the causal flow: which plays the greater part in creating the self-concept, the family or the school? Evidence suggests that schools tend to heighten the self-concepts of obedient and submissive middle-class pupils but have the opposite effect on blacks. Furthermore, studies of teacher expectations of student performance show that students who were expected to do well increased their performance levels, whereas those who were expected to do poorly were less successful (Rosenthal and Jacobson 1968).

Becker's work ignores the formal aspects and goals of educational institutions and asks instead what students learn from each other. His interest in student culture was elaborated in two books, *Boys in White* (1961), a study of medical students, and *Making the Grade* (1968), a study of undergraduate students at the University of Kansas. Becker feels that the essential functions of college are probably not reflected in grades or tests, or even in the diploma, but rather in the informal learning that takes place as students run student government, organize political and social activities, and hunt for spouses. In these activities, where students are given responsibility (as they are not in the classroom), they learn to become more mature, competent people by rehearsing for life and by learning work-relevant occupational skills. He shows in *Making the Grade* not only that the grading and academic system does not teach very much (implied), but also that it turns the *means* of motivation (the grading system) into an *end* (grades are sought for themselves), making much of education a mismanaged ritual.

In the selections in this section, some of the obvious, or manifest, functions of education may be identified—providing facts and concepts, producing willing workers, modifying attitudes—as may some less obvious, or latent, functions—developing interpersonal competence, rehearsing for responsibilities, gaining political savvy. The manifest functions are contained in the official rhetoric of the institution and espoused by those in positions of authority, whereas the latent functions are most significant to many of the subordinate members of the same institutions. These internal tensions and contradictions underlie many of the demands for relevance, change, and the restructuring of education. What is education, and who is it for, after all?

Inequalities in Educational Opportunities in the United States

Ernest Q. Campbell and James S. Coleman

The Civil Rights Act of 1964 required that a survey be conducted to determine the lack of availability of equal educational opportunities for individuals by reason of race and other factors at all levels of public instruction in the United States, its territories and possessions.[1] This paper is a summary of some of the findings of that survey, limited to a comparison of

Reprinted by permission of the authors from a paper presented to the American Sociological Association, August 31, 1966.

[1]*Equality of Educational Opportunity,* Superintendent of Documents Catalog No. FS 5.238:38001, U.S. Government Printing Office, 1966.

Negroes and whites, to the first twelve grades of school, and to the fifty states plus the District of Columbia.

Sample and Method

The sampling plan selected school systems (high schools plus their feeder schools) in seven geographical regions divided into two strata representing the metropolitan and non-metropolitan areas in each region. The selection proceeded in such a way as to heavily magnify the chance that schools with a large non-white enrollment would be included and the final sample take includes approximately thirty-five percent non-white. In the first stage of the sample the nation was divided into metropolitan and other counties. The largest metropolitan areas were selected with certainty and the others by probabilities which depended on the proportion of non-white population. Counties outside metropolitan areas were selected with probabilities which increased with increasing proportion of non-white population.

In the second sample stage a list of high schools was made for each selected county and metropolitan area and then high schools were selected by probabilities which increased with increasing proportion of non-white enrollment. Feeder schools which sent ninety percent or more of their graduates to a high school drawn in the sample were included with certainty and those that had fewer than ninety percent were selected by a probability equal to the proportion they fed to the high school. Then the sample schools, all superintendents, principals and teachers, were included in the survey as were pupils in the twelfth, ninth, sixth, and third grades and in half of the first grades. Pupils in the first grade were given a very short simple test which their teachers helped them individually in completing; twelfth grade students were given a forty-seven page combination questionnaire and test booklet that required between four to five hours to complete. Around seventy percent of all schools drawn in the sample cooperated with the study and the final sample yield includes approximately 645,000 school children. Analysis of data concerning non-participating schools and systems suggests that their participation would not have materially altered the conclusions of the study.

Verbal and non-verbal reasoning tests were given in all five grades and in all except the first grade a reading comprehension and a mathematics achievement test were given. In addition, ninth and twelfth grade students took a general information test that covered four broad areas—practical arts, natural sciences, social studies and humanities—and was designed to give some measure of the depth of a school's training.

The Definitions of Inequality

Congress in requesting the survey did not define what it meant by educational inequalities, and it was necessary to consider a variety of possible definitions and to attempt to provide data appropriate to each. One common and traditional conception of inequality rests in the characteristics of the instructional staff and the physical facilities of the school: such things as the age, condition, and cost of the school plant; pupil–teacher ratios, the variety of instructional facilities and curricula; and such characteristics of the teachers as their salaries and experience. It would be argued that if Negroes attend older schools or less well-equipped ones or are taught by less well-trained teachers an inequality in educational opportunity exists.

A second definition of inequality is provided by the 1954 Supreme Court decision that segregated education is by definition unequal education. Thus data that reflect the probability that a white student will attend school with whites and the Negro student with Negroes might be said to index inequality of educational opportunity by this definition.

A third conception of inequality, perhaps implicit in the prior one, argues that the educationally relevant backgrounds from which students come invariably affect the quality and level of course work, conversation, and other interactions that occur in the classroom and hence that students who attend school with students from homes unlikely to support and reinforce the educational process are subject to inequality of opportunity.

A fourth and final view of educational inequality focuses not on the input of resources into the school but on the outcomes of the school's educational effort. That is, equality of educational opportunity would be said to exist if the public schools produced students who, as groups, are equally well prepared to compete for jobs and other rewards available in the society they will live in. Since the fundamental task of the schools is to prepare students for adult life, if the quality of that preparation varies systematically across groups such that some are competitively disadvantaged compared to others it would be argued that the nation's schools have failed to provide equal educational opportunity. This position argues that the allocation of resources should be determined so that quite apart from where children begin they have a real opportunity to end at the same point. If, on the other hand, the public schools fail to produce graduates to whom the labor market, the colleges and universities, and society at large can respond without regard to race insofar as educational performance is relevant to their judgment, then there has not been a true equality of educational opportunity.

This paper deals briefly with each of these measures of educational opportunity and will concentrate in two separate ways on the latter named.

A. School Facilities

The survey determined the availability of a great variety of school facilities and it is impossible to represent the results in any simple summary form. Overall it can perhaps be said that a degree of educational inequality does exist in the United States such that whites are more likely than Negroes to have available a large variety of school facilities. However, it is rare on any given facility that the same direction of inequality holds across all regions considered in the survey. That is, if in any given region on any given factor there is an inequality that favors whites it is highly probable that in some other region there is an inequality that favors Negroes on the same factor. Also within any cluster of factors it is quite uncommon that the direction of inequality is consistent across the various components of the cluster. Our discussion will consider differences at the national level only, although the reader will find it much more advantageous to examine differences by region as given in the accompanying table.

School children differ relatively little in the physical school facilities available. In elementary schools they all have about the same number of pupils per instruction room and per teacher and the same number of makeshift instruction rooms. There is a difference that favors whites in the relative prevalence of science laboratories at the secondary school level. Centralized school libraries are available to almost all secondary school children in the country and to around three-quarters of the elementary school children. Very small differences by race of student are observed. However, when the average number of volumes in the library per student is computed, it is observed that the average white child attends a school that has more books per student in the library. Negro pupils in both elementary and secondary schools are more often found to attend schools within walking distance of the public library. Free textbooks are available almost equally to students of all races at the elementary level while at the secondary level the average Negro attends a school which has a higher percentage of free textbooks. On the other hand, textbooks are more often in short supply in schools attended by Negro pupils, especially in the elementary grades.

There are no important national differences in the recency of textbooks used by Negroes compared to whites. Negro pupils generally receive free lunches and free milk somewhat more often than do white pupils, and a higher percent of Negro pupils attend schools where there is a full or part-time nurse. There are not noticeable differences in the nation in the service of school psychologists available to the different races. Free kindergartens are generally more available to Negro pupils, at least in the nation's metropolitan regions. A higher percentage of white pupils attend both regionally and state accredited schools, and white pupils tend to have more art and music teachers in their schools than do Negro pupils. There is no general tendency for Negro pupils to differ from whites on the length of school day or on the expected amount of daily homework. The average white is more likely to attend a secondary school that offers a college preparatory curriculum and he is somewhat more likely to enroll in a school that offers a commercial curriculum. Negroes are slightly less likely than whites to be in a school classed by the principal as academic in its primary curricular emphasis. The average Negro pupil is much less likely to attend a school to which representatives of predominantly white colleges are sent for recruitment purposes. Negroes are deficient relative to whites in the availability of remedial reading and arithmetic classes and in the availability of accelerated curriculums. According to the principal's report, achievement and intelligence tests are widely used in both elementary and secondary schools and there are no noteworthy differences by race in regard to achievement testing in the schools they attend. But Negroes are less often than whites attending secondary schools which give interest inventories. In every region more Negro students are enrolled in schools which ability-group pupils at the elementary level; more pupils are in the lowest tracks in schools attended by Negroes than in schools attended by whites, whereas in most regions the average white pupil attends the schools which have a slightly larger proportion of pupils in the highest track. Negro students are less likely than whites to attend a school in which students who fail a course are required to repeat the entire grade, at least at the elementary level. When we look at extra curricular activities the most important conclusion is that there is little difference between Negroes and whites in their availability overall.

B. Characteristics of Staff

Negro pupils are more likely to be taught by teachers who are locality-based in the sense that they are products of the area in which they teach and secured their public school training nearby. Negro pupils are more likely to have teachers who have lived in larger towns and cities than have the teachers of white pupils. Teachers of Negro students grew up in homes in which the educational attainments of parents were on the average somewhat less than is the case for the teachers of white students. Generally no race differences in the sex composition of faculties is observed nor are there gross differences in the average age of teachers, but there are sharp differences in the racial composition of the faculty. The average Negro elementary student attends a school in which sixty-five percent of the faculty are Negro and the average white elementary student attends a school in which ninety-seven percent of the faculty are white. At secondary levels the corresponding figures are fifty-nine percent and ninety-seven percent. Sixty-one percent of Negro secondary students attend schools with Negro principals and ninety-five percent of white students attend schools with white principals. Negro principals are rare outside the southern states, but wherever they appear they are in charge of schools with a concentration of Negro students. Negro pupils are neither more nor less likely than whites to be taught by teachers with advanced degrees. The average Negro pupil is more likely, however, to be taught by teachers who score low on a short thirty-item verbal facility test that was administered to teachers on a voluntary basis. Negro pupils have teachers with slightly greater experience both in total years and in length of experience in the current school. Their teachers report reading more professional education journals and more time spent in class preparation. The general impression for the nation is that the average white and average Negro pupil do not differ in the type of college in which their teachers were trained, but the level of degree offered by the college does differ with teachers of Negro pupils more likely to be products of colleges that do not offer advanced degrees. Teachers of Negro pupils are much more likely to have been educated in colleges that had a large enrollment of Negro pupils and teachers of white pupils are likely to have had limited contact with Negroes as fellow students when they were in college. Teachers of the average Negro are somewhat less likely to be members of scholastic honorary societies such as Phi Beta Kappa or Kappa Delta Pi, more likely to have attended institutes that offer special training in professional upgrading, more likely to have participated in teachers' associations as officers or active workers, more likely to have attended institutes that offer special training in teaching or counselling the culturally disadvantaged. Race of student has no appreciable relation to the salary earned by either teacher or principal, nor to teacher absenteeism rates. A smaller proportion of the teachers of whites plan definitely to remain in teaching until retirement although more teachers of whites would reenter teaching if they had the decision to make over again. Average class size tends to be one to two students larger for the teachers of Negroes than for the teachers of whites at the elementary school level, whereas it is two to three students larger for the teachers of Negroes at the secondary school level. Faculties are somewhat more stable in schools attended by Negroes and are more likely to fall under a tenure system. The National Teacher Examination or similar test is used more often in schools attended by the average Negro. The average white child is considerably more likely to be taught by teachers who express a special preference for teaching children of white-collar and professional workers, for teaching Anglo-Saxon children, and for teaching white pupils. They are also more likely to prefer to teach high ability students and to support the concept of the neighborhood elementary school, to fail to favor compensatory educational programs for the culturally disadvantaged, and to reject the idea that it is educationally sound to have white teachers for non-white pupils and non-white teachers for white pupils.

C. Characteristics of Fellow Students

An important part of a child's school environment consists not of the physical facilities of the school, the curriculum, and the teachers, but of his fellow students. These provide challenges to achievement or distractions from achievement; they provide the opportunities to learn outside the classroom through association and casual discussions. Indeed it seems likely that when the average citizen thinks of a good school in a community he most often measures it by the kind of student body it contains and implicitly recognizes that whatever the quality of the staff, curriculum and facilities, the level of instruction must be geared to the student body itself. To the extent, then, that schools are homogeneous in the composition of their student bodies, homogeneous as to race, socio-economic origins, or whatever may seem of relevance, it may be argued that the school holds the child in the environment of his origins and keeps out of his reach the environment of the larger society.

The average white elementary school child attends a school where eighty-seven percent of his classmates are white and the average Negro attends a school where sixteen percent of his classmates are white. The average Negro is more often in classes with pupils whose mothers are not high school graduates. Negro children are especially likely to be in classes with a large number of students from broken homes and are more often in classes with children who come from large families. The average Negro has fewer fellow students who come from homes that have such material possessions as telephones, vacuum cleaners, and automobiles. On the other hand, we do not observe a difference by race in the percent of fellow pupils who report their parents to be highly interested in their education and, indeed, the average Negro child has more fellow students whose parents attend the PTA or other parent association meetings. Negro children attend classes with fellow students who report less reading matter in their homes. This applies to daily newspapers, encyclopedias, and the number of books.

Negro students attend schools in which a larger proportion of students drop out before finishing. If we assume that aspirations and performance can be dulled by association with those who will drop out of school we must also assume that they can be raised by association with those who will go to college. The average Negro is less likely to attend a school in which the students have read a college catalog or talked with a college official about going to college, and fewer of his fellow classmates—at least in preceding grades—have in fact gone on to college. More of the classmates of whites than of Negroes are in a college preparatory curriculum and more are taking courses ordinarily required for college. Negroes also attend schools in which fewer of their classmates report high overall grade averages. There is, however, some conflicting evidence. Negroes and whites are about equally exposed to classmates who report definite intentions to go to college and who have been encouraged to attend college by their teachers or counselors. Indeed the average Negro is more exposed to fellow students who report high interest in school and frequent reading activity, as he is more often exposed to fellow students who report strong aspirations to be among the best students in the school. Negro and white elementary children are about equally likely to attend school with pupils who report being one of the best students in my class and who agree with the statement that "I sometimes feel I just can't learn." At the secondary level the classmates of Negroes are somewhat less likely to agree that "I sometimes feel I just can't learn" or that "I would do better in school if teachers didn't go so fast."

D. Test Results and Their Predictions

The differences between whites and Negroes in test performance are great indeed. Negro averages tend to be about one standard deviation below those of the whites. The disadvantage appears to be about the same for all areas tested.[2] The regional variation is much greater for Negroes than for whites. The achievement disadvantage suffered by whites as a result of living in the rural south compared to the urban north is about fifteen percentile points in the distribution of white scores, whereas the disadvantage suffered by twelfth grade Negroes as a result of living in the rural south

[2]Verbal ability and non-verbal ability in all five grades; reading comprehension and mathematics achievement in all except grade one; and five areas of general information at grades twelve and nine only.

Table 1-A. Selected Comparisons Between Negroes and Whites, *Elementary* School Level, for the Nation and by Region, Fall 1965

Item	United States			Nonmetropolitan								
				North & West			South			Southwest		
	N	W(N)	W	N	W(N)	W	N	W(N)	W	N	W(N)	W
a) Percent of students in school plants less than 20 years old	63	62	60	48	47	54	72	42	34	73	58	40
b) Av. no. of pupils per teacher	29	29	28	26	27	25	32	27	27	23	24	26
c) Volumes per student in school library	3.76	5.02	5.20	1.81	2.57	5.44	3.27	5.66	5.60	6.13	4.37	7.31
d) Av. no. of days school in session	180	179	179	178	179	178	177	178	177	175	175	175
e) Av. annual percent of teachers leaving school	7.5	9.3	10.3	12.3	11.4	10.3	5.8	8.0	10.2	6.5	9.3	16.3
Percent of students in school with:												
f) Cafeteria (solely)	38	40	37	41	43	33	46	67	64	47	52	54
g) Gymnasium (solely)	15	18	21	9	17	8	15	36	31	15	27	21
h) School has a centralized school library	73	78	72	44	47	58	74	79	77	48	70	75
i) One or more full-time librarians serving school library	30	26	22	4	7	13	32	23	22	5	6	11
j) State accreditation	57	66	64	67	76	71	57	73	71	91	94	77
k) No art teacher	68	74	57	61	60	53	88	92	91	89	91	89
l) No music teacher	38	24	25	6	13	14	49	47	40	51	37	31
m) Speech therapist (full- and part-time)	54	49	60	51	48	59	17	12	14	37	47	27

Table 1-A (continued).

n) Remedial reading teacher (full- and part-time)	39	30	39	37	40	46	15	19	11	12	7	26
o) No intelligence tests	11	7	5	14	18	5	19	15	8	9	6	9
For schools attended by the average (white, Negro) student the:												
p) Percent of teachers who spent most of their lives in the local area	53	42	40	34	36	40	54	59	55	40	32	31
q) Teacher's race or origin:												
Negro	65	11	2	17	2	1	90	18	2	75	7	1
White	32	87	97	82	97	99	8	81	96	24	91	96
r) Av. verbal facility of teachers and counselors[1]	20.2	22.6	23.4	22.7	23.5	23.7	17.5	21.1	22.5	20.4	23.5	22.4
s) Av. annual teacher's salary (in $1,000)	6.0	5.9	6.0	5.8	5.8	5.7	4.6	4.8	5.0	5.5	5.4	5.4
t) Teacher's rating of student effort[2]	1.9	2.4	2.4	2.0	2.2	2.4	2.0	2.2	2.3	2.2	2.1	2.4
u) Teacher's rating of student ability[2]	1.9	2.4	2.4	1.9	2.1	2.3	2.1	2.3	2.3	2.2	2.2	2.3
v) Percent of white pupils is	16	76	87	54	76	89	10	77	89	16	68	67
w) Percent of classmates whose mother completed high school	33	45	48	35	39	51	24	37	38	28	38	39
x) Percent of schoolmates with daily newspaper in home	61	75	77	60	67	75	40	56	59	54	63	56
y) Percent of schoolmates with encyclopedia in home	54	73	75	62	68	72	36	60	65	48	65	64

Table 1-A (continued).

Item	Metropolitan														
	Northeast			Midwest			South			Southwest			West		
	N	W(N)	W	N	W(N)	W	N	W(N)	W	N	W(N)	W	N	W(N)	W
a.	31	40	59	28	66	63	77	74	75	52	84	89	76	80	80
b.	27	27	26	29	29	28	28	29	30	30	41	42	30	32	31
c.	3.02	5.33	4.65	2.39	4.00	5.03	3.34	4.16	4.50	2.95	2.26	2.28	6.58	7.57	7.27
d.	183	181	182	183	179	180	181	178	180	176	178	177	178	179	184
e.	7.5	7.2	7.9	8.2	13.0	12.2	4.2	9.2	9.2	7.1	12.1	11.2	14.3	10.3	9.5
f.	41	47	45	24	16	22	34	41	32	48	45	38	34	6	14
g.	46	41	49	36	18	19	6	5	5	13	19	17	0	0	8
h.	83	95	89	57	75	70	79	70	69	59	36	33	81	98	95
i.	46	34	43	22	15	15	38	40	50	11	5	12	19	14	13
j.	49	49	52	75	72	83	55	80	55	89	77	76	40	28	29
k.	27	21	16	33	11	20	76	93	91	77	92	88	72	91	85
l.	18	13	11	13	5	6	48	49	62	63	35	37	35	28	40
m.	94	94	90	98	95	79	35	19	43	48	14	15	87	100	99
n.	73	52	58	60	22	17	28	23	31	18	25	29	66	46	70
o.	27	15	9	1	0	1	7	3	0	3	3	2	0	0	0
p.	64	53	51	55	40	39	69	37	37	35	18	18	24	29	24
q.	31	11	2	40	3	2	96	14	4	65	17	1	22	4	2
	67	88	97	58	96	98	2	85	96	32	82	98	69	91	95
r.	21.8	22.7	23.4	22.4	23.4	23.4	19.2	22.9	23.1	20.9	22.7	24.3	22.2	23.0	23.5
s.	7.2	7.4	7.1	7.0	6.7	6.5	5.4	5.1	5.0	5.8	5.1	5.1	7.8	7.8	7.3
t.	1.8	2.6	2.6	1.7	2.4	2.4	2.0	2.4	2.4	2.1	2.3	2.3	1.7	2.4	2.6
u.	1.7	2.6	2.6	1.6	2.4	2.4	2.0	2.4	2.4	2.1	2.3	2.3	1.5	2.3	2.5
v.	33	73	88	23	87	90	3	80	89	20	70	83	17	70	80
w.	39	55	52	36	49	51	33	45	44	40	41	43	35	48	50
x.	75	85	86	70	84	84	64	79	84	67	69	76	67	83	82
y.	71	84	84	61	79	80	51	75	80	57	66	72	64	82	83

[1] Best possible score = 30
[2] Low score = low rating

Explanation of Columns:
N = Negro, W = White, and W(N) = whites in same county as Negroes, derived by weighting the schools attended by whites in each county proportionally to the number of Negroes in that county.

compared to the urban north is about thirty percentile points in the distribution of Negro scores. Or, differently, the disadvantage suffered by Negroes in comparison to whites is about nine points in standard scores (mean of fifty and sigma of ten) in the metropolitan north but about twelve points in the rural south. In general, Negro scores differ little by region in the first grade but increasingly as school proceeds. In no region are there experiences that decrease the racial difference over the period of school. It is clear that the educational disadvantage with which a group begins remains the disadvantage with which it finishes school. In fact, in some areas of the country, notably the south and southwest, the opportunities are not even enough for Negroes to maintain their position relative to that of whites, measured in standard deviation terms. Measured in grade-level terms, the gap widens at higher grades in all regions. Thus, the Negro child, since his school does not attempt or fails in the attempt to compensate for the cultural disadvantages with which he begins school, can expect to start his adult life with the handicap given him by the culture in which he resides compounded by the missed opportunities in schooling that this handicap has caused.

These test scores may be used in a very direct way as a measure of educational inequality. They describe what students know at different points in their schooling and when they finish school. And they are directly pertinent to the argument that educational inequality exists in proportion as the products of schools are unequally equipped to compete for college scholarships, the job market, or in other areas to which school-taught skills are relevant. In other words, to the extent that achievement tests measure the skills necessary for further education and for occupational advancement in our urban industrial society, any difference in achievement test results may be interpreted as an educational disadvantage. But the test results may also be used to determine what things about schools make an educational difference, and thereby help us escape from the mire we are in when we look at a great variety of school facilities and other characteristics of schools and wonder whether the differences we observe do, in fact, make a difference. We can ask two related questions: first, whether given features of schools make any difference in what students achieve, second, what variation is there by race in access to those features of schools that do in fact make a difference in what students achieve?

Based on regression analysis, the most general statement we can make is that schools are very similar in the effect that they have on pupils' achievement when pupils' socio-economic background is taken into account.[3] In other words, differences between schools account for only a small

[3]Prediction is to the verbal ability score, based on these findings: 1) the percent of variance that lies between schools is somewhat greater for this than for the "achievement" tests; 2) school-to-school variations as a percent of total variation decline less from lower to higher grades on this test than on the achievement tests; 3) holding family background constant, a higher proportion of variance in individual scores is explained by school characteristics on the verbal ability than on the achievement test scores; 4) the relation between family background factors and reading comprehension does not decline more over the years of school than does the relation between family background and verbal ability, though it should if schools affect reading comprehension more than they affect verbal ability.

Table 1-B. Selected Comparisons Between Negroes and Whites, *Secondary* School Level, for the Nation and by Region, Fall 1965

				Nonmetropolitan								
	United States			North & West			South			Southwest		
Item	N	W(N)	W	N	W(N)	W	N	W(N)	W	N	W(N)	W
a) Percent of students in school plants less than 20 years old	60	50	53	64	65	35	79	47	52	76	65	44
b) Av. no. of pupils per teacher	26	24	22	20	20	20	30	26	25	20	20	21
Percent of students in schools with:												
c) Space and equipment available for laboratory work in physics	80	90	94	80	80	90	63	81	83	74	87	93
d) Foreign language labs with sound equipment	49	58	56	32	36	24	17	22	32	38	36	19
e) Free textbooks	70	60	62	42	42	53	51	51	43	94	91	92
f) Sufficient no. of textbooks	85	86	95	99	94	99	79	88	91	97	100	100
g) Psychologist (full- or part-time)	23	24	31	16	16	20	1	2	4	1	0	0
h) College prep. curriculum	88	97	96	98	96	95	74	91	92	81	94	83
i) Commercial curriculum	75	94	92	97	97	92	49	89	92	39	81	70
j) Accelerated curriculum in one or more subjects	61	63	66	42	41	46	46	48	58	25	15	25
k) Opportunities for seniors to obtain advanced college credit	67	65	80	73	73	72	54	66	75	39	79	61
For schools attended by the average (white, Negro) student the:												
l) Av. no. of Negro colleges sending representatives to visit school is	3.0	0.2	0.1	0.3	0.0	0.0	2.7	0.2	0.1	2.5	0.0	0.1
m) Av. no. of white colleges sending representatives to visit school is	5.3	12.2	13.0	9.4	10.1	10.1	1.2	7.6	9.1	1.3	9.2	5.6

Table 1-B (continued).

n) Teacher's race or origin:												
Negro	59	6	2	11	4	2	85	3	2	70	2	1
White	38	93	97	88	95	97	13	97	98	27	98	98
o) Av. verbal facility of teachers and counselors is[1]	21.2	22.9	23.2	22.6	22.9	23.5	19.4	22.9	23.2	22.2	23.8	23.5
p) Av. annual teacher's salary (in $1,000) is	6.4	6.4	6.6	6.0	6.0	6.3	4.9	5.2	5.2	5.6	5.8	5.8
q) Teacher's rating of student effort is[2]	1.8	2.2	2.3	2.0	2.0	2.3	1.9	2.2	2.2	1.8	2.1	2.2
r) Teacher's av. rating of student ability is[2]	2.0	2.3	2.4	2.1	2.1	2.3	2.1	2.3	2.3	2.0	2.3	2.3
s) Av. no. of problems with students and their homes reported by teachers	.20	.13	.11	.15	.14	.10	.20	.11	.12	.18	.14	.13
t) Av. no. of problems in school functioning reported by teachers is	.11	.09	.08	.08	.07	.07	.14	.07	.08	.08	.07	.07
u) Percent of teachers who prefer to teach children of professional and white-collar workers is	8	20	17	10	12	11	7	18	16	7	12	12
v) Percent of teachers who prefer to teach children who are white is	6	42	28	25	27	22	7	73	60	8	37	35
w) Percent of teachers who believe in neighborhood schools is	74	80	81	80	81	79	70	80	80	81	82	82
x) Percent of white pupils is	24	83	91	76	84	94	11	91	93	19	83	83
y) Percent of classmates with real father living at home is	64	81	83	80	82	84	65	83	84	64	80	85
z) Percent of schoolmates with vacuum cleaner in home is	58	83	89	86	89	92	34	68	75	46	75	73
aa) Percent of schoolmates with encyclopedia in home is	69	82	82	76	78	78	52	74	75	66	77	75
bb) College attendance rate of last year's graduating class is	35	46	46	39	40	41	27	41	41	45	51	56
cc) Percent enrolled in college prep. curriculum is	32	39	41	29	30	35	22	33	33	28	33	32

Table 1-B (continued).

Item	Metropolitan														
	Northeast			Midwest			South			Southwest			West		
	N	W(N)	W	N	W(N)	W	N	W(N)	W	N	W(N)	W	N	W(N)	W
a.	18	47	64	33	38	43	74	55	84	76	31	43	53	55	79
b.	24	22	20	25	25	24	26	24	25	25	26	26	23	24	23
c.	92	97	99	94	98	96	83	96	100	96	100	97	76	76	100
d.	47	80	79	68	48	57	48	65	72	69	90	97	95	94	80
e.	98	96	91	67	48	39	58	33	34	98	100	97	99	99	86
f.	94	99	99	98	99	100	69	68	97	94	56	57	96	99	96
g.	30	58	40	73	42	55	0	1	1	4	0	3	70	71	72
h.	93	98	99	99	100	100	87	100	100	89	85	82	100	100	100
i.	85	94	93	99	98	96	71	96	100	70	73	71	100	100	100
j.	60	85	82	64	70	78	72	79	81	87	53	55	74	45	73
k.	64	85	82	70	68	92	75	57	85	83	89	83	73	45	74
l.	1.4	1.1	0.2	1.3	0.2	0.1	6.4	0.1	0.5	4.3	0.2	0.2	0.3	0.2	0.1
m.	9.4	15.8	18.2	5.9	11.5	15.5	3.6	13.9	14.2	3.9	6.4	6.1	11.9	16.0	14.3
n.	18	9	2	35	2	1	94	5	1	77	26	0	14	9	2
	79	89	96	64	97	97	3	93	99	20	69	96	82	87	94
o.	22.0	22.6	22.7	21.8	22.7	23.2	20.6	23.0	22.6	21.0	21.7	23.5	23.3	23.3	23.5
p.	7.8	7.9	7.6	7.2	7.1	7.2	5.5	5.3	5.4	6.1	5.6	5.5	8.8	8.7	8.3
q.	1.8	2.6	2.4	1.9	2.4	2.4	1.9	2.1	2.3	2.0	2.3	2.0	1.6	2.0	2.3
r.	1.8	2.6	2.5	2.1	2.5	2.5	2.1	2.2	2.4	2.2	2.4	2.2	1.5	2.0	2.4
s.	.18	.10	.10	.18	.12	.11	.20	.13	.11	.20	.14	.16	.25	.19	.14
t.	.11	.08	.08	.10	.08	.08	.12	.11	.09	.09	.11	.12	.11	.11	.09
u.	16	21	21	9	17	21	5	28	25	6	8	13	10	16	22
v.	6	9	13	6	30	24	2	61	59	4	27	38	5	8	11
w.	74	77	79	82	85	86	72	83	87	77	78	84	67	74	76
x.	45	76	90	45	88	91	3	91	95	13	70	94	35	56	79
y.	67	77	83	70	85	84	58	82	84	55	83	84	62	70	74
z.	78	90	94	79	94	95	47	84	90	65	81	85	82	88	91
aa.	82	86	87	80	88	86	67	85	88	73	77	83	78	81	83
bb.	33	54	53	33	41	45	33	47	52	39	35	33	49	52	53
cc.	39	55	53	43	45	46	34	38	44	29	38	31	34	40	46

[1] Best possible score = 30

[2] Low score = low rating

Explanation of Columns:

N = Negro, W = White, and W(N) = whites in same county as Negroes, derived by weighting the schools attended by whites in each county proportionally to the number of Negroes in that county.

part of the differences in individual pupil achievement (ten to twenty percent for whites and Negroes). Within the structure imposed by the fact that most of the total variance in pupil achievement consists of differences of individual scores in a school about the school average—the within-school variance—we will note that schools do differ in the degree of their impact on various racial groups; specifically, the average white student's achievement is less affected by schools' curricula, facilities, and teachers than is the achievement of the average Negro. The implication is that improving the school of a Negro pupil will increase his achievement more than will improving the school of a white pupil increase his achievement.

Over eighty percent of the variation in achievement for each racial group is variation within the same student body. Furthermore, the existence of variations among schools does not itself indicate whether these differences are due to school factors, pupil background differences, or community differences in support of school achievement. A substantial part of school-to-school variation in achievement appears not to be a consequence of effects of school variations at all but of variations in family backgrounds of the entering student bodies. These two results taken together can be seen as a measure of the weakness of schools' influences. They simply have not found ways to break into the strong influences that family backgrounds and student body factors exert; schools do not develop an autonomous influence upon a child's achievement. Thus we see why minorities that begin with an educational disadvantage continue to exhibit this disadvantage throughout the twelve grades of school; the schools are unable to exert independent influences to make achievement levels less dependent on the child's background. Insofar as variations in school factors do make a difference in achievement they make most difference for children of minority groups. It is those children who come least prepared to school and whose achievement in school is generally low for whom the characteristics of a school make the most difference. The data indicate that those least sensitive to the schools' influences are, in general, those children from groups where achievement is highest when they begin school in the first grade, and the most sensitive are those with lowest initial levels of achievement.

We turn first to examine the effect of student background factors on achievement. By taking the school to school variations as given and examining the added variance accounted for by family background characteristics we show what portion of the within school variance can be accounted for by these factors. The amount of within school variance accounted for by eight factors[4] taken together is of the same order of magnitude as the variance associated with school to school factors. It is well to remember here that many other aspects of the child's background are not measured and thus the variance accounted for in the present analysis is a kind of lower bound to the actual effects of background differences.

[4]Urbanism of background; parents' education; structural completeness of home; size of family; material items in the home; reading materials in the home; parents' interest in school; parents' education desires for child.

Table 2. Grade Level Lag of Negro Compared to White Students for Three Achievement Tests at Three Grade Levels: Comparisons Within Regions,[a] Fall 1965

	Test:	Verbal Ability			Reading Comprehension			Math Achievement		
AREA	Grade:	6	9	12	6	9	12	6	9	12
Non Metro										
South		1.8	2.9	3.7	2.2	2.9	3.9	1.9	2.8	4.8
Southwest		1.7	2.9	3.9	2.3	3.0	4.0	2.1	2.9	4.8
North		1.7	2.3	3.3	2.0	2.3	3.3	2.0	2.7	4.4
Metro										
Northeast		1.6	2.4	3.3	1.8	2.6	2.9	2.0	2.8	5.2
Midwest		1.6	2.2	2.9	1.7	2.2	2.5	2.0	2.5	4.6
South		1.5	2.5	3.3	1.8	2.6	3.5	2.0	2.5	4.4
Southwest		1.4	2.3	3.6	1.7	2.3	3.7	1.7	2.3	5.1
West		1.6	2.3	3.4	1.9	2.6	3.0	2.1	2.8	4.5

[a]In each cell, the value shows how far Negroes in the given Grade and Region are behind Whites in the same Grade and Region, in grade level terms.

Source: Derived from Tables 3.121.1, 3.121.2, and 3.121.3, *Equality of Educational Opportunity,* U.S. Government Printing Office, 1966.

We turn now to examine the effects of various school characteristics on pupil achievement. We prefer to separate school characteristics into three groups: First facilities, curriculum, and other characteristics of the school itself; second, characteristics of the teaching staff; and, third, characteristics of the student body. Having seen that school-to-school differences in achievement are a small part of the total variation, we are cautioned against attributing large effects to any component.

The first step is to determine the relative effects of the three components. We observe that the attributes of other students account for far more variation in the achievement of minority group children than do any attributes of school facilities and slightly more than do attributes of staff. Of the five student body measures used, it appears particularly that as the educational aspirations and backgrounds of fellow students increase the achievement level increases even when the student's own background characteristics are controlled. A portion of the supporting analysis appears in the tables. School variables are allowed to account for as much variance as they can and then characteristics of fellow students are added to see how much additional variance is explained. Even under this severe restriction, the explained variance is often more than doubled and always sharply increased. Comparisons of student body effects by race suggest that the environment provided by a student body is asymmetric in its effects in that it has its greatest effect on those from educationally deficient backgrounds. It is indeed those Negroes who are in the South whose achievement appears to vary most greatly with variations in the characteristics of their fellow students. The highest achieving groups show generally less dependence of achievement on characteristics of fellow students.

It is also found that as the proportion white in a school increases the achievement of students in both racial groups increases. This relationship increases as grade in school increases, being absent at grade three, stronger at grade nine, and strongest at grade twelve. This higher achievement of all racial and ethnic groups in schools with greater proportions of white students is largely, perhaps wholly, accounted for by effects associated with the student body's educational background and aspirations. Thus the real influence comes not from racial composition per se, but from the better educational background and higher educational aspirations that are, on the average, found among white students.

Our next concern is with the effects of school facilities and curriculum. For schools attended by Negroes in the South, but among no other groups, high per pupil instructional expenditure is associated with higher achievement at grades six, nine, and twelve after six background differences of students are controlled (2.98 percent of variance explained). Considering that the variance in per pupil expenditure among Negroes and whites in the South is only one-tenth to one-third as great as that for other parts of the nation, the contrast between this relationship for southern Negroes and its

Table 3. School Variations in and Pupil Background Effects on Verbal Achievement

		Negro South	Negro North	White South	White North
Percent of variance in individual verbal achievement scores accounted for by school-to-school variation[a]					
	Grade 12	22.54	10.92	10.11	7.84
	Grade 9	20.17	12.67	9.13	8.69
	Grade 6	22.64	13.89	11.05	10.32
	Grade 3	34.68	19.47	17.73	11.42
	Grade 1	23.21	10.63	18.64	11.07
Percent of variance in individual verbal achievement scores accounted for by eight pupil background factors					
	Grade 12	15.79	10.96	20.13	24.56
	Grade 9	15.69	11.43	23.12	22.78
	Grade 6	15.44	10.25	19.91	15.57

[a]1/9 to 1/3 of this due to eight pupil background factors.
Source: Based on Tables 3.22.1 and 3.221.3, *Equality of Educational Opportunity.*

Table 4. School and Student Body Characteristics Effects on Verbal Achievement

	Negro South	Negro North	White South	White North
Percent of variance in individual verbal achievement, with six pupil background characteristics controlled, accounted for by—				
—11 school characteristics				
Grade 12	8.64	3.14	3.16	1.87
Grade 9	7.52	1.45	1.60	.73
Grade 6	4.90	.77	.57	.32
Grade 3	.80	2.96	.83	.33
Grade 1	2.14	2.38	.96	.83
—11 school characteristics plus six student body characteristics				
Grade 12	12.69	7.73	4.61	2.94
Grade 9	12.66	4.62	2.82	2.34
Grade 6	7.77	2.73	1.92	3.63
Grade 3	1.40	5.13	1.91	1.46
Grade 1	2.93	3.28	1.53	2.35

Source: Based on Table 3.23.2, *Equality of Educational Opportunity.*

relative absence elsewhere is even more marked. It appears, however, that expenditure differences are really a surrogate for other differences in the community and this is evidenced by the fact that when student body characteristics are taken into account the unique contribution of per pupil expenditure for southern Negroes nearly vanishes. One variable that explains a relatively large amount of variance among Negroes at grades nine and twelve under the condition of controlling for student background and per pupil instructional expenditure but nothing else, is school size (2.55 percent grade twelve; 1.32 percent grade nine). Most of its apparent effect vanishes if various other facilities and curricular differences are controlled. That is, higher achievement in larger schools is largely accounted for by the additional facilities they include. Tracking shows no relation to achievement and comprehensiveness of the curriculum shows very small and inconsistent relations. An accelerated program in the curriculum does show a consistent relation to achievement at grade twelve, both before and after other curriculum and facilities measures have been controlled. The number of volumes per student in the school library shows small and inconsistent relations to achievement. However, both the number of science laboratories (1.62 percent for Negroes, grade twelve) and the number of extracurricular activities (1.64 percent for Negroes, grade twelve) gave a consistent relation of moderate size to achievement.

Our effort to find effects, even small ones, of various facilities and curriculums, should not obscure the more central fact: School facilities and curriculum are the major variables by which attempts are made to improve schools; yet differences between them are so little related to achievement levels of students that with few exceptions their effects fail to appear even in a survey of this magnitude.

Next, the effects of teacher characteristics. Altogether, teachers' char-

Table 5. Unique Contributions to Variance in Verbal Achievement, of Various Individual Facilities and Curricular Measures, Under Specified Analytical Conditions

	Negro South	Negro North	White South	White North	Negro Total	White Total
Percent of variance in individual verbal achievement, with six background variables controlled, accounted for by—						
—per pupil expenditure						
Grade 12	2.98	.09	.06	.29	2.62	.80
Grade 9	2.89	.02	.21	.14	2.55	.64
Grade 6	3.49	.14	.15	.05	2.17	.36
—then adding *each* of the following (Reported for grade 12 only)						
Volumes in library	1.37	(−).28	.03	(−).12	.04	(−).11
Science Labs	1.93	.97	.87	.33	1.61	.62
Extracurric. activities	1.10	1.07	1.57	.43	1.64	.04
Accelerated curriculum	.30	.96	.42	.66	.59	.67
Comprehension of curric.	.57	.22	.33	(−).05	.61	.00
Tracking	(−).02	.11	(−).03	(−).01	(−).01	( ).02
Size	3.72	.40	1.13	.02	2.55	(−).22
Guidance	3.04	.38	2.23	.28	2.61	.16
Urbanism	2.80	.30	.98	.06	2.12	.04
—then adding *all* of those listed above						
Grade 12	8.64	3.14	3.16	1.87	6.96	2.53
Grade 9	7.52	1.45	1.60	.73	5.19	1.15
Grade 6	4.90	.77	.57	.32	2.77	.47

Source: Based on Table 3.24.2, *Equality of Educational Opportunity.*

Table 6. Effects of Selected Teacher Variables on Verbal Achievement, Under Specified Analytical Conditions

	Grades				
	12	9	6	3	1
With four pupil background variables controlled, percent of variance in individual verbal achievement scores explained cumulatively by adding teacher variables (averaged over the school) in listed order:					
NEGRO VERBAL ACHIEVEMENT					
(A) Teachers' family educational level	2.26	1.42	.58	.03	.03
(B) Years experience	3.37	1.53	.61	1.50	.14
(C) Localism	3.38	1.54	.93	2.34	.26
(D) Teachers' educational level	4.87	3.20	.93	2.40	.26
(E) Vocabulary test score	7.05	5.05	2.82	2.74	.34
(F) Middle class performance	8.09	5.42	3.03	2.76	.35
(G) Proportion white	8.23	5.55	3.33	2.83	.52
WHITE VERBAL ACHIEVEMENT					
(A)	.10	.14	.21	.01	.00
(B)	.12	.22	.21	.05	.15
(C)	.47	.47	.49	.21	.19
(D)	1.08	.60	.51	.23	.21
(E)	1.21	.62	.67	.27	.27
(F)	2.07	.69	.82	.56	.33
(G)	2.10	1.04	1.20	.59	.37

Source: Based on Table 3.25.2, *Equality of Educational Opportunity.*

acteristics account for a higher proportion of student achievement than do other aspects of the school, excluding student body characteristics. Teacher variables selected for special examination were the average educational level of the teachers' families, average years of experience, localism, average level of education of the teachers themselves, average score on self-administered vocabularly test, teachers' preference for teaching middle class white-collar students, and proportion of teachers in the school who were white. The first important result is that the effect of teachers' characteristics shows a sharp increase over the years of school. Also the apparent effect of teacher characteristics for children is directly related to their need for good teachers. That is, good teachers matter more for children from groups with educationally deficient backgrounds. There is a strikingly stronger effect of teacher variables for Negroes than for whites. The variables which show most effect are the teachers' family educational level, the teachers' own education, and the score on the vocabulary test. The strongest result to derive from these tabulations is that teachers' verbal skills have a strong effect first showing at the sixth grade. The second and less strong effect for Negroes is that the teachers' educational level, or some variable for which this is a surrogate, begins to make a difference at grades nine and twelve.

Lastly, we turn to look at the effects of attitude on achievement. Three were examined: the students' interest in school and his reported casual reading; his self-concept specifically with regard to learning and success in school; and his sense of control of the environment.[5] Taken alone these attitudinal variables account for more of the variation in achievement than any other set of variables (all family background variables together or all school variables together). When added to any other set of variables they increase the accounted for variation more than does any other set of variables. Perhaps it is reasonable that self-concept should be so closely related to achievement since it represents the individual's own estimate of his learning ability. However, the other variables are not so logically related to achievement. One's interest in learning, it can be assumed, partly derived from family background and partly from his success in school; thus it is partly a cause of achievement, partly determined by past achievement. Of the three attitudinal variables, however, this is the weakest, especially among minority groups. For Negroes the child's sense of control of environment becomes the strongest predictor of achievement. (The questions on which this scale is based are a statement that "Good luck is more important than hard work for success," a statement that "Every time I try to get ahead something or someone stops me," and a statement that "People like me don't have much of a chance to be successful in life.") For grades twelve and nine Negroes of both sexes who give "control" responses score higher on the test than do whites who give "no control" responses.

The implications of these findings are immense, for it may be that a causal chain runs by which experiencing an unrewarding environment leads to beliefs in the inefficacy of one's own behaviors which leads to behaviors not characterized by diligent, extended effort toward achievement and thus to low achievement levels in fact. We have seen that the larger task is less to secure an equitable input of resources into the nation's schools than to increase the effectiveness of this input measured by the responses Negro children make to and the benefits they derive from their schooling. It now appears that a critical step may be the development of an ordered set of increasingly more challenging, but rewarding activities by which the disadvantaged child gains an enlarging sense of the relevance of his efforts to affect the outcomes he wishes to secure.

[5]Full measures available in grades twelve, nine, and six only.

What Do They Really Learn at College?

Howard S. Becker

When we talk of education, we ordinarily refer to the conventional institutions in which it is carried on: elementary schools, secondary schools, colleges and universities, graduate and professional schools. When we talk of what students learn at school, we usually refer to the things adults want them to learn there. What do people learn as they grow up in our society? Where do they learn it? It may be that the important things that happen to students in college do not happen in the library, the laboratory, or in the classroom.

Most middle-class boys and girls graduate from high school and go on to college. Many, perhaps most, college-goers learn in college precisely what they need to know to get along as adults in a middle-class world. The middle-class worlds of business and the professions demand a number of specific skills and abilities and the experience of college is such as to provide college students with training in precisely those skills and abilities. I shall discuss a number of the demands made by the adult middle-class world, indicating in each case how the world of the college is organized to provide relevant training. Most of what I will talk about is not conventionally regarded as an important part of the college curriculum; nevertheless, these are matters which are important for college students while they are in school and afterward. They know it and they act accordingly.

Independence from Home

Ours is one of the most mobile societies ever known. People move frequently and they move great distances. Unlike nomadic groups, they do not move together, taking their families and communities with them. They move because opportunity beckons elsewhere and it beckons to individuals, not groups. Moving for the sake of opportunity is very common in the middle class. As more and more people enter itinerant professions or go to work for one of the national organizations which ships its men around from city to city, more and more members of the middle class find themselves, as young adults, leaving their homes, neighborhoods, and families behind and setting out for new territory. Friends, instead of being furnished almost automatically by family connections and neighborhood contiguity, must be made without that help. To make the break from family and community requires an independence of spirit that does not come naturally.

Going away to college provides a rehearsal for the real thing, an opportunity to be away from home and friends, to make a new life among strangers, while still retaining the possibilities of affiliation with the old. In the dormitory, and even more so in the fraternity and sorority, one finds himself on his own but at the same time surrounded by strangers who may become friends. One has the experience of learning to shift for oneself and making friends among strangers.

Further, all the little chores that one's family did for you now have to be taken care of in some other way. You get your own meals, take care of your own room, make your own bed, clean your own clothes. These are small things but difficult until one has learned to do them. They are a kind of training for the passage from home, whether it is geographical or simply the making of a new home upon marriage. Going away to college provides an opportunity to play at moving away from home for good and it prepares the youngster for the world in which he will have to live.

Dating, Marriage, and Poise

We normally expect young people to achieve some kind of workable relationship with members of the opposite sex, to learn how to get along with them and eventually to choose or be chosen for marriage. For middle-class youth, the problem is complicated by the requirement of the adult work world that he choose a wife who will be "culturally adequate" for the circles his business or profession will require him to move in. He must acquire the ability to attract and marry the kind of woman who can run a proper house for him and entertain for him. And for women, this means that they must learn how to perform these functions in an adequate middle-class way. It means for both men and women that they must learn the kind of manners, poise, and cultural skills necessary to move in such a world and to attract such a mate.

Again, the college (and particularly the large state university) provides the proper kind of training. Although it is not part of the curriculum, training in manners, poise, and cultural skills is given in a wide variety of places on the campus. Fraternities and sororities specialize in it. Pledges are taught in formal classes how to introduce themselves to strangers, how to ask for a date or accept one, how to behave on a date, how to handle silverware at a formal dinner, and so on. The need for this training is obvious if one watches incoming freshmen during orientation week. The people who prepare dinners for these students know that, in order to avoid embarrassments, they had better not serve any strange dishes which require more than rudimentary skill with silver. The formal training is reinforced by constant practice. A stranger who walks into a fraternity house finds himself assaulted by a stream of young men rushing up to introduce themselves, fearing that if they do not one of the active members will punish them.

The Marriage-Hunting Ground

The dating system and the round of formal and informal social functions provided by both the Greek system and the university proper provide a fine training ground for meeting the opposite sex and finding a proper mate. Some pledges are required to have a certain minimum number of dates per month; most students feel some vague pressure to date, even though they find it anxiety-provoking. By participating in a round of parties and social functions, students learn the kind of manners and poise necessary for the social life of the country club or civic organization, skills that will stand them in good stead in their later middle-class lives.

In addition, many, though by no means all, students receive training in dealing socially with "important people." Fraternities, dormitories, and other kinds of student groups make a practice of inviting important people, both campus personages and visitors, to meet with them. Students may have experience socializing with the governor of the state, the chancellor of the university, national political figures, or important visitors from overseas.

Work Skills

The middle-class occupational world demands a number of generalized work skills from its recruits. They must, first of all, acquire some skills needed for their prospective occupations which the university is set up to teach. It may be that they need to learn the analytic techniques of chemistry or engineering; they may need to learn the skills of reading, writing, and the use of a library. Whatever it is, the university has courses which teach them some of the knowledge and technique necessary to hold a job.

We must not overstate this. Many business, industries and professional and graduate schools feel that an undergraduate college cannot, or at least does not, teach the required skills in the proper way. They prefer to train their recruits from scratch. To this end, many firms have in-service training programs which provide the specific knowledge recruits need.

More important than the specific knowledge and techniques necessary for entrance into an occupation is a more generalized kind of work skill, one that in older days was referred to as "stick-to-it-iveness." The entrant into the middle-class occupational world must have the ability to see a job through from beginning to end, to start a project and keep his attention and energy focused on it until it is completed.

The ability to get things done does not come naturally to young people; it is a hard-won skill. In acquiring it, the middle-class youth must learn to defer immediate gratifications for those that are longer in coming; he must learn to give up the pleasures of the moment for the larger rewards that await a big job well done. Most students have not had to learn this in high school, where the parade of daily requirements and assignments places the emphasis on receiving the immediate gratification of having done this day's job well.

College . . .

For many students, it is only when one reaches college that one is required to plan ahead in units of four or five months, keeping attention focused on the long-range goal of passing the course without the constant prodding of the daily assignment. In learning to organize himself well enough to get a good grade in a college course, in learning to keep his mind on one job that long, the college student learns the middle-class skill of getting things done, so important in business and industry.

Finally, the middle-class world demands of those who enter it that they be able to juggle several things at once, that they be able to handle more than one job at a time and to keep them straight. He must learn to manage his time successfully and not fritter it away in actions that produce no reward. At least some college students get magnificent training in how to budget time and energy. The kind of student, of whom there are many, who does well in his courses and at the same time is, let us say, a high-ranking officer in several campus-wide organizations and an officer of his fraternity or dormitory, learns that he cannot waste his time if he is to achieve anything. He learns to set aside particular times for study and not to allow anything to intervene; he learns to handle organizational matters with dispatch; he learns to give up or strictly ration the joys of watching television and drinking beer with the boys. He learns, in short, how to have a time for everything and to do everything in its time.

Organizational Skills

The typical middle-class career now takes place in a bureaucratic organization. Even the professions, which used to be the stronghold of the individual practitioner, now tend increasingly to find the locus of their activities in a complex organization rather than a professional office; the doctor spends more of his time in the hospital and is responsive to the social control of the bureaucratically organized hospital, rather than practicing independently in his own office. The recruit to the middle-class occupational world requires, if he is to operate successfully in it, the ability to get along in a mass of organization and bureaucracy. If the rules and constraints of large organizations frighten or anger him, he will not be able to achieve what he wants nor will he be an effective member of the organization.

Among the specific things an effective member of a large organization must know and be able to do we can include the following: He must be willing and able to take the consequences for his own actions, to see ahead far enough to realize how what he does will affect others and the organization. He must have some skill in manipulating other people, in getting them to do what he wants without the use of force or coercion; he must learn to be persuasive. He must have the ability to compromise, to give up some of what he wants in order to gain the rest; he must not be a narrow-minded fanatic, who either has his way or not at all. And he must, finally, be knowledgeable and skillful in manipulating the rules and impersonal procedures of bureaucratic organizations to his own advantage, rather than being stymied and buffaloed by them.

Rehearsal for Management

The network of extracurricular organizations characteristic of the large state university provides a perfect context in which to learn these skills. The student can participate in student politics, either as an active candidate or as a behind-the-scenes organizer. He can become an officer of one of the organizations that helps run campus activities. He can work on the student newspaper. He may be an officer of his fraternity or dormitory. A large number of students have experiences in one or more such organizations during their four years in college.

Melville Dalton, in tracing the antecedents of successful industrial managerial careers, argues that experience in this realm of campus life is a perfect background for success in industry.

Our observations at the University of Kansas corroborate Dalton's findings. Let me point out some sources of experience, important for the recruit to the middle-class occupational world. Many officers of campus organizations find themselves exercising responsibility for large amounts of money; they may administer budgets running as high as $50,000 a year. Some of them administer programs of activity in which it is necessary to coordinate the efforts of several hundred or more of their fellow students. You have only to think, for an example, of the effort and organization necessary for the traditional Homecoming Weekend at any big university.

Some students even have the experience of discovering that the important people with whom they come in contact have feet of clay. As they deal with officers of the university in the course of their organizational work, they discover that these officers may ask them to do things they regard as improper. A typical case, which occurs in many universities, arises when some university officer requests or attempts to coerce the student newspaper into not publishing matter he believes harmful to the university. The student reporters and editors discover, in such a situation, that university officials are, after all, only human too; it is a shocking and educational discovery for a nineteen-year-old to make.

Motivation

The recruit to the middle-class world must, finally, learn to attach his own desires to the requirements of the organizations he becomes involved in. He must learn to have what we might call *institutional motivation.* He must learn to want things simply and only because the institution in which he participates says these are the things to want.

College provides practice at this linking of personal and institutional desires. The student learns that he requires, at the least, a degree and that he must do whatever it is the college asks of him in order to get that degree. This attachment to the long-range goal furnishes him with the motivation to continue in classes that bore or confound him, to meet requirements that seem to him foolish or childish. The college student learns to want to surmount the obstacles posed for him by the college, simply because they are there. He learns to regard these external obstacles as marks of his own ability and maturity, and because he interprets the obstacles that way, sees his success in college as a sign of his own personal worth. The ability to link institutional and personal desires is an important prerequisite for occupational success in adult life.

Through participation in the college community, the student comes to define himself as the kind of person who ought to have the skills of the middle-class occupational world. He pins his self-respect, his sense of personal worth, on acquiring them. He feels that he will have properly become an adult only when he has all these qualities and skills. He directs his effort and organizes his life in such a way as to achieve them and thus to prove to himself and others that he has grown up. It may be that these are the really important things he learns at college.

It is too bad that convention requires the college studiously to ignore what it really teaches students.

8 Youth and Religion

Religion, one of our major institutions, can be seen as a formal structure operating to solve persistent social problems. Religion deals in general with man's relationship to eternal life. The theological core of religion is concerned with explanations of the world and of the significant symbols and beliefs associated with membership in the church. "Membership" in an organized religion involves at least two dimensions: *beliefs,* or commitments to the theological tenets of the denomination; and *actions,* such as attendance, contributions, and active involvement in church affairs. The former deals with general attachment, whereas the latter deals with activity in a given congregation.

Religious denominations differ, of course, in the degree to which they are "orthodox," the degree to which their membership believes in a personal God, a divine saviour, and the promise of an eternal life. Within a given denomination there are typically cleavages based on socially meaningful categories such as age, ethnicity, social class, race, and sex. The clergy, or the professionally religious, are typically more attached to the theological core of the denomination than are their congregations. Thus there are natural, almost "built in," tensions in any congregation and within any religious organization. However, the majority of a denomination's members must feel involved and must be active in the institution if it is to survive in its present form.

Glock and Stark report, on the basis of a national survey, that ". . . the current *religious revolution is being accompanied by a general decline in commitment to religion* . . . religious beliefs that have been the bedrocks of Christian faith for nearly two millennia are on their way out, and . . . this *may very* well be the dawn of a post-Christian era."

They make this prediction on the basis of a decline in what they call commitment, and a growth of "ethicalism," that is, a vision of the church as a social instrumentality without its mythological, sacred, and ritualistic foundations. The church is now seen by a great many of its members as a means to attaining social justice rather than personal salvation. Sociologists Glock and Stark note that the church without its former functions and sources of attachment for members may well drift into a new social form, a new type of institution.

One of the most telling changes in belief and support of the historical church is among the young. In Glock and Stark's survey, people over fifty, regardless of denomination, showed a greater attachment to the traditional orthodox views of the church than did those under fifty. The changes in religious commitment between 1948 and 1967 among college students (shown in Hastings and Hoge) support the general trends identified by Glock and Stark, but show specifically that the faith of the students' parents declined less than that of the young during the same period. Even when changes in the social composition of the student body from 1948 to 1967 were taken into account, diminished traditional religious commitment (with accompanying liberalization of beliefs), reduced religious activity, more and earlier questioning of religion during adolescence, and fewer designations of religious preference were discovered among the youth in the 1967 sample. These findings, those suggesting a link between closeness to parents and religious practices (except among the Protestants), and the authors' inference that religious activity may be inversely related to political activitism on the campus are discussed further in the context of youth and politics by Flacks, Braungart, and Orum and Orum.

The young, source of new strength to the church as an institution, do not seem attracted to the church (if one can assume that attitudes and reports of behavior are strong indicators of future trends). Commenting on their findings, Glock and Stark write:

> . . . there has been an important generational break with traditional religion. This break consistently occurs between those who have reached maturity since the beginning of World War II—those who were 25 or less in 1940—and those who were raised in a pre-war America. In this as well as in many other ways, World War II seems to mark a watershed between the old America of small-town, rural, or stable-urban-neighborhood living, and the contemporary America of highly mobile urban living.

These changes may leave the church an "empty shell" populated only by the old, for as is the case with many other institutions, religion has not remained a viable alternative for the young.

What will be the consequences of the changing meanings of religion? Will this change be, or is it already, the stimulus for alternatives such as the occult, Far Eastern religions, astrology, and belief in magic? Will these "religions" fill the same functions that conventional religion has fulfilled? They may be one of the many signs of a counter-culture containing parallel institutions, or alternatives to the conventional social order.

Will Ethics Be the Death of Christianity?

Charles Y. Glock and Rodney Stark

Perhaps at no time since the conversion of Paul has the future of Christianity seemed so uncertain. Clearly, a profound revolution in religious thought is sweeping the churches. Where will it lead? Is this a moment of great promise, or of great peril, for the future of Christianity?

Some observers believe we have already entered a post-Christian era—that the current upheavals are the death throes of a doomed religion. Yet many theologians interpret these same signs as the promise of renewed religious vigor. They foresee the possibility of a reconstructed and unified church that will recapture its relevance to contemporary life. A great many others, both clerics and laymen, are simply mystified. In the face of rapid changes and conflicting claims for the future, they hardly know whether to reform the church, or to administer it last rites. Probably the majority of Christians think the whole matter has been greatly exaggerated—that the present excitement will pass and that the churches will continue pretty much as before. Our own research, however, suggests that *the current religious revolution is being accompanied by a general decline in commitment to religion.*

The fact is that in the current debate about the future of Christianity there has been an almost total lack of evidence. The arguments have been based on speculation, hope, and even temperament, but rarely on fact. Mainly this has been because so few hard facts about contemporary religion have been available. Our own findings do not entirely fill this vacuum. Still, what we have learned provides a number of clues about the trends in religious commitment, and permits a cautious assessment of the direction in which Christianity is headed. We have reached two main conclusions: that the religious beliefs that have been the bedrocks of Christian faith for nearly two millennia are on their way out; and that this *may* very well be the dawn of a post-Christian era.

While many Americans are still firmly committed to the traditional, supernatural conceptions of a personal God, a Divine Saviour, and the promise of eternal life, the trend is away from these convictions. Although we must expect an extended period of doubt, the fact is that a demythologized modernism is overwhelming the traditional Christ-centered, mystical faith.

Of course, rejection of the supernatural tenets of Christianity is not a strictly modern phenomenon. Through the ages men have challenged these beliefs. But never before have they found much popular support. Until now, the vast majority of people have retained unshaken faith in the other-worldly premises of Christianity.

Today, skeptics are not going unnoticed, nor are their criticisms being rejected out of hand. For the modern skeptics are not the apostates, village atheists, or political revolutionaries of old. The leaders of today's challenge to traditional beliefs are principally theologians—those in whose care the church entrusts its sacred teachings. It is not philosophers or scientists, but the greatest theologians of our time who are saying "God is dead," or that notions of a God "out there" are antiquated. And their views are becoming increasingly popular.

Erosion of Orthodoxy

Although only a minority of church members so far reject or doubt the existence of some kind of personal God or the divinity of Jesus, a near majority reject such traditional articles of faith as Christ's miracles, life after death, the promise of the second coming, and the virgin birth. An overwhelming majority reject the existence of the Devil. This overall picture, however, is subject to considerable variation among the denominations. Old-time Christianity remains predominant in some Protestant bodies, such as the Southern Baptists and the various small sects. But in most of the main-line Protestant denominations, and to a considerable extent among Roman Catholics, doubt and disbelief in historic Christian theology abound. In some denominations the doubters far outnumber the firm believers.

We are convinced that this widespread doubt of traditional Christian tenets is a recent development. What evidence there is supports this assumption. For if there has been an erosion of faith, we would expect many people to have shifted from denominations with unswerving commitment to that faith to denominations with more demythologized positions. Our data show that this is exactly what has happened. Because these denominational shifts indicate changes in religious outlook only indirectly, they do not *prove* our point. But they are very consistent with it.

More direct evidence of an erosion in orthodox belief is provided by contrasts in the percentages of orthodox believers in different age groups. Among people 50 years of age or older, we found that age made very little difference in the percentage subscribing to traditional beliefs. Similarly, among those under 50, orthodoxy differed little by age. But Christians over 50 are considerably *more* likely than younger people to hold orthodox views. The difference occurs in every denomination and is quite substantial.

These findings suggest that there has been an important generational break with traditional religion. The break consistently occurs between those who have reached maturity since the beginning of World War II—those who were 25 or less in 1940—and those who were raised in a pre-war America. In this as well as in many other ways, World War II seems to mark a watershed between the older America of small-town, rural, or stable-urban-neighborhood living, and the contemporary America of highly mobile urban living.

Recent Gallup Poll findings indicate that the decline in American church attendance that began in the late 1950's is accelerating. This decline has been particularly sharp among young adults. The number who attend every week dropped 11 percent between 1958 and 1966. Furthermore, the Gallup interviewers found that Americans overwhelmingly believe that religion is losing its influence in contemporary life. In 1957 only 14 percent of the nation's Christians thought religion was losing its influence and 69 percent thought it was increasing; ten years later, 57 percent thought religion was losing ground and only 23 percent thought it was gaining. This would seem to mark an enormous loss of confidence in religion during the past decade.

Aside from this statistical evidence, there are numerous more obvious signs that a religious revolution is taking place. The radical changes in the Roman Catholic Church flowing from the reforms of Pope John XXIII and Vatican II are perhaps the most dramatic indications. Of equal significance is the ecumenical movement. Prevailing differences in doctrinal outlook still impede the unification of Christian denominations. But though such differences seemed to preclude all prospects of unification several generations ago, today doctrinal barriers have broken down enough so that some mergers have already taken place, and clearly more are in the offing.

The mergers are taking place among denominations with the least residual commitment to traditional faith. More traditional denominations still resist the prospects of ecumenism. Thus it seems clear that a loss of concern for traditional doctrine is a precondition for ecumenism. And this in turn means that the success of ecumenism today represents a trend away from historic creeds.

These major signs of the depth and scope of religious change are accompanied by a spate of minor clues: the popularity of Anglican Bishop John A. T. Robinson's *Honest to God* and Harvey Cox's *The Secular City;* the widespread discussion of the "death of God" theology in the mass media; and the profound changes in the Westminster Confession recently adopted by the Presbyterian Church. All of these are compelling evidence of ferment. Nor is this exclusively a Protestant phenomenon. Almost daily the press reports nuns leaving their orders because they believe they can pursue their missions more effectively outside the church. Priests advocate "the pill." The number of Catholics taking up religious vocations has dropped sharply. Catholics ponder Teilhard de Chardin as seriously as Protestants reflect on Dietrich Bonhoeffer, the German theologian imprisoned and executed by the Nazis. A leading Jesuit theologian is quoted in *Newsweek* as admitting, "It is difficult to say in our age what the divinity of Christ can mean."

Demythologizing the Church

The seeds of this revolution were planted a long time ago. Since Kierkegaard, the "death of God" has been proclaimed—although subtly—by the theologians who have counted most. It is only because what they have been saying privately for a long time is now being popularized that the religious revolution seems such a recent phenomenon. For example, during the recent attempts to try him for heresy, Episcopalian Bishop James A. Pike defended himself by saying he had merely told the laity what the clergy had taken for granted for years. Moreover, the majority of Episcopalian church members hold theological views quite similar to Bishop Pike's. This presents an ironic picture of Sunday services in many churches. Both pastor and congregation reject or at least doubt the theological assumptions of the creeds they recite and the rituals in which they participate, but neither acknowledges this fact.

The heart of the religious revolution is the demise of what has been proclaimed as the core of Christian faith for nearly 2000 years: a literal interpretation of the phrase "Christ crucified, risen, coming again." Now, in many theological circles both the fact of the current revolution and its demythologizing character are considered obvious. But what many consider obvious is, in this instance, terribly important—perhaps vastly more important than contemporary churchmen recognize.

In most of the commentary on the major transformations of our religious institutions, the key terms are change, renewal, and improvement. Churchmen view the massive change in belief that is taking place not as a transition from belief to unbelief, but as a shift from one form of belief to another. The theologians who are leading this procession do *not* regard themselves as pallbearers at the funeral of God. It is *not* the end of the Christian era that they expect, but the dawn of a new and more profound period of Christianity.

The subtleties of what is being proposed in place of the old beliefs seem elusive, however. As sociologists, we find it difficult to imagine a Christian church without Jesus Christ as Divine Saviour, without a personal God, without the promise of eternal life. The "new breed" of theologians, as we understand them, are telling us we are wrong—that we rigidly identify Christianity with an old-fashioned fundamentalism that modern Christianity has long since discarded. Still, we find it difficult to grasp the substance of their alternatives. Conceptions of God as ultimate concern, as love, as poetry, as the divine essence in all of us—the ground of our being—have powerful esthetic and rhetorical appeal. But how do they differ from humanism? And more important, how can such conceptions induce the kind of commitment necessary to keep the church, as an organization, alive?

For some contemporary churchmen, the new theology does mean the eventual abandonment of today's church and its replacement by a still vaguely defined spiritual community. But the vast majority of clerics expect no such thing. They expect the new theology to be effectively accommodated in the present church. They recognize that this accommodation will require some changes in the church's present organization and modes of operation, but they think that these changes *can* be made.

So far, the new theology has not altered the basic structure, form, or functioning of the institutional church. The churches continue to predicate their structure and activities upon a conception of a judging, personal, active God, whether or not the theological views predominant among clergy and laity still conceive of God in these terms. Historically, the central concern of the churches has been the relationship between man and God. Part of their efforts have been directed to propitiating this active God, to teaching what must be done to escape his wrath and obtain his blessings. Such common religious terms and phrases as "praise," "worship," "seeking comfort and guidance," "bringing the unconverted to faith," and "seeking forgiveness for sins" all presuppose the existence of a conscious, judging God who intervenes in human affairs. An elaborate conception of God and his commandments is the *raison d'être* for church worship services, mission societies, adult Bible classes, baptism, and communion.

Admittedly, there have been some superficial alterations. There have been various liturgical experiments. Sometimes the mass is recited in English rather than in Latin. Pastors have made some changes in the content of their sermons. But, by and large, the churches are still organized and conducted as they have been in the past. The traditional creeds are still recited—"I believe in God the Father almighty, maker of heaven and earth . . ."—and the old hymns regularly sung—"I Know that My Redeemer

Liveth." There has been no substantial change in the sacraments. And, with some rare exceptions, there are no loud, or even soft, cries from the pulpit that Christ did not walk on water or that God does not see and hear all.

Restraints on the Clergy

The general absence of institutional change does *not* mean that the clergy is more committed to traditional tenets than the laity. On the contrary, rejection of traditional Christian supernaturalism is perhaps even more widespread among the clergy than among the laity and follows essentially the same pattern of variation by denomination. A recent study comparing our findings on church members with national samples of clergy showed that laymen and clergymen in a given denomination are nearly identically distributed on questions of belief. (See "A Protestant Paradox—Divided They Merge," by Jeffrey K. Hadden, *TRANS-action,* July/August 1967.) For example, while 34 percent of Methodist laymen and 92 percent of Missouri Synod Lutheran laymen accept the virgin birth, 28 percent of Methodist clergy and 90 percent of Missouri Lutheran clergy accept this article of faith.

However, even if liberal ministers would like to alter the forms of the church on the basis of their new theology, they are not likely to find their congregations ready to permit it. This is because in all denominations supporters of the old theology still persist. What's more, they are likely to be their churches' most active laymen.

Thus the liberal pastor faces formidable restraints. His religious convictions might dispose him to reforms—to deleting, for example, references to traditional supernaturalism in the worship service, or to preaching the new theology from the pulpit and teaching it in Sunday school. But he is unlikely to have a congregation that would tolerate such changes. Even in congregations where orthodox members are in the minority, such changes are unlikely. The minority will oppose them vigorously, while the plain fact is that the more liberal members are not likely to care much one way or the other.

This discrepancy between institutional inertia and theological revolution presents the churches with growing peril. Can the old institutional forms continue to draw commitment and support from people whose theological outlook is no longer represented in these forms—or at least maintain support until the theological revolution becomes so widespread that institutional changes are possible? More serious, can a Christianity without a divine Christ survive in *any* institutional form?

Our findings provide no final answer to these questions. They do, however, provide some important clues as to what will happen should future developments follow the present course. Evidently belief in traditional Christian doctrines, as they are now constituted, is vital to other kinds of religious commitment. While the churches continue to be organized on the basis of traditional orthodoxy, people who lack the beliefs that are needed to make such organization meaningful are falling away from the church.

Today, the acceptance of a modernized, liberal theology is being accompanied by *a general corrosion of religious commitment.*

Orthodoxy and Commitment

Among both Protestants and Roman Catholics, orthodoxy is very strongly related to other aspects of religious commitment. (See Table 1.) The highly orthodox are much more likely than the less orthodox to be ritually involved in the church, and they far surpass the less orthodox on devotionalism (private worship, such as prayer), religious experience, religious knowledge, and particularism (the belief that only Christians can be saved). Only on ethicalism among Protestants—the importance placed on "loving thy neighbor" and "doing good for others"—is the pattern reversed. By a slight margin, it is the least orthodox who are most likely to hold the ideals of Christian ethics.

Granted, it could be convincingly argued that devotionalism, religious

Table 1. Unorthodox Protestants Stress Ethics

	Orthodoxy Index		
	Low	Medium	High
Percentage high on ritual involvement			
Protestants	19%	39%	71%
(Sample)	(595)	(729)	(705)
Catholics	19	36	55
(Sample)	(64)	(115)	(304)
Percentage high on devotionalism			
Protestants	20	49	79
Catholics	18	58	80
Percentage high on religious experience			
Protestants	25	57	86
Catholics	29	49	70
Percentage high on religious knowledge			
Protestants	15	19	46
Catholics	0	5	7
Percentage high on particularism			
Protestants	9	25	60
Catholics	15	28	40
Percentage high on ethicalism			
Protestants	47	46	42
Catholics	48	48	56

As this table shows, both Protestants and Catholics who are highly orthodox are also the most likely to be ritually involved in the church, and to surpass the less orthodox in devotionalism (private worship, such as prayer); religious experiences (a mystical experience, or the like); religious knowledge; and particularism (the belief that only Christians can be saved). Among Protestants, however, the *least* orthodox are somewhat more likely to hold the ideals of Christian ethics.

experience, knowledge, particularism, and perhaps even ritual involvement are not intrinsically necessary to the existence of Christian institutions. The fact that these forms of commitment decline as traditional belief declines could be interpreted as reflecting changes in modes of religious expression, rather than as an erosion of religious commitment. After all, the new theology implies not only a departure from old-time supernaturalism, but from religious practices that reflect supernaturalism. The clergy of the new reformation can hardly expect their adherents to break out "speaking in tongues."

But it is implausible to speak simply of change, rather than of decline, unless religious institutions retain a laity committed in *some* fashion. The churches cannot survive as formal organizations unless people participate in the life of the church and give it financial support. Without funds or members, the churches would be empty shells awaiting demolition.

This could just happen. (See Table 2). Among both Protestants and Catholics, church attendance is powerfully related to orthodox. Only 15 percent of those Protestants with fully modernized religious beliefs attend church every week, as opposed to 59 percent of those who have retained traditional views. Among Catholics, the contrast is 27 percent versus 82 percent. Similarly, the table shows that membership in one or more church organizations is strongly related to orthodoxy. Furthermore—and perhaps most important—financial support for the churches is mainly provided by those with orthodox views.

These findings show how the institutional church, predicated as it is on traditional theological concepts, loses its hold on its members as these

Table 2. The Orthodox Support the Church Most

	Orthodoxy Index		
	Low	Medium	High
Percentage attending church every week			
Protestants	15%	31%	59%
Catholics	27	60	82
Percentage belonging to one or more church organizations			
Protestants	46	61	72
Catholics	14	24	46
Percentage contributing $7.50 or more per week to their church			
Protestants	17	23	44
Catholics	2	4	8
Percentage of Catholics who contribute $4 or more per week to their church	13	19	26

It is the orthodox religionists, as this table shows, who attend church more, who belong to more than one church organization, and who contribute the most financially. This is why the fewer orthodox supporters the church has, the less its organizational support.

concepts become outmoded. Consequently, if the erosion of traditional beliefs continues, as presumably it will, the church—as long as it remains locked in its present institutional forms—stands in ever-increasing danger of both moral and financial bankruptcy. The liberal denominations are particularly vulnerable because the demise of traditional theology and a concomitant drop in other aspects of commitment is already widespread in these bodies.

In coming days, many conservative Christians will undoubtedly argue and work for an about-face. But it seems clear to us that a return to orthodoxy is no longer possible. The current reformation in religious thought is irrevocable, and we are no more likely to recover our innocence in these matters than we are to again believe that the world is flat.

Is there any way the impending triumph of liberal theology can be translated into the renewed church that liberal clergymen expect? Or must liberalism lead inevitably to the demise of organized faith? It is here the future is most murky. The alternatives to orthodoxy being advocated by the new theologians and their supporters are still rather formless. It is too soon to know just where they will lead. However, it seems clear that their central thrust is toward the ethical rather than the mystical.

Shift toward Ethicalism

This shift is more than a change in emphasis. The ethics of the new theologies differ sharply from the old. No longer are Christian ethics defined as matters of personal holiness or the rejection of private vices. They are directed toward social justice, toward the creation of a humane society. As theologian Langdon Gilkey put it, . . . there has been a "shift in Christian ethical concern from personal holiness to love of neighbor as the central obligation. . . ." In the new ethical perspective, the individual is not neglected for the sake of the group, but the social situation in which people are embedded is seen as integral to the whole question of what is ethical. The long Christian quest to save the world through individual salvation has shifted to the quest to reform society.

Consequently, the new theology is manifested less in what one believes about God than in what one believes about goodness, justice, and compassion. A depersonalized and perhaps intuitively understood God may be invoked by these theologies, but what seems to count most is not how one prepares for the next life—the reality of which the new theology seems to deny—but what one does to realize the kingdom of God on earth.

Among some modern Christians, ethicalism *may* provide a substitute for orthodoxy. Ethicalism is most prevalent in denominations where orthodoxy is least common. Furthermore, individual church members whose religious beliefs are the least orthodox score higher on ethicalism than the most orthodox.

But from an institutional point of view, is ethicalism a satisfactory substitute for orthodoxy? Can ethical concern generate and sustain the kinds of practical commitment—financial support and personal participation—that the churches need to survive?

If the churches continue their present policy of business as usual, the answer is probably No. The ethically oriented Christian seems to be deterred rather than challenged by what he finds in church. The more a man is committed to ethicalism, the less likely he is to contribute funds or participate in the life of the church. We suspect that, in the long run, he is also less likely to remain a member.

Tables 3 and 4 show the joint effects of orthodoxy and ethicalism on financial contributions and church attendance. Table 3 shows that, among Protestants, the more a church member is committed to ethics, the less likely he is to contribute money to his church, regardless of his level of orthodoxy. The best contributors are those of unwavering orthodoxy, who reject the religious importance of loving their neighbors or doing good for others. A similar relationship exists among Roman Catholics. Regardless of orthodoxy, the higher his score on the ethicalism index, the less likely a parishioner is to give money to the church. Member commitment to Christian ethics seems to cost the churches money.

Table 3. Who Contributes the Most Money?

	Ethicalism Index		
	High	Medium	Low
	Percentage who contribute $7.50 or more per week to their church		
Protestants—Orthodoxy Index			
High	38%	43%	58%
(Sample)	(304)	(240)	(111)
Medium	18	25	43
	(333)	(321)	(44)
Low	18	20	12
	(241)	(251)	(34)
Catholics—Orthodoxy Index	Percentage who contribute $4 or more per week to their church		
High	27	45	*
	(150)	(122)	(4)
Medium	16	18	*
	(48)	(56)	(4)
Low	7	21	*
	(30)	(28)	(1)

Among both Protestants and Catholics the more a church member is committed to ethicalism—placing importance on "loving thy neighbor" and "doing good for others"—the less likely he is to give money to his church. The best contributors are those with unwavering orthodoxy and the least commitment to ethicalism.

*Too few cases for a stable percentage.

Table 4 shows the joint impact of ethicalism and orthodoxy on church attendance. Here again, among Protestants, it is clear that the higher their ethicalism, the less likely they are to attend church regularly. The best attenders are the highly orthodox who reject ethical tenets. Among Roman Catholics, it is unclear from these data whether or not ethicalism has any effect at all upon church attendance.

These findings were rechecked within liberal, moderate, and conservative Protestant groups, and within specific denominations as well. Invariably, a concern with ethics turned out to be incompatible with church attendance and contributions. Furthermore, these same relationships held true for participation in church organizations and activities.

Today's churches are failing to engage the ethical impulses of their members. Regardless of whether they retain orthodox religious views, to the extent that people have accepted Christian ethics, they seem inclined to treat the church as irrelevant. Obviously, this bodes ill for the future of the churches. It means that the churches have to find a substitute for orthodoxy that will still guarantee their organizational survival. And while *some* form of ethicalism might work as a theological substitute for orthodoxy, clearly the existing efforts along this line have not succeeded.

Sooner or later the churches will have to face these facts. This will require a forthright admission that orthodoxy is dead. Furthermore, it will

Table 4. Who Attends Church the Most?

	Percentage who attend church every week Ethicalism Index		
	High	Medium	Low
Protestants—Orthodoxy Index			
High	55%	58%	67%
(Sample)	(328)	(247)	(113)
Medium	29	31	52
	(347)	(331)	(44)
Low	19	22	10
	(255)	(165)	(39)
Catholics—Orthodoxy Index			
High	82	82	*
	(161)	(124)	(4)
Medium	65	60	*
	(51)	(57)	(4)
Low	30	27	*
	(30)	(30)	(2)

Among Protestants, the higher the ethicalism, the lower the church attendance. The best attenders are the highly orthodox who do not stress Christian ideals. The data for Catholics are unclear.

*Too few cases for a stable percentage.

also require—and here's the real hurdle—a clear alternative. It will require a new theology, ethically-based or otherwise, and radical changes in forms of worship, programs, and organization to make them consistent with and relevant to this new theology.

But even successfully fulfilling these tasks will not ensure the survival of the church. Indeed, the immediate effect will almost certainly be to alienate those members committed to old-time orthodoxy and thus to sharply reduce the base of support on which the churches presently depend. The gamble is that these people can be replaced by renewing the commitment of those members whose interest in the church is presently waning, and by winning new adherents among those who do not now belong to any church.

Clearly, among the conservative churches such a radical change of posture is not likely. The impact of modernized theology on these bodies has so far been indirect, in the loss of members who switch to more liberal denominations. To the extent that these losses remain endurable, the conservative clergy and laymen can continue to ignore the current crisis.

Reclaiming the Dormant Christians

If institutional reforms are to come, the liberal churches must lead the way. Our findings suggest that not only are the liberal churches in the best position to make such changes, but that their existence may very well depend on their doing so.

At present, the liberal bodies are functioning as way stations for those who are moving away from orthodoxy, but who are still unwilling to move entirely outside the church. The new members may prove to be only a passing phenomenon, however, unless the liberal churches can find a way to *keep* them. And the churches' current organizing practices are clearly unequal to this task. For it is the liberal churches that are currently in the poorest organizational health.

Most liberal Christians are dormant Christians. They have adopted the theology of the new reformation, but at the same time they have stopped attending church, stopped participating in church activities, stopped contributing funds, and stopped praying. They are uninformed about religion. And only a minority feel that their religion provides them with answers to the meaning and purpose of life, while the overwhelming majority of conservatives feel theirs *does* supply such answers. The liberal congregations resemble theater audiences. Their members are mainly strangers to one another, while conservative congregations are close-knit groups, united by widespread bonds of personal friendship.

In the light of these facts, the liberal churches do not seem organizationally sound in comparison with the conservative ones.

Although all these signs point to the need for a radical break with traditional forms in the liberal churches, it seems quite unlikely that this will happen any time soon. For one thing, there is no sign that the leaders

Table 5. Liberal Churches May Be in Trouble

	Members of Liberal Protestant Churches[a]	Members of Moderate Protestant Churches[b]	Members of Conservative Protestant Churches[c]	Members of Roman Catholic Parishes
Percentage high on orthodoxy	11	33	81	61
Percentage high on ritual involvement	30	45	75	46
Percentage high on devotionalism	42	51	78	65
Percentage high on religious experience	43	57	89	58
Percentage high on religious knowledge	17	25	55	5
Percentage who feel their religious perspective provides them with the answers to the meaning and purpose of life	43	57	84	68
Percentage who attend church weekly	25	32	68	70
Percentage who have 3 or more of their 5 best friends in their congregation	22	26	54	36
Percentage who contribute $7.50 or more per week to their church	18	30	50	6

Compared with the conservative Protestant denominations, the liberal churches are in poor organizational health. Liberal religionists, as the table shows, attend church less, contribute less money, and have a generally weaker religious commitment. Still, the liberals know more about religion than Catholics, and contribute more money to their church than Catholics.

[a]Congregationalists, Methodists, Episcopalians.

[b]Disciples of Christ, Presbyterians, American Lutherans, American Baptists.

[c]Missouri Synod Lutherans, Southern Baptists, Sects.

of these bodies recognize the situation that confronts them. Here and there one hears a voice raised within the clergy, but such spokesmen are a minority with little power to lead. What's more, leadership is not the only thing lacking. There is no clearly formulated blueprint for renovating the churches. The critical attack on orthodoxy seems a success, but now what? The new theologians have developed no consensus as to what they want people to believe, or as to what kind of new church they want to build.

What we expect is that all of the Christian churches will continue a policy of drift, with a rhetoric of hope and a reality of business as usual. There will be more mergers and more efforts to modernize classical interpretations of the faith, but these will go forward as compromises rather than as breaks with the past. Perhaps, when the trends we see have caused greater havoc, radical change will follow. Institutions, like people, have a strong will to survive. But institutions *do* die, and often efforts to save them come too late.

Only history will reveal the eventual fate of Christianity. As matters now stand, there seems to be little long-term future for the church as we know it. A remnant church can be expected to last for a time, if only to provide the psychic comforts that are currently dispensed by orthodoxy. But eventually substitutes for even this function are likely to emerge, leaving churches of the present form with no effective rationale for continuing to exist.

This is *not* to suggest that religion itself will die. As long as questions of ultimate meaning persist, and as long as the human spirit strives to transcend itself, the religious quest will continue. But whether the religion of the future will be in any sense Christian remains to be seen. Clearly it will *not* be, if one means by "Christian" the orthodoxy of the past and the institutional structures built upon that orthodoxy. But if one can conceive of Christianity as a continuity in a search for ethics, and a retention of certain traditions of language and ritual, then perhaps Christianity *will* survive.

The institutional shape of religion in the future is as difficult to predict as its theological content. Conceivably it may take on a public character, as suggested recently by sociologist Robert Bellah, or the invisible form anticipated by another sociologist, Thomas Luckmann. Or it may live on, in a form similar to the religions of Asia, in a public witness conducted by priests without parishes. Quite possibly, religion in the future will be very different from anything we can now expect.

The portents of what is to come could easily seem trivial today. William Butler Yeats, in a poem celebrating the slow death of ancient paganism and the coming birth of a still unformed Christianity, asked a question that we may well ask of our own religious future:

> And what rough beast, its hour come round at last,
> Slouches towards Bethlehem to be born?

*Religious Change Among College Students Over Two Decades**

Philip K. Hastings and Dean R. Hoge

Many observers have noted recently that college students are turning away from traditional religion. It is assumed by almost everyone that the campuses are becoming secularized. Among Christian theologians the topics of secularization, secular society, and the "world come of age" have become major preoccupations. Other observers (cf. Greeley, 1969) have noted that religious concerns and orientations to sacredness are stronger than ever on campus, even though the newest manifestations are in nontraditional terms. At the same time enrollment in religion courses has risen on many campuses in recent years. It would be helpful for interpreting the present situation to have indications of trends over several decades. This paper reports on an effort to measure trends in traditional religious attitudes and practices[1] from 1948 to 1967 at Williams College.

Past studies of changes in students' traditional religious attitudes and practices have been rather scattered. The earliest trend study was done by Leuba (1934) in one women's college in 1914 and 1933. He found a decline of about *30* percentage points in those expressing belief in personal immortality. Gilliland (1953) found increases in traditional beliefs at Northwestern University between the middle 1930s and 1949, and Bender (1958) found increasing religious values on the Allport–Vernon *values study* at Dartmouth College from 1940 to 1956. At Ripon College, Dudycha (1950)

Reprinted by permission of the publisher from *Social Forces* 49 (September 1970): 16–28.

*A portion of the analysis in this study was supported by National Institute of Health Fellowship No. 2-FI-MH-30, 523-03.

[1]The concept "religion" is ambiguous and needs specification. A distinction is necessary between "personal religion" and "traditional religion." The former term refers to an individual's system of meanings and commitments, somewhat in the sense of Tillich's "ultimate concern." One's orientation to the main Judeo-Christian traditions may be extensive or slight, conscious or unconscious, avowed or denied. The latter term refers to the organized religious systems and organizations in American society. The main focus of this study is on the relationship of these two entities—the type and amount of conscious traditional religious orientation, attitudes, and practices in each student's personal religion. In this paper the term "religion" unless specified refers to "traditional religion."

found few changes in religious beliefs from 1929–30 to 1949. Argyle (1958) reviewed all available evidence and concluded that traditional religion had waned among most social groups in America from about 1900 to 1940, whereafter it had grown in numbers and influence. Between 1955 and 1964 Young *et al.* (1966) found a decrease in favorable religious attitudes at the University of Texas. Gallup polls found that in 1965, *62* percent of American students thought that religion was "losing its influence" on American life, and in 1969 it was *78* percent.[2] The available data suggest that religious attitudes and practices among college students were more orthodox and stronger in the early 1950s than in the 1930s but that since the late 1950s they have declined. Changes in specific attitudes and practices are unknown, as are the explanations for any of the changes.

Method

This paper reports on religious change at Williams College, a high quality independent eastern liberal arts college of about *1,200* undergraduate men. Its admission standards are among the highest in the nation. The students come from all regions; in 1968, *21* percent were from New England and *39* percent were from the middle Atlantic states. Williams College draws its students from the same general pool as many other quality eastern colleges and may be seen as rather typical of many such colleges. It is probably more liberal in religious orientation than most denominational colleges and state universities.

In the fall of 1946 Gordon W. Allport and his associates surveyed students at Harvard College and Radcliffe College, and in April 1948 the same instrument was employed in a survey of Williams College students.[3] From a random sample *205* questionnaires were returned for a completion rate of *96* percent. In April 1967 the same questionnaire was pretested and found to be reliable for a replication study. It was slightly enlarged and then delivered to a random sample stratified by college class. A total of *206* were returned for a completion rate of *93* percent.

Fred C. Copeland, Director of Admissions, said that the main changes in admission policies since World War II were three. First, Williams accepts many more public school graduates today than two decades ago. Second, college board scores have risen; from the fall of 1946 to the fall of 1966 the mean verbal scores rose *87* points and the mean mathematical scores rose *85* points. Third, Williams today recruits actively throughout the nation so that it achieves a geographically more diverse student body than before. This has not necessarily produced social and economic diversity, since the best applicants for admission from the various regions tend to be from upper-middle class groups generally resembling one another. It is thought

[2]Reported in *The New York Times,* June 1, 1969.

[3]For the Williams data, cf. Hastings (1948) and for the questionnaire, cf. Allport *et al.* (1948).

that the average socioeconomic level of students has fallen slightly due to the active recruiting program, increased scholarship aid, and more universalistic admission policies.

The 1948 and 1967 sample groups differed in several respects, reflecting these admission policies. Of the *205* students surveyed in 1948, *113* were veterans and *92* were nonveterans. For measuring change all comparisons must be made between the 1967 sample and the 1948 nonveterans. The mean age of the 1948 nonveterans was *18.9* years, and in 1967 it was *20.0* years. This difference occurred because more of the 1948 nonveterans were underclassmen than upperclassmen. Fathers' education levels rose during the two decades. In 1948 about *75* percent of the nonveterans' fathers had college degrees, and in 1967 the figure was *80* percent. In 1948 about *26* percent of the fathers had graduate or professional degrees, and in 1967 it was *45* percent. Fathers' occupations changed only in that about *9* percent fewer of the fathers in 1967 were business executives and about the same percentage more were professional men, mostly in medicine and education.

Sizes of hometowns were very nearly the same in 1948 and 1967. Those from public high schools increased from about *37* percent of the 1948 nonveterans to 55 percent in 1967. Major courses also changed; there were increases of about *7* percent in the humanities and about *3* percent in the social sciences, with a decrease of about *10* percent in the natural and biological sciences.

The main purpose of this research is to ascertain actual changes over nineteen years and also the amount of change not directly traceable to changes in admissions practices. The latter may be more confidently generalized to larger groups of students in similar colleges. As we shall see below, the effect of changes in admissions on the survey results is small.

The analysis ignores the 1948 veterans. It may be noted that they reported less orthodox religious beliefs and practices than the nonveterans. *Five* percent fewer felt the need for a religious orientation or belief, *10* percent fewer reported at least occasional prayer, *4* percent fewer had theistic or deistic conceptions of the Deity, and *15* percent fewer believed in personal immortality.

Religious Background and Preference

An item in the questionnaire asked about the amount of religious influence in students' upbringing, and the 1967 responses closely matched those in 1948—about two-thirds said it was "very marked" or "moderate."[4] Succeeding items asked about the character of this influence (if there was any), about present feelings of need for religious orientation or belief, and about present preference of existing religious systems. Table 1 shows students' religious backgrounds and present preference of traditions.

In both 1948 and 1967 the number of students choosing the three

[4]For more data and technical detail on any item or procedure, cf. Hoge (1969).

Table 1. Net Changes from Religious Background to Present Choice of Religious Tradition

	Percentages					
	1948 Nonveterans (N=92)			1967 (N=206)		
	Back-ground	Choice	Change	Back-ground	Choice	Change
Roman Catholic	15	14	−1	12	9	−3
Anglo-Catholic, East Orthodox	7	4	−3	4	†	−4
Protestant Christianity	65	38	−27	57	19	−38
Liberalized Protestantism	5	6	+1	3	6	+3
Ethical but not theological Christianity	4	14	+10	4	19	+15
Some form of Judaism	4	1	−3	15	8	−7
Other	1	2	+1	3	10	+7
No influence	0	—		2	—	
Multiple responses	—	0		—	8	
New type of religion needed	—	7		—	12	
None needed or doubtful need	—	14		—	8	
Total	101*	100		100	99	

*Due to rounding, columns may not add up to *100* percent.
†Less than ½ percent.

major religious traditions (Protestant, Catholic, and Jewish) was smaller than the number reared in those traditions. The "loss" was greater in 1967 than in 1948. Many of the students changed to "none needed," "new type of religion needed," or "ethical but not theological Christianity." The written-in comments plus all available evidence suggest that those departing from the main traditional groups propose not basic departures from them but rather further development and evolution of the Judeo-Christian traditions, especially toward greater individualistic and humanistic ethical emphases. Orientation to non-Western religious traditions is slight.

The figures in Table 1 are "net change" including both those who changed *away from* their home religious traditions and others who changed *to* them. It is also possible to calculate the percentage of those reared in each tradition designating that tradition as their preference. The figures in 1948 are approximately *73* percent for the Catholics, *58* percent for the Protestants, *22* percent for the Jews, and *36* percent for the *liberal* Protestants and *ethical* Christians. In 1967 they are *65* percent for the Catholics, *34* percent for the Protestants, *50* percent for the Jews, and *53* percent for the *liberal* Protestants and *ethical* Christians. For example, in 1967, out of *113* men reared in the Protestant tradition *38* (or *34* percent) gave it as their preference, *7* made multiple choices, *2* shifted to Catholicism, *1* shifted to Judaism, *27* shifted to *liberal* Protestantism or *ethical* Christianity, *10* had other preferences, and *28* made no choice or called for a new type of religious tradition.

The "holding power" of the Catholic and Protestant groups has weakened over two decades, while in the Jewish and liberal groups it has strengthened. Put more generally, the liberal groups have strengthened and the conservative groups have weakened. For both liberal and conservative groups the picture is one of considerable disaffection, with large numbers of students departing entirely from having any traditional religious identification at all.

Religious Beliefs

In Table 2 are four items asking about religious beliefs. The trend is away from orthodox beliefs, and the amount of change is quite uniform from item to item. Those feeling a need for religious orientation or belief, however they define it, have declined from *85* percent to *65* percent.[5]

Those holding favorable attitudes toward the organized church have declined from *64* percent to *42* percent. Many more students in 1967 checked the noncommittal and mildly unfavorable responses, but few in either 1948 or 1967 checked the most strongly critical responses. The Williams' students have become more indifferent but not more hostile.

Belief in an omnipotent Creator declined *18* points, and belief in a deistic conception declined *3* points. During pretesting we tried to ascertain the meaning of the frequent choices in 1967 of "none of these alternatives." It seems to mean in most cases that the respondent lacks a thought-out view and that he hesitates to commit himself to any alternative in the questionnaire. It does not mean that the questionnaire is too inarticulate to fit precisely enough the students' particular views. The students with strong religious influence in upbringing tended not to check "none of these alternatives."

Belief in personal immortality declined *21* points. The main change is toward the view that one's immortality consists entirely in his influence upon children and social institutions.

Another item asked about views of the Person of Christ. In 1948, *38* percent believed that Christ is the human incarnation of God; in 1967 it was *20* percent.

Three items dealt less directly with traditional doctrines. One stated, "If religion is to play a useful role in life, it should be regarded entirely as

[5]When the 1967 sample is compared with the 1948 nonveterans the differences significant at the *.05* level are: for percentages in the ranges *0* to *20* and *80* to *100,* about *7* points; for percentages in the ranges *20* to *80,* about *10* points.

a natural human function. It should have nothing whatever to do with supernatural notions." In 1948, *55* percent agreed, and in 1967, *42* percent

Table 2. Four Items on Religious Beliefs

	Percentages	
	1948 Nonveterans (N=92)	1967 (N=206)
"Do you feel that you require some form of religious orientation or belief in order to achieve a fully mature philosophy of life?"		
Yes	85	65
No	5	22
Doubtful	10	13
"The Church"*		
The Church is the one sure and infallible foundation of civilized life.	8	1
On the whole the Church stands for the best in human life.	56	41
There is certain doubt. Possible that the Church may do some harm.	12	19
The total influence may be on the whole harmful.	3	11
Stronghold of much that is unwholesome and dangerous to human welfare.	2	4
Insufficient familiarity.	5	7
A different attitude.	14	18
"The nature of the Deity"*		
Infinitely wise omnipotent Creator.	29	11
Infinitely intelligent and friendly Being.	27	24
Vast, impersonal spiritual source.	13	13
I neither believe nor disbelieve in God.	18	13
The only power is natural law.	1	8
The universe is merely a machine.	1	1
None of these alternatives.	11	28
"Immortality"*		
Personal immortality.	38	17
Reincarnation.	3	2
Continued existence as part of a spiritual principle.	9	11
Influence upon children and social institutions.	23	39
Disbelieve in any of these senses.	2	7
None of these alternatives.	25	24

*The responses here are abbreviations; for the full responses see Allport *et al.* (1948).

agreed. The trend is away from natural religion as well as away from orthodox beliefs, even though the students more liberal on other belief items tended to agree on this one.

A second item quoted Marx that religion is an opiate of the people and prevents their social uplift, therefore organized religion must be resisted. In 1948, *3* percent agreed, and in 1967, it was *9* percent. Opposition to organized religion among these students is slight, and apparently Marxist ideas are not central to that opposition.

A third item stated that denominational distinctions, at least within Protestant Christianity, are out of date and may as well be eliminated quickly. In 1948, *60* percent agreed, and in 1967 it was only *49* percent. Support for ecumenism has fallen off since 1948, and it is difficult to understand why. The students disagreeing with this item tend to be Protestant and orthodox in beliefs. Apparently denominationalist sentiments have strengthened among students in recent years.

Religion and Science

The perceived relation between religion and science has been much debated and discussed (cf. Stark, 1963; Lehman and Shriver, 1968). The tendency in recent years is for Christian theologians to stress that there never was a true conflict between Christian theology and modern science or if there was a real conflict it has now been successfully accommodated. Table 3 shows the responses to an item asking about the conflict.

The 1967 students perceived considerably more conflict than did the 1948 students. Those who checked the fourth or fifth responses in 1967 were asked to indicate whether scientific or religious formulations must give way

Table 3. "How Do You Feel About the Frequently Mentioned Conflict Between the Findings of Science and the Principal (Basic) Contentions of Religion?"

	Percentages	
	1948 Nonveterans (N=87)	1967 (N=198)
Religion and science clearly support one another.	38	16
Conflict is negligible (more apparent than real).	32	35
Conflict is considerable but probably not irreconcilable.	21	21
Conflict is very considerable, perhaps irreconcilable.	7	16
Conflict is definitely irreconcilable.	2	12
Total	100	100

to the other. Of this group *91* percent said that religion must give way and *9* percent said that science must give way. Those who see no conflict between religion and science tend to be those with the most orthodox responses on other belief items. The major course groups[6] did not differ significantly in their perception of the religion and science conflict.

Here is a basic change in orientation from the "fundamentalist–modernist" controversies of the early twentieth century in which the most orthodox religious spokesmen were the most antiscience. Now the most orthodox students perceive no conflict between religion and science, and only the less religious students see a basic conflict.

Religious Practices

Table 4 shows two items asking about religious practices. A third item dealt with church attendance, but since Williams College had compulsory chapel until 1962 the responses are not usable. Over two decades both prayer and experiences of religious reverence have declined sharply. The smaller decline in religious experiences is probably due to the broader conceptualization of what might be included.

Table 4. Two Items on Devotional Practices During Past Six Months

	Percentages	
	1948 Nonveterans (N=92)	1967 (N=206)
Prayed		
Daily	19	9
Fairly frequently	20	15
Occasionally	23	18
Rarely	23	23
Never	15	35
Experienced feeling of reverence		
Daily	12	3
Frequently	15	16
Occasionally	26	23
Rarely	22	23
Never	24	35

[6]The course groups were categorized into natural and biological sciences, social sciences, humanities, and "other."

Change Within Each Tradition

Table 1 showed that fewer students in 1967 than in 1948 considered any of the existing organized religious traditions satisfactory for them. The students have changed faster than the traditions. It is possible to estimate relative changes in the traditions by comparing the 1948 and 1967 responses of those students choosing to remain within them. Table 5 shows the responses of those students expressing a need for a religious orientation and designating one tradition as satisfactory.

Those remaining within the Catholic tradition in 1967 seem less orthodox than those in 1948 (due to the small *N* we must be cautious). Those remaining within the Protestant tradition in 1967 are slightly more orthodox than those doing so in 1948. In the "other" group there is little change. Combining Tables 1 and 5 we see that the Catholic group has weakened slightly in holding power and liberalized somewhat; the Protestant group

Table 5. Religious Beliefs and Practices of Those Expressing Need for Religion and Choosing One Tradition as Satisfactory

	Percentages					
	1948 All Men			1967		
	Cath. (N=19)	Prot. (N=114)	Other* (N=35)	Cath. (N=17)	Prot. (N=32)	Other* (N=81)
Belief in Deity:						
Theistic or Deistic†	100	61	37	77	66	33
All other positions	0	39	63	23	34	67
Belief in immortality:						
Personal, or reincarnation†	95	32	23	65	38	15
All other positions	5	68	77	35	62	85
Prayer:						
Daily, frequently, occasionally	89	67	43	82	78	46
Rarely, never	11	33	57	18	22	54
Feeling of reverence:						
Daily, frequently, occasionally	89	61	52	71	78	49
Rarely, never	11	39	48	29	22	51

*Mostly liberalized Protestant and ethical but not theological Christianity.
†First and second responses on the items about Deity and immortality.

has weakened greatly in holding power and turned slightly more conservative; the Jewish and liberal Christian groups (combined) have strengthened considerably in holding power and changed little in orientation. Protestantism especially has lost the loyalty of a large "outer circle" of adherents, leaving only a smaller and more conservative group.

Religious Development

The questionnaire included a series of items about religious upbringing and development. Three are shown in Table 6. Those reacting against the beliefs taught them have increased by *15* percentage points since 1948. This finding coincides with the lower holding power of both Catholicism and Protestantism reported above. The median age when the doubts started fell almost one year from 1948 to 1967. It is probably traceable in part to rising admission standards at Williams College, but even without rising standards it is part of a general trend over several decades toward greater individualism and autonomy among students. Researchers have generally found that liberal religious attitudes are associated with greater personal autonomy of individuals (cf. Argyle, 1958:80–86). In this association the direction of causation is unclear. Probably any causation from individual autonomy to liberal religious beliefs and practices is less important than external factors acting on both of them concurrently.

Most research on religion and the life cycle shows that orthodox beliefs and practices tend to decrease starting about age *16* and continuing until about age *30,* whereafter they slowly increase again (Argyle, 1958:59–70). Also ages *15* and *16* are crucial for development of religious viewpoints

Table 6. Reaction to Home Religious Teachings

	Percentages	
	1948 Nonveterans (N=88)	1967 (N=199)
"If you were brought up under some religious influence has there been a period in which you have reacted either partially or wholly against the beliefs taught?"		
Yes	57	72
No	27	19
Doubtful	16	9
(If so:) "When did the doubts start?" (median age)	16.4	15.5
(If so:) "Would you say that at the present time you":		
Are in substantial agreement with the beliefs taught.	24	15
Are in partial agreement with them.	70	67
Wholly disagree with them.	6	18

and commitments, for they are the period of most frequent conversion experiences. Among the Williams' nonveterans in 1948, *66* percent reported important religious "awakening" during adolescence. The median age was *16.1* years.

Various information suggests that adolescence and the changes associated with it are now occurring earlier in the upper-middle class life cycle than formerly. Measures of the age of onset of menses in girls show a fall of about four months per decade in Western Europe over the past century, and recent trends in America are the same (Tanner, 1962:152). Physical maturation is probably also earlier in boys. Alongside the earlier physical adolescence come patterns of earlier dating, earlier separation from parental tutelage, and possibly earlier emotional development. The earlier age of religious reaction seems, however, only partially related to the particular religious beliefs held during college, for age differences in religious beliefs and practices in the 1967 data are slight.

The third item in Table 6 shows that those reacting against the religious beliefs taught them tend to remain in only partial agreement with those beliefs. More wholly disagree with them in 1967 than in 1948.

The students most likely to react against the beliefs taught them are those from more conservative families and with less-educated parents. In 1967 among those from Catholic families *87* percent reacted against the beliefs taught them, as opposed to *71* percent of those from non-Catholic families. From 1948 to 1967 the reactions within the Catholic background group increased *25* percentage points, compared with an increase of *4* percentage points in the non-Catholic group. In 1967 the figure for Protestants was *73* percent; for Jews it was *60* percent; and for *liberal* Protestants and *ethical* Christians it was *69* percent. The median age of reaction in 1967 among the Catholics was *16.8* years; among the Protestants it was *15.5* years; and among the Jews it was *16.0* years. The students with stronger religious influence during upbringing tend to react oftener but at a later age than the others. Stronger home loyalties delay the criticism.

Table 7 shows students' estimates of which factors have caused them to feel religious. From 1948 to 1967 the more emotional factors (sex turmoil, fear or insecurity, gratitude, etc.) seem to have declined in importance. The rise in "a mystical experience" may be related to emphasis on immediate experiences in the current student movements and experimentation with drugs. This suggestion is strengthened by the intercorrelation of *.346* between "reading outside of school and college" and "a mystical experience," the strongest intercorrelation of responses in the item. The fewer checks on items referring to emotional factors are probably related to reduced acceptance of emotionality and sentimentality by college students in most normal social interaction.[7] Accepted forms of expressive behavior have apparently been differentiated from traditional religious forms.

[7]At Haverford College, Heath (1969a) has found evidence of more restricted emotionality and less acceptance of emotional expression among students in the middle 1960s than those two decades earlier.

Table 7. "If at Any Time You Felt Yourself to be Religious, Which Factors in the Following List do You Consciously Recognize to Have Been Contributing Reasons? Check as Many as Apply."

	Percentages	
	1948 Nonveterans (N=92)	1967 (N=206)
Parental influence	49	61
Personal influence of others	38	40
Sorrow or bereavement	20	20
Sex turmoil	17	9
A mystical experience	3	14
Conformity with tradition	35	38
Fear or insecurity	38	28
Gratitude	32	20
Studies in school or college	21	20
Reading outside of school and college	24	17
Aesthetic appeal	22	21
Church teachings	42	32

Table 8 shows an item asking the students to compare their own religious belief with that of their father and mother. Both the 1948 and the 1967 students report less firm faith than their parents. From 1948 to 1967 the difference has increased—that is, the generation gap has grown. The gap from the mothers grew about as much as that from the fathers. This item confirms the greater rebellion of the 1967 students from their home religious culture.

The distance between the students and their mothers is greater than that between the students and their fathers. This pattern is consistent with the findings of almost all studies, that women are more traditionally religious than men. In most homes the women seem to be the more important bearer of the religious tradition.

The 1967 students know more about their parents than did the 1948 students, suggesting that religious beliefs are discussed more openly in the homes in the late 1960s than in the late 1940s. The 1967 students have relatively well-informed reactions to the religious beliefs taught them.

The fact that students report less religious belief than their parents is no measure of social change, for it is traceable to changes during the life cycle. As already noted, religious commitments and practices tend to be less prevalent during the twenties than later in life during the forties and fifties. It is probable that the specific emphases and patterns also change; available

Table 8. "How, in General, Does the Firmness of Your Belief in Religion Compare with Your Mother's Belief? With Your Father's Belief?"

	Percentages					
	1948 Nonveterans		1967		Change	
Own Belief Is	Mother's	Father's	Mother's	Father's	Mother	Father
More firm	7	14	10	15	+3	+1
Less firm	39	20	55	37	+16	+17
About the same	30	33	19	35	−11	+2
Don't know	24	33	16	13	−8	−20
Total	100	100	100	100		

evidence does not tell us. But a certain "generation gap" between students and their parents is normal.

The increasing generation gap seen in Table 8 is, however, an indication of social change. When combined with the declining orthodoxy seen in Table 2 it suggests that the students changed more from 1948 to 1967 than the parents. Change among the parents appears small. This pattern is confirmed by nationwide polls–change among the total adult population during the 1950s and early 1960s is less than change among young persons (cf. Marty *et al.,* 1968). The change among students resembles that among the more educated, more affluent, and younger groups in the total population. The young people have declined in orthodox religious beliefs and practices during the period from 1952 to 1965, but the *45* to *54* year group have changed little. Table 8 shows that religious beliefs both change over the life cycle and also change from decade to decade regardless of one's location in the life cycle. Studies of trends must be cognizant of both.

An item in 1967 asked how college experiences had affected the respondent's religious orientation and his interest in the problems religion seeks to answer. Sixteen percent said college had made them "more religious," *31* percent said "less religious," and *53* percent said "no effect." Also *63* percent said it had made them "more interested in the problems religion seeks to answer," *10* percent said "less interested," and *28* percent said "no effect." An item asked how interested the students are in the problems religion seeks to answer. Thirty-seven percent said "very interested," *41* percent said "moderately interested," and *22* percent said "little interested." These responses correlate only weakly with items indicating religious orthodoxy. Religious interest is largely independent of any particular religious orientation. It appears to strengthen during college, and it leads in various directions.

An item asked how many students had taken courses in religion prior to that semester, and *18* percent had done so. The effects were mainly (a) to make them more concerned with religious questions, (b) to leave them with the feeling that only a personal, individual religion could fulfill their religious needs, and (c) to weaken their ties to a particular organized religion. The students reporting weakened ties to organized religion tended to have Protestant backgrounds, and those reporting emphasis on a personal, individual religion tended to have little religious influence in upbringing.

Adjusted Responses

In order to generalize from these samples to broader groups of college students it is necessary to eliminate the effects of changes in the samples from 1948 to 1967. As already noted, the 1967 sample was slightly older than the 1948 sample: it had more Jewish background students and fewer with Protestant and Catholic backgrounds; its fathers were better educated, and more of them were professional men; more were from public schools rather than private schools, and more majored in the humanities and social sciences; and scholastic aptitudes were considerably higher. In the 1967 data the only one of these changes having a systematic relationship to religious attitudes and practices was religious background. With the others there were only a few scattered relationships. Also no noteworthy relationships appeared between the religious items and family income, college class, and size of hometown. The last of these may give pause to those who attribute secularization to city residence; when age, education, and socioeconomic status are held fairly constant, as in our sample, no differences appear between rural and urban students.

We lack direct correlations between college board scores and religious attitudes, but other studies show either no relationship or a very weak association between higher scores and more liberal religious orientations (Hoge, 1969; Argyle, 1958:92–96). In private colleges such as Williams the relationships are usually very weak or absent.

The great homogeneity of the college is probably responsible for the comparative unimportance of major course groups as determinants of religious attitudes and practices. The lack of difference between freshmen and seniors is somewhat atypical for such studies; a majority of studies find declining religious orthodoxy and practices from freshman to senior year (cf. Feldman and Newcomb, 1969).

By a system of weighting it is possible to calculate "adjusted responses" indicating what the 1967 responses would have been if all relevant background characteristics of the two samples had been constant. Most of the adjusted responses show slightly less change than the actual responses. In Table 2 the decline on the first two items about religious beliefs would have been *1* percent smaller; the decline on the last two items (first two responses on each) would have been *3* percent smaller. In Table 3 the changes on the first two responses would have been *1* percent greater. In Table 4 the adjusted responses are within *1* percent of the actual responses. In Table 6 those reacting to the religious beliefs taught them would rise from *72* to *77* percent. The median age of reaction would rise from *15.5* to

16.6 years, and the number now agreeing with their parents would decline from *15* to *12* percent. In Table 7 the adjusted responses closely resemble the actual responses. In summary, the changes in students' backgrounds account for a small amount of the changes from 1948 to 1967. The most important change in backgrounds was the increase in Jewish students. The changes from the 1948 responses to the 1967 adjusted responses may probably be generalized to other colleges similar to Williams.[8]

Four Dimensions

The 1967 questionnaire included several items not in the 1948 questionnaire and not reported here. From the total set four indices could be constructed. First is a *religious interest* index constructed from (a) the item asking about the need for a religious orientation, (b) the item asking how much interest the respondent has in the "problems religion seeks to answer," and (c) an item asking if the respondent has read modern theologians or religious thinkers. Second is a *religious sentiments* index, constructed from (a) the item on prayer, (b) the item on feelings of reverence, (c) an item asking about the respondent's religious needs and sentiments compared with other people, and (d) four responses from Table 7 concerning emotional experiences. Third is an *orthodox* belief index, constructed from (a) the item on the Deity, (b) the item on immortality, (c) the item about Christ–on which all Jewish responses were scored as missing data, (d) the item on natural religion, and (e) an item asking about belief in a personal God. Fourth is a *churchmanship* index, constructed from (a) an item about church attendance, (b) the item about attitudes toward the church, (c) the item about denominational distinctions ("no opinion" is scored medium low, other responses medium high), and (d) an item about formal church membership. Church attendance is weighted twice.

All items are scored approximating equal intervals if possible, but otherwise dichotomized into high and low. It is recognized that some approximation enters into the indices by this procedure. Index scores are the means of items scores. The intercorrelations are shown in Table 9.

The two dimensions most closely related are the *religious sentiments* index and the *orthodox belief* index; they should probably be considered a single dimension. The one most weakly related to the others is the *religious interest* index, probably because it was intended to measure broad religious concerns generally independent of any particular tradition. The relatively strong correlations between *churchmanship* and both *religious sentiments* and *orthodox beliefs* show that support for and participation in the organ-

[8]This suggestion is confirmed by two other studies. A replication of the 1946 survey of Harvard and Radcliffe students done in 1966 found changes very similar to those at Williams College (cf. Hoge, 1969). Also a study of Haverford College freshmen from the late 1940s to 1966 shows declining religious orthodoxy and practices starting in the early 1950s (cf. Hoge, 1969; Heath, 1969b).

Table 9. Interrelation of Indices, 1967*

	Religious Interest	Religious Sentiments	Orthodox Belief
Religious sentiments	.33		
Orthodox belief	.25	.66	
Churchmanship	.21	.45	.51

*All are significant at the *.01* level.

ized church is rather closely associated with traditional beliefs and commitments. This finding does not support some current theories attributing the flourishing state of many churches to extra-religious and extra-traditional factors (cf. Stark and Glock, 1968, for conclusions similar to ours).

We could not construct indices from the 1948 data, but available tables show that the interrelations of the various items are generally the same in 1948 and 1967.

Relation of Attitudes and Practices to Backgrounds

The 1967 questionnaire had an extensive list of background variables, and as already noted the relations between many of them and religious attitudes and practices are weak.

An item asked about the birthplaces of parents and grandparents in an effort to test the Herberg (1960:chap. 3) theory that the "third generation" of immigrant groups tends to uphold more strongly the religious tradition than the second generation. The students from each religious tradition were categorized by immigrant generation, and no relationships at all were found with religious attitudes and practices. There is a slight suggestion that Jewish identification might diminish in the third and fourth generations. These findings are not what Herberg would predict. They coincide with the findings of Lazerwitz, who has done extensive research on the problem without uncovering support for the "third generation" hypothesis (cf. Lazerwitz and Rowitz, 1964). The pattern usually found is a gradual liberalization from generation to generation.

The background variable most strongly predicting religious attitudes and practices is a measure of religious influence in upbringing. From two items we created an index of religious influence in childhood, and it correlated *.20* with the need for a religious orientation, *.20* with interest in religious problems, *.39* with the *orthodox belief* index, and *.34* with frequency of prayer. Another item asked about church attendance of parents, and it correlated about *.18* to *.24* with orthodoxy of beliefs and frequency of prayer. The correlations are stronger in the Jewish group than elsewhere.

An item asked how close the respondent's relationship is with each of his parents. A *close to parents* index correlated *.22* with the need for a religious orientation, *.21* with the *orthodox belief* index, *.24* with frequency of prayer, and only very weakly with interest in religious problems. Closeness to parents is a factor in religious attitudes and practices of all students except the Protestants. It was found that students from Jewish, *liberal* Protestant, and *ethical* Christian homes are significantly closer to their fathers than are those from Catholic and Protestant homes. Also students from lower-income homes report significantly closer relationships to their mothers than those from higher-income homes.

The strongest predictor of religious attitudes and practices besides home religious influence is religious tradition. On all the indicators those from Catholic homes are the most orthodox, those from Jewish, *liberal* Protestant, and *ethical* Christian homes the least orthodox, and the Protestants between.

Parents' education is related weakly to several of the religious items; in each case higher parents' education is associated with a more liberal religious orientation. An item asked about students' "occupational intentions and interests." Those intending business careers tend to be a bit more traditionally religious than the others. This relationship is probably traceable to home culture.

Besides these, the background variables were very weak in predicting religious attitudes and practices. Home influences are by far the most important. The sociological variables included in this study are generally not very strong predictors of religious attitudes and practices. Psychological factors in home life and educational experiences, not studied here, seem at least equally important.

Conclusions

From 1948 to 1967 Williams College students' religious beliefs have liberalized and their religious practices have diminished. The more orthodox responses to the items on religious beliefs declined about *18* to *22* percentage points. For a nineteen-year period this is considerable change.

Other research indicates that a high point of religious orthodoxy and commitment among college students occurred sometime in the early 1950s.[9] The 1948 to 1967 changes are probably similar to or smaller than changes from about 1952–55 to 1967. The rapid decline in traditional religious commitment during the late 1950s and early 1960s probably accounts for much of the discussion of "secularization" recently.

This research has been more successful in eliminating possible explanations for the change than in putting forth convincing explanations. Changes in college culture are not responsible for the religious changes, since the latter exist among freshmen as well as seniors. Changing back-

[9]This was shown at Haverford College (see footnote 8) and also in the study by Lazarsfeld and Thielens (1958).

grounds of students admitted to Williams College account for only about *1* to *3* percentage points of the changes.

The Herberg "third generation" hypothesis is not supported by these data, nor is an explanation based on urbanization trends. The upgrading of admission standards at Williams College remains a possible explanation for some of the changes. The strength of this explanation is unknown, but the weak correlations between college board scores and religious attitudes at other colleges suggest that it is at best a partial explanation. Greater individualism and autonomy of students, as shown by the greater number reacting to religious beliefs taught them, is another likely explanation, since other research shows an association between individual autonomy and liberal religious orientation. Also we found an association between religious orthodoxy and closeness to parents.

Economic explanations seem difficult to support. What economic indicator plausibly related to personal religious commitments rose from about 1940 to the early 1950s, then fell from the late 1950s to 1967?

Since the change at Williams College generally agrees with change among better educated and more affluent young people in the national population (cf. Marty *et al.,* 1968), the main explanations are probably broad and general rather than specific and local. Since the trends over two decades are not the same as over four decades, the explanations must be related to phenomena of the last decade or two.

A relationship probably exists between this lessening of religious commitment and the increasing protest activity among students. The early 1950s were the time of the "silent generation" and also the high point of traditional religious attitudes. Since then students have increased their political action commitments and lessened their commitments to traditional religion (for more data cf. Hoge, 1969). Also since the middle 1950s anxieties about communism and internal subversion have subsided in upper-middle class America. A plausible hypothesis is that the trends toward greater religious orthodoxy among college students in the 1940s and early 1950s were a product of the same social forces producing the "silent generation." Since then, opposite forces have become dominant. This hypothesis is supported by the history of American student political activism which shows great activity in the middle 1930s and after the middle 1960s but almost none in the early 1950s (cf. Lipset, 1966)—a curve exactly the inverse of the traditional religious commitments curve. Furthermore, studies of student activists have generally found that the activists are not traditionally religious but hold intense political commitments (cf. Flacks, 1967).

Such an explanation would point to world and national events such as the decline of the Cold War, the Kennedy years, and others, which seemed to encourage greater political involvement and commitment among students throughout the late 1950s and early 1960s. The decline of the Cold War perhaps also encouraged a liberalization of traditional religious commitments. Such an explanation might prove powerful in explaining some of the shifts from traditional religious commitments to political commitments up until 1967. It would not help us understand if the total amount of commitments outside the most personal and "privatistic" changed during that time. Probably traditional religious commitments are associated with privatism, and both declined after the middle 1950s. This form of explanation would need refinement to handle some of the most recent social withdrawal tendencies seen in hippie and cultic groups. Our present research cannot speak to these topics, but they deserve careful study, for they may provide us a greater understanding of college students today.

References

Allport, G. S.; Gillespie, J. M.; and Young, J. "The Religion of the Post-War College Student." *Journal of Psychology* 25 (January 1948):3–33.

Argyle, M. *Religious Behaviour.* London: Routledge & Kegan Paul, 1958.

Bender, I. E. "Changes in Religious Interest: A Retest After 15 Years." *Journal of Abnormal and Social Psychology* 57 (July 1958):41–46.

Dudycha, G. J. "The Religious Beliefs of College Freshmen in 1930 and 1949." *Religious Education* 45 (May–June 1950):165–69.

Feldman, K. A., and Newcomb, T. M. *The Impact of College on Students.* San Francisco: Jossey-Bass, 1969.

Flacks, R. "The Liberated Generation: An Exploration of the Roots of Student Protest." *Journal of Social Issues* 23 (July 1967):52–75.

Gilliland, A. R. "Changes in Religious Beliefs of College Students." *Journal of Social Psychology* 37 (February 1953):113–16.

Greeley, A. M. "There's a New-Time Religion on Campus." *The New York Times Magazine* (June 1, 1969):14–28.

Hastings, P. K. "Religious Attitudes Among Post-War College Students, Williams College, 1948." Unpublished paper, 1948.

Heath, D. H. *Growing Up in College: Liberal Education and Maturity.* San Francisco: Jossey-Bass, 1969a.

———. "Secularization and Maturity of Religious Beliefs." *Religion and* Health 8 (October 1969b):335–58.

Herberg, W. *Protestant–Catholic–Jew.* New York: Doubleday, 1960.

Hoge, D. R. "College Students' Religion: A Study of Trends in Attitudes and Behavior." Vol. 1. Unpublished Ph.D. dissertation, Harvard University, 1969.

Lazarsfeld, P. F., and Thielens, W. *The Academic Mind.* Glencoe, Ill.: Free Press, 1958.

Lazerwitz, B., and Rowitz, L. "The Three Generations Hypothesis." *American Journal of Sociology* 69 (March 1964):529–38.

Lehman, E. C., Jr., and Shriver, D. W., Jr. "Academic Discipline as Predictive of Faculty Religiosity." *Social Forces* 47 (December 1968):171–82.

Leuba, J. H. "Religious Beliefs of American Scientists." *Harper's Monthly Magazine* 169 (August 1934):292–300.

Lipset, S. M. "Student Opposition in the United States." *Government and Opposition* 1 (April 1966):351–74.

Marty, M. E.; Rosenberg, S. E.; and Greeley, A. M. *What Do We Believe?* New York: Meredith Press, 1968.

Stark, R. "On the Incompatibility of Religion and Science: A Survey of American Graduate Students." *Journal for the Scientific Study of Religion* 3 (Fall 1963):3–20.

Stark, R., and Glock, C. Y. *American Piety.* Berkeley: University of California Press, 1968.

Tanner, J. M. *Growth at Adolescence,* 2nd ed. Oxford: Blackwell, 1962.

Young, R. K.; Dustin, D. S.; and Holtzman, W. H. "Change in Attitude Toward Religion in a Southern University." *Psychological Reports* 18 (February 1966):39–46.

9 Youth and Politics

Politics is the study of power. When societies undergo rapid rearrangements in other spheres, the political order is subject to parallel changes. In this context, the flow, creation, and consequences of power are of great interest to our discussion. We are now in a period of great flux, and students are interested and involved in the processes of change, especially as they affect politics. Student interest in politics, marked early in the sixties by their involvement in the civil rights movement, has now become institutionalized in some schools. In the fall of 1970, many universities adopted the Princeton plan, to allow students free time for campaigning during the two weeks prior to the November elections. The level of interest and participation was high, and many signs indicate increased involvement.

Many people ask what is the basis for this new participation and involvement, and for the apparent increase in radical ideologies. Richard Flacks, in the first selection, presents a careful analysis of the student movement and some possible future trends. Flacks, himself one of the founders of SDS while a student at the University of Michigan, did important early research on the attitudes and values of the families of members of the SDS and also studied the members themselves. Flacks found no evidence of what the mass media insists on calling the "generation gap." Rather, he found a continuity between the middle-class, educated, humanistic values of the parents and their children. Citing his research and more recent evidence, Flacks argues that major change is occurring now in American society, and that it is likely to continue. The young, products of rapid technological change, mobility, growth in numbers, and disillusionment created by the events of the late sixties, are seen as harbingers of further change.

Flacks argues that the values of the children of the middle classes will form the basis of a new socially conscious white-collar, service-oriented stratum in American society. They will value self-expression, autonomy, and idealism, but reject nationalism, materialism, and acquisitiveness. Flacks feels that other explanations of the student movement, which describe it as a "romantic last gasp" or merely as a transitional phenomenon, underestimate the degree of commitment of the young to these values. He points out that the political environment is critical—further wars such as the Vietnam conflict, increased racial turmoil, and the like are certain to increase and stimulate further youth activity.

Other selections in this section attempt to broaden the study of student politics and movements, with a wide variety of evidence to explain the extensiveness of changes in values, specific social settings, and institutions that affect political activity. It is important that this work attempts to broaden the study of student politics from exclusive concern with psycho-social issues of identity and personality.

Kahn and Bowers, in a United States student sample, found an important effect of social context (university or university department) on the political values of students. For example, if a person with a given personality enters an excellent university, he will be more likely to become an activist than if he enters a lesser university. Within the same universities, the same student will be more likely to become an activist if he enters social science than if he majors in engineering (the probability that a person actually might initially consider these two very different possibilities is not high).

The survey approach used by Kahn and Bowers and Braungart is particularly appropriate because it allows an examination of some of the very sensitive and insightful explanations advanced by Keniston on the basis of a very small sample of elite students at Harvard. Other studies, such as those done by Flacks at the University of Chicago and by Heist at Berkeley, support some of Keniston's ideas. Interviews and psychological testing by Braungart, on the other hand, surveyed students at ten universities, both public and private (see his footnote 2 for a complete list), and sought to test the thesis that radicals are more alienated from their parents than other groups, and that among radical males, more identify with their mothers than with their fathers. The mother, according to Keniston's work, was the source of nurturance and creative, expressive values, whereas the father was disliked among the radicals and had little influence among the culturally disaffected. Braungart did not find this pattern: all the members of SDS were more alienated from *both* parents than were members of other organizations in his sample. Males did not identify more with mother than father. A notable aspect of Braungart's research is his use of "control" or comparison groups covering a range of political values from right to left, that is, Young Americans for Freedom, Young Republicans, uninvolved college students, Young Democrats, and SDS. This research strategy allows comparisons of youths sharing many characteristics, and allows statistical controls to infer which values and attitudes are distinctive of given groups, which are common among all, and which are not shared by any groups.

It is difficult to evaluate some aspects of Braungart's work. We do not know from his paper what it is that creates or underlies the distance or alienation between parent and child—is it politics, immorality, or differences in other social values? Can we make predictions such as those advanced by Flacks from this study? We are not told by any of these studies about the other significant commitments of students (for example, work, romance and marriage, "success"); nor do we know how important students' politics are relative to their future plans. Will today's SDS member be tomorrow's IBM programmer?

Orum and Orum's study of black student involvement in politics tested several models of explanation for political participation: the vulgar Marxian model (class struggle is endemic to capitalistic society, but does not deterministically lead to revolution), the rising expectations model (people tend to revolt when events have taken an upswing), and the relative deprivation model (people who feel deprived of political power relative to a significant comparison group will tend to revolt). Their research does not establish a clear case for any of the three general explanations. What implications does this have for relationships between white and black political movements, especially for the future coalescence of white and black radical groups?

*Social and Cultural Meanings of Student Revolt: Some Informal Comparative Observations**

Richard Flacks

I

The phenomenon of student rebellion has in the past few years come to appear international in scope. During this period, student demonstrations and strikes have paralyzed universities and shaken the political systems in societies as far apart, culturally and geographically, as Japan and France, Mexico and West Germany, Italy and Brazil, Czechoslovakia and the United States.

The simultaneity of these outbursts and the similarities in style and tactics of the student movements have led many observers to assume that there is a world-wide revolt of the youth, which is new historically, and which derives from a single set of causes.

It is obvious, however, that student movements, acting in opposition to established authority, are not at all new. For example, student revolu-

Reprinted by permission of the author and the publisher, The Society for the Study of Social Problems, from *Social Problems* 17 (Winter 1970):340–57.

*Paper prepared for presentation at meetings of American Association for the Advancement of Science, Dallas, Texas, December 1968.

tionary activity was a constant feature of Russian life during the 19th century. It played a major role in the revolution of 1848 in Central Europe. The communist movements in China and Vietnam grew out of militant student movements in those countries. In Latin America, student movements have been politically crucial since the early part of this century. Youth and student movements were a dramatic feature of life in pre–World War I Germany; the Zionist movement among European Jews had its roots in the German youth movement. Since World War II, student movements have helped bring down regimes in Asia and Latin America. It is clear that the events of recent months are in certain respects merely further expressions of a long tradition of student rebelliousness (cf. Altbach, 1967, for an overview of this tradition).

But just as it would be a mistake to think that the student revolts are historically new, it would also be an error to uphold the conventional wisdom which asserts that youth are "naturally" rebellious, or idealistic. There are, of course, good reasons for believing that some segments of the youth are likely to be particularly disposed to revolt, particularly attracted to new ideas, particularly prepared to take direct action in behalf of their ideals. But it is by no means true that rebellious, experimental, or idealistic behavior is a general characteristic of young people—indeed, it is probably the case that in any historical period the majority of the young, as Bennett Berger has remarked, are not "youthful." Moreover, it is even less true that youthful impulses in support of radical change inevitably take the form of distinct, autonomous political movements against the established political system. For instance, such movements have been quite rare in the U.S. and other advanced Western countries until the present decade. Although significant minorities of students and other young people have been active participants in movements for social change in the U.S., Britain, France, and the smaller capitalist democracies, these societies have not had movements created by and for youth, independent of adult organizations, containing a strong element of rebellion not only against injustice but against the authority of the older generation. The feeling that there is something new about generational revolt is not accurate in global terms; but it is substantially correct for societies like our own.

There is a need for a theoretical framework to account for the emergence of oppositional movements among youth—a framework which can embrace the fact that such movements have become a feature, not only of developing pre-industrial societies, but of apparently stable advanced industrial nations as well. In searching for such a framework, two classical theoretical perspectives might be expected to provide some help. One would be Marxian theory, which, after all, was created in an effort to account for the rise of revolutionary movements in contemporary society. But Marxism, since it emphasizes the role of classes are revolutionary agencies, has a difficult time assimilating student revolutionary action. First, students do not themselves constitute a class. Second, students do occupy class positions, but these are typically privileged ones. Indeed, one fact about the American student movement is that participation in it tends to be associated with high family status and income (Westby and Braungart, 1966; Flacks, 1970), and the same pattern may be found in other countries as well. Thus, a problem for Marxian theory of revolution would be to account for the mass defection of students from their families' class, and for the tendency of privileged youth to identify with the plight of the dispossessed in their society. This is particularly problematical in the advanced industrial societies: here we have a situation in which at the present time organized political and cultural opposition to capitalism appears to be more extensive and militant among students than among workers. There is no straightforward way to derive this fact from the body of Marxian theory.

A second theoretical perspective which one might find useful is that of Parsons. Indeed, one of the few theories about the conditions giving rise to generational conflict is that of Eisenstadt (1956) whose perspective flows directly from Parsons (cf. Parsons, 1962, for a recent formulation).

This perspective focusses less on the revolutionary thrust of student and youth movements than on their functional character. What is most salient to Parsons and Eisenstadt is the formation of distinctive groups or movements among persons at the same stage in the life-cycle. The appearance of such groupings among youth is seen as a consequence of the differentiation of the family from the occupational structure, resulting in a sharp discontinuity between the values and role-expectations operative within the family and those prevailing in the larger society. As youth move out of the family and experience such discontinuities, major problems of socialization are created by the necessity for them to successfully orient toward occupational roles. Such problems are not manageable within the family, nor within the institutions of formal schooling. What is needed are institutions which can combine some of the features of family life with those of the occupational structure. Youth groups, youth cultures, and youth movements serve this function of aiding the transition to adulthood by combining relations of diffuse solidarity with universalistc values.

This perspective predicts that the sharper the disjunction between family values and those in the larger society, the more distinctive and oppositional will be the youth culture. In particular, one would expect that students in societies undergoing a rapid breakdown of traditional authority, and in which new bases of legitimation had not yet been established, would most acutely experience problems of achieving adult status and would be most likely to form autonomous, oppositional movements. By the same token, young people in the advanced, stable, industrial, democratic societies, although experiencing marked discontinuity between familial and occupational roles, would not experience the same intense cultural dislocation found in developing countries. For, although familial and occupational roles are disjunctive in advanced industrial countries, families in these societies tend to be congruent in their values and expectations with other institutions. Thus, the industrialized societies would exhibit distinctive youth cultures, but these implicitly support other socializing agencies in identity formation and orientation toward adulthood. In short, the Parsons–Eisenstadt perspective leads us to expect student movements in societies where traditional authority is disintegrating under the impact of industrialization, Western ideas, and modernizing trends, and where families continue to adhere to traditional culture. Depicting industrial societies as ones in which both parental and political authority support modernity and change, this perspective leads us to expect a distinctive youth culture, but not an "alienated" oppositional, revolutionary one in societies like our own (Eisenstadt, 1956; Parsons, 1962).

As I have suggested, this perspective was a viable one—until this decade. Now each passing year makes it less and less easy to assume the stability of the developed Western societies, less and less safe to adopt the view that the U.S. represents some culmination point in cultural development, or that there is a fundamental congruence among socializing, political and economic institutions and the values which prevail within them in our society.

A comparative perspective on student movements and generational revolt leads us to seek a theoretical framework which transcends the Marxian view of the sources of revolutionary impulse in capitalist society, and the Parsonian view that such impulses are not characteristic of advanced industrial society. If such a framework existed it would undoubtedly constitute a synthesis of Eisenstadt's insight that student movements are a symptom of cultural disintegration and the Marxian insight that capitalism and its culture are themselves unstable and capable of being negated.

II

If recent events lead us to discard the view that student movements are characteristic only of societies in which traditional culture and authority are breaking down, we nevertheless ought to be able to specify why such movements have been endemic under such conditions. The Parsons–Eisenstadt hypothesis provides us with at least a partial answer: the university student in an agrarian society is someone who is compelled to abandon the values with which he was raised, who is exposed to a set of new cultural influences, but who is becoming an adult in an historical period in which the new values have not been clarified, new roles have not been created, new authority has not been established or legitimated. The student movement, with its diffuse, fraternal interpersonal life, its identification with the masses of the people, its disdain for privilege and authority—combined with a commitment to rationalism, democracy, nationalism and other "modern" values—enables them to develop the political skills and motives which may be necessary to challenge the established elites, enables them to undergo the personal transition which is an aspect of the historical transition through which the whole society is going.

In addition to this hypothesis, which locates the sources of "strain" in the cultural and psychological consequences of modernization, there are additional and equally powerful factors at work in such societies which make such movements extremely likely. (A summary of such factors appears in Lipset, 1968.)

There is, for example, the widely remarked fact that typically in developing countries there is an "overproduction" of educated youth—the available jobs for university graduates often are not commensurate with the training or aspirations they have as a result of their educational attainment. Prospective or actual unemployment, and the frustration of aspiration, is presumably a politicizing experience for many educated youth in such societies.

Another politicizing and radicalizing feature of these societies is the backwardness and authoritarianism of political authority. Political authority in these societies plays a paradoxical role for students; on the one hand, it sponsors the formation and expansion of a university system in order to promote technical progress, while simultaneously it resists the political, social, and cultural transformations which such progress requires. In this situation, students inevitably come into conflict with the state and other established elite institutions. The more intransigent the established elites are with respect to nationalist, democratic, and modernizing aspirations, the more likely it is that the student movement becomes the breeding ground for a "counter-elite" and the spearhead of revolutionary politics (Ben-David and Collins, 1967).

Still another factor likely to generate discontent is the quality of life in the universities of these societies. Living and working conditions are likely to be extremely impoverished. The schools are likely to be overflowing; the quality of instruction and facilities for study are likely to be totally inadequate; and material poverty among students is likely to be substantial.

If cultural disintegration, overproduction of the educated, reactionary regimes, and university conditions generate discontent leading to politicization and radicalism, additional factors promote the emergence and growth of autonomous student movements in developing nations. For example, the autonomous character of student movements in these countries is facilitated by the absence of other oppositional forces. To the extent that peasants, workers and other strata are poorly organized or passive or suppressed, students, with their high degree of interaction and their sophistication may become the only group in a society capable of initiating oppositional activity. Moreover, students may have a degree of freedom for political action which is not available to other opposition forces. This freedom may in part be due to the fact that many student activists are the offspring of elite or upper status families, in part because of the recognition of the fact that students are indispensable to the future of the society, in part because of an established tradition of university autonomy which makes it illegitimate for police power to invade the campus. Given the relative leniency toward students and the ambivalence of authorities toward them, instances of repressive action taken against students are likely to be especially discrediting to the regime. Thus, the weakness of other oppositional forces, the wide opportunities for intensive interaction available to students, the large numbers of students likely to be concentrated in particular locales, and the special freedom for political expression which they are likely to have all combine to foster the growth of a student movement as an independent oppositional movement.

The conditions we have been describing may be regarded as the "classic" pattern presaging the emergence of students as a revolutionary force. Put another way, these conditions help us understand why student oppositional movements have been a regular feature of developing societies.

III

Our analysis has suggested that the classical student movement is a symptom of marked cultural incoherence, of political stagnation, and of severe problems of identity for educated youth in the face of the social and technological changes associated with the process of "modernization." Because this analysis emphasizes that student movements are an aspect of the modernization process, it appears to be quite inadequate for accounting for the rise of student movements in societies like our own, which are not agrarian, which are not dominated by traditional culture and authority, which are not struggling to achieve national identity and independence, where democratic, rationalistic and egalitarian values prevail, where families orient their offspring toward active achievement in a technological society, where the freedom to organize political opposition is available and used. At least at first glance one would be led to believe that the advanced industrial capitalist societies of the West would provide the least hospitable soil for a revolt of educated youth.

Yet a student movement has grown up over the past decade in American society. Over these years, it has become increasingly radicalized, and indeed now includes an avowedly revolutionary wing. Like the classical movements, it contains a strong component of generational revolt—that is, of implicit and explicit hostility to the authority of older generations, and an emphasis on the moral superiority of the young as such and on their capacity to be an agency of social transformation. Like the classical movements, the student movements of the West are intensely anti-authoritarian, egalitarian, and populist. They also resemble the classical type in being completely independent of other, "adult" political groups.

Are there any ways to comprehend the appearance of such a movement in American society that will account for its comparability with classical student movements?

The most parsimonious hypothesis, perhaps, would focus on possible similarities between the immediate situation of the student in the advanced industrial societies and in the developing countries. For example, it seems plausible that the rapid expansion of higher education and the great influx of young people to the universities has led to a devolution in the quality of educational institutions and of student life in the U.S. and Western Europe. It is also plausible that the rapid growth in the numbers of educated youth has produced the same kind of sectional unemployment of the educated which is present in the developing nations.

There may be considerable validity to these hypotheses, indeed, much of the commentary on the present student revolt has emphasized these factors as crucial ones. But it is much harder to see how they can be applied to the American case. For instance, data on the distribution of student protest on American campuses quite clearly show that the student movement had its origins at the highest quality state universities and prestigious private universities and colleges, that the movement continues to have its widest following on such campuses, and that it has only recently spread to schools of lower prestige and quality (Peterson, 1966; 1968). There is, in short, a negative correlation between the quality of an institution and the proportion of its student body which is activist, and between the selectivity of an institution and the radicalism of its student body.

It is equally hard to make a case that the student movement in the U.S. originates in overproduction of educated youth. In the first place, there is no dearth of opportunity for college graduates. Still, one might hypothesize that students who are attracted to the movement experience "relative deprivation"—for example, they may be students who cannot hold their own in academic competition. However, the data on student protesters indicate otherwise, there is, in fact, a tendency for activists to have above average academic records in high school and college, and most of the several studies on student protesters indicate they include a disproportionate underrepresentation of students with poor academic records (Flacks, 1967; 1970). Student protesters come from families with high income and occupational status; they tend to be most prevalent at the top schools; they have above average aptitude for academic work, and perform at above average levels. If there is an overproduction of educated youth in this society at this time, it is hard to see how this would affect the structure of opportunities available to the academic elite from which activists tend to be recruited.

It seems clear that any effort to explain the rise of a student movement in the U.S. must take account of the fact that the movement originated among highly advantaged students, that it did not begin as a revolt against the university, and that its active core contains many students whose aptitudes, interests, values, and origins suggest a strong orientation to intellectual and academic life.

Indeed, one of the most striking findings about American activists has to do with their intellectualism. I refer here not only to the variety of studies which find activists exhibiting intellectual interests and achievements superior to those of the student body as a whole. More persuasive and more sociologically relevant are findings concerning the socioeconomic backgrounds of participants in protest activity. These findings may be briefly summarized as follows: activists are disproportionately the sons and daughters of highly educated parents; in a large proportion of cases, their parents have advanced graduate and professional degrees; a very high percentage of activists' mothers are college graduates; the parents tend to be in occupations for which higher education is a central prerequisite: professions, education, social service, public service, the arts; both businessmen and blue and white collar workers tend to be underrepresented among the parents of activists; family interests—as they are expressed in recreation, or in dinner-table conversation, or in formal interviews—tend to be intellectual and "cultural" and relatively highbrow; these are families in which books were read, discussed, and taken seriously, in which family outings involved museums and concert-halls rather than ball-parks and movies, etc. They were families in which "values" were taken seriously—conventional religion and morality were treated with considerable skepticism, while at the same time strong emphasis was placed on leading a principled, socially useful, morally consistent life. They were, finally, families in which education was regarded with considerable reverence and valued for its own sake, rather than in utilitarian terms.

In short, the student movement originated among those young people who came out of what might be called the "intellectual" or "humanist" subculture of the middle class. In the last two years, it has become considerably more heterogeneous, but it was created almost exclusively by offspring of that particular stratum. (A more detailed review of these findings appears in Flacks, 1970.)

At first glance, it would seem that nothing could be more incomparable than the situation of these middle class American youth and the situation of educated youth in underdeveloped countries. The former, as we have said, can look forward to an array of high status occupational opportunities. Their lives as students are well-subsidized, comfortable, and intellectually rich. Their parents are highly "modern" people, playing central cultural roles, well-informed about and sympathetic with the latest cultural developments. All of this is especially true in comparison with the position of educated youth in developing countries, whose futures are extremely uncertain, whose lives as students are likely to be meager and oppressive, whose families are likely to be locked into traditional ways and attitudes and stand as positive hindrances to the emancipation of their children.

These contrasts are striking, but they may be quite superficial. What I want to do is to restate some of the major factors which we have seen to be central in accounting for the appearance of classical student movements—and try to determine whether comparable factors are at work in American society, especially in relation to the situation of students who come out of the educated middle class.

1. We have said, after Eisenstadt, that a central determinant of the appearance of youth and student movements is sharp discontinuity between values embodied in the family and those emerging in other institutional contexts. From this perspective, as we have suggested, the student movement serves as a "secondary institution"—a way of re-establishing family-like solidarity to ease the achievement of independent adult identities and role-orientations. For youth in developing countries, discontinuity arises because of the fundamental conflict between the traditional orientation of the family and the modernizing orientations encountered in the university and the cosmopolitan community associated with it.

This kind of discontinuity could not be one experienced by the offspring of the educated middle class in America—if anything, students from this stratum are likely to experience less disjunction between familial and university values than any other groups of students. But there are grounds for feeling that humanist youth in America do experience a kind of discontinuity between family and larger society that may have comparable implications for the establishment of identity.

Our studies (cf. Flacks, 1967) of the parents of student activists show that these parents differ from others in the middle class in the following respects:

First, as mentioned above, there is a strong commitment to intellectuality and "culture" and a considerable disdain for mass culture and mass leisure. Their children were expected to be intellectually aware and serious, artistically creative or at least appreciative, serious about education and self-development.

Second, these parents were unusual in their political awareness and their political liberalism. Although they were not necessarily politically active, they tended to stress to their children the necessity for social responsibility and service, and active citizenship, and encouraged their children to support racial equality, civil liberties, and other liberal political goals. In this respect, these families were likely to see themselves, correctly, as different from the vast majority of politically passive or conservative families in their community.

Third, these parents were overtly skeptical about conventional middle-class values, life-styles, and religious orientations. Most of these parents were explicitly secular; those who were actively religious tended to belong to particularly liberal religious denominations or to have a strong social gospel kind of religious commitment. Many of these parents were articulate critics of conventional middle-class mores—by which, in particular, they had in mind sexual repressiveness, materialism, status-striving, and strict methods of rearing children. Many were quite explicit in hoping that their children would be more successful than they had been in leading self-fulfilling, socially responsible lives rather than participating in the "rat race," the "suburban way of life," the "commercial world."

Finally, these parents tended to express these values implicitly through the structure of the family and the styles of child rearing which they adopted. These were parents who encouraged "self-expressive" and "independent" behavior in their children, who interacted with each other and with their children in relatively "democratic" ways, who refused to impose conventional stereotypes of masculine and feminine conduct on their children (e.g., they tended to foster aesthetic and intellectual interests in their boys and assertive behavior on the part of their girls). It was not that these parents were unusually "permissive" or over-indulgent—for instance, their very explicit expectations about intellectuality and social responsibility indicate that they did not adopt a "laissez-faire" attitude toward their children. But they rather consciously organized family life to support anti-authoritarian and self-assertive impulses on the part of their children and rather clearly instructed them in attitudes favoring skepticism toward authority, egalitarianism and personal autonomy (Flacks, 1967, 1970; Keniston, 1968b).

Now what happens when these intellectual, anti-authoritarian, socially conscious, somewhat unconventional children move on to school and street and peer group? I think it is clear that they are likely to experience a considerable discontinuity between the values they encounter in these settings and the values with which they were raised. They are likely to find authority in school to be petty, arbitrary, repressive. They are likely to feel considerable isolation from the conventional culture of their peers. They are likely to be particularly sensitive to the hypocrisies, rigidities, and injustices of particular institutions and of the society as a whole as they experience it.

Most American youth experience some dislocation as they move from their families into the larger society, if for no other reason than that the rapidity of social change prevents any family from adequately preparing its offspring for the world as it actually is developing, and because proper, moral behavior for children in the American family is inescapably different from proper, moral behavior in the competitive, impersonal society beyond. The existing primary and secondary institutions—school and youth culture—which Parsons and others have expected to be serviceable in easing the transition to adulthood, have failed to incorporate humanist youth, who were in fact raised to question many of the fundamental premises of these institutions. As more and more such youth have entered upon the scene, they have tended to find each other and to create a kind of counter-culture, much as black urban youth, similarly unincorporated, have created theirs. This new humanist youth culture embodies norms concerning sex-role behavior, worthwhile activity, and personal style which are quite opposed to those which prevail in conventional adolescent society; it expresses values which seem quite subversive of conventional middle-class aspirations, and an attitude toward adult authority which is quite clearly defiant. The American student movement is an expression of that new youth culture, although by no means the only one.

In a peculiar sense, then, the appearance of a student movement and a rebellious youth culture in American society in recent years supports the Eisenstadt hypothesis that such phenomena are rooted in sharp discontinuities between family values and values in the larger society. It is a peculiar kind of support for that hypothesis because, unlike the classical case, the discontinuities we refer to do not have to do with incongruence between a traditional family and a modernizing culture. If anything, the reverse may be the case.

2. As we have suggested, a second major factor contributing to the rise of classical student movements has been the "overproduction" of educated youth—a factor which appears to be largely absent in the American situation. Nevertheless, there are severe problems for humanist youth with respect to vocation. These problems have to do, not with the scarcity of opportunity, but with the irrelevance of the opportunities which do exist. One of the most characteristic attributes of students in the movement (and an attribute which they share with a large number of apolitical students) is their inability to decide on a career or a vocation. This indecision is less the result of the wide range of choices available, than of the unsatisfactory

quality of those choices. What is repellent about the existing opportunities is not their incompatibility with the status or financial aspirations of these youth—but that they are incompatible with their ideals. Business careers are rejected outright as acquisitive, self-seeking, and directly linked to that which is defined as most corrupting in American society. Careers in government or conventional politics are regarded as either self-deluding or "selling out." Professional careers—particularly such established professions as law and medicine—are attractive to some, but only if one can become a doctor or lawyer outside of the conventional career lines; otherwise such careers are regarded as just as acquisitive as business. Teachers and social workers are seen as agents of social control; a few are attracted to scholarship or science, but with profound anxiety. To take an ordinary job is to give up any chance for leading a free life. In general, embarking on a career within the established occupational structure is regarded as morally compromising because it leads to complicity with established interests or because it requires abandoning personal autonomy or because it draws one away from full commitment to radicalism or because it signifies acceptance of the norms and standards of bourgeois society or because it means risking corruption because of material comfort and security.

Although some of these attitudes are undoubtedly the result of participation in the movement rather than a determinant of such participation, it is clear that an underlying revulsion with conventional adult roles and established, institutionalized careers predates movement involvement for many students. One reason for believing that it does is the fact that such revulsion is observable among young people who do not become political activists; indeed, a widespread restlessness about becoming committed to conventional careers and life-styles is evident on the American campus. This has been particularly surprising for those of us who remember the decade of the Fifties and the prevailing feeling of that era—namely, that affluence was producing a generation which would be particularly conformist, complacent, status-conscious, and bourgeois.

It now appears that the opposite may be equally true. Although people with high status and material security may typically be motivated to maintain their position, it is also the case that being born into affluence can foster impulses to be experimental, risk-taking, open to immediate experience, unrepressed. For some at least, growing up with economic security in families of secure status can mean a weakening of the normal incentives of the system and can render one relatively immune to the established means of social control, especially if one's parents rather explicitly express skepticism about the moral worth of material success. Post-war affluence in our society then has had the effect of liberating a considerable number of young people from anxieties about social mobility and security, and enabled them to take seriously the quest for other values and experiences. To such youth, established careers and adult roles are bound to be unsatisfying. What is the sense, after all, of binding oneself to a large organization, of submitting to the rituals, routines and disciplines of careerism, of postponing or foregoing a wide range of possible experience—when there is little chance of surpassing one's father, when the major outcome of such efforts is to acquire goods which one has already had one's fill of, when such efforts mean that one must compromise one's most cherished ideals?

In newly-industrializing societies, students become revolutionaries, or bohemians, or free intellectuals and artists, because established careers commensurate with their education had not been created. In our society, large numbers of students do the same, not because opportunities for conventional achievement are absent but because they are personally meaningless and morally repugnant. We began with the proposition that a blockage of economic opportunity for the educated is a determinant of student movements. Our comparative analysis leads us to a reformulation of this proposition—any condition which leads to a weakening of motivation for upward mobility increases the likelihood of student rebellion—such conditions can include either blocked opportunity *or* high levels of material security. In short when numbers of youth find occupational decisions extremely difficult to make, their propensity for collective rebellion is likely to increase.

3. What we have so far been discussing may be described as a kind of cultural crisis—the emergence of a sector of the youth population which finds its fundamental values, aspirations, and character structure in sharp conflict with the values and practices which prevail in the larger society. We have said that, in certain respects, this conflict is similar to that experienced by youth in societies undergoing rapid transition from traditional to "modern" culture; and in both cases, we find these youth responding to their crisis by banding together in movements of opposition to the older generations and attempting to generate what amounts to a counter-culture.

In some ways, this kind of crisis is not new in American society. For more than a century, at least, small groups of intellectuals have expressed their revulsion with industrial capitalism, and the commercialism, philistinism, and acquisitiveness they saw as its outcome. By the turn of the century, what had largely been an expression of genteel criticism was supplanted by a more vigorous and intense revolt by some educated youth—expressed through bohemianism and through a variety of political and social reform movements. Indeed, opposition to Victorian morality and business culture has been characteristic of American intellectuals in this century (Hofstadter, 1966); and the emergence of large numbers of humanist youth out of relatively intellectual families is an indication of the impact this opposition has had on the society. What was once the protest of tiny pockets of intellectuals and artists has become a mass phenomenon, in part because the ideas of these earlier critics and reformers were taken up in the universities and became part of the world-view of many members of the educated middle class. These ideas influenced not only sentiments regarding commercialism, material success and intellectuality, they also had a direct bearing on the treatment of women and the raising of children, since an important element of anti-bourgeois thinking had to do with the emancipation of women and the liberation of the child from repressive and stultifying disciplines.

What is new in this decade is, first of all, the degree to which this cultural alienation has become a mass phenomenon—an extensive, rooted subculture on the campus and in major cities, with a wide and steadily growing following. Equally important, the present movement is new in the degree to which it has expressed itself through political opposition—an opposition which has become increasingly revolutionary, in the sense that it has increasingly come to reject the legitimacy of established authority and of the political system itself.

As we have previously pointed out, political rebellion by students in other countries has largely been a response to authoritarian, reactionary regimes—regimes which were incapable of or unwilling to adapt to pressures for modernization, and which tended to meet such pressures by attempting to repress them. Thus, classical student movements tend to arise out of the cultural crisis created by the processes of modernization, and tend to go into active political opposition when the political system stands against those processes.

It is perhaps hard for American social scientists to understand why American students should undergo a similar reaction to the American political system. After all, many of them have spent years demonstrating that the system was pluralist, democratic, egalitarian, and highly flexible; thus, while it may be rational for Russian, Chinese, or Latin-American students to have become revolutionary in the face of tsars, war-lords, and dictators, it is, for them, irrational for students in the U.S. and other Western countries to adopt revolutionary stances against liberal, democratic regimes. (For one example cf. Glazer, 1968.)

To understand why the cultural alienation of intellectual youth in America has become politicized and radicalized requires an historical analysis—the details of which are beyond the scope of this paper. Without attempting such an analysis we can, I think, at least point to some of the most relevant factors.

The first point would be that culturally alienated intellectuals in America have not historically been revolutionary. They have, instead, either been anti-political or have placed their hopes in a variety of progressive, reform movements. In part they have been sustained by the view that the national political system, whatever its flaws, had progressive potential because of its democratic character. They have also been sustained by comparisons between the American system and the rest of the world.

During the New Deal and World War II period, a kind of culmination was reached in the formulation of an ideological perspective for the educated class in America. At the heart of this perspective was the view that inequality, injustice, and business culture could be controlled and offset by effective political and social action through the Federal government. The rise of labor as a political force, the passage of social legislation, and the subsidization of reform by the government would create the conditions for a just and humane society. Not incidentally, the expansion of the public sector would also create vast new vocational opportunities for educated people with humanitarian concerns—in education, in social service, in public health, mental health, child care, public planning, and all the rest. Thus the creation of the welfare state and an American version of social democracy was crucial for the expanded intelligentsia, not only because it provided a solution to the social ills that contributed to their alienation, but also because it offered a way to realize themselves vocationally outside of the business economy and in terms of their values. It is perhaps important to mention that it was in this ideological milieu that the parents of the present generation reached maturity.

In the past twenty years, however, two things have been happening simultaneously: on the one hand, the ranks of the educated middle class have greatly expanded, due in considerable degree to government support of higher education and of public sector types of occupations which required advanced education; on the other hand, the social benefits anticipated from this development have not been forthcoming—that is, liberal politics have not eradicated gross social inequality, have not improved the quality of public life, and perhaps above all have not created a pacific, internationalist global posture on the part of the American government. Instead, the educated middle-class person is likely to see his society as increasingly chaotic and deteriorating, to feel that enormous waste of material and human resources is taking place, and to believe that his nation is not a liberalizing force internationally, but perhaps the reverse.

The offspring of this stratum, as they began to throng the nation's universities in the early Sixties, entered political involvement at just the point where their parents had begun to experience disillusionment with progressive ideology. But the early phase of the student movement tended to continue traditional middle-class faith in the democratic process. The New Left, in its beginnings, rejected all received ideology; for fairly obvious reasons, it found neither social democracy, nor Marxism–Leninism, nor liberalism at all adequate foundations for renewing radical politics. Indeed, in an early age, many New Leftists would not have attempted to create a youth-based radicalism at all; they would instead have found their way into one or another established radical or reform movement. It is important to realize that the exhaustion of existing ideologies in post-war Europe and America meant that young people with radical impulses had to start afresh. The starting point in the U.S. was to take democratic ideals seriously; to try to make the system work, by participating in and catalyzing grass-roots protest against glaring injustice—particularly against segregation and the threat of nuclear holocaust. Such an outlook included a fairly explicit expectation that the creation of protest and ferment from below would provide an impetus for major change at the top—on the part of the Federal government (in behalf of the constitutional rights of Negroes, for example) and on the part of established agencies of reform such as the churches, the universities, the labor movement. Until about 1964, this political model seemed to be working to a considerable extent—civil rights laws were passed, the Kennedy Administration was moving toward detente with the Soviet Union, a war on poverty was declared, and a spirit of social renovation seemed to be taking hold in the society. In this situation, the SDS and other student radicals retained a considerable willingness to operate within the conventional political system; it is well to remember, for example, that in the election campaign of 1964, SDS adopted the slogan, "Part of the Way with LBJ."

The escalation of the war in Vietnam marked a turning point for radical students—it began a process of progressive disillusionment with the political system, a process which, for many, has culminated in a total rejection of its legitimacy. I cannot here recount in any adequate way the series of events which contributed to this process; but it is clear that the war itself was crucial to it, as was the use of the draft to prosecute that war and to "channel" young men educationally and occupationally, as was the failure of the war on poverty (a failure directly experienced by many young activists as they tried to work in poverty areas), as was the transformation of the black movement from a struggle for integration to a far more radical struggle for "liberation" and economic equality, as was the revelation that many universities actively contributed to the war effort and military research, as was the increasing use of the police to suppress protest demonstrations in the streets and on the campuses, as was the failure of the political parties to recognize their liberal, dovish constituencies. In short, for young people who identified with the cause of racial equality, who despised war and militarism, and who had hoped to construct lives based on humane, intellectual, and democratic ideals, by 1968 American society did seem largely reactionary, authoritarian, and repressive. (A more detailed review of this history appears in Skolnick, 1969: 87–105.)

This perception is heightened and reinforced by other, more fundamental beliefs. For example, it is very difficult to accept the amount of squalor, inequality, and misery in this society if one is aware of the fact that the society has the material resources to guarantee a decent private and public life to the whole population. It is very difficult to accept war and the arms race and the expansion of militarism when one is convinced that these institutions have the capacity to destroy the human race. And, finally, it is very difficult to maintain a calm long-run perspective, if one believes that the society has the capacity—in its technology, in its large-scale organizational structure, and in the character structure of millions of its members—to obliterate personal autonomy, individuality, and free expression. Many radical students, in other words, have a profound pessimism about the chances for democracy, personal freedom and peace (for an empirical demonstration of this pessimism, cf. Westby and Braungart, 1970); this pessimism, however, leads toward activism rather than withdrawal because many are convinced that the probable future is not a necessary one. The events of the past four or five years have overwhelmingly confirmed their sense of the main social drift, but what has sustained the impulse to act has been the rapid growth of resistance among many in their generation.

Briefly, then, our argument to this point has been something like the following: the expansion of higher education in our society has produced a social stratum which tends to rear its children with values and character structures which are at some variance with the dominant culture. Affluence and secure status further weaken the potency of conventional incentives and undermine motivations for upward mobility. The outcome of these processes is a new social type or subculture among American youth—humanist youth. Such youth are especially sensitized to injustice and authoritarianism, are repelled by acquisitive, militaristic, and nationalistic values, and strive for a vocational situation in which autonomy and self-expression can be maximized. They have been politicized and radicalized by their experiences in relation to the racial and international crises, and by the failure of established agencies of renewal and reform, including the universities, to alleviate these crises. They also sense the possibility that opportunities for autonomy and individuality may be drying up in advanced technological societies. One of the reasons that their political expression has taken generational form is that older ideologies of opposition to capitalism and authoritarianism have failed in practice.

We have also been saying that, although it is clear that the situation of these youth is enormously different from the situation of educated youth in underdeveloped countries, there are important analogies between the two. Both groups of youth confront the problem of discontinuity between family tradition and the values of the larger society. Both confront major problems of vocation and adult identity. Both confront political systems which are stagnated and repressive, and find few resources and allies external to themselves as they attempt to change that system.

There is a final issue in the comparative analysis of student movements that I want to raise. In our discussion of the classical movements, we suggested that the appearance of such movements was a clear sign that processes of fundamental social and cultural change were at work, and that these movements were not simply the result of certain pressures operating on a particular group of young people in a society but more importantly were indications that traditional, agrarian society was being transformed by processes of industrialization and modernization. It is clearly important to ask whether the appearance of student movements in advanced industrial societies are similarly signs that a new social and cultural era is struggling to emerge.

There are those who believe that the current crop of student revolutionaries is not the vanguard of a new social order, but rather, in the words of Daniel Bell, "the guttering last gasps of a romanticism soured by rancor and impotence" (Bell, 1968). In this view, student unrest in industrial societies is regarded as analogous to the protests of the first waves of industrial workers who resisted their uprooting by the machine. Now, it is argued, high-status intellectually and artistically inclined youth resist their incorporation into large-scale organizations—an incorporation which, nevertheless, is as inevitable as was the imposition of the factory on the rural lower classes.

Such a view does implicitly recognize that a major social transformation may be in the making. What I find objectionable in it is the implication that the new radicalism of the young is irrelevant to the nature of that transformation.

An alternative view would emphasize the possibility that large scale social, political, and cultural changes are occurring, that these are reflected in the social origins and focal concerns of student rebels, and that the existence of student rebellion may be a determining feature of this process of change.

First, at the cultural level, the student movement and the new alienated youth culture appear to reflect the erosion, if not the collapse, of what might be called the culture of capitalism—that cluster of values which Max Weber labelled the "Protestant Ethic"—a value system which was appropriate for the development of capitalism and the entrepreneurial spirit but which has lost its vitality under the impact of the bureaucratic organization of the economy, the decline of entrepreneurships, and the spread of affluence. The erosion of this culture is reflected in the transformation of family structure and child rearing practices, in the changing relations between the sexes, in the replacement of thrift with consumership as a virtue. As Schumpeter (1950) predicted many years ago, bourgeois culture could not survive the abundance it would generate. Thus, the cultural crisis experienced very sharply and personally by humanist youth really impinges on the whole society. It is a crisis because no coherent value system has emerged to replace what has deteriorated; but it is hard not to believe that the anti-authoritarian, experimental, unrepressed, and "romantic" style of the youth revolt does in fact represent the beginnings of the effort to create a workable new culture, rather than the "last gasps" of the old. Such a view gains support when one observes the degree to which the youth revolt has affected popular culture and attracted the interest, if not the total involvement, of large numbers of young people in this country and abroad.

A second major social change which underlies the student movement is the rise of mass higher education. If the student movement is any indication of the possible effects of higher education, then one might have the following expectations about the coming period. First, the number of people in the middle class with critical attitudes toward the dominant culture will rapidly rise. In my view, critical feelings about capitalist culture—particularly negative attitudes toward symbols and ideology which support competitive striving, acquisitiveness, narrow nationalism, and repressive moral codes—are enhanced by exposure to higher education. Such feelings are further reinforced by entrance into occupations which are structurally not bound into the private, corporate economy—for example, occupations associated with education, social service, social planning, and other intellectual or human service work. These occupations embody values which tend to be critical of the culture and of the going system and tend to have an ethic which emphasizes collective welfare rather than private gain. It is important to recognize that the current student activists were born into the social stratum defined by these occupations, and many students with activist sympathies end up in these occupations. Data collected by Lubell (1968) show a general tendency for students oriented toward such occupations to move toward the left, politically. In a certain sense, then, the student movement may be seen as an outgrowth of a new level of occupational differentiation, i.e., the development of a distinct stratum organized around these occupations. This stratum is one of the most rapidly growing occupational sectors, and its political impact can already be seen, not only on the campus, but in such developments as the "new politics" movement during the recent elections. I am not arguing that this "new middle class" of intellectuals, professionals, upper white-collar workers, technical workers, public employees, etc., is politically homogeneous, or class-conscious, or radical. Indeed, it contains many antagonisms, and its participants are hardly ready for massive collective action, much less the barricades. But it does seem to me that the student movement, with its opposition to nationalism and militarism, its identification with egalitarian ideals, and particularly its opposition to bureaucratic and rigid authority in the university represents a militant version of the kinds of attitudes which are increasingly likely to prevail in the stratum to which I am referring. It seems particularly likely that the spread of mass higher education will mean increasing pressure against bureaucratic forms of authority and for "participatory democracy" within the institutions in which the newly educated work. The political trajectory of the educated class will, in large measure, be a function of the responsiveness of the political and economic system to their demands for more rational domestic and international policies, more personal autonomy and participation in decision-making, and a more authentic and humane cultural and public life. More Vietnams, more racial turmoil, more squalor in the cities, more political stagnation, more debasement of popular culture—in short, more of the status quo is likely to increase the availability of members of this stratum for radical politics.

One may continue at great length to enumerate other cultural and social changes which seem to be implied by the appearance of a student movement in our society. For example, it clearly signifies a process of change in the position of youth in the society—a change which involves protest against the subordination of youth to rigid and arbitrary forms of authority in the school system and in the general legal system, and which also may involve an extension of youth as a stage of life beyond adolescence (Keniston, 1968a). The student movement may also signify a general decline in the legitimacy of military authority and nationalist ideology—a decline associated with rising education levels, with changing character structure, and with the impact of mass communications.

My point in mentioning all of these potential cultural and social transformations is not to stake a claim as a prophet, but rather to urge that we take seriously the possibility that the appearance of student movements in advanced industrial societies really does signify that a new social and cultural stage is in the process of formation. A comparative perspective leads us to that hypothesis, because the classical student movements were, as we have suggested, just such signs. If we were to take the student movement in our own country seriously in this sense, then we would, I believe, be less likely to assume the stability of our social and political order and the cultural system sustaining it, less likely to dismiss campus unrest as a momentary perturbation or a romantic last gasp, less likely to focus on particular tactics and bizarre outcroppings of the youth revolt. Instead, we would open up the intellectual possibility that our kind of society can undergo major transformation, that it can generate, as Marx anticipated, its own "internal contradictions" and "negations," and that the future need not be like the present only more so.

References

Altbach, P. "Students and Politics." In Seymour Martin Lipset, ed., *Student Politics,* pp. 175–87. New York: Basic Books, 1967.

Bell, Daniel. "Columbia and the New Left." *The Public Interest* 61 (Fall 1968).

Ben-David, J., and Collins, R. "A Comparative Study of Academic Freedom and Student Politics." In S. M. Lipset, ed., *Student Politics,* pp. 148–95. New York: Basic Books, 1967.

Eisenstadt, S. N. *From Generation to Generation.* Glencoe, Ill.: The Free Press, 1956.

Flacks, R. "The Liberated Generation: An Exploration of the Roots of Student Protest." *Journal of Social Issues* 23 (July 1967):52–75.

———. "Who Protests: The Social Bases of the Student Movement." In J. Foster and D. Long, eds., *Protest! Student Activism in America,* pp. 134–57. New York: William Morrow and Company, 1970.

Glazer, N. "Student Power at Berkeley." *The Public Interest* 61 (Fall 1968).

Hofstadter, R. *Anti-Intellectualism in American Life.* New York: Vintage, 1966.

Keniston, K. "Youth as a Stage of Life." Mimeographed. New Haven, Conn.: Yale University Press, 1968a.

———.*Young Radicals.* New York: Harcourt, Brace and World, 1968b.

Lipset, S. M. "Students and Politics in Comparative Perspective." *Daedalus* 91 (1968):97–123.

Lubell, S. "That 'Generation Gap'." *The Public Interest* 52 (Fall 1968).

Parsons, T. "Youth in the Context of American Society." *Daedalus* 91 (1962): 97–123.

Peterson, Richard F. *The Scope of Organized Student Protest in 1964–65.* Princeton, N.J.: Educational Testing Service, 1966.

———. *The Scope of Organized Student Protest in 1967–68.* Princeton, N.J.: Educational Testing Service, 1968.

Schumpeter, J. *Capitalism, Socialism and Democracy.* New York: Harper and Bros., 1950.

Skolnick, Jerome. *The Politics of Protest.* New York: Simon and Schuster, 1969.

Westby, D., and Braungart, R. G. "Class and Politics in the Family Backgrounds of Student Political Activists." *American Sociological Review* 31 (October 1966): 690–92.

———. "Activists and the History of the Future." In J. Foster and D. Long, eds., *Protest! Student Activism in America,* pp. 154–83. New York: William Morrow and Company, 1970.

The Class and Status Bases of Negro Student Protest[1]

Anthony M. Orum and Amy W. Orum

Most contemporary analysts of social and political movements subscribe to the view that such movements originate from a number of different circumstances. Smelser, for instance, argues that social movements may emerge in response to conditions as diverse as economic depressions, wars, and actions of agencies like the police force.[2] Others assign the major impetus for social movements to economic and status-related deprivations.[3] Threats to the maintenance or improvement of a group's economic resources and status accoutrements, they argue, eventually can produce sufficient discontent to permit social movements to arise.

In the case of the present Negro protest movement in the United States, observers frequently trace its roots to barriers to Negroes' economic and status-related achievements.[4] With few exceptions, however, the connection between protest activity and economic or status-related deprivation among Negroes has been based on insufficient evidence.[5] By examining data

Reprinted by permission of the authors and the publisher, from the *Social Science Quarterly* 49 (December 1968):521–33.

1This article represents a revised portion of the senior author's doctoral dissertation, "Negro College Students and the Civil Rights Movement" (unpublished Ph.D. diss., University of Chicago, 1967). Norman Bradburn provided helpful suggestions on an earlier draft of this article.

2Neil Smelser, *A Theory of Collective Behavior* (New York: Free Press, 1963), Chs. 10 and 11.

3See especially the studies by Richard Hofstadter, "The Pseudo-Conservative Revolt," and "Pseudo-Conservatism Revisited: A Postscript," and by Seymour M. Lipset, "The Sources of the Radical Right," and "Three Decades of the Radical Right: Coughlinites, McCarthyites, and Birchers," in Daniel Bell, ed., *The Radical Right* (Garden City, N.Y.: Doubleday and Co., Inc., 1963), pp. 63–86, 259–377.

4See, for instance, William F. Soskin, "Riots, Ghettos, and the 'Negro Revolt,'" in Arthur M. Ross and Herbert Hill, eds., *Employment, Race and Poverty* (New York: Harcourt, Brace and World, Inc., 1967), p. 209.

5Studies of participation in the Negro protest movement mainly deal with the participation of students. These studies only briefly consider the relationship between economic and status-related factors and participation. See J. R. Fishman and F. Solomon, "Youth and Social Action: I. Perspective on the Student Sit-In Movement," *The American Journal of Orthopsychiatry,* 33 (Oct., 1963), pp. 872–82; Donald R. Matthews and James on Negro college students, the present study seeks to shed light on this matter. Specifically, we ask: To what extent is the participation of Negro college students in the Negro protest movement a response to economic or status-related deprivation?

Perspectives and Research on the Negro Protest Movement

The literature about economic or status-related conditions and the Negro protest movement can best be viewed in terms of three explanations outlined by Geschwender.[6] In this section we shall examine the evidence for each explanation. The first interpretation, the "vulgar Marxist" orientation, claims that fundamental economic impoverishment may create the dissatisfaction required for a social movement to emerge.[7] Meier and other social scientists as well as Negro political leaders emphasize the importance of such basic economic motivations for the present Negro protest efforts.[8] For instance, in 1963, Whitney Young, Jr., a moderate Negro spokesman, dramatized the economic plight of Negroes by calling for a domestic "Marshall Plan" to help offset unemployment and poverty among Negroes.[9]

W. Prothro, *Negroes and the New Southern Politics* (New York: Harcourt, Brace and World, Inc., 1966); John M. Orbell, "Protest Participation Among Southern Negro College Students," *American Political Science Review,* 61 (June, 1967), pp. 446–56; Ruth Searles and J. Allen Williams, Jr., "Negro College Students' Participation in Sit-Ins," *Social Forces,* 40 (March, 1962), pp. 215–20; F. Solomon and J. R. Fishman, "Youth and Social Action: II. Action and Identity Formation in the First Student Sit-In Demonstration," *The Journal of Social Issues,* 20 (April, 1964), pp. 36–45; and Howard Zinn, *SNCC: The New Abolitionists* (Boston: Beacon Press, 1964). The only reported research on this topic among adults is in Gary T. Marx, *Protest and Prejudice: A Study of Belief in the Black Community* (New York: Harper and Row, 1967).

[6]Geschwender provides a very interesting explication of five hypotheses about the relation between certain social and economic conditions and the rise of the Negro protest movement. James A. Geschwender, "Social Structure and the Negro Revolt: An Examination of Some Hypotheses," *Social Forces,* 43 (Dec., 1964), pp. 248–56.

[7]The type of evidence that supports this point of view can be found in: Leonard Broom and Norval Glenn, *Transformation of the Negro American* (New York: Harper and Row, 1965), Chs. 5 and 6; Rashi Fein, "An Economic and Social Profile of the Negro American," in Talcott Parsons and Kenneth B. Clark, eds., *The Negro American* (Boston: Houghton Mifflin Co., 1966), pp. 102–33; Dale W. Hiestand, *Economic Growth and Employment Opportunities for Minorities* (New York: Columbia University Press, 1964); Herbert Hill, "Racial Inequality in Employment: The Patterns of Discrimination," in Arnold Rose, ed., *Annals of the American Academy of Political and Social Science,* Special Issue on The Negro Protest, 357 (Jan., 1965), pp. 30–47; Thomas Pettigrew, *A Profile of the Negro American* (Princeton, N.J.: D. Van Nostrand Co., Inc., 1964), esp. p. 189; and U.S. Department of Labor, "The Employment of Negroes: Some Demographic Considerations," in Raymond J. Murphy and Howard Elinson, eds., *Problems and Prospects of the Negro Movement* (Belmont, Calif.: Wadsworth Publishing Co., Inc., 1966), pp. 116–24.

[8]August Meier, "Civil Rights Strategies for Negro Employment," in Ross and Hill, eds., *Employment, Race and Poverty,* pp. 175–204.

[9]Whitney M. Young, Jr., "Domestic Marshall Plan," in *New York Times Magazine,* October 6, 1963, cited in Murphy and Elinson, eds., *Problems and Prospects,* pp. 45–49.

Miller argues that "usually the long-term economically depressed are unlikely candidates for a dynamic political movement, but the race ethnic dimension, as well as the economic factor, is propelling the poor, whether Negro, Mexican-American, or Puerto Rican."[10] In addition, organizations engaged in the Negro protest movement, like the Student Nonviolent Coordinating Committee (SNCC), focus their campaigns on basic economic issues and problems. Such organizations often have demanded increased job opportunities for Negroes, sometimes in preference to voting rights or benefits in housing, frequently have employed economic boycotts to secure fair treatment for Negroes by white-owned or operated businesses, and, most recently, have urged the full-scale development of business enterprises in the ghettos.[11]

The second explanation, the "rising expectations" view, argues that if people of longstanding impoverishment are subject to heightened aspirations, due to partial fulfillment of certain goals, then they may become dissatisfied with gradual improvement of their situation and seek to channel their energies into a social movement. A number of writers accept this point of view as an interpretation of the present Negro protest efforts.[12] Kristol, for instance, remarks that "American Negroes . . . feel . . . that they have a special claim upon American society: they have had some centuries of resignation and now would like to see tangible benefits, quickly."[13] Evidence from public opinion polls conducted in the 1950's and 1960's indicates that Negroes had comparatively high expectations regarding their future. A 1954 nationwide study revealed that 64 per cent of the Negroes felt life would become better as compared with only 53 per cent of a matched group of whites who had this feeling.[14] Approximately 10 years later Brink and Harris found somewhat larger proportions of Negro respondents answering positively to similar questions.[15] However, such high aspirations of Negroes may quickly be transformed into anger and frustration when confronted with insurmountable barriers to their fulfillment. Along these lines, the discovery that the Negro–white income gap increases with additional education prompted Siegel to comment: "We might speak of the motivation provided the civil rights movement by the discovery on the part of thousands of

[10]S. M. Miller, "Poverty and Politics," in Irving Louis Horowitz, ed., *The New Sociology* (New York: Oxford University Press, 1964), pp. 297, quoted in Michael Harrington, "The Economics of Protest," in Ross and Hill, eds., *Employment, Race and Poverty*, p. 236.

[11]Broom and Glenn, *Transformation,* pp. 69–72; Jack L. Walker, "Protest and Negotiation: A Case Study of Negro Leadership in Atlanta," *Midwest Journal of Political Science,* 7 (May, 1963), pp. 99–124.

[12]Broom and Glenn, *Transformation,* p. 59; Pettigrew, *A Profile,* pp. 170–91; and Everett Carll Ladd, Jr., *Negro Political Leadership in the South* (Ithaca, N.Y.: Cornell University Press, 1966), p. 24.

[13]Irving Kristol, "It's Not a Bad Crisis To Live In," *New York Times Magazine,* January 22, 1967, p. 70.

[14]Cited in Pettigrew, *A Profile,* pp. 184–85.

[15]William Brink and Louis Harris, *The Negro Revolution in America* (New York: Simon and Schuster, 1964), p. 238.

young Negroes that their coveted education wasn't worth much on the open market."[16]

The third thesis, the "relative deprivation" perspective, states that discontent, and subsequently, social rebellion, may occur among people who evaluate their achievements by reference to the standards and accomplishments of some similarly situated persons who differ only in terms of having different or more numerous advantages. Karl Marx provided the essence of this notion by observing:

> A house may be large or small; as long as the surrounding houses are equally small it satisfies all social demands for a dwelling. But let a palace arise beside the little house, and it shrinks from a little house to a hut.[17]

In the case of the Negro protest activities, many observers claim that certain segments of the Negro community, especially for middle class, experience dissatisfaction as a result of comparing their achievements with those of their white counterparts.[18] The evidence for this argument certainly appears convincing. While Negro unemployment, for example, seems to have declined over the past 20 years, it has increased relative to that of whites.[19] In addition, the few studies of Negro participation in the Negro protest movement indicate that the more socially advantaged persons are over-represented in the protest activities. A recent study by G. Marx, for instance, demonstrates that Negroes who have more educational, occupational, and social privileges were more apt to be militant about the need for Negroes to gain equal rights.[20] After finding that middle-class Negro college students were over-represented among student participants, Searles and Williams suggest that many student participants adopted their white middle-class counterparts as a reference group.[21] Similar evidence on the background of Negro student protesters also is presented by Matthews and Prothro and Orbell.[22]

Each of the above interpretations attempts in a somewhat different

[16]Paul M. Siegel, "On the Cost of Being a Negro," *Sociological Inquiry,* 35 (Winter, 1965), p. 57. Siegel's results are also pertinent to the discussion on "relative deprivation."

[17]Karl Marx, "Wage-Labor and Capital," in Karl Marx and Friedrich Engels, *Selected Works* (Moscow, 1958), I, p. 93, quoted in Ladd, *Negro Political Leadership,* p. 24.

[18]This explanation is found in many discussions of the Negro protest movement. For illustrations: see Broom and Glenn, *Transformation,* p. 106; Joseph Gusfield, *Symbolic Crusade: Status Politics and the American Temperance Movement* (Urbana: University of Illinois Press, 1963), p. 22; Lewis M. Killian and Charles Grigg, *Racial Crisis in America: Leadership in Conflict* (Englewood Cliffs, N.J.; Prentice-Hall, Inc., 1964), pp. 133–34; Pettigrew, *A Profile,* pp. 178–79; and Daniel Thompson, "The Rise of the Negro Protest," in Rose, ed., *Annals of American Academy,* pp. 19–20.

[19]U.S. Department of Labor Report in Murphy and Elinson, eds., *Problems and Prospects,* p. 121.

[20]Gary T. Marx, *Protest and Prejudice,* pp. 55–70.

[21]Searles and Williams, "Negro College Students' Participation," p. 219.

[22]Matthews and Prothro, *Negroes and the New Southern Politics,* p. 419; and Orbell, "Protest Participation," p. 448. Orbell, incidentally, used the same data as Matthews and Prothro.

manner to account for the current momentum of Negro protest efforts by virtue of economic or status-related deprivations among Negroes. In the analysis which follows, an attempt is made to determine whether the phenomenon of fundamental poverty, relative deprivation, or rising expectations is more characteristic of protest participants than of nonparticipants among Negro students.

Data

The data upon which this study is based are part of a nationwide sample survey conducted in 1964 by the National Opinion Research Center (NORC). The purpose of the survey was to collect information on the graduate plans of seniors at colleges and universities throughout the nation. In April and May of 1964 a questionnaire was sent to a representative group of seniors at these institutions. In addition, a sample was chosen of seniors at predominantly Negro senior colleges and universities, designed to represent all students who received their bachelor's degrees in the spring of 1964.[23] Members of the NORC staff, together with personnel from the Department of Labor, identified 77 schools primarily attended by Negroes.[24] This list was comparable with one compiled independently and, for all practical purposes, exhausted the population of four-year predominantly Negro colleges and universities in the United States.[25] A two-stage probability design was employed in choosing the sample of students. Altogether, a total of 50 schools and roughly 7,000 students were included in the original sample.

Although respondents represent about one-third of all Negro college seniors who graduated in the spring of 1964, about 3,500 students, the response rate was only 49 per cent. In contrast, the response rate to the nationwide 1964 study was 74 per cent. No conclusive evidence was obtained to explain this low rate among Negroes, but one investigation suggests that a major factor was the greater length of the Negro college student questionnaire.[26] The low response rate probably accounts for certain biased characteristics of respondents. Those students who responded were more likely to be women, to have higher grade-point averages, and to have majors in areas such as the physical sciences and humanities. These biases, however, were similar in type and magnitude to those in the nationwide study. Hence, there appears to be no reason for anticipating that the biases affected the representativeness of this sample.

[23]The results of this study of Negro seniors' career plans are reported in Joseph H. Fichter, "Neglected Talents: Background and Prospects of Negro College Graduates," National Opinion Research Center, Feb., 1966, multilithed.

[24]This group of schools does not include the fairly large number of predominantly Negro junior colleges in the United States.

[25]The other list was assembled by McGrath. See Earl J. McGrath, *The Predominantly Negro Colleges and Universities in Transition* (New York: Bureau of Publications, Teachers College, Columbia University, 1965).

[26]Fichter, "Neglected Talents," App. 1.

Findings

The information on the participation of students in the protest activities comes from two separate questions. Students were asked, first of all, what major protest events had occurred on their campuses. As can be seen in Table 1, most students claimed that economic boycotts were the major activity at their school, an answer that confirms other evidence on the popularity of economic boycotts among Negro college students.[27] In addition, students were questioned about their own roles in these efforts. Approximately 70 per cent of the students reported participation and, of this group, 32 per cent claimed to be active participants or leaders. A comprehensive measure of participation probably should account for both the degree and type of involvement, but the ambiguity of the question on type of activity prevented our creating such a measure. Instead we chose to distinguish between students who said that they were nonparticipants and those who reported taking an inactive, active, or leadership role.[28]

SOCIOECONOMIC STATUS AND PARTICIPATION. Most evidence concerning

Table 1. Proportion of Students Reporting Major Types of Protest Activities on Their Campus

	Per Cent	N
Holding rallies	36	1,244
Public addresses by civil rights leaders	40	1,378
Participation in "freedom rides"	19	655
Participation in boycott moves against segregated businesses	64	2,170
Sit-ins in segregated public places	61	2,098
Fund raising for civil rights movement	35	1,185
Voter registration campaigns	48	1,652
Marches on city hall	42	1,441
Participation in March on Washington	23	802
None of these	12	405
No answer	—	125
Total	380	13,155
Total N		3,423[a]

[a]Variations in total sample size from table to table are due to rounding off to nearest whole number.

[27]Broom and Glenn, *Transformation.*

[28]Also examined were the correlates of activism by distinguishing between activists, leaders or very active participants, and nonactivists, inactive participants. The characteristics of the activists did not differ much from those who were inactive participants. As a consequence, results were presented only on the dimension of participation.

the link between economic or status factors and involvement in the Negro protest movement is based on the background characteristics of participants and nonparticipants. Without exception, such evidence indicates that Negroes from middle-class, or in general, more privileged background were more apt to be protest participants. In Table 2 we have assembled information on fathers' education, family income, and protest participation that allow us to re-examine these results. The education of students' fathers shows no association with participation, whereas the income of students' families has a slight positive relationship with participation. Students from high SES backgrounds were slightly more apt to participate in protest activities. The "relatively deprived" students, those from families with high education but low income, were no more likely to be protest participants than were their economic peers from families with less education.

It will be recalled from our earlier discussion that one interpretation of the Negro protest movement concerns the relative deprivation of Negroes as compared with their white counterparts. Although the data do not permit systematic exploration of this hypothesis, we can examine the relative deprivation of Negro students in their college settings. Table 3 presents data on the SES composition of the school, the SES background of students, and protest participation.[29] If the relative-deprivation argument is correct, then we would anticipate more extensive participation among students whose SES background is lower than that of their fellow students. Specifically, students from homes of low SES should be more likely to participate in

Table 2. Father's Education, Family Income, and Protest Participation (per cent participating)

Father's Education	Family Income Less than $5,000/yr.	$5,000 or more/yr.
Some high school or less	69	74
N=	(1,389)	(471)
High school graduate or more	69	74
N=	(456)	(617)
Total N		3,424[a]

[a]Variations in total sample size due to rounding.

[29]An index of socioeconomic status was created by combining responses to questions on father's education, family income, and occupation of the chief wage earner. In terms of this index, a family of high socioeconomic status would be comprised of a man whose education included at least some college training, whose head—most often a man—held a professional, managerial, or clerical position, and whose annual income was at least $7,500. Of course such families appear to be more prevalent among the parents of the Negro student population than among the Negro population in general.

schools in which there is a medium or high proportion of students from high SES backgrounds. An examination of data in Table 3, however, reveals virtually no difference in participation among students from low- and high-SES families in the different settings.[30]

STUDENT OCCUPATIONAL ASPIRATIONS AND PARTICIPATION. Some additional depth to our analysis of SES factors and participation in the protest activities is provided by examining students' choices of occupational careers. In order to make this analysis, we first examined the relationship between students' career preferences as freshmen and participation. Using freshman career preferences, the preference in 1960, rather than senior preferences, acts as a control for the possibility that protest participation from 1960 through 1964 might have had either beneficial or adverse consequences for students' aspirations.[31] Among both men and women we found that stu-

Table 3. Socioeconomic Status Composition of Schools, Socioeconomic Status Background of Students, and Protest Participation (per cent participating)

School SES (Proportion of students from high SES families)	Students' SES Low	High	Participating Total Per Cent
Low	61	65	61
N=	(850)	(99)	(949)
Medium	76	73	75
N=	(677)	(175)	(852)
High	77	75	76
N=	(634)	(498)	(1,132)
Total N			3,423[a]

[a]Variations in total sample size due to rounding.

[30]The careful reader will note that the class composition of the school is related to the rate of participation. Specifically, the greater the proportion of students from high socioeconomic status (SES) homes, the greater is the rate of participation. This association can be explained by other variables that are related to the proportion of high SES students. For instance, schools of high quality generally have a greater proportion of students from high SES backgrounds and also have higher rates of student participation. See Matthews and Prothro, *Negroes and the New Southern Politics,* pp. 424–29; Orbell, "Protest Participation," pp. 448–50; and Anthony M. Orum, "Negro College Students and the Civil Rights Movement" (unpublished Ph.D. diss., University of Chicago, 1967), Ch. 6. The measures of school quality employed in these studies are based upon such indexes as the proportion of Ph.D.'s on the faculty, student–faculty ratio, ratio of library books per student, and number of books in the library.

[31]Pettigrew, for instance, claims that involvement in the protest might have advantageous effects for the self-respect and esteem of Negroes. He states that "the remedial powers of the movements themselves alter their followers in the process. . . . Negro Americans are learning how to be first-class citizens at the same time they are winning first-class citizenship." (Pettigrew, *A Profile,* p. 167.)

dents with high career aspirations as freshmen were somewhat more apt to participate in the protest events.[32] Among, 1,028 male students, 79 per cent of those with high aspirations were participants as compared to 76 per cent of those with low aspirations. Among 1,859 females, the percentages were 72 and 66, respectively. The relationship was stronger for women, but was not very strong in either case.

Let us suppose, however, that a shift in students' career aspirations from their freshman through senior year accompanied differential involvement in the protest movement. For example, some students may have shifted their aspirations from "high" to "low" during their college years because of their dissatisfaction with prospects for occupational success. And, as a consequence, they might have been more likely than other students to participate in the protest movement. Examination of the data in Table 4, however, indicates that such an argument is unwarranted.

PERCEPTION OF EMPLOYMENT OPPORTUNITIES AND PARTICIPATION. Both the "rising expectations" and, to a lesser degree, the relative-deprivation explanations suggest that protest activity may arise among Negroes who confront unanticipated limits on their opportunities. Negro students tend, as a

Table 4. Sex, Freshman Career Preference, Senior Career Preference, and Protest Participation (per cent participating)

Sex	Freshman Career Preference	Senior Career Preference Low	High
Male	Low	74	78
	N=	(392)	(109)
	High	77	81
	N=	(167)	(340)
Female	Low	65	69
	N=	(1,123)	(127)
	High	72	72
	N=	(27)	(283)
Total N			3,423[a]

[a]Variations in total sample size due to rounding.

[32]In order to measure the level of students' career aspirations, an index developed by James Davis was employed. It is based upon the number of years of postgraduate education required for a particular occupation. The careers tend to be ranked by skill level or loosely speaking, occupational status. See James A. Davis, *Great Aspirations* (Chicago: Aldine Press, 1964). Sex was used as a control variable in this and subsequent analyses. There were two reasons for this procedure. First, the anticipated associations between economic or status-related factors and participation might have been stronger for men, since occupational data often demonstrate that Negro males seem to face a greater inequality of opportunity than Negro females, particularly in the white-collar occupations. Second, Negro college men were more likely to participate in the protest than Negro women. This difference might have confounded other differences in the association between economic or status-related factors and participation.

group, to be one of the more upwardly mobile segments of the Negro community. Yet their earnings are not commensurate with their educational attainment.[33] For that matter, their opportunities for employment in the professions and in business also may not be commensurate with their education.[34] Consequently, those Negro students who recognize the existence of such barriers might turn to the Negro protest movement to relieve their discontent.

Such arguments are examined here by looking at the association between students' perception of employment opportunities and protest participation. Students were asked the following question about job opportunities in the nation: "In your view, when will Negroes have equal job opportunities as compared with whites of the same educational level?" Students' responses to this question, together with the extent of their participation, are presented in Table 5. Among both male and female students, perception of opportunities for employment in the nation bore no relationship to the extent of participation. A similar absence of association is found between participation and the perception of employment opportunities in both the North and South.

The analysis above assumes that many students thought that the expansion of employment opportunities for Negroes was an important goal of the Negro protest movement and, thus, joined the movement when confronted with limits on their own mobility. Undoubtedly, some dissatisfied students did not regard the protest movement as a vehicle for such purposes and therefore did not choose to participate in the protest. In order to take account of this possibility, let us examine the relationship between perception of employment opportunities and participation among students who did think that expanded opportunities were the most important goal. As the data in Table 6 indicate, even among the students who believed ex-

Table 5. Sex, Perception of Employment Opportunities in the Nation, and Protest Participation (per cent participating)

	Perception of Opportunities	
Sex	Equal now/ten years	Equal twenty years or more
Male	77	77
N=	(510)	(501)
Female	66	67
N=	(1,032)	(780)
Total N		3,422[a]

[a]Variations in total sample size due to rounding.

[33]Siegel, "On the Cost."

[34]For instance, see Hill, "Racial Inequality," pp. 30–47.

Table 6. Gamma Coefficients for Association between Perception of Employment Opportunities and Participation, Controlling for Most Important Goal of Protest Movement and Sex

	Most Important Goal			
	Employment Opportunities		All Others	
Type of Opportunity	Male	Female	Male	Female
Employment opportunities in the nation[a]	+.06	−.01	−.02	−.04
Employment opportunities in the South	+.08	−.03	−.05	−.06
Employment opportunities in the North	+.05	−.06	+.01	−.03

[a]In each case, participation is counted as positive (+) and nonparticipation as negative (−). Thus, a gamma coefficient with a plus sign (+) means that students who thought equal employment opportunities for Negroes would be obtained in twenty years or more were more likely to be participants than students who thought such opportunities would be achieved more rapidly.

panded job opportunities were the most significant aim of the Negro protest movement, the perception of employment opportunities had neither a consistent nor a strong association with participation.

Occupational aspirations, perception of opportunities and participation. Although this investigation has provided less than convincing evidence for the connection between economic or status-related factors and protest participation, one additional hypothesis. It is plausible to argue that the occupational aspirations of students would, in Lazarsfeld's terms, specify the relationship between perception of opportunities and participation.[35] More precisely, we might anticipate that only among the Negro students with high aspirations will the perception of limited employment opportunities lead to protest participation. Table 7 presents data necessary to test this hypothesis. Although freshman career preference continues to be slightly related to participation, students' perception of employment opportunities has no association with participation, even among students with high aspirations.

[35]Patricia L. Kendall and Paul F. Lazarsfeld, "Problems of Survey Analysis," in Robert K. Merton and Paul F. Lazarsfeld, eds., *Continuities in Social Research: Studies in the Scope and Method of "The American Soldier"* (New York: Free Press, 1950), pp. 154–65.

Discussion

There are three traditional explanations which have been used to account for the growth of the Negro protest movement in terms of economic and

Table 7. Sex, Perception of Employment Opportunities in the Nation, Freshman Career Preference and Protest Participation (per cent participating)

Sex	Opportunities	Freshman Career Preference: Low	High
Male	Equal now/ten years	77	80
	N=	(250)	(208)
	Twenty years or more	78	82
	N=	(199)	(263)
Female	Equal now/ten years	66	73
	N=	(672)	(271)
	Twenty years or more	66	71
	N=	(474)	(235)
Total N			3,424[a]

[a]Variations in total sample size due to rounding.

status-related deprivations. The "vulgar Marxist" explanation argues that fundamental economic impoverishment of Negroes produces the necessary conditions for the spread of Negro protest efforts. This argument received no confirmation from our evidence on the participation of Negro college students. Students from poor families—lower socioeconomic status—were about equally likely to participate in protest activities as were students from wealthy backgrounds, higher SES.

The "rising expectations" thesis claims that many Negroes are unhappy with the pace of their recent achievements and, consequently, have channeled their frustrations into the protest activities. In order to test this argument, we looked at relationships among students' career aspirations, perception of employment opportunities, and protest participation. If this argument were correct, the perception of limited opportunities should have been associated with participation. However, this hypothesis received no support. We also found that there was no association between the perception of employment opportunities and participation even among students with high aspirations, who might be most dissatisfied with limited opportunities. Finally, we expected that many students who had lowered their career aims during college were unhappy with their occupational prospects and, therefore, would be most prone to participate. Instead, we discovered that students with high career aspirations throughout college were most likely to participate.

The third interpretation claims that the Negro protest movement arose largely as a means for expressing the discontent of many Negroes, especially middle-class Negroes, who feel "relatively deprived" compared with their Negro or white peers. In order to assess the effect of individual "deprivation" we examined the SES characteristics of student participants and nonparticipants, in general, and in different college settings. We found that students from relatively deprived backgrounds, homes in which the father's education was high and family income low, had no greater likelihood of participation than any other group. We also anticipated that students whose parents' SES was lower than that of the majority of their fellow students would feel relatively deprived and would be most likely to participate. There was no confirmation of this hypothesis. Of course, none of this evidence provides a basis for dismissing the importance of the relative deprivation that Negro students might feel toward their white counterparts.

By and large, all these results contradict those of previous research. Matthews and Prothro as well as Orbell discovered that students from higher SES homes were more likely to be participants than were students from lower SES homes.[36] Searles and Williams also uncovered a similar finding.[37] The present study, however, differs in several respects from earlier research. First, it is based on a much larger and somewhat more representative sample of Negro students and therefore may furnish more reliable evidence of the link between economic and status-related factors and participation. In addition, it was conducted two years after the other studies and reveals about twice as much overall participation. During the intervening two years, it seems likely that many students of lower-class origins became involved in the protest movement. Consequently, the earlier class differences between participants and nonparticipants would tend to disappear.

The different results also could be associated with the fact that the earlier studies used samples of students from all college classes, i.e., freshman through senior, whereas the present research dealt with seniors only. This analysis might indirectly confirm what Newcomb and other social scientists have observed about college students' political behavior: namely, that the impact of background factors such as parents' SES is gradually muted by salient dimensions of the college environment.[38] Along these lines, Matthews and Prothro's research demonstrates that characteristics of the college setting are much better predictors of students' participation in the protest movement than are economic or status-related background variables.[39]

In summary, we have found that several major interpretations of the

[36]Matthews and Prothro, *Negroes and the New Southern Politics*.

[37]Searles and Williams, "Negro College Students' Participation."

[38]Theodore M. Newcomb, *Personality and Social Change* (New York: The Dryden Press, 1943).

[39]Matthews and Prothro, *Negroes and the New Southern Politics*, esp. p. 429.

growth of the Negro protest movement fail to explain student participation in these activities. The inadequacy of these interpretations might be due to the type of group analyzed in this study, or to their limited applicability as explanations of the Negro protest. In either case, the evidence from this research indicates that a re-evaluation should be made of these interpretations. Such a reassessment, moreover, should be conducted not only in light of the results from this study, which deals with Negro protest efforts of the past, but also with an eye to changes occurring in the character of the movement, especially in the strategies of protest organizations.

Parental Identification and Student Politics: An Empirical Reappraisal[1]

Richard Braungart

In his first major work on American college students, *The Uncommitted,* growing out of a clinical study of a small number of alienated Harvard youth, Keniston discovered his students were reacting against weak father images (Keniston, 1965). Fathers were perceived as frustrated men, dominated by their wives, who "sold out" what idealism they had to a materialistic and chaotic world. These uncommitted or alienated youth empathized with their mothers, the latter of whom, according to Keniston, transferred their own ambitions, needs for achievement and independence onto their sons. As a result, many of these male youth identified more with their mothers, whom they perceived to be the legitimate centers of influence and power in the family.

In his more recent work, Keniston described (leftist) politically active youth in much the same manner (Keniston, 1967, 1968). In his discussion of committed youth, the author found that the dominant ethos of activist-prone families were equalitarian, permissive, democratic and highly individuated. More often than not, it was the mothers of these actively dissenting

Reprinted by permission of the author from a paper presented to the American Sociological Association, 1970.

[1]The data on which this investigation is based are drawn from the author's doctoral dissertation. This paper was supported in part by a grant from the General Research Board, The University of Maryland. Funds for the collection of data were provided by a research grant from The Pennsylvania State University. The author thanks Margaret M. Braungart for her assistance in the data collection and processing phases of this study and for her helpful suggestions. Acknowledgment is gratefully made to those young people who took part in the survey, who, in effect, made this research possible.

youth who appeared the most likely carrier and epitome of such values given their freedom from professional and financial commitments (Keniston, 1967:120–21; 1968:52–55). Once again, Keniston maintained that (leftist) male activist youth were likely to identify more with their mothers than with their fathers.

> While no empirical study has tested this hypothesis, it seems probable that in many activist-producing families, the mother will have a dominant psychological influence on her son's development (Keniston, 1967:120).

He clarified this by suggesting that:

> These hypotheses about the family background and psychodynamics of the protester are speculative, and further research may prove their invalidity. But regardless of whether *these* particular speculations are correct, it seems clear that, in addition to the general social, demographic and attitudinal factors mentioned in most research, more specific familial and psychodynamic influences contributed to protest-proneness (Keniston, 1967: 121).

Alienating families and protest-prompting families were differentiated in this way. In both families, the sons' emotional ties were directed toward their mothers. In the alienating family, the mother–son relationship was characterized by maternal control and intrusiveness. Conversely, in the protest-prompting families, mothers were highly individuating forces in their sons' lives, encouraging them toward independence and autonomy. In both family constellations the sons were disappointed with their fathers. Alienated youth were determined to avoid the fate that befell their fathers; protesting youth aspired to live out the values their fathers had not always "worked hard enough to practice" (Keniston, 1967:121; 1968:349–50).

Keniston went on to say that as a distinct group, leftist-prone political activists possessed an unusual "capacity for nurturant identification"—that is, empathy for the underdog, the oppressed and needy—that did not exist in the same degree of intensity with apolitical and conservative youth. This presumably explained their support for insurgent movements throughout the world and in American ghettos. It is most likely the origins of such a capacity came from homes with active mothers whose own work and values embodied nurturant concern for others (Keniston, 1967:120). Flacks found this to be true in his research on Chicago activists whose mothers were more likely employed professionally in service roles such as teaching and social work (Flacks, 1967:52–75). While these mothers were employed, along with the fathers, it was still the mothers of these activist youth who symbolized relative freedom from competitive and financial burdens and transmitted familial values to their sons. Lifton reported a strong son–mother emotional tie in his research on politically active Japanese youth (Lifton, 1963:223). Parsons and Bales (1955) noted that in American society, there was no neat, bisexual symmetry in the socialization of the father–son and mother–daughter relationships. Daughters usually identified with mothers; sons did not always identify with their fathers. While the son's sex identification is with the father, the latter is often an absentee parent. Therefore, the American male has typically had more female exposure both at home and in elementary school.

In this paper an attempt is made to test the type of family constellation presumed to exist in the homes of protest-prompting families. If previous assumptions are correct, we would expect the following proposition to be supported in a larger and more diverse sample of activist and nonactivist college students: *parental identification of sons and mothers is differentially related to student political activism.* Deductively, this proposition is tested through two hypotheses:

H_1: Male youth in general identify more with their mothers than their fathers.

H_2: The number of males when compared with females who identify more with their mothers than their fathers is more prevalent among left-wing student activists.

Sample

In order to test the hypotheses under investigation, students representing both flanks of the campus ideological spectrum were compared, employing sets of Likert-type attitude response items, to determine the effect family constellation has upon collegiate political activity. During the academic year 1966–1967, a sample of 1246 college students, including members of the Students for a Democratic Society (SDS), Young Democrats (YD), a Control Group (CG) of nonactivist, apolitical college youth, Young Republicans (YR), and the Young Americans for Freedom (YAF) were surveyed from 10 universities in New York, Pennsylvania, Maryland, and from two national conventions of SDS and YAF.[2] The four political activist groups were selected for study inasmuch as they represent the legitimate and radical political elements on most American college and university campuses; they are the largest campus-based political activist groups in the United States; and they best articulate the changing political anchorages, cleavages and conflicts that have emerged during the decade of the 1960's. The control group of apolitical Introductory Sociology students was collected for comparative analysis between the two student political wings.

Findings

In Table 1 and Table 2 we can see that the majority of males and females in our total sample agree they feel close to or can identify with both parents when responding to the questions: "My relationship with my father is

[2]These institutions include: the State University of New York at Binghamton, City University of New York, Brooklyn College, Pennsylvania State University, University of Pennsylvania, University of Pittsburgh, Carnegie-Mellon University, Temple University, University of Maryland and Johns Hopkins University.

Table 1. Total Percentage Distribution of Identification with Mother Versus Identification with Father for Males (N=686)[a]

Identification with Father	Identification with Mother		
	Disagree	Undecided	Agree
Disagree	25.3	6.3	14.4
Undecided	2.3	5.3	6.3
Agree	4.7	3.6	31.6

$x^2 = 199.2$, $p < .001$, gamma $= .6553$

[a]Table percentage total equals 100.0 percent.

very close, with much communication and mutual understanding," and "My relationship with my mother is very close, with much communication and mutual understanding."[3] That is, the plurality or 31.6% of the males and 36.3% of the females agree they can identify with both parents. On the other hand, 25.3% of the males and 20.0% of the females indicate that they cannot identify with both parents, or feel alienated or estranged from both parents. Of those who feel they can identify with one parent but not the other, 14.4% of the males and 20.3% of the females identify more with their mothers than their fathers, while only 4.7% of the males and 3.6% of the females identify more with their fathers than their mothers. This is a 9.7 (maternal/paternal) differential for males and a 16.7 differential for females. Therefore, while males appear to feel closer to their mothers than their fathers when a choice is made between the two parents, this pattern is not exclusive to males, and we note the maternal identification is stronger for females than for males.

The chi-squares and gammas in Table 1 and Table 2 indicate a significant and structurally (linearly) consistent relationship between identification with mother versus identification with father for both males and females. The largest percentage of our youth (both male and female) are consistent in their identification and attachment toward both parents. We would expect this relationship to exist in the general student activist and nonactivist population with the same probability and consistency reported

[3]We of course realize and admit that the Likert-type attitudinal dimensions employed in our analysis at best are surface measures of parental identification and do not directly tap the more proximal and ego-involved familial relationships of youth with their parents. However, such questions do suggest a "gut" or affective response to cognitive stimuli which, if valid, should square with the more intensive and personalized interview data. Much more information is needed in this area if we are to adequately understand the psychodynamics of parental identification employing both survey and interview techniques.

with our data. Of course, when male youth choose between identifying with mother vis-à-vis identifying with father, they more often than not identify with the former rather than the latter. And further, when the same comparison is made with females, we discover that this maternal relationship is stronger with females. We would reject H_1 on the grounds that the plurality of males do not identify more with one parent over the other. But we must add, for the minority of males indicating a parental preference, mothers are endorsed over fathers.

In Tables 3 and 4, when we control parental identification by student activist group, we are able to see that SDS males and females are the most alienated from both parents of all our groups (38.0% for males, 33.3% for females), and YD males (8.5%) and females (10.0%) are the least alienated from both parents. YR males and females have the highest percentage agreeing they can communicate with both parents (40.9% for males, 50.1% for females), followed closely by YD males (38.0%) and females (40.1%). YD males (19.7%) and females (33.3%) have the highest incidence of all groups identifying more with mothers than with fathers, while SDS males (10.7%) and YAF females (11.4%) have the lowest percentage identifying more with mothers than with fathers. Although less than 10% of any group say they identify more with fathers than mothers, the Control Group males (6.1%), followed closely by YAF males (5.1%) and YAF females (8.6%) have a higher percentage than the other student groups showing father identification. Generally speaking, we can say that Tables 3 and 4 closely resemble Tables 1 and 2. That is, with few exceptions, the youth in our sample identify equally with both parents rather than with one parent more often than not when controlled by group, and this is illustrated by the strong positive gammas in our tables. In addition, for those who identify with one parent but not the other, we find that mothers are endorsed consistently over fathers, and this relationship is not influenced by political group membership. We can conclude therefore that, although leftist male students iden-

Table 2. Total Percentage Distribution of Identification with Mother Versus Identification with Father for Females (N=449)[a]

Identification with Father	Identification with Mother: Disagree	Undecided	Agree
Disagree	20.0	4.2	20.3
Undecided	2.4	3.6	7.4
Agree	3.6	2.2	36.3
$x^2 = 98.3$, $p < .001$, gamma = .6279			

[a]Table percentage equals 100.0 percent.

Table 3. Total Percentage Distribution of Identification with Mother Versus Identification with Father for Males by Student Group[a]

Identification with Father	Identification with Mother		
	Disagree	Undecided	Agree
SDS (N=150)			
Disagree	38.0	8.0	10.7
Undecided	4.0	5.3	4.0
Agree	3.3	4.0	22.7
$x^2=54.1$, $p<.001$, gamma=.7290			
YD (N=71)			
Disagree	8.5	8.5	19.7
Undecided	4.2	7.0	8.5
Agree	2.8	2.8	38.0
$x^2=11.7$, $p<.05$, gamma=.4798			
CG (N=231)			
Disagree	24.2	7.4	15.6
Undecided	1.7	4.3	6.1
Agree	6.1	4.3	30.3
$x^2=49.3$, $p<.001$, gamma=.5874			
YR (N=76)			
Disagree	15.8	5.3	14.5
Undecided	0.0	3.9	11.8
Agree	3.9	3.9	40.9
$x^2=19.7$, $p<.01$, gamma=.6445			
YAF (N=157)			
Disagree	27.4	2.5	14.0
Undecided	1.9	6.4	5.1
Agree	5.1	2.5	35.1
$x^2=72.6$, $p<.001$, gamma=.6957			

[a]Group percentage total equals 100.0 percent

tify more with their mothers than their fathers when a choice is made between the two parents, so do all the political groups in our sample and to a greater degree than SDS. And when male activists are compared with female activists, the latter tend to exhibit stronger identification with mothers than fathers.[4] In light of these data, we reject H_2 which suggests that the

[4]The controlling of the family status factors, social class, ethnicity, religion and family politics did not significantly alter the above relationships (see Braungart, 1969).

number of males when compared with females who identify more with their mothers than their fathers is more prevalent among left-wing student activists.

These findings are verified further when past and present attitudes of attachment and hostility toward father and mother, and communication with father and mother, are compared by sex and student group. In Table 5, we can see that, contrary to the predicted relationship between leftist student group membership and male attachment and communication with

Table 4. Total Percentage Distribution of Identification with Mother Versus Identification with Father for Females by Student Group[a]

Identification with Father	Identification with Mother		
	Disagree	Undecided	Agree
SDS (N=78)			
Disagree	33.3	3.9	16.7
Undecided	3.9	5.1	6.4
Agree	0.0	2.5	28.2
$x^2 = 33.4$, $p < .001$, gamma = .7798			
YD (N=30)			
Disagree	10.0	6.7	33.3
Undecided	0.0	3.3	3.3
Agree	3.3	0.0	40.1
$x^2 = 6.5$, n.s., gamma = .5385			
CG (N=276)			
Disagree	17.7	4.4	21.7
Undecided	2.2	2.9	8.3
Agree	4.4	1.1	37.3
$x^2 = 49.5$, $p < .001$, gamma = .6032			
YR (N=30)			
Disagree	16.7	3.3	13.3
Undecided	3.3	0.0	10.0
Agree	0.0	3.3	50.1
$x^2 = 10.6$, $p < .05$, gamma = .8298			
YAF (N=35)			
Disagree	20.0	2.9	11.4
Undecided	2.9	8.6	2.9
Agree	8.6	11.4	31.3
$x^2 = 10.4$, $p < .05$, gamma = .5019			

[a]Group percentage total equals 100.0 percent

Table 5. Differences Between Means Reported for Past Attitudes, Present Attitudes and Communication with Father and Mother by Sex and Student Group[a]

Past Attitudes, Present Attitudes and Communication with Parents by Sex	SDS	YD	Group CG	YR	YAF
Males					
Past attitude toward father	3.80	4.06	4.07	3.99	4.16
Past attitude toward mother	4.32	4.62	4.58	4.41	4.44
Difference	−.52	−.56	−.51	−.42	−.28
t-test	$p<.001$	$p<.001$	$p<.001$	$p<.001$	$p<.001$
Present attitude toward father	3.81	4.16	4.03	4.12	4.09
Present attitude toward mother	3.82	4.18	4.20	4.29	4.13
Difference	−.01	−.02	−.17	−.17	−.04
t-test	n.s.	n.s.	$p<.05$	n.s.	n.s.
Communication with father	4.25	5.11	4.80	5.28	4.90
Communication with mother	4.82	6.00	5.52	6.13	5.52
Difference	−.57	−.89	−.72	−.85	−.62
t-test	$p<.01$	$p<.01$	$p<.001$	$p<.001$	$p<.01$
Females					
Past attitude toward father	4.16	4.48	4.38	4.57	4.09
Past attitude toward mother	4.22	4.65	4.55	4.63	4.31
Difference	−.06	−.17	−.17	−.06	−.22
t-test	n.s.	n.s.	$p<.05$	n.s.	n.s.
Present attitude toward father	3.70	3.96	4.21	4.57	4.19
Present attitude toward mother	3.79	4.56	4.40	4.77	4.41
Difference	−.09	−.60	−.19	−.20	−.22
t-test	n.s.	$p<.05$	$p<.01$	n.s.	n.s.
Communication with father	4.13	4.83	4.92	5.93	5.37
Communication with mother	5.17	7.06	6.35	6.83	5.28
Difference	−1.04	−2.23	−1.43	−.90	+.09
t-test	$p<0.01$	$p<.001$	$p<.001$	$p<.05$	n.s.

[a]Data in this table are based on three sets of attitudes scaled in the following fashion: first, "My attitude toward my father when I was a child was one of": and "My attitude toward my mother when I was a child was one of": (1) strong hostility, (2) mild hostility, (3) indifferent, (4) mild attachment and (5) strong attachment; second, "My present attitude toward my father is one of": "My present attitude toward my mother is one of": (1) strong hostility, (2) mild hostility, (3) indifferent, (4) mild attachment and (5) strong attachment; third, "My relationship with my father is very close, with much communication and mutual understanding" and "My relationship with my mother is very close, with much communication and mutual understanding": ranging from (1) strongly disagree to (9) strongly agree.

mother, the reverse, if anything, appears to be true. That is, the mean attitude scores of our mainstream, conservative and apolitical students, and to a lesser extent radical right-wing students, toward their mother is generally higher than in our radical left-wing student group, higher also for females than for males. Consequently, this evidence supports the decision to reject H_2.

Discussion

There appears to be an impression among some of the researchers in the area of student politics that leftist male youth tend to identify more with their mothers than with their success-oriented and often "absentee" fathers, while rightist males manifest a weak son–mother relationship (Block, Haan, and Smith, 1968). This was tested in the proposition: parental identification of son and mother is differentially related to student political activism.

Upon inspection of survey data collected from 1246 college youth including members of SDS, YD, YR, YAF and a Control Group of nonactivists, we found that left-wing males when compared with right-wing males do not identify more with their mother than their father, nor is there greater mother identification among left-wing females vis-à-vis right-wing female student activists. These conclusions were derived from the hypotheses set: (1) *male youth in general do not identify more with their mothers than their fathers*—they identify equally with both parents, not significantly more with one than the other; and (2) *the number of males when compared with females who identify more with their mother than their father is not more prevalent among left-wing student activists*—of those identifying more with one parent than the other, both sexes tend to identify more with mothers than fathers, and this maternal relationship is greater for females than males; moreover, left-wing activists identify less with mothers than the other student groups.

We found that students tend to be rather consistent in their evaluation of their closeness to their mother and father. That is, more often than not, if a student indicated he felt close to (or alienated from) his mother, he also indicated he felt close to (or alienated from) his father. Therefore, the very concept of identifying more or less with one parent vis-à-vis the other did not appear to be applicable to many of the students in our sample. However, when exploring the minority of students who state a preference for one parent over the other, we found, as Keniston indicated, males in general say they can identify and communicate with their mothers but not their fathers (Keniston, 1968). However, this was not characteristic only of left-wing males. In fact, males from the other student groups indicate a greater percentage of mother rather than father identification than do our SDS males. And in keeping with Parsons and Bales' assumptions, females tend to identify with mothers to a greater extent than males (Parsons and Bales, 1955). On this subject, Block, Haan, and Smith presented evidence that conservative males often exhibited a weak son–mother relationship (Block,

Haan, and Smith, 1968:220–21). In our research, we found that the conservative YAF males appear to feel closer to their mothers than do SDS males. SDS males and females are the most alienated from both parents of all student groups, while mainstream YD and YR indicate closeness to both parents. Our Control Group males are similar to YAF males in terms of the percentage distribution of parental feelings, indicating less communication and consistency than YD and YR males but greater parental identification than SDS males. Interestingly, of those few youth who evinced greater father than mother identification, the Control Group males and YAF females had the highest percentage of all the groups.

Conclusion

The findings in this paper were unable to support the proposition which states that parental identification is related to the direction of student political activism. Our results revealed that: (1) students in general were consistent in their attitude toward both parents, that is, the plurality of students in our sample did not identify more with one parent vis-à-vis the other; (2) of those identifying more with one parent over the other, both sexes tended to identify more with mothers than fathers, albeit this maternal relationship was greater for females than males; and finally (3) left-wing activist males identified less with their mothers than the other student groups in our collegiate sample. These findings suggest a reappraisal of much of the student politics literature which claims that a strong mother–son identification and relationship exists in the family backgrounds of left-wing male student activists.

References

Block, J. H., Haan, N., and Smith, M. B. "Activism and Apathy in Contemporary Adolescents." In J. F. Adams, ed., *Understanding Adolescence,* pp. 198–231. Boston: Allyn and Bacon, 1968.

Braungart, R. G. "Family Status, Socialization and Student Politics: A Multivariate Analysis." Unpublished Ph.D. dissertation, The Pennsylvania State University, 1969.

Flacks, R. "The Liberated Generation: Exploration of the Roots of Student Protest." *Journal of Social Issues* 23 (July 1967):52–75.

Keniston, K. "The Sources of Student Dissent." *Journal of Social Issues* 23 (July 1967):108–37.

———. *The Uncommitted.* New York: Harcourt, Brace and World, 1965.

———. *The Young Radicals.* New York: Harcourt, Brace and World, 1968.

Lifton, R. J. "Youth in Postwar Japan." In E. Erikson, ed., *Youth: Change and Challenge,* pp. 217–42. New York: Basic Books, 1963.

Parsons, T., and Bales, R. F. *Family Socialization and Interaction Process.* Chicago: Free Press, 1955.

*The Social Context of the Rank-and-File Student Activist: A Test of Four Hypotheses**

Roger M. Kahn and William J. Bowers

A new "student movement" has emerged on the American college campus. Its participants include the vanguard of contemporary civil rights activists, anti-poverty workers, anti-militarists, and peace agitators, as well as those calling for the democratization of our major institutions—especially the educational ones. The Movement seems to be increasing both in its intensity and in the magnitude of its support among young people.

Social scientists have begun to turn their attention to this Movement, particularly to the kinds of students who have become involved in it. Somers (1965) and Watts and Whittaker (1966) examined students during the Free Speech Movement at Berkeley; Flacks (1967) investigated students at the University of Chicago during anti-draft protests; Braungart (1966) studied the participants at conventions of two activist organizations (SDS and YAF); and Keniston (1968) studied radical students who staffed a national summer project of anti-war activity.

For the most part, however, these studies overlooked the typical college student activists. Instead, the investigations focused on the most active students, those assuming leadership roles in the Student Movement, as indicated by their attendance at an annual organizational meeting or participation in full-time work on a national peace project. Moreover those students who participate in political activism at such top ranking institutions as Berkeley and Chicago may not typify the student activist at most colleges and universities.

These and other studies consistently reveal at least four major findings: (1) that activist students come from high status families (Braungart, 1966:10–12, Flacks, 1967:55–56; Kahn, 1968:13–17); (2) that these students have a strong academic commitment (Flacks, 1967:56; Heist, 1965); (3) that most major in the social sciences and humanities (Keniston, 1968:307); and

Reprinted by permission of the authors and the publisher, the American Sociological Association, from *Sociology of Education* 43 (Winter 1970):38–55.

*This is a revision of a paper presented by the first author at the American Sociological Association meetings in San Francisco, August 1969. We would like to thank Hanan Selvin and Stephen Cole for comments on the earlier draft.

(4) that most have strong intellectual orientations (Flacks, 1967:70; Heist, 1965; Keniston, 1968:70–74, 87ff).

The Data

These four hypotheses were examined with data from a nationwide survey in 1966 of the attitudes and behavior of college students. This survey was conducted as part of a follow-up to a 1963 survey of academic dishonesty. The data for the earlier study were gathered in two stages. First, a stratified sample of 100 institutions was chosen to represent all regionally accredited colleges and universities. Then, within each school, samples of 75 to 100 students were drawn randomly from the directories or listings of the registrars. To avoid response bias by institution, special efforts were made to reach non-respondents at institutions with low response rates. Sixty per cent of the students in the original study returned questionnaires; this rate was relatively uniform by type of institution. (For further details of the research design and sampling procedures, see Bowers, 1964: appendix C.)

In 1966 these schools were asked to participate in a follow-up study. The names of students who were freshmen in the original study were sent to the registrars for current addresses and other information; 97 institutions provided current addresses. A follow-up questionnaire then was sent to each respondent in the earlier study for whom a current address was available; 946 returned it, a 57 per cent response. Of the respondents in the follow-up study, 690 were college seniors at the same school in which they had been freshmen; 166 were students who had transferred from one school into another (however, on the measure of school quality used below they were classified according to the school they first attended), and 90 students were drop-outs who had not enrolled elsewhere. (For a detailed discussion of the sample and procedures employed in collecting the data, see Kamens, 1968: appendix A.) This group of students—most, but not all, of them college seniors in the spring of 1966—comprise the subjects for the present analysis.

Students who answered affirmatively to either of the following questions were classified as activists: "Have you ever participated in a social protest demonstration or march?" "Have you ever violated the law in a deliberate act of civil disobedience on behalf of a social cause?" The responses to these questions are presented in Table 1; the data reveal that about one-fifth of the respondents had participated in one or the other of these actions.

These questions, which indicate only minimal activist commitment, do not necessarily get at the "hard core" activists who become full-time Movement workers or political organizers. Presumably they tap the students who the organizers organize and are best described as rank-and-file student activists.[1]

[1]The only other study of activism based on a national sample of students, to the best of my knowledge, is by Astin (1968). Bowers (1970), using the same data referred to

Table 1. The Extent of Activism Among College and University Students

Answered Affirmatively to:	Number	Per cent
Have you ever participated in a social protest demonstration or march?	168	17.8
Have you ever violated the law in a deliberate act of civil disobedience on behalf of a social cause?	34	3.6
Have engaged in civil disobedience and/or protest demonstrations[a]	177	18.7
		(N=946)

[a]Only nine of the people who had participated in civil disobedience had not been involved also in social protest demonstrations or marches.

Findings

HYPOTHESIS 1: ACTIVIST STUDENTS COME FROM STATUS FAMILIES. The data provide information on the students' social backgrounds, including mother's and father's education, father's occupation, and family income. The relationship between each of these indicators of family status and student participation in protest activities is shown in Table 2. Twenty-two per cent of students whose mothers had obtained a college degree, in contrast to only 12 per cent of those whose mothers did not finish high school, were student activists. Student activism also is related positively, but less strongly, to father's education.

Father's occupation has a direct relationship to student political activism. Among the sons and daughters of blue-collar workers, 17 per cent were activists; among students whose fathers are professionals, the comparable figure rises to 24 per cent. (Interestingly, the children of white-collar workers, including executives and managers, are more like blue-collar workers' children than they are like professionals' offspring, at least in regard to student activism.) Furthermore, students whose families had high incomes were more apt to be activists than were students coming from families with relatively low incomes (27 and 15 per cent respectively).

These four variables, maternal and paternal education, paternal occupation, and family income, were used to construct an index of socioeconomic status. Each was scored 0, 1, and 2 for low, medium, and high, respectively. Students who scored 0–3 on the index were classified as low, 4–6 as medium, and 7 or 8 as high in SES.

The data in Table 2 show that of those students who came from families high on the SES index, 30 per cent were activists, as compared to only

in this paper, discusses student activism relative to other forms of campus conduct. National surveys of college administrators (Peterson, 1966, 1969) have focused on the breadth of student protests, noting especially the issues on which they have centered.

Table 2. Per Cent Activist by Indicators of Social Class and SES Index

	Parental Education		
	Less Than High School Graduate	High School Graduate or Some College	College Graduate or More
Mother	12 (152)	20 (494)	22 (263)
Father	16 (223)	19 (365)	22 (323)
	Father's Occupation		
	Blue Collar	White Collar (including Executives and Managers)	Professional
	17 (251)	19 (444)	24 (201)
	Family Income		
	$7,499 or less	$7,500–9,999	$10,000 or More
	15 (298)	22 (146)	27 (268)[a]
	SES Index		
	Low	Medium	High
	17 (285)	22 (257)	30 (120)

[a]The N's for this item are reduced substantially because the "Don't Know's" are excluded. They also are excluded in the computation of the SES index appearing in this table and in Table 3.

17 per cent of the students from families low on the SES index. Whatever the measure used to indicate students' family backgrounds, then, the higher the parents' status, the more likely was the student to become involved in student political activism.

Family status is known to be associated with the quality of the educational institution a student attends (Feldman and Newcomb, 1969:148). Moreover, as the names of Berkeley, Wisconsin, Michigan, Harvard, and Columbia suggest, the more prestigious schools are the ones where student activism is the most pronounced.[2] Perhaps the relationship between SES

[2]Peterson's survey (1969) of university officials indicates that at the higher quality institutions, the frequency of student protests is greater than at the lower quality ones.

and student activism is a consequence largely of the quality of the schools that the high status respondents attended. Does, in fact, the direct relation between SES and activism hold at all colleges and universities or does it tend to disappear within levels of academic excellence?

In order to examine this, a measure of college quality was used which distinguishes among four different levels of educational institutions.[3] The three lowest categories of school quality are differentiated according to the proportion of applicants accepted for admission. The "not very selective" category indicates that 80 per cent or more of the applicants were accepted; the "moderately selective" category, 50–79 per cent; and the "highly selective" category indicates that less than 50 per cent were accepted (data from Hawes, 1961). The "top ranking" category, like the "highly selective" one, indicates that less than 50 per cent of the applicants to a particular school were admitted. In addition, however, a reputational prestige measure was used to isolate further the very best schools in the nation (from Berelson, 1960:124ff). Although the proportion of students accepted by an educational institution was taken as an adequate measure of its quality, it was considered desirable to distinguish the very top schools in the sample. Table 3 presents the relationship between SES and activism within each of these categories of school quality.

When school quality is controlled, the impact of family status on student activism is reduced drastically; in fact, the original relationship altogether disappears in three of the four quality contexts. At the most prestigious schools, the low SES students are most likely to be activists; at the less selective schools (both "moderately" and "not very" selective categories), the medium status students are slightly more apt to participate in social

Table 3. Per Cent Activist by SES Index and School Quality

	Quality of School			
SES Index	Top Ranking	Highly Selective	Moderately Selective	Not Very Selective
High	41 (39)	27 (49)	15 (26)	13 (15)
Medium	38 (34)	19 (75)	18 (90)	20 (51)
Low	50 (18)	13 (60)	14 (97)	14 (105)
Totals	42 (91)	19 (194)	15 (213)	16 (171)

[3]Four predominantly black universities have been excluded from the above categories and are not represented in this analysis. For a discussion of the difficulty of qualitatively equating white and black educational institutions, see Jencks and Riesman (1967).

protest and civil disobedience. Only at the "highly selective" (but not "top ranking") educational institutions does the original positive relationship between SES and student activism persist.

Two related explanations may account for these findings. First, the social status composition of the student bodies varies with school quality. The top ranking schools had a large proportion of students from relatively high status families (high SES is the modal category). A predominantly high SES student body may develop a tolerant climate or activist "sub-culture." This may permit, or even directly encourage, students at all SES levels to participate in social or political action.

By contrast, however, at the lower two levels of school quality, low SES student background was modal. A predominantly low SES student body may generate a more restrictive or intolerant climate in which students—even those whose social status backgrounds might have indicated a predisposition toward activism—with liberal or radical beliefs and values feel socially isolated or "queer" about becoming active, and, therefore, refrain from doing so. Only at the "highly selective" colleges and universities is the student body composed of roughly equal numbers of students from all the levels of socioeconomic status. Perhaps under this condition, no one status group disproportionately influences the student culture. Students' predispositions toward activism, as established by their social backgrounds, may have been relatively free to manifest themselves.

Secondly, the social-political "climate" established by higher educational institutions of top standing, quite apart from the composition of their student bodies, in fact may encourage activism among students. In these schools, administrative "attitudes," as well as actual rules and regulations governing student conduct, are likely to be flexible and permissive regarding various forms of student behavior, including student activism (Williamson and Cowan, 1966). Moreover, there is evidence that activist faculty members tend to be located in the nation's top ranking educational institutions (Ladd, 1969). At the moderately and not very selective colleges and universities, on the other hand, the administrative climate may be rigid and repressive, thus, actually discouraging student social and political activism.

It seems likely that the concentration of high SES students in the better colleges and universities, combined with a relatively tolerant administrative climate, encourages the emergence of a student activist sub-culture and activist social-political behavior. Certainly, the fact that the rate of activism at the top institutions is very much greater than at the other levels of institutional quality, suggests that these schools have been able to develop a distinct atmosphere conducive to student activism.

The data in Table 3 also reveal that the rate of activism in the highly selective schools differed from the moderately and not very selective ones only among students from high status families. Perhaps high SES students at less selective schools take as their reference group their counterparts in the top ranking colleges and universities. Students at the most prestigious schools frequently set the styles and standards that eventually are adopted by students in other educational contexts (e.g., Ivy League clothing). Presumably, the first to follow the lead of students at the top ranking schools will be the high status students at the next level of institutional quality. Thus, the overall pattern of relationships between SES and activism within categories of school quality may represent an early stage in the diffusion of student activism from the top ranking schools to other academic institutions.

Our interpretations here are necessarily *ex post factum* conjecture. Significantly, however, our data generally do not confirm earlier findings that show activists at a given school coming disproportionately from higher SES backgrounds. It may be that the leaders and organizers of activist demonstrations do come from higher status families, but our evidence on rank-and-file activism suggests little, if any, social class bias in recruitment to student activism, *once institutional quality is taken into account.*

HYPOTHESIS 2: ACTIVISTS COME FROM THOSE STUDENTS WITH STRONG ACADEMIC COMMITMENTS. The data in Table 4 show two indicators of academic commitment—hours spent studying and grade point average—as they relate to student activism. Of those students who studied thirty or more hours per week, 22 per cent were activists, in contrast to only 14 per cent of the students who studied less than twenty hours per week. Similarly, 22 per cent of the students whose grade average was B-plus or above, but only 15 per cent of those with averages of C or less, were activists. Academic performance and student activism appear to have been modestly, but directly, related.

However, when measures of academic performance are controlled by school quality (Table 5), the relationship becomes more complex. At the two lower levels of educational quality, the observed differences on both measures are eliminated almost completely. In fact, among the least selective colleges, there appears to be a slight inverse relationship between grades and activism. Among the highly selective and the top ranking schools, however, one finds a strong positive association between both study-

Table 4. Per Cent Activist by Indicators of Academic Commitment

Hours Studying and Doing Assignments Per Week		
30+	20–29	0–19
22 (449)	18 (305)	14 (99)
Total Grade Average[a]		
B+ or Above	B to C+	C or Below
22 (140)	18 (471)	15 (175)

[a]Obtained from institutional records; most of the students were juniors or seniors.

Table 5. Per Cent Activist by Indicators of Academic Commitment and School Quality

	Quality of School			
Hours Studying	Top Ranking	Highly Selective	Moderately Selective	Not Very Selective
30+	47 (74)	21 (136)	14 (162)	14 (102)
20–29	22 (27)	16 (70)	14 (103)	18 (82)
0–19	17 (6)	9 (22)	11 (36)	12 (26)
Grades				
B+ and above	47 (17)	32 (37)	14 (49)	11 (37)
B to C+	47 (60)	16 (136)	11 (153)	16 (122)
C or Below	27 (26)	13 (40)	13 (70)	16 (39)

ing a great deal and getting high grades and participating in student political activism. The most striking relationship is found in the nation's top colleges and universities. At these schools, almost half of the students with excellent academic performance were activists (47 per cent of those who studied most and 47 per cent of those with top grades).

The relationship between academic performance and activism, then, depends on the quality of the educational institution. At the nation's better colleges and universities, apparently the academic context itself encourages activism among the more academically committed students. More than others, these schools are supposed to promote high academic standards and to encourage a critical perspective in a wide variety of areas, including the institutions of contemporary society. Their best students should be those most affected by these environmental influences, and, hence, the most perceptive social critics and reformers. Furthermore, as noted above, the most activist faculty members also tend to be found in the nation's high ranking educational institutions; presumably, the top students at these colleges and universities have the closest contact with faculty members and are the ones most influenced by their attitudes and activist behavior.

HYPOTHESIS 3: ACTIVISTS COME FROM THOSE STUDENTS MAJORING IN THE SOCIAL SCIENCES AND HUMANITIES. Quite apart from how hard students study and the grades they get, *what* they study may be related to their involvement in social protest activities. Table 6 shows the level of activism among students in four different areas of academic specialty: the social sciences, humanities, physical sciences, and pre-professional programs. (History, area studies, and languages are grouped with the humanities; pre-professional

Table 6. Per Cent Activist by Field of Study

Social Sciences	Humanities	Physical Sciences	Pre-professional Programs
23 (164)	21 (274)	13 (131)	12 (301)

programs include business and commerce, engineering, and education.) Again, the data seem to confirm the findings of earlier studies that activism is more common among social science and humanities majors; the percentage of activist students in these fields was almost twice that of students majoring in pre-professional programs or in the physical sciences.

Typically, high quality institutions tend to provide a broad and general education, emphasizing the liberal arts. This suggests that the higher rates of activism among social science and humanities majors reflect the effects of school quality on student activism. Table 7 tests this possibility, showing the relationship between field of study and activism within categories of institutional quality. (Because of the gap in activism between the social sciences and humanities on the one hand, and the physical sciences and pre-professional programs on the other, as shown in Table 6, we have dichotomized field of study in Table 7.)

The humanities and social sciences had higher rates of activism in all contexts; however, the differences between these two broad areas of study were far from uniform. The percentage differences by field of study increased regularly (i.e., −3, −6, −9, and −13) with school quality. Apparently, increasing school quality tends to bring out a latent tendency toward activism among the social science and humanities students. The base figures in Table 7 show that the proportion of students majoring in these fields also increases with school quality. But this by no means accounts for the relationship between school quality and activism; for example, humanities and

Table 7. Per Cent Activist by Field of Study and School Quality

	Quality of School			
Field of Study	Top Ranking	Highly Selective	Moderately Selective	Not Very Selective
Social Sciences and Humanities	43 (80)	22 (116)	16 (149)	16 (93)
Physical Sciences and Pre-professional Programs	30 (30)	13 (112)	10 (156)	13 (121)

social science majors in the leading institutions had substantially higher rates of activism than did their counterparts in schools of lesser quality. For both broad areas of study, the top ranking schools had substantially higher rates of activism.

While physical science and pre-professional programs emphasize the mastery of specific technical knowledge for future vocational application, the humanities and social sciences at least partially encourage the development of critical abilities and perspectives with respect to society and social institutions. It seems likely that students who apply their critical faculties to contemporary society observe many contradictions and injustices. Furthermore, in the presence of strong student values to act upon one's beliefs, in the absence of administrative sanctions against such actions, and with a large proportion of social science and humanities majors (all conditions that are apt to be found at the top ranking colleges and universities), it seems likely that students will try to eliminate the contradictions and inequities that they perceive. That is, they become student activists.

HYPOTHESIS 4: ACTIVISTS COME FROM THOSE STUDENTS WITH STRONG INTELLECTUAL ORIENTATIONS. In an effort to measure students' intellectual orientations, they were asked to indicate how important each of the following was to them: (1) ideas and intellectual problems; (2) appreciation of the arts; and (3) intellectual skill and knowledgeability. Table 8 shows the correspondence between students' responses to these questions and their involvement in student activism. In each case, the more important these values were said to be, the more likely was the respondent to be an activist.

The three items were combined to form an index of intellectual ori-

Table 8. Per Cent Activist by Indicators of Intellectual Orientation Plus Intellectual Orientation Index

	Indicators of Intellectual Orientation		
	Degree of Importance		
	Great Deal	Fair Amount	Not Much, Not At All
How Important Are the Following to You?			
Ideas and Intellectual Problems	25 (336)	17 (437)	12 (132)
Appreciation of the Arts	26 (269)	18 (364)	15 (271)
Intellectual Skill and Knowledgeability	21 (332)	19 (465)	13 (69)
	Intellectual Orientation Index		
	27 (273)	17 (529)	9 (99)

Table 9. Per Cent Activist by Intellectual Orientation Index and School Quality

Intellectual Orientation Index	Quality of School			
	Top Ranking	Highly Selective	Moderately Selective	Not Very Selective
High	45 (41)	29 (66)	18 (85)	21 (58)
Medium	37 (59)	16 (129)	13 (173)	13 (145)
Low	22 (9)	6 (32)	3 (36)	8 (13)

entation. "Not very important" was scored 0, "fairly important" was scored 1, and "very important" was scored 2 for each item. Respondents with combined scores of 0 or 1 were classified as "low," those with scores of 2, 3, or 4 as "medium," and those scoring 5 or 6 as "high" on the index. As the data in Table 8 show, there is a substantial relationship between intellectual orientation and student activism. There is a spread of 18 percentage points between the "lows" and the "highs" on the index; the former were three times as likely to be activists as were the latter.

Significantly, when the effect of intellectual orientation is examined within the context of school quality (Table 9), a fairly strong relationship remains at all levels of quality. At lower quality schools, the relationship between intellectual orientation and activism is slighty reduced, while at the top ranking and highly selective schools the percentage difference increases slightly. Yet, irrespective of the quality of the college or university, a consistent pattern was maintained; students with high intellectual orientations were much more likely to be activists than those without such orientations. This suggests that for today's college students, actively expressing social and political values is an important component of having a strong intellectual commitment, regardless of institutional setting.

THE ROLE OF SCHOOL QUALITY. Although the analysis has focused on the effects of individual commitments, interests, and orientations within categories of school quality, perhaps the most impressive finding of this research has to do with the role of institutional quality itself in promoting student activism. In part, the better schools may achieve a high rate of student activism through their ability to stimulate hard work, to promote an intellectual orientation, and to encourage work in the humanities and social sciences.[4] But beyond this, we have found that school quality exerted an independent influence toward activism, particularly among those students

[4]An analysis of the joint effects of academic commitment, field of study, and intellectual orientation shows that each contributes independently to activism at the leading and highly selective institutions.

who were most disposed in that direction. It was not the presence of these students so much as it was the ability of the leading institutions to "turn them on" that accounted for their higher levels of participation in student political activity.

Yet, a question might be raised about the choice of institutional quality as the contextual variable relating to activism. While previous studies have shown a relationship between quality and the incidence of protest demonstrations (cf. Peterson, 1969), other associated factors such as school size may be more important determinants of student activism. In fact, a very recent study concluded that, "school size accounted for almost all of the explained variance" in the number of demonstrations per school. "School quality and community size accounted for almost none of the variance" (Scott and El-Assal, 1969:707).[5] Thus, schools that have unusually high rates of activism may be distinguished more by their size than by the quality of their academic programs. To test this possibility, Table 10 shows the joint effects of school quality and school size. (Since both independent variables are college characteristics, percentages are apt to be less stable than in previous tables. Cells with ten or fewer students usually will represent only one institution.)

The top ranking institutions were substantially higher in rates of activism than were other schools in four of the five categories of school size. The very largest institutions (5,000 or more undergraduate enrollment) were the one exception. Although the pattern is somewhat less regular for the highly selective schools, their rates of activism were higher than those of the less selective schools within three of the five size categories.

Thus, controlling for school size has little, if any, systematic effect on the relationship between school quality and activism. Only among the very largest schools does the effect of quality seem to be suppressed; this effect is dependent upon a very few students from only two schools. It should be noted that there is little overall relationship between school size and activism. The rate increases slightly up to the largest size category at which point it drops below all previous values (see the "All Schools" column in Table 10).

Thus, controlling for school size, substantial differences remain, particularly between the top ranking schools—the nation's most prestigious institutions—and all the others.[6] These are the schools charged with educating

[5]Actually, this conclusion is not justified. They are reporting the results of a stepwise regression in which school size was the first variable to be introduced because it had the highest zero order correlation with protest demonstrations. If they had introduced quality first, however, it would have "accounted for almost all of the variance" leaving "almost none of the variance" for whatever variables followed—the whole set is highly intercorrelated. Since there is no clear causal order among these variables, a more adequate picture of their respective contributions would have been provided by subtracting their common explained variance and presenting the amount of variance explained that was uniquely attributable to each.

[6]Although Scott and El-Assal (1969) find a strong relationship between school size and the number of protest demonstrations per school, they mention in a footnote that there is virtually no difference among schools in the number of protests per *thousand stu-*

Table 10. Per Cent Activist by School Quality and School Size

Size of Undergraduate Enrollment	Quality of School				
	Top Ranking	Highly Selective	Moderately Selective	Not Very Selective	All Schools
0–499	40 (10)	8 (24)	16 (108)	18 (56)	17 (198)
500–999	48 (52)	15 (65)	10 (134)	0 (21)	18 (272)
1,000–2,999	40 (20)	20 (85)	22 (37)	14 (80)	20 (222)
3,000–4,999	38 (8)	29 (24)	0 (15)	23 (31)	22 (78)
5,000 or more	15 (20)	16 (32)	9 (12)	14 (29)	14 (93)

the elite in American society; their purposes and ideals are well articulated, and they have a clearly defined charter (Meyer, 1970). Moreover, they also are the colleges and universities associated most closely with the most powerful institutions in society—government, industry and commerce, and the military. Because of their conspicuous position of power and influence within higher education, the top ranking schools are particularly vulnerable to criticism. Ideologically and politically they represent the best targets for protest, especially to the extent that activists are concerned with issues such as "university complicity" in the Vietnam War and reforms in higher education. Therefore, part of the explanation for the higher rates of activism at the nation's leading educational institutions simply may be their greater vulnerability to attack.

Conclusions

In this paper four hypotheses were tested using a sample of students from a wide cross-section of colleges and universities in the United States. Although activist students tend to come from high status backgrounds as predicted in the first hypothesis, it is particularly significant that school quality generally interprets this relationship. That is, the relationship between SES and student political activism largely disappears within quality contexts. Thus, the higher rate of activism among students from high status families is primarily a result of the fact that they are concentrated in the higher quality schools. This concentration may foster the emergence of a student activist sub-cul-

dents. "Large size does not produce a higher rate of demonstrations than small size" (p. 707). To the extent that the number of protests at an institution is a function of the number of protesters, our findings on the effects of school size are consistent with theirs.

ture; the schools, themselves, are especially likely to encourage activist commitment and behavior. These colleges and universities are "where the action is."

The second hypothesis, that academic commitment and student activism are directly related, also appears to be confirmed in this national sample of college students. However, when school quality is controlled, academic performance is unrelated to student activism at the lower quality schools; at these schools relatively few students are activists, whatever their academic commitments. At the better educational institutions, where the rates of activism are high, those students who perform well academically are much more likely to be activists than are the students who do not. Students at these schools—particularly the better students—presumably are stimulated to apply their critical abilities to contemporary social issues. Also they are more likely than students at institutions of lesser academic rank to come in contact with activist faculty members.

The third hypothesis, that activist students are more common among the social science and humanities majors than among those in the physical sciences and pre-professional programs, appears to be confirmed in the national sample. Controlling for school quality, however, shows that this difference varies consistently with the academic quality of the institution. Presumably the social sciences and humanities encourage a critical appraisal of contemporary society; yet, the likelihood that students in these fields, as compared to their more technically oriented counterparts, will convert their critical perspectives into social and political action definitely is enhanced by the quality of the educational institution they attend.

The fourth hypothesis, that there is a direct connection between intellectual orientation and student activism, was confirmed without qualification. At all levels of educational institution, students who were intellectually oriented were substantially more likely to be activists than were their classmates. This suggests that students who think of themselves as intellectuals may feel that they should participate actively in contemporary social and political issues. This contrasts sharply to the stereotype of the "ivory-tower" intellectual, but does coincide with the Marxist notion of the intellectual's role.[7]

Perhaps the most important finding relates to the effect of institutional quality on activism. The quality of the school itself—and not its size—is directly and strongly related to student activism. Clearly, there is something apart from a student's social background, his academic commitment, his field of study, or his intellectual orientation that promotes activist involvement at the better quality colleges and universities. The top ranking schools, in particular, somehow encourage activism among their most able and intellectually oriented students. Thus, the determinants of student po-

[7]Flacks (1970a, 1970b) presents a stimulating analysis of the new class of young activist intellectuals, stressing especially their role in contemporary movements for social change.

litical activism, rather than merely being characteristics of the individual activist students themselves, also are to be found in the quality of the educational institutions that they attend.

Besides providing a stimulus to intellectualism and critical social thought, the top quality institutions may contribute to activism in another way—as symbolic and strategic targets. We noted above that these schools often set the standards and styles for the entire system of higher education. Where educational reform is the subject of protest, if the protest is successful, it is likely to have reverberations and ramifications throughout the entire educational system. Furthermore, these institutions generally play an important role in community and national affairs, making them especially vulnerable to the judgments of social critics. In other words, as the nation's leading institutions, these schools may stimulate protest by providing a supportive climate and a symbolic and strategic target for the student activist.

In the four years intervening since the data were collected, the Student Movement has undergone considerable change. The focus of attention has shifted from civil rights to educational reform and anti-war protest. Participation has become more widespread and more intense. More students on more campuses have become involved. As the Student Movement broadens its base, opportunities for young people to participate probably will not be as restricted by type of student or by type of institutional context as they were in the past. Thus, the rank-and-file student activists of today may represent a greater diversity of orientations and commitments and may come from a wider range of institutions than they did four years ago.

This investigation of student activism should make it clear that in addition to individual data, both institutional data and an analysis of the issues the students themselves are addressing are required for insight into the sources of the Student Movement. Such data, in conjunction with the findings reported here, will enable us to document the development of the Student Movement over the past several years.

References

Astin, Alexander W. "Personal and Environmental Determinants of Student Activism." Paper delivered at the APA meetings, San Francisco, 1968.

Berelson, Bernard. *Graduate Education in the United States.* New York: McGraw-Hill, 1960.

Bowers, William J. *Student Dishonesty and Its Control in College.* New York: Bureau of Applied Social Research, Columbia University, 1964.

———. "Recent Trends in Campus Deviance." Russell B. Stearns Study (unpublished paper), 1970.

Braungart, Richard G. "S.D.S. and Y.A.F.: Backgrounds of Student Political Activists." Paper read at the annual meeting of the American Sociological Association (mimeographed), 1966.

Feldman, Kenneth A., and Newcomb, Theodore M. *The Impact of College on Students.* San Francisco, Calif.: Jossey-Bass, Inc., 1969.

Flacks, Richard W. "The Liberated Generation: An Exploration of the Roots of Student Protest." *Journal of Social Issues* 23 (1967):52–75.

———. "The Revolt of the Young Intelligentsia: Revolutionary Class-Consciousness in Post-Scarcity America." In Norman Miller and Rod Aya, eds., *Revolution Reconsidered.* New York: The Free Press, 1970a.

———. "Social and Cultural Meanings of Student Revolt: Some Informal Comparative Observations." *Social Problems* 17 (1970b):340–57.

Hawes, Eugene R. *A Guide to Colleges,* 2nd edition. New American Library, 1961.

Heist, Paul. "Intellect and Commitment: The Faces of Discontent." In O. W. Knorr and W. J. Minter, eds., *Order and Freedom on the Campus: The Rights and Responsibilities of Faculty and Students.* Boulder, Colo.: Western Interstate Commission for Higher Education, 1965.

Jencks, Christopher, and Riesman, David. "The American Negro College." *Harvard Education Review* 37 (1967):3–60.

Kahn, Roger M. "Class, Status Inconsistency, and Student Political Activism." Unpublished M.A. paper, Department of Sociology, Northeastern University, 1968.

Kamens, David H. "Institutional Stratification and Institutional Commitment: Contextual Effects on College Dropout." Unpublished dissertation, Columbia University, 1968.

Keniston, K. *The Young Radicals: Notes on Committed Youth.* New York: Harcourt, Brace and World, 1968.

Ladd, Everett C., Jr. "Professors and Political Petitions." *Science* 163 (March 28, 1969):1425–30.

Meyer, John W. "The Charter: Conditions of Diffuse Socialization in Schools." In W. Richard Scott, ed., *Social Processes and Social Structure,* pp. 564–78. New York: Holt, Rinehart and Winston, 1970.

Peterson, Richard E. *The Scope of Organized Student Protest in 1964–65.* Princeton, N.J.: Educational Testing Service, 1966.

———. *The Scope of Organized Student Protest in 1967–68.* Princeton, N.J.: Educational Testing Service, 1969.

Scott, Joseph W., and El-Assal, Mohamed. "Multiversity, University Size, University Quality and Student Protest: An Empirical Study." *American Sociological Review* 34 (October 1969):702–8.

Somers, Robert H. "The Mainsprings of the Rebellion: A Survey of the Berkeley Students in November, 1964." In S. M. Lipset and Sheldon S. Wolin, eds., *The Berkeley Student Revolt, Facts and Interpretations,* pp. 530–57. Garden City, N.Y.: Doubleday and Company, 1965.

Watts, William A., and Whittaker, D. "Free Speech Advocates at Berkeley." *Journal of Applied Behavioral Science* 2 (1966):41–62.

Williamson, E. O., and Cowan, John L. *The American Student's Freedom of Expression.* Minneapolis, Minn.: University of Minnesota Press, 1966.

10 Social Change and Youth

Perhaps because they lack the number and depth of commitments to the established social order that characterize most adults of comparable social class, the young are the most sensitive indicators of social change. In the ideal model of cultural transmission (the passage of the accumulated culture of one generation to the next), what is taught, demonstrated, and implied or taken for granted by the older generation would overlap completely with what is learned, observed, and inferred by youth. "Change" can be measured by the degree to which the culture of the young and the culture of the older generation is not continuous, integrated, and coherent. The dependence of the young on the old, already insured in part by the biological immaturity of men until well into their late teens, is maximized in traditional cultures. Little change takes place. On the other hand, in some societies, such as ours, the rapid rate of change is unprecedented and relatively unchecked by morality. One of the great certainties of our life is change itself. Inevitably, it seems, any change affects the young more than the old. In this situation, as Margaret Mead (1970) claims, it may well be that the young have much more to teach the old than vice versa. The dependency equation is reversed. The young are expected to fill the parents in on the latest "new math," fashions, political movements, etc., and to interpret the dismal daily events assaulting us from the daily papers.

Several observers argue that rapid change separates the past and future, making the past recede, and making the future more distant and problematic (Keniston 1965). The present, almost by default, looms large. It undercuts ties between the young and the old. Keniston, for example, argues that "an increasing number of young people . . . are alienated from their parents' conceptions of adulthood, disaffected from the mainstreams of traditional public life, and disaffiliated from many of the historical institutions of our society" (1965). The lack of commitment in the young grows from their inability to see in their parents' behavior models relevant to their own behavior; but as Braungart points out, this may be true only of elite groups.

But there does seem to be an emerging style of the later twentieth century, a psychosocial superficiality and adaptivity which Lifton calls "Protean Man." Instead of focusing on the changes in social structure (which he clearly takes into account), Lifton attends to the consequences of an apparent lack of deep commitment to adult values and roles. In addition to citing the importance of drastic and disruptive change, Lifton concerns himself with the symbols people use to order their social relations. He finds modern man *symbolically dislocated,* seemingly torn out of the context of the social institutions on which he depends. Self and institutional order no longer mesh from the point of view of the actor, but seem to float without clear connection. The mass media themselves contribute to the changing nature of man, for they supply many of the stimuli and images that seem to flood over us. Powerlessness comes not only from a failure to see the self as capable of control, but also from seeing this experience in the context of rapid change caused by other sources.

Youth culture, as Eisenstadt shows, is a mode of accommodation to the stresses caused by discontinuity between early learning and expectations and later experiences. But the culture of modern youth itself is important not only for its functions and form, but for its *content.* That is, the very existential nature of the present youth movement is critical. Emphasis on the present is the most important theme in the youth culture. The "presentness" of all experience makes lasting commitments to ideas unlikely, and drives many of the youth to experiential domains they can control—their bodies and their minds. They very rationally seek domains where they can control their experiences. The drug culture indicates the importance of expressive symbols and experience.

Granted the pervasiveness of change, and its sources, what will be the future of the present youth movement? Flacks foresees the continuing importance of the youth culture because of: (1) the collapse of the Protestant ethic, combining deferred gratification, hard work, and asceticism as the central value support of the capitalistic system; (2) the rise of higher education; and (3) the growth of the white-collar service and educational stratum. In a sense then, Flacks sees that youth will continue in the present pattern to become a politically conscious stratum, especially in the present social context of international war, racial stress and reaction, campus turmoil, urban decline, and political inactivity. The future would hold a continuing new cultural stratum, both a result and a cause of the post-industrial culture, according to Flacks. An alternative approach sees the youth culture not as the last gasp of a romantic reaction to the inevitable conquest of all by technology, nor as a continuing influence in the mainstream of American political and social life, but as a functional alternative to commitment to the increasing demands of the post-industrial society. As Wilensky (in Becker, ed. 1966) and others have shown, the effects of automation and cybernetics are differential, affecting most the middle mass, creating some jobs and destroying others. At the top, according to Wilensky, there will remain a large mass of people with high work demands, long hours, and little leisure. At the same time, many hard, dirty, and demanding jobs will be eliminated. Thus, a middle mass requiring skill and training will emerge, the same mass Flacks sees as central. However, the extent of their political power is problematic, as both writers would agree.

As the post-industrial consumer-oriented society grows, there will be a need for new mechanisms to assign people to roles, especially to their occupational roles, and the social control required will also be altered in shape and content. Perhaps society, instead of using the labels "mental illness" and "crime" as means to control "unproductive" elements—that is, instead of confining them and thereby eliminating them from the competitive labor market—will develop new alternatives to the present work–family–home–religion types of social control. Communes, urban mate-swapping, reservations of nudists, macrobiotic cults, and the like may become available as optional life styles (Toffler 1970). There may be governmental support for sabbaticals, research, or sensual, psychedelic experiences. Adults in life crises, instead of going to a mental health center, may retire to a Zen archery camp. It is clear that government action during the next 25 years to create alternatives to the work career is imperative.

Protean Man

Robert Jay Lifton

I should like to examine a set of psychological patterns characteristic of contemporary life, which are creating a new kind of man—a "protean man." As my stress is upon change and flux, I shall not speak much of "character" and "personality," both of which suggest fixity and permanence. Erikson's concept of identity has been, among other things, an effort to get away from this principle of fixity; and I have been using the term self-process to convey still more specifically the idea of flow. For it is quite possible that even the image of personal identity, in so far as it suggests inner stability and sameness, is derived from a vision of a traditional culture in which man's relationship to his institutions and symbols are still relatively intact—which is hardly the case today. If we understand the self to be the person's symbol of his own organism, then self-process refers to the continuous psychic re-creation of that symbol.

I came to this emphasis through work in cultures far removed from my own, studies of young (and not so young) Chinese and Japanese. Observations I was able to make in America, between and following these East Asian investigations, led me to the conviction that a very general process was taking place. I do not mean to suggest that everybody is becoming the same, or that a totally new "world-self" is taking shape. But I am convinced that a universally shared style of self-process is emerging. Considering once more the three-way interplay responsible for the behavior of human groups —universal psychobiological potential, specific cultural emphasis, and prevailing historical forces—my thesis is that the last factor plays an increasingly important part in shaping self-process.

In work done in Hong Kong (in connection with a study of the process of "thought reform"—or "brainwashing"—as conducted on the mainland), I found that Chinese intellectuals of varying ages had gone through an extraordinary array of what I then called identity fragments—of combinations

Reprinted by permission of Random House, Inc. from *History and Human Survival*, 1970, pp. 316–31, and by permission of Robert Jay Lifton, c/o International Famous Agency. First published in the U.S. by *Partisan Review*, Winter 1968.

of belief and emotional involvement—each of which they could readily abandon in favor of another. I remember particularly the profound impression made upon me by the extraordinary psychohistorical journey of one young man in particular: beginning as a "filial son" or "young master," that elite status of an only son in an upper-class Chinese family, with all it meant within the traditional social structure; then feeling himself an abandoned and betrayed victim, as traditional cultural forms collapsed midst civil war and general chaos, and his father, for whom he was always to long, was taken from him by political and military duties; then a "student activist" in militant rebellion against the traditional cultural structures in which he had been so recently immersed (as well as against a Nationalist regime whose abuses he had personally experienced); which led him to Marxism and to strong emotional involvement in the Communist movement; then, because of remaining "imperfections," becoming a participant in a thought reform program which pressed toward a more thoroughgoing ideological conversion; but which, in his case, had the opposite effect, as he was alienated by the process, came into conflict with the reformers, and fled the country; then, in Hong Kong, struggling to establish himself as an "anti-Communist writer"; after a variety of difficulties, finding solace and significance in becoming a Protestant convert; and following that, still just thirty, apparently poised for some new internal (and perhaps external) move.

Even more dramatic were the shifts in self-process of young Japanese whom I interviewed in Tokyo and Kyoto from 1960 to 1962, and then again in 1967. I need only mention those depicted in the young Japanese businessman I refer to in the first essay as Kondo, all of which took place before he was 25.

There are, of course, important differences between the protean life styles of the two young men, and between them and their American counterparts—differences which have to do with cultural emphases and which contribute to what is generally called national character. But such is the intensity of the shared aspects of historical experience that contemporary Chinese, Japanese, and American self-process turn out to have striking points of convergence.

I would stress two general historical developments as having special importance for creating protean man. The first is the worldwide sense of what I have called historical (or psychohistorical) dislocation, the break in the sense of connection which men have long felt with the vital and nourishing symbols of their cultural tradition—symbols revolving around family, idea-systems, religions, and the life cycle in general. In our contemporary world one perceives these traditional symbols (as I have suggested elsewhere, using the Japanese as a paradigm) as irrelevant, burdensome, or inactivating, and yet one cannot avoid carrying them within or having one's self-process profoundly affected by them. The second large historical tendency is the *flooding of imagery* produced by the extraordinary flow of post-modern cultural influences over mass-communication networks. These cross readily over local and national boundaries, and permit each individual to be touched by everything, but at the same time cause him to be overwhelmed by superficial messages and undigested cultural elements, by headlines and by endless partial alternatives in every sphere of life. These alternatives, moreover, are universally and simultaneously shared—if not as courses of action, at least in the form of significant inner imagery.

We know from Greek mythology that Proteus was able to change his shape with relative ease—from wild boar to lion to dragon to fire to flood. But what he did find difficult, and would not do unless seized and chained, was to commit himself to a single form, a form most his own, and carry out his function of prophecy. We can say the same of protean man, but we must keep in mind his possibilities as well as his difficulties.

The protean style of self-process, then, is characterized by an interminable series of experiments and explorations—some shallow, some profound—each of which may be readily abandoned in favor of still new psychological quests. The pattern in many ways resembles what Erik Erikson has called "identity diffusion" or "identity confusion," and the impaired psychological functioning which those terms suggest can be very much present. But I would stress that the protean style is by no means pathological as such, and in fact may well be one of the functional patterns of our day. It extends to all areas of human experience—to political as well as sexual behavior, to the holding and promulgating of ideas, and to the general organization of lives.

I would like to suggest a few illustrations of the protean style, as expressed in America and Europe, drawn both from psychotherapeutic work with patients and from observations on various forms of literature and art.

One patient of mine, a gifted young teacher, spoke of himself in this way:

> I have an extraordinary number of masks I can put on or take off. The question is: Is there, or should there be, one face which should be authentic? I'm not sure that there is one for me. I can think of other parallels to this, especially in literature. There are representations of every kind of crime, every kind of sin. For me, there is not a single act I cannot imagine myself committing.

He went on to compare himself to an actor on the stage who "performs with a certain kind of polymorphous versatility"—and here he was referring, slightly mockingly, to Freud's term, "polymorphous perversity" for diffusely inclusive (also protean) infantile sexuality. And he asked:

> Which is the real person, so far as an actor is concerned? Is he more real when performing on the stage—or when he is at home? I tend to think that for people who have these many, many masks, there is no home. Is it a futile gesture for the actor to try to find his real face?

My patient was by no means a happy man, but neither was he incapacitated. And although we can see the strain with which he carries his "polymorphous versatility," it could also be said that, as a teacher and a thinker, and in some ways as a man, he was well served by it.

In contemporary American literature Saul Bellow is notable for the protean men he has created. In *The Adventures of Augie March,* one of his earlier novels, we meet a picaresque hero with a notable talent for adapting himself to divergent social worlds. Augie himself says, "I touched all sides, and nobody knew where I belonged. I had no good idea of that myself." And a perceptive young English critic, Tony Tanner, tells us, "Augie indeed celebrates the self, but he can find nothing to do with it." Tanner goes on to describe Bellow's more recent protean hero, Herzog, as "a representative modern intelligence, swamped with ideas, metaphysics, and values, and surrounded by messy facts. It labors to cope with them all."

A distinguished French literary spokesman for the protean style—in his life and in his work—is, of course, Jean-Paul Sartre. Indeed, I believe that it is precisely because of these protean traits that Sartre strikes us as such an embodiment of twentieth-century man. An American critic, Theodore Solotaroff, speaks of Sartre's fundamental assumption that "there is no such thing as even a relatively fixed sense of self, ego, or identity—rather there is only the subjective mind in motion in relationship to that which it confronts." And Sartre himself refers to human consciousness as "a sheer activity transcending toward objects," and "a great emptiness, a wind blowing toward objects." Both Sartre and Solotaroff may be guilty of overstatement, but I doubt that either could have written as he did prior to the last thirty years or so. Solotaroff further characterizes Sartre as

> . . . constantly on the go, hurrying from point to point, subject to subject; fiercely intentional, his thought occupies, fills, and distends its material as he endeavors to lose and find himself in his encounters with other lives, disciplines, books, and situations.

This image of repeated, autonomously willed death and rebirth of the self, so central to the protean style, becomes associated with the themes of fatherlessness—as Sartre goes on to tell us in his autobiography with his characteristic tone of serious self-mockery:

> There is no good father, that's the rule. Don't lay the blame on men but on the bond of paternity, which is rotten. To beget children, nothing better, To have them, what iniquity! Had my father lived, he would have lain on me at full length, and would have crushed me. Amidst Aeneas and his fellows who carry their Anchises on their backs, I move from shore to shore, alone and hating those invisible begetters who bestraddle their sons all their life long. I left behind me a young man who did not have time to be my father and who could now be my son. Was it a good thing or bad? I don't know. But I readily subscribed to the verdict of an eminent psychoanalyst: I have no superego.

We note Sartre's image of interchangeability of father and son, of "a young man who did not have time to be my father and who could now be my son" —which in a literal sense refers to the age of his father's death, but symbolically suggests an extension of the protean style to intimate family relationships. And such reversals indeed become necessary in a rapidly changing world in which the sons must constantly "carry their fathers on their backs," teach them new things which they, as older people, cannot possibly know. The judgment of the absent superego, however, may be misleading, especially if we equate superego with susceptibility to guilt. What has actually disappeared—in Sartre and in protean man in general—is the *classical* superego, the internalization of clearly defined criteria of right and wrong transmitted within a particular culture by parents to their children. Protean man requires freedom from precisely that kind of superego—he requires a symbolic fatherlessness—in order to carry out his explorations. But we shall see that, rather than being free of guilt, his guilt takes on a different form from that of his predecessors.

There are many other representations of protean man among contemporary novelists: in the constant internal motion of "beat generation" writings, such as Jack Kerouac's *On the Road;* in the novels of a gifted successor to that generation, Brian [*sic*] Donleavy, particularly *The Ginger Man;* and of course in the work of European novelists such as Günter Grass, whose *The Tin Drum* is a breathtaking evocation of prewar Polish–German, wartime German, and postwar German environments, in which the protagonist combines protean adaptability with a kind of perpetual physical–mental "strike" against any change at all.

In the visual arts, perhaps the most important of postwar movement has been aptly named "Action Painting" to convey its stress upon process rather than fixed completion. And a more recent and related movement in sculpture, called Kinetic Art, goes further. According to Jean Tinguely, one of its leading practitioners, "Artists are putting themselves in rhythm with their time, in contact with their epic, especially with permanent and perpetual movement." As revolutionary as any style of approach is the stress upon innovation per se which now dominates painting. I have frequently heard artists, themselves considered radical innovators, complain bitterly of the current standards dictating that "innovation is all," and of a turnover in art movements so rapid as to discourage the idea of holding still long enough to develop a particular style.

We also learn much from film stars. Marcello Mastroianni, when asked whether he agreed with *Time*'s characterization of him as "the neocapitalist hero," gave the following answer:

> In many ways, yes. But I don't think I'm any kind of hero, neocapitalist or otherwise. If anything, I am an *anti*-hero or at most a *non*-hero. *Time* said I had the frightened, characteristically twentieth-century look, with a spine made of plastic napkin rings. I accepted this—because modern man is that way; and being a product of my time and an artist I can represent him. If humanity were all one piece, I would be considered a weakling.

Mastroianni accepts his destiny as protean man; he seems to realize that there are certain advantages to having a spine made of plastic napkin rings, or at least that it is an appropriate kind of spine to have these days.

John Cage, the composer, is an extreme exponent of the protean style, both in his music and in his sense of all of us as listeners. He concluded a recent letter to *The Village Voice* with the sentence "Nowadays, everything happens at once and our souls are conveniently electronic, omni-attentive." The comment is McLuhan-like, but what I wish to stress particularly is the idea of omni-attention—the sense of contemporary man as having the possibility of "receiving" and "taking in" everything. In attending, as in being, nothing is "off limits."

To be sure, one can observe in contemporary man a tendency which seems to be precisely the opposite of the protean style. I refer to the closing-off of identity or constriction of self-process, to a straight-and-narrow specialization in psychological as well as in intellectual life, and to a reluctance to let in any "extraneous" influences. But I would emphasize that where this kind of constricted or "one-dimensional" self-process exists, it has an essentially reactive and compensatory quality. In this it differs from earlier characterlogical styles it may seem to resemble (such as the "inner-directed" man described by Riesman, and still earlier patterns in traditional society). For these were direct outgrowths of societies which then existed, and in harmony with those societies, while at the present time a constricted self-process requires continuous psychological work to fend off protean influences which are always abroad.

Protean man has a particular relationship to the holding of ideas which has, I believe, great significance for the politics, religion, and general intellectual life of the future. For just as elements of the self can be experimented with and readily altered, so can idea systems and ideologies be embraced, modified, let go of, and re-embraced, all with a new ease that stands in sharp contrast to the inner struggle we have in the past associated with these shifts. Until relatively recently, no more than one major ideological shift was likely to occur in a lifetime, and that one would be long remembered as a significant individual turning-point accompanied by profound soul-searching and conflict. But today it is not unusual to encounter several such shifts, accomplished relatively painlessly, within a year or even a month; and among many groups, the rarity is a man who has gone through life holding firmly to a single ideological vision.

In one sense, this tendency is related to "the end of ideology" spoken of by Daniel Bell, since protean man is incapable of enduring an unquestioning allegiance to the large ideologies and utopian thought of the nineteenth and early twentieth centuries. One must be cautious about speaking of the end of anything, however, especially ideology, and one also encounters in protean man what I would call strong ideological hunger. He is starved for ideas and feelings that can give coherence to his world, but here too his taste is toward new combinations. While he is by no means without yearning for the absolute, what he finds most acceptable are images of a more fragmentary nature than those of the ideologies of the past; and these images, although limited and often fleeting, can have great influence upon his psychological life. Thus political and religious movements, as they confront protean man, are likely to experience less difficulty convincing him to alter previous convictions than they do providing him a set of beliefs which can command his allegiance for more than a brief experimental interlude.

Intimately bound up with his flux in emotions and beliefs is a profound inner sense of absurdity, which finds expression in a tone of mockery. The sense and the tone are related to a perception of surrounding activities and beliefs as profoundly strange and inappropriate. They stem from a breakdown in the relationship between inner and outer worlds—that is, in the sense of symbolic integrity—and are part of the pattern of psychohistorical dislocation I mentioned earlier. For if we view man as primarily a symbol-forming organism, we must recognize that he has constant need of a meaningful inner formulation of self and world in which his own actions, and even his impulses, have some kind of "fit" with the "outside" as he perceives it.

The sense of absurdity, of course, has a considerable modern tradition, and has been discussed by such writers as Camus as a function of man's spiritual homelessness and inability to find any meaning in traditional belief systems. But absurdity and mockery have taken much more extreme form in the post–World War II world, and have in fact become a prominent part of a universal life-style.

In American life absurdity and mockery are everywhere. Perhaps their most vivid expression can be found in such areas as pop art and the more general burgeoning of "pop culture." Important here is the complex stance of the pop artist toward the objects he depicts. On the one hand, he embraces the materials of the everyday world, celebrates and even exalts them —boldly asserting his creative return to representational art (in active rebellion against the previously reigning nonobjective school), and his psychological return to the "real world" of *things*. On the other hand, everything he touches he mocks. "Thingness" is pressed to the point of caricature. He is indeed artistically reborn as he moves freely among the physical and symbolic materials of his environment, but mockery is his birth certificate and his passport. This kind of duality of approach is formalized in the stated "duplicity" of Camp, an ill-defined aesthetic in which all varieties of mockery converge under the guiding influence of the homosexual's subversion of a heterosexual world.

Also relevant is a group of expressions in current slang, some of them derived originally from jazz. The "dry mock" has replaced the dry wit; one refers to a segment of life experience as a "bit," "bag," "caper," "game" (or "con game"), "scene," "show," or "scenario"; and one seeks to "make the scene" (or "make it"), "beat the system," or "pull it off"—or else one "cools it" ("plays it cool") or "cops out." The thing to be experienced, in other words, is too absurd to be taken at its face value; one must either keep most of the self aloof from it, or if not, one must lubricate the encounter with mockery.

A similar spirit seems to pervade literature and social action alike. What is best termed a "literature of mockery" has come to dominate fiction and other forms of writing on an international scale. Again Günter Grass's *The Tin Drum* comes to mind, and is probably the greatest single example of this literature—a work, I believe, which will eventually be appreciated as much as a general evocation of contemporary man as of the particular German experience with Nazism. In this country the divergent group of novelists known as "black humorists" also fits into the general category—related as they are to a trend in the American literary consciousness which R. W. B. Lewis has called a "savagely comical apocalypse" or a "new kind of ironic literary form and disturbing vision, the joining of the dark thread of apocalypse with the nervous detonations of satiric laughter." For it is precisely death itself, and particularly threats of the contemporary apocalypse that protean man ultimately mocks.

The relationship of mockery to political and social action has been less apparent, but is, I would claim, equally significant. There is more than coincidence in the fact that the largest American student uprising of recent decades, the Berkeley Free Speech Movement of 1965, was followed immediately by a "Filthy Speech Movement." While the object of the Filthy Speech Movement—achieving free expression of forbidden language, particularly of four-letter words—can be viewed as a serious one, the predominant effect, even in the matter of names, was that of a mocking caricature of the movement which preceded it. But if mockery can undermine protest, it can also enliven it. There have been signs of craving for it in major American expressions of protest such as the rebellion of the blacks and the opposition to the war in Vietnam. In the former a certain chord can be struck by the comedian Dick Gregory, and in the latter by the use of satirical skits and parodies, that revives the flagging attention of protesters becoming gradually bored with the repetition of their "straight" slogans and goals. And on an international scale, I would say that, during the past decade, Russian intellectual life has been enriched by a leavening spirit of mockery—against which the Chinese leaders are now, in pressing ahead with their Cultural Revolution, fighting a vigorous but ultimately losing battle.

Closely related to the sense of absurdity and the spirit of mockery is another characteristic of protean man which I call "suspicion of counterfeit nurturance." Involved here is a severe conflict of dependency, a core problem of protean man. I originally thought of the concept several years ago while working with survivors of the atomic bomb in Hiroshima. I found that these survivors both felt themselves in need of special help, and resented whatever help was offered them because they equated it with weakness and inferiority. In considering the matter more generally, I found that this equation of nurturance with a threat to autonomy was a major theme of contemporary life. The increased dependency needs resulting from the breakdown of traditional institutions lead protean man to seek out replacements wherever he can find them. The large organizations (government, business, academic, etc.) to which he turns, and which contemporary society increasingly holds out as a substitute for traditional institutions, present an ambivalent threat to his autonomy in one way; and the intense individual relationships in which he seeks to anchor himself in another. Both are therefore likely to be perceived as counterfeit. But the obverse of this tendency is an expanding sensitivity to the inauthentic, which may be just beginning to exert its general creative force on man's behalf.

Technology (and technique in general), together with science, have special significance for protean man. Technical achievement of any kind can be strongly embraced to combat inner tendencies toward diffusion, and to transcend feelings of absurdity and conflicts over counterfeit nurturance. The image of science itself, however, as the ultimate power behind technology and, to a considerable extent, behind contemporary thought in general, becomes much more difficult to cope with. Only in certain underdeveloped countries can one find, in relatively pure form, those expectations of scientific-utopian deliverance from all human want and conflict, which were characteristic of eighteenth- and nineteenth-century Western thought. Protean man retains much of this utopian imagery, but he finds it increasingly undermined by massive disillusionment. More and more he calls forth the other side of the God–devil polarity generally applied to science, and sees it as a purveyor of total destructiveness. This kind of profound ambivalence creates for him the most extreme psychic paradox: the very force he still feels to be his liberator from the heavy burdens of past irrationality also threatens him with absolute annihilation, even extinction. But this paradox may well be—in fact, I believe, already has been—the source of imaginative efforts to achieve new relationships between science and man, and indeed, new visions of science itself.

I suggested before that protean man was not free of guilt. He indeed suffers from it considerably, but often without awareness of what is causing his suffering. For his is a form of hidden guilt: a vague but persistent kind of self-condemnation related to the symbolic disharmonies I have described, a sense of having no outlet for his loyalties and no symbolic structure for his achievements. This is the guilt of social breakdown, and it includes various forms of historical and racial guilt experienced by whole nations and peoples, both by the privileged and the abused. Rather than a clear feeling of evil or sinfulness, it takes the form of a nagging sense of unworthiness all the more troublesome for its lack of clear origin.

Protean man experiences similarly vague constellations of anxiety and resentment. These too have origin in symbolic impairments and are particularly tied in with suspicion of counterfeit nurturance. Often feeling himself uncared for, even abandoned, protean man responds with diffuse fear and anger. But he can find neither a good cause for the former, nor a consistent target for the latter. He nonetheless cultivates his anger because he finds it more serviceable than anxiety, because there are plenty of targets of one kind or another beckoning, and because even moving targets are better than none. His difficulty is that focused indignation is as hard for him to sustain as is any single identification or conviction.

Involved in all of these patterns is a profound psychic struggle with the idea of change itself. For here too protean man finds himself ambivalent in the extreme. He is profoundly attracted to the idea of making all things, including himself, totally new—to what I have elsewhere called the "mode of transformation." But he is equally drawn to an image of a mythical past of perfect harmony and prescientific wholeness, to the "mode of restoration." Moreover, beneath his transformationism is nostalgia, and beneath his restorationism is his fascinated attraction to contemporary forms and symbols. Constantly balancing these elements midst the extraordinarily rapid change surrounding his own life, the nostalgia is pervasive, and can be one of his most explosive and dangerous emotions. This longing for a "Golden Age" of absolute oneness, prior to individual and cultural separation or delineation, not only sets the tone for the restorationism of the politically Rightist antagonists of history: the still-extant Emperor-worshipping assassins in Japan, the *colons* in France, and the John Birchites and Ku Klux Klanners in America. It also, in more disguised form, energizes that transformationist totalism of the Left which courts violence, and is even willing to risk nuclear violence, in a similarly elusive quest.

Following upon all that I have said are radical impairments to the symbolism of transition within the life cycle—the *rites de passage* surrounding birth, entry into adulthood, marriage, and death. Whatever rites remain seem shallow, inappropriate, fragmentary. Protean man cannot take them seriously, and often seeks to improvise new ones with whatever contemporary materials he has available, including cars and drugs. Perhaps the central impairment here is that of symbolic immortality—of the universal need for imagery of connection, antedating and extending beyond the individual life span, whether the idiom of this immortality is biological (living on through children and grandchildren), theological (through a life after death), natural (*in* nature itself which outlasts all), or creative (through what man makes and does). I have suggested that this sense of immortality is a fundamental component of ordinary psychic life, and that it is now being profoundly threatened: by simple historical velocity, which subverts the idioms (notably the theological) in which it has traditionally been maintained; and, of particular importance to protean man, by the existence of nuclear weapons, which, even without being used, call into question all modes of immortality. (Who can be certain of living on through children and grandchildren, through teachings or kindnesses?)

Protean man is left with two paths to symbolic immortality which he tries to cultivate, sometimes pleasurably and sometimes desperately. One is the natural mode we have mentioned. His attraction to nature and concern over its desecration have to do with an unconscious sense that, in whatever holocaust, at least nature will endure—though such are the dimensions of our present weapons that he cannot be absolutely certain even of this. His second path is that of "experiential transcendence"—of seeking a sense of immortality in the way that mystics always have, through psychic experience of such great intensity that time and death are, in effect, eliminated. This, I believe, is the larger meaning of the "drug revolution," of protean man's hunger for chemical aids to "expanded consciousness." And indeed all revolutions may be thought of, at bottom, as innovations in the struggle for immortality, as new combinations of old modes.

We have seen that young adults individually, and youth movements collectively, express most vividly the psychological themes of protean man. And although it is true that these themes make contact with what we sometimes call the "psychology of adolescence," we err badly if we overlook their expression in all age groups and dismiss them as "mere adolescent phenomena." Rather, protean man's affinity for the young—his being metaphorically and psychologically so young in spirit—has to do with his never-ceasing quest for imagery of rebirth. He seeks such imagery from all sources: from ideas, techniques, religious and political systems, mass movements, and drugs; or from special individuals of his own kind whom he sees as possessing that problematic gift of his namesake, the gift of prophecy. The dangers inherent in the quest seem hardly to require emphasis. What perhaps needs most to be kept in mind is the general principle that renewal on a large scale is impossible to achieve without forays into danger, destruction, and negativity. The principle of "death and rebirth" is as valid psychohistorically as it is mythologically. However misguided many of his forays may be, protean man also carries with him an extraordinary range of possibility for man's betterment, or more important, for his survival.

References Cited in Section Introductions

Becker, Howard S.; Geer, B.; and Hughes, E. C. *Making the Grade.* New York: John Wiley, 1968.

Becker, Howard S.; Geer B.; Hughes, E. C.; and Strauss, A. *Boys in White.* Chicago: University of Chicago Press, 1961.

Bendix, R., and Lipset, S. M., eds. *Class, Status and Power: Social Stratification in Comparative Perspective,* 2nd ed. New York: The Free Press, 1966.

Davis, F. James. "Crime Waves in Colorado Newspapers." *American Journal of Sociology* 57 (January 1952):325–30.

Eisenstadt, S. N. *From Generation to Generation.* New York: The Free Press, 1956.

Griswold, H. Jack; Misenheimer, M.; Powers, A.; and Tromanhauser, E. *An Eye for an Eye.* New York: Holt, Rinehart and Winston, 1970.

Lenski, Gerhard. *Power and Privilege.* New York: McGraw-Hill, 1966.

Kozol, Jonathan. *Death at an Early Age.* New York: Bantam Books, 1968.

Matza, David. *Becoming Deviant.* Englewood Cliffs, N.J.: Prentice-Hall, 1969.

Mead, Margaret. *Culture and Commitment.* New York: Doubleday, 1970.

Moore, Barrington. "Thoughts on the Future of the Family" in *Political Power and Social Theory.* New York: Harper Torchbooks, 1965.

Robinson, John, and Hirsch, Paul. "Teenage Response to the New Rock and Roll." Unpublished paper, 1969.

Rosenthal, Robert, and Jacobson, Lenore. *Pygmalion in the Classroom.* New York: Holt, Rinehart and Winston, 1968.

Roszak, Theodore. *The Making of a Counter Culture.* New York: Doubleday, 1969.

Scott, John F. "The American College Sorority: Its Role in Class and Ethnic Endogamy." *American Sociological Review* 30 (August 1965):514–27.

Sennett, Richard. *The Uses of Disorder.* New York: Alfred A. Knopf, 1970.

Suttles, Gerald. *The Social Order of the Slum.* Chicago: University of Chicago Press, 1969.

Toffler, Alvin. *Future Shock.* New York: Random House, 1970.

Turner, Ralph H., and Surace, S. "Zoot-Suiters and Mexicans: Symbols in Crowd Behavior." *American Journal of Sociology* 62 (1956):14–20.

Watts, William A., and Whittaker, David. "Profile of a Non-Conformist Youth Culture." *Sociology of Education* 41 (Spring 1968):178–200.

Wilde, William. "Official News." Unpublished Ph.D. dissertation, Department of Sociology, Northwestern University, 1968.

Wilensky, Harold. "Work as a Social Problem." In *Social Problems,* edited by Howard S. Becker. New York: John Wiley, 1966.